U0051664

空中英語教室

全新修訂版

完勝大考！
英語7000單字

中級篇 | 2001~4500字

空中英語教室編輯群／著

笛藤出版

近年來，坊間其實已經有眾多紙本、甚至是電腦化的字彙學習輔助教材，提供英語教師和學生許多字彙學習上的選擇。但是在選擇適當教材時，教師和學生最常問的一個問題就是哪一本或是那一種教材才是最有效的學習資源。但是坊間教材之間就形式內容而言，大致是大同小異（譬如大都是按照字母順序編排，都有例句）。但是如何產生、挑選、編纂字彙教材內容才往往是區隔教材良劣的關鍵。坊間紙本字彙學習書往往可以分成四個類型：

（一）按照字母或是字根字首順序編排、無前後文、無例句，但提供音標、詞性、中文解釋。

（二）和前面第一類型內容幾乎一樣，但不再是無前後文；但在大部分的情況下每一單字僅搭配一個例句。

（三）含有第二類型的內容，且多了英文同（反）義字，提供學生類同字的聯想。

（四）在最新的含有字頻資訊，提供學生對於字彙重要性判斷的參考。

其中，第二類型的字彙學習資源書雖然補足了第一種類型資源書沒有的例句，但是單一例句往往無法精確地幫助學生釐清許多英語字彙（尤其是一字多義）之間的精確語用資訊。第三種字彙資源書，雖然提供了同義字，但是根據 Alan Baddeley (2003) 對於人類短期記憶的研究，在遭遇到陌生的初學字彙時，同時間呈現與初學字彙意義、概念上互相關聯（但是沒前後文的）字串（如：huge, big, long, tall, large）並不會特別幫助學生對這些初學字彙的立即回想（immediate recall）。Baddeley 發現意義、概念上互相關聯的同義字只有在被打散時（譬如：呈現在不同的例句、或情境中，才能有效的幫助學生記得初學字彙的學習。若字彙只提供單一例句，有點像把一隻鑰匙跟很多其他類似的鑰匙放在一起；這樣的安排，會讓學生事後得單憑記憶，在很多類似的鑰匙中找出他們所需要的鑰匙。但是若是透過不同的（兩個或兩個以上）例句，就像給予學生不同的情境記憶標籤，幫助學生將新學的字彙和其他的同義字在不同情境的記憶中做連結與代換，進而幫助學生建立新學字彙與同義字之間的記憶標籤。空英這次編纂的紙本字彙資源書中，針對一字多義的字彙提供至少兩種例句，提供學生不同的前後文情境來連結初學字彙與對應同義字。此外，空英編纂的字彙資源書並參酌字庫、歷屆學測指考內容，補充最常用同義字及重要搭配語，進而達到上述第四類型字彙學習資源書的優點。

不同於坊間字彙學習資源書僅有紙本或是僅有 app 版本，空中英語教室所編製的字彙學習書同時具有紙本與手機 app 版本。有了 app 版本最大的好處，除了提供行動學習的工具，最重要的是app 補足了紙本字彙資源學習書所無法提供的發音。同時，除了單字本身的發音，在 app 中更提供例句的發音。這樣的好處是可以讓學生同時接觸到單字單獨呈現與在有前後文的例句中的發音（不論在中文與英語中，有許多字在單獨發音及有前後文句子當中的發音是有細微差異的，例如連音與局部變音）。藉由空英老師字正腔圓的道地發音音檔，學生可以在課室內與課室外的環境中，得到更多的輔助。當然學生更可以在 app 版本中，標示自己覺得最困難、最重要、或是最喜歡的單字，提供日後複習時的電子書籤。以上這些用心的特點，讓空英的單字書所匯集的 7000 英文單字能更有效地深植在學生的腦海中，成為輔助英語字彙學習有效工具。

國立台灣師範大學英語學系 副教授 劉宇挺

① 本書收錄實用中級字彙，其中包括相同拼法，不同詞性的字彙等約 2500 字。以點、線、面擴展方式學習該單字用法，使用讀者能夠有效率增加字彙量。

② 收錄進階詞彙，如同義字、搭配詞及實用片語等，使讀者快速了解該單字的延伸用法，進而在語言學習上更加活用單字。

③ 本書以單元學習的方式，分為 80 回，以每 25 字歸納為一回，並在每回結束時，設計 10 題練習題，以有效評核學習狀況，使讀者能夠循序漸進的習得單字。

④ 本書特別收錄 50 組發音容易混淆的單字及 50 組拼字容易混淆的單字，透過字詞對照，可明確

⑤ 分辨其用法，使讀者的學習能夠更加事半功倍。

　本書字表中收錄 784 個單字，曾出現在歷屆學測，指考及統測考題中。

⑥ 另附有完勝大考 7000 單字雲 _ 中級 -- 專屬序號，幫助讀者學習不間斷，充份利用零碎時間，走到哪聽到哪，走到哪背到哪。

※ 完勝大考 7000 單字雲及單字書內容的差異：

① 單字雲：主要單字及例句，並附音檔。
　　◆提供多樣互動練習題　◆聽發音猜中文意思
　　◆聽發音猜英文拼法　◆聽發音猜單字

② 單字書：提供主要單字及例句，並補充實用片語、搭配詞並搭配詞例句。
　　單字書另提供 80 回，每回 10 題，便於讀者更深入學習單字的使用情境。

◎ 詞性縮寫
v. = Verb 動詞
n. = Noun 名詞
adj. = Adjective 形容詞
adv. = Adverb 副詞
prep. = Preposition 介系詞
conj. = Conjunction 連接詞

◎音標參考 DICT.TW 線上字典 / Macmillan Dictionary / Cambridge Dictionary

同：同義詞
搭：搭配詞
▶ ：例句
99：學測或指考或統測年度

---

104 103 101 97

inspire [ɪnˈspaɪr] *v.* 激勵；啟發；鼓舞；激動

同 **arouse / motivate**

 實用片語
inspire with 激勵，激發

▶ His music inspires me every time I hear it.
每次聽到他的音樂，我都會受到音樂的激勵。

▶ She inspired us all with her personal story.
她用她個人的故事激勵我們。

目次 Contents

完勝大考 7000 單字雲開通説明

親愛的讀者 您好：

恭喜您獲得【完勝大考 7000 單字雲】專屬 QR Code，請按以下步驟開通：

➡ 請掃下方 QR Code 進入【完勝大考 7000 單字雲服務首頁】，輸入空英官網會員帳號及密碼直接登入。若非空英官網會員，請按【註冊】，並填妥相關欄位成為空英會員。

序號：5m8g9pcS6j6M
對象：購完勝大考7000
字中級篇修訂版附贈
級別：中

★注意事項：

(1) 完勝大考 7000 單字雲 - 中級服務網址：https://7000wi.studioclassroom.com

(2) 完勝大考 7000 單字雲的音檔服務係為雲端服務，無離線收聽的功能。

(3) 任何可上網的裝置，都可以使用服務網址收聽音檔。

(4) 序號開通後，若書籍轉給他人使用，只能以原帳號接續使用，無法轉移。

若您在操作上有任何疑問，或完勝大考 7000 單字雲無法正常使用，請洽空中英語教室客服專線 (02)2533-9123。

單字
Vocabulary

收錄 2494 字

► 80 回單字（每回 25 字）
　　每回 25 個實用單字，附上音標、詞性、例句、同義字、搭配字
　　等說明，循序漸進增加字彙量。

► 80 回練習題（每回 10 題）
　　每回單字後面皆有練習題，馬上驗收前面所學，加深學習印象。

► 10 回易混淆形義字（每回 5 組）
　　每 10 回單字與練習題後嚴選出拼法、發音相似，意思與詞性卻
　　完全不同的單字組，使用時請特別注意。

a.m./am/A.M./AM [ˌeɪˈem] *adv.* 上午

▶ Is 7:00 a.m. too early to meet for breakfast?
早上七點碰面吃早餐會不會太早啊？

---

abandon [əˈbæn.dən] *v.* 拋棄；放棄

搭 **abandon dream** 放棄夢想
同 **discard / withdraw**
實用片語
abandon ship 棄船而逃

▶ Because her father left her family, Brenda feared her husband might one day abandon her too.
由於布蘭達的父親離棄了家人，她害怕她的丈夫將來也會拋棄她。

▶ The company is facing a crisis, and the manager is abandoning ship.
公司面臨危機，因而那經理棄船而逃了。

---

abdomen [ˈæb.də.mən] *n.* 腹部；胃

同 **belly / tummy**

▶ After doing sit-ups, Bryan always feels pain in his abdomen.
布萊恩每次做完仰臥起坐，都會感到腹部疼痛。

▶ The left side of her abdomen is in a lot of pain.
她左邊的腹部很痛。

---

aboard [əˈbɔːrd]

① *adv.* 在交通工具上；上交通工具

② *prep.* 在交通工具上；上交通工具

實用片語
go aboard 登船，登機

▶ She climbed aboard just as the train was leaving.
她在火車正要離站時上了車。

▶ The entire family is aboard the ship.
那一家人都在這艘船上。

▶ Please ask everyone to go aboard.
請要求所有人登船。

---

absolute [ˈæb.sə.luːt] *adj.* 完全的；絕對的

搭 **absolute power** 絕對權力
同 **total / complete**

▶ There was absolute silence as the girl delivered her incredible speech.
當女孩發表她的精彩演說時，現場是鴉雀無聲。

---

absolutely [ˌæb.səˈluːt.li] *adv.* 絕對地

同 **certainly / exactly**

▶ My sister absolutely loved her new gift.
我的姊妹非常喜歡她新收到的禮物。

absorb [əbˈzɔːrb] *v.* 吸收

搭 **absorb heat** 吸熱

同 **consume / ingest**

實用片語
absorb into 吸收

▶ Tim's shirt absorbed all of Tina's tears as she cried on his shoulder.
當提娜靠在提姆的肩上哭泣時，他的襯衫吸收了提娜所有的眼淚。

▶ Nutrients are absorbed into the bloodstream.
營養在血液中被吸收。

---

abstract [ˈæbˌstrækt] *adj.* 抽象的

搭 **abstract concept** 抽象概念

同 **conceptual / symbolic**

實用片語
abstract idea 抽象概念

▶ The artist's work portrayed abstract ideas such as love and justice.
這位藝術家得作品描繪了像是愛以及公正這樣的抽象意念。

▶ Some people regard happiness as an abstract idea.
有些人將快樂視為一種抽象概念。

---

academic [ˌæk.əˈdem.ɪk] *adj.* 學術的

同 **scholarly / theoretical**

▶ Ron continued his academic career by applying to graduate school.
榮恩申請了研究所，以繼續他的學術生涯。

102
accent [ˈæk.sənt] *n.* 口音

搭 **speak with accent** 說話有口音

同 **tone / pronunciation**

實用片語
with accent 有口音

▶ It took me a while to adjust to Kim's Australian accent.
我花了不少的時間去適應克姆的澳洲口音。

▶ Mr. Jones speaks with an American accent.
瓊斯先生說話有美國口音。

99
acceptable [əkˈsept.ə.bəl] *adj.* 可接受的

搭 **acceptable standard** 可接受的標準

同 **adequate / agreeable**

▶ Rude behavior is not acceptable during class.
上課時，不可以有粗魯的行為。

96
acceptance [əkˈsep.təns] *n.* 錄取；接受

同 **approval / admission**

▶ Ron received a letter of acceptance from his favorite graduate school.
榮恩收到他最喜歡的研究所給他的錄取函。

---

accepted [əkˈsep.tɪd] *adj.* 受到認可的；公認的

同 **authorized / endorsed**

▶ Our college professor uses an accepted style of teaching.
我的大學教授使用一種受到認可的教學方式。

access [ˈæk.ses]

① *n.* （使用某物的）權利；使用途徑

搭 **permit access to** （某事物）存取許可

同 **entry / admission**

② *v.* 讀取（電腦資訊）

實用片語
access to 存取權

▶ Students don't have access to the teachers' lounge.
學生沒有進入教師休息區的權利。

▶ You can't access your email without the proper password.
你如果沒有正確的密碼就無法取讀你的電子郵件。

▶ Linda was finally granted access to the customer database.
琳達最後終於獲准取得客戶資料庫的存取權。

---

accident [ˈæk.sə.dənt] *n.* 意外事件；事故

搭 **prevent accident** 預防意外發生

同 **mishap / hazard**

▶ In case of a car accident, wear your seat belt at all times.
你全程都要繫上安全帶，以預防發生車禍。

---

accidental [ˌæk.sə.ˈden.təl] *adj.* 偶然的

同 **unexpected / unplanned**

▶ Running into his ex-girlfriend at the mall was purely accidental.
在購物中心撞見前女友完全是偶然的。

---

accompany [əˈkʌm.pə.ni] *v.* 陪伴

同 **escort / follow**

實用片語
accompany someone on 伴隨某人

▶ Would you like to accompany me to the concert?
你願意陪我去聽音樂會嗎？

▶ My wife often accompanies me on my trips.
我的太太常常伴隨我渡過各個旅程。

---

accomplish [əˈkɑːm.plɪʃ] *v.* 完成；實現

搭 **accomplish mission** 達成任務

同 **achieve / realize**

實用片語
mission accomplished 任務完成

▶ It's impossible to accomplish everything on this to-do list in one day.
想要在一天內完成這些所有的待辦事項根本是不可能的。

▶ I've finished all the tasks you assigned. Mission accomplished.
我已經完成所有你指派的任務。任務完成。

---

accomplishment [əˈkɑːm.plɪʃ.mənt]
n. 成就；成績

同 **achievement / performance**

▶ Someone with all of your accomplishments should feel proud of himself.
任何擁有你這般成就的人，都應該自以為榮。

account [əˈkaʊnt]

① *n.* 敘述

同 **explanation / narrative**

② *v.* 說明；解釋

同 **regard / state**

實用片語
on account of 由於；基於

▶ Mike gave an incredible account of his life in Africa.
麥克對他在非洲的生活有不可思議的描述。

▶ The thief couldn't account for his whereabouts.
這小偷無法交代自己的行蹤。

▶ He is not allowed to play computer games on account of his bad score.
由於他的成績不好，他被禁止玩電腦遊戲。

---

accountant [əˈkaʊn.tənt]

n. 會計師；會計人員

同 **bean counter / auditor**

▶ I may be good at math, but I don't want to be an accountant.
我的數學或許不錯，但是我並不想成為一位會計師。

---

accuracy [ˈæk.jə.ə.si] *n.* 準確（性）；正確（性）

① *n.* （使用某物的）權利；使用途徑

搭 **ensure accuracy** 確保正確性

同 **correctness / certainty**

▶ The psychologist always seems to describe people with accuracy.
那位心理學家好像都有辦法準確地描述他人。

---

 accurate [ˈæk.jə.ət]

adj. 準確的；精確的；正確的

同 **factual / specific**

▶ The weatherman gave an accurate weather report this morning.
今早氣象播報員的氣象報告很準確。

---

 accuse [əˈkjuːz] *v.* 指控；控告

搭 **accuse the police** 指控警察

同 **blame / charge**

實用片語
accuse of 指責，控告

▶ Why did you accuse me of eating your ham sandwich? I don't even like ham.
你為什麼指控我吃了你的火腿三明治？我根本不喜歡火腿。

▶ Don't accuse me of forgetting to turn off the lights.
不要指責我忘記關燈。

---

accustomed [əˈkʌs.təmd]

adj. 習慣的；通常的

同 **adapted / acquainted**

實用片語
accustomed to 習慣於

▶ I am accustomed to waking up early.
我已經習慣了早起。

▶ I am accustomed to sleeping late in the evening.
我已經習慣晚上很晚睡覺。

I. Derivatives

1. Breaking the cup was purely _____ (accident), he did not mean to do it.

2. The witness said he was _____ (absolute) certain about what he saw.

3. It was a great _____ (accomplish) for the athlete to win two gold medals in the Olympics.

4. Debbie works as an _____ (account) in a big accounting firm.

5. The new business was anxious about their _____ (accepted) into the national trade union.

II. Vocabulary Choice

(A) abdomen (B) absorb (C) accent (D) abstract (E) aboard

(F) abandoned (G) account (H) absolute (I) accident (J) access

1. Her father _____ her when she was a baby, so her grandmother raised her.

2. That Charlize Theron speaks perfect English without a foreign _____ makes people forget she's South African.

3. After eating a lot of spicy food tonight, Peter felt a great deal of pain in his _____ .

4. Michael couldn't _____ his email account because he forgot his password.

5. For safety and security reasons, certain items are not permitted _____ a plane as carry-on baggage.

ache [eɪk]

① *n.* 疼痛

同 **pain / soreness**

② *v.* 疼痛

同 **hurt / suffer**

實用片語
ache for 渴望

▶ How do I get rid of this ache in my back?
我該如何擺脫背痛呢？

▶ His heart ached when his girlfriend broke up with him.
他的女朋友和他分手時，他很心痛。

▶ The mother ached for her son to return home.
這位母親很渴望看到她兒子回家。

---

achieve [əˈtʃiːv] *v.* 達成

搭 **achieve goal** 達成目標

同 **accomplish / attain**

實用片語
achieve the impossible 完成不可能的任務

▶ You can achieve anything if you put your mind to it!
如果你全心全意，就能完成任何事情！

▶ We can achieve the impossible if we work together.
若我們一起合作，我們就可以達成不可能的任務。

98

achievement [əˈtʃiːv.mənt] *n.* 成就

同 **success / triumph**

實用片語
crowning achievement 至高成就

▶ Getting into an Ivy League school is an amazing achievement.
能夠進入一所常春藤聯盟的學校，可說是了不起的成就。

▶ Mr. Chen has had success in business but in his eyes his crowning achievement is becoming a father.
陳先生的事業已經很成功，但他感到最高的成就是在他當爸爸的那天。

---

acid [ˈæs.ɪd]

① *n.* 酸

② *adj.* 酸的

同 **sour / tart**

實用片語
come the acid （說話）很不客氣

▶ George was rushed to the hospital after acid splashed on his face.
喬治在被強酸濺到臉上之後，馬上被送到醫院。

▶ Many people fear that acid rain will cause them to lose their hair.
很多人都擔心酸雨會讓他們掉髮。

▶ Don't come the acid with me.
別對我大呼小叫地。

acquaint [əˈkweɪnt] v. 使認識；介紹

同 familiarize / accustom

實用片語
acquaint with 使熟悉，使相識

▶ The manager wants to acquaint the new worker with his entire team.
經理要新的員工認識他的整個團隊。

▶ Let me acquaint you with my friends.
容我介紹你跟我朋友認識一下。

acquaintance [əˈkweɪn.təns]

n. 熟人；相識的人；（與人）相識

同 companion / friend

實用片語
nodding acquaintance 一面之緣

▶ I have many acquaintances, but only a few true friends.
我有很多熟識，但只有幾位是真心的朋友。

▶ I have a nodding acquaintance with the company president.
我跟公司總裁只有一面之緣。

acquire [əˈkwaɪɚ] v. 獲得

搭 acquire knowledge 學習知識

同 gain / achieve

▶ Mary acquired two houses - one that she bought, another as an inheritance.
瑪莉得到兩棟房子 — 一棟是她買的，另一棟是繼承來的。

acre [ˈeɪ.kɚ] n. 英畝

▶ The forest behind my house stretches hundreds of acres.
我房子後面的樹林延伸到數百英畝。

activity [ækˈtɪv.ə.tɪ] n. 活動

搭 marketing activity 行銷活動

同 exertion / exercise

實用片語
hive of activity 一片繁忙，榮景

▶ My favorite weekend activity is playing soccer with my friends.
我週末最喜愛的活動是和朋友踢足球。

▶ On weekend, the shopping center is a hive of activity.
週末時，購物中心內總是一片繁忙。

actual [ˈæk.tʃu.əl] adj. 實際的

搭 actual measurement 實際測量

同 certain / genuine

▶ The actual cost of this house is much more than the price listed in the newspaper.
買這房子的實際花費，比報紙上刊登的售價更高。

actually [ˈæk.tʃu.ə.li] adv. 實際上

同 indeed / in reality

▶ He is actually a very famous performer in Asia.
他其實是亞洲一位非常著名的演出家。

(104)

adapt [əˈdæpt] *v.* 適應

同 **revise / readjust**

實用片語
adapt to 適應於

▶ I'm trying my best to adapt to the culture here, but it's not always easy.
我已經盡我所能適應這裡的文化，但並不總是那麼容易。

▶ You will quickly adapt to the new environment.
您將可迅速適應新環境。

---

(96)

additional [əˈdɪʃ.ən.əl] *adj.* 額外的

搭 **additional spending** 額外花費
同 **further / extra**

▶ Would you like any additional toppings on your pizza?
你想不想在你的披薩上再額外加其他配料？

---

adequate [ˈæd.ə.kwət] *adj.* 足夠的

同 **sufficient / enough**

▶ Is this sentence adequate to help you understand the meaning?
這個句子是否足夠幫助你瞭解它的意思？

---

adjective [ˈædʒ.ek.tɪv] *n.* 形容詞

▶ Using adjectives will help make your essay interesting.
使用一些形容詞會讓你的文章更有趣味。

---

(96)

adjust [əˈdʒʌst] *v.* 調整

搭 **adjust temperature** 調整溫度
同 **modify / alter**

實用片語
adjust to 調適

▶ Mark, please adjust your tie so you don't look so sloppy.
馬克，請你調整一下你的領帶，才不會看起來那麼邋遢。

▶ It took me several years to adjust to the warm weather in Taiwan.
我花了許多年適應台灣的溫暖氣候。

---

adjustment [əˈdʒʌst.mənt] *n.* 調整；調節

同 **alteration / improvement**

▶ I need to make some adjustments to my spending habits.
我必須調整我的花費習慣。

---

(100)

admirable [ˈæd.mə.rə.bəl]
adj. 值得讚揚的；令人欽佩的

搭 **admirable quality** 值得欽佩的特質
同 **commendable / valuable**

▶ Helping those children was an admirable act of love.
幫助那些小朋友是一件值得讚揚的愛心行為。

admiration [ˌæd.məˈreɪ.ʃən]

n. 敬佩；欽佩；讚美

同 **applause / esteem**

▶ Sherry has lots of admiration for her favorite teacher.
雪莉對她最喜愛的老師充滿了敬佩。

---

admire [ədˈmaɪr] *v.* 欽佩；欣賞

搭 **admire greatly** 極度地佩服

同 **appreciate / adore**

實用片語
admire for 讚賞

▶ The person I admire the most is my grandmother.
我最欽佩的人是我的奶奶（外婆）。

▶ I really admire Mr. Chen for his courage.
我真的很讚賞陳先生的勇氣。

---

admission [ədˈmɪʃ.ən] *n.* 進入許可

同 **entrance / acceptance**

▶ Admission to the school is only given to those with a GPA of 3.8 or higher.
那所學校的入學許可只發給那些學業總平均三點八以上的人。

---

admit [ədˈmɪt] *v.* 承認

搭 **admit guilt** 認罪

同 **accept / permit**

實用片語
admit to 承認

▶ Even proponents of the technology admit that it doesn't always work as well as it should.
即使是那項科技的擁護者也承認，它沒能一直正常運作。

▶ Mr. Chen admits to feeling exhausted.
陳先生承認感到筋疲力盡。

---

adopt [əˈdɑːpt] *v.* 採取

同 **approve / embrace**

▶ The company adopted a new system in its factory.
該公司在工廠裡採用了新系統。

---

advanced [ədˈvænst] *adj.* 先進的

搭 **advanced technology** 高科技

同 **cutting-edge / state-of-the-art**

實用片語
advanced in years 年歲已高

▶ Simon loves to read about advanced civilizations of the ancient world.
賽門喜歡閱讀有關古代先進文明的內容。

▶ My grandmother is advanced in years and can't hear very well.
我的祖母年歲已高，且聽力不大好。

advantage [əd`væn.tɪdʒ]

n. 優勢；好處；優點

搭 **competitive advantage** 競爭優勢

同 **benefit / superiority**

實用片語
take advantage of 利用

▶ Being able to speak English is an advantage when you travel.
會說英語在旅行時是一種優勢。

▶ I try to take advantage of every opportunity that comes my way.
我試著利用我遇上的所有機會。

Exercise 2

I. Derivatives

1. The brave man did an _____ (admire) job in trying to break the windows of a burning tour bus to rescue the tourists.

2. The police have suspected for a long time that he planned to kill the bus passengers, but they could never _____ (actual) prove their suspicions.

3. Steve recently ran into an old _____ (acquaint) from his years in teaching and he hardly recognized her.

4. Romance of Three Kingdoms has been described as a great _____ (achieve) of Chinese literature.

5. Since Tom will start his new job next week, he has to make some _____ (adjust) to his daily routine as soon as possible.

II. Vocabulary Choice

(A) adjectives   (B) additional   (C) accuse   (D) acres   (E) achieve

(F) acquire   (G) acids   (H) adapt   (I) admits   (J) adequate

1. Passion fruits contain _____ and sugars, nutrients and non-nutritive elements that make the fruits tasty and healthy.

2. Cindy and Debbie bought _____ foreign currency for their trip in case their credit cards got lost.

3. The college is surrounded by 90 _____ of unspoilt views of the countryside.

4. The words "interesting", "red", "absolute" and "small" are all _____ .

5. My boss _____ that the project he has assigned us is not easy to complete.

Unit 3

adventure [əd'vɛn.tʃə] *n.* 探險；冒險

同 **exploit / experience**

▶ I like to travel around the world looking for new adventures.
我喜歡環遊世界，尋找新的探險。

---

adverb ['æd.vɝːb] *n.* 副詞

▶ Use adverbs like "quickly" and "quietly" when describing the thief's actions.
當在形容小偷的行為時，可使用像是「快速地」，「輕聲地」這樣的副詞。

---

advertise ['æd.vɚ.taɪz] *v.* 為⋯廣告

搭 **advertise product** 為產品廣告

同 **exhibit / promote**

實用片語
advertise for 登廣告

▶ You need to advertise your restaurant if you want more customers.
如果你想要更多顧客上門，就必須登廣告，宣傳你的餐廳。

▶ We need to advertise for some new sales reps.
我們需要登廣告徵一些新的銷售代表。

---

advertisement / ad ['æd.vɝː.taɪz.mənt] *n.* 廣告

同 **announcement / notice**

▶ The diet advertisement I saw on television made me want to lose weight.
我在電視上看到的減肥廣告讓我想要減肥。

---

advice [əd'vaɪs] *n.* 建議；勸告

搭 **constructive advice** 建設性的忠告

同 **guidance / suggestion**

實用片語
sage advice 睿智的忠告

▶ If you want advice on dating, you should talk to your mother.
如果你想要約會的建議，就應該跟你媽媽談談。

▶ The elder manager gives sage advice.
資深經理給了一些睿智的忠告。

---

advise [əd'vaɪz] *v.* 建議；勸告

搭 **strongly advise** 強列建議

同 **instruct / suggest**

實用片語
keep someone advised 讓某人隨時知道進展

▶ The doctor advised me to stop smoking.
醫生建議我停止吸菸。

▶ Please keep me advised of new progress made in this project.
請隨時讓我知道此專案的進展。

adviser / advisor [ədˈvaɪ.zɚ ; ədˈvaɪ.zɚ]

n. 顧問；指導教授

搭 **personal advisor** 私人顧問

同 **mentor / teacher**

▶ The President of the United States is surrounded by advisors to help him make decisions.

美國總統周遭有顧問可以協助他作決策。

95

affect [əˈfekt] *v.* 影響

同 **influence / impact**

▶ The death of her classmate affected her.

她同班同學的過世對她造成影響。

95

afford [əˈfɔːrd] *v.* 負擔得起；付得起；買得起

搭 **afford the luxury** 買得起高檔貨

同 **allow / sustain**

實用片語
afford to 可負擔得起

▶ I can't afford to stay at a five star hotel, but I can afford to stay at a three star hotel.

我負擔不起五星級旅館的住宿費，但負擔得起三星級的。

▶ I can't afford to eat in expensive restaurants.

我負擔不起在昂貴的餐廳用餐。

---

afterwards [ˈæf.tɚ.wɚdz] *adv.* 以後；之後

同 **eventually / later**

▶ We went to the movies, and afterwards we got some ice cream.

我們去看了電影，後來又去吃了冰淇淋。

---

aged [ˈeɪ.dʒɪd / eɪdʒd] *adj.* 年邁的；舊的

同 **elderly / ancient**

▶ The aged man walked slowly to his apartment.

這位老人家慢慢地走到他的公寓。

97

agency [ˈeɪ.dʒən.si] *n.* 署；代辦處；代理商

搭 **travel agency** 旅行社

同 **company / firm**

▶ This space agency prepares astronauts for traveling to the moon.

這個太空總署會幫助太空人做好登上月球的準備。

---

agent [ˈeɪ.dʒənt] *n.* 仲介；代理商

同 **assistant / officer**

實用片語
free agent 自由球員

▶ Peter suggested that Molly hire an agent to help her find acting jobs.

彼得建議茉莉去請個仲介幫她介紹表演的工作。

▶ After he is released from the Nets, he will be a free agent.

在他被 NETS 釋出後，他是個自由球員。

96

aggressive [ə'gres.ɪv]

adj. 積極進取的;有幹勁的;侵略的

搭 **aggressive attitude** 積極的態度

同 **energetic / bold**

▶ Some people think you should be more aggressive in a competitive job market.

有些人認為在這個競爭激烈的人力市場中,你應該要再積極進取一點。

---

agreeable [ə'griː.ə.bəl] *adj.* 令人愉快的

搭 **perfectly agreeable** 完全可接受

同 **enjoyable / pleasant**

▶ Can you please try to be more agreeable so we can find a solution to our problem?

能不能請你再隨和一點,所以我們才能為我們的問題找出解決方案?

---

agriculture ['æg.rə.kʌl.tʃɚ] *n.* 農業

同 **farming / cultivation**

▶ If you want a career in farming, you should study agriculture.

如果你想要務農,就應該攻讀農學。

AIDS / acquired immune deficiency syndrome [eɪdz] *n.* 愛滋病

▶ Doctors are working to find a cure for AIDS.

醫生們正努力找出治好愛滋病的方法。

---

air-conditioner / air-con

['er kən.dɪʃ.ən.ɚ / 'er kɑːn] *n.* 空調機;冷(暖)氣機

▶ Please turn on the air-conditioner, it's getting way too hot.

請打開空調,實在太熱了。

---

alcohol ['æl.kə.hɑːl] *n.* 酒精

▶ Harry's alcohol addiction ruined many of his relationships.

哈利的酒癮破壞了他很多的人際關係。

103

alert [ə'lɝːt]

① *adj.* 清醒的;機警的

搭 **mentally alert** 精神警醒

同 **attentive / sharp**

② *v.* 向…報警

同 **warn / inform**

實用片語
alert the public 警示大眾

▶ I tried to stay alert in class, but I was too tired.

我試著在課堂上保持清醒,但是實在是太累了。

▶ Alert the police if you see the thief.

如果你看到小偷,要趕快報警。

▶ You need to alert the public of drinking too much coffee.

您需要警示大眾飲用過多咖啡的問題。

③ *n.* 警報

搭 **issue alert** 發出警告

同 **alarm / signal**

實用片語
on the alert 提高警覺

▶ Typhoon alert: everyone stay indoors.
颱風警報：所有人留在屋內。

▶ You should be on the alert for thieves.
您應提高警覺小心扒手。

---

alley [ˈæl.i] *n.* 小巷

同 **lane / pathway**

實用片語
right up someone's alley 拿手，得心應手

▶ To get to the cafe, go through the alley and make a left.
去咖啡店的方向是，穿過小巷子後左轉。

▶ Computer programming is right up my alley.
編寫電腦程式我很拿手。

---

allowance [əˈlaʊ.əns] *n.* 零用錢

搭 **receive allowance** 收到零用錢

同 **wage / stipend**

實用片語
make allowance for 留有餘裕

▶ My siblings and I get a weekly allowance if we do our chores.
我的手足和我只要做好我們的家事，就可以每週拿到零用錢。

▶ I am making allowance for 20 extra attendees.
我會考慮多留二十個與會者的座位。

---

aluminum [ˌæl.jəˈmɪn.i.əm] *n.* 鋁

▶ The nice thing about aluminum is it cools down quickly after it's out of the oven.
鋁的好處就是，它一出了烤箱就會很快的冷卻。

---

amateur [ˈæm.ə.tʃə]

① *n.* 業餘愛好者

同 **novice / apprentice**

② *adj.* 非職業的；業餘的

搭 **amateur gardener** 業餘園丁

同 **novice / beginner**

▶ Sonny is a great artist, but he is an amateur and doesn't make any money from his paintings.
索尼是位很棒的藝術家，但他只是位業餘者，完全不靠賣畫賺錢。

▶ I paid way too much money for that amateur performance.
我花了太多錢去看那場不到職業水準的表演。

---

amaze [əˈmeɪz] *v.* 使驚奇；使驚訝

同 **astonish / impress**

▶ The young girl's ice skating performance amazed the audience.
年輕女孩的滑冰表演讓觀眾驚嘆不已。

Exercise 3

I. Derivatives

1. One of David's dream jobs is to work for the Central Intelligence _____ (agent) when he grows up.

2. This company is good at using very creative _____ (advertise) to sell their products.

3. Ariel works as a special _____ (advise) to the president on children's issues.

4. My grandmother _____ (age) so beautifully that people can't believe she is almost 85 years old.

5. The sunny weather was very _____ (agree) for spending the day at the beach.

II. Vocabulary Choice

(A) aggressive   (B) advanced   (C) adopt   (D) alcohol   (E) adventure
(F) allowance   (G) air-conditioner   (H) agriculture   (I) agent   (J) afford

1. I can't _____ another trip abroad this year as I have already used up my yearly travel budget.

2. Daniel is very _____ in his job and he believes that he can become the CEO of the company one day.

3. My father gave me a weekly _____ of NT$500 in my childhood and I spent it all on games.

4. Driving a car or riding a motorcycle after drinking _____ is dangerous and illegal.

5. Over 70 per cent of the Indian population depends on _____ for their living.

Unit 4

amazed [ə'meɪzd] *adj.* 吃驚的；感到驚奇的

同 **astonished / stunned**

▶ Stephanie was amazed when she heard she got the job.
史緹芬妮聽到自己得到那份工作時，感到相當吃驚。

(98)

amazement [ə'meɪz.mənt] *n.* 驚奇

▶ To his amazement, he received a perfect score on his science test.
他很驚訝他的科學考試居然得了滿分。

(103)

amazing [ə'mezɪŋ] *adj.* 驚人的；令人吃驚的

搭 **amazing story** 令人驚訝的故事

同 **incredible / awesome**

▶ The change in his behavior after his teacher scolded him was amazing.
在被老師罵過之後，他的行為改變真是叫人吃驚。

ambassador [æm'bæs.ə.dɚ] *n.* 大使

同 **representative / consul**

▶ The ambassador of France will arrive in New York tomorrow morning.
法國大使明天上午會抵達紐約。

(100)

ambition [æm'bɪʃ.ən] *n.* 雄心；抱負

同 **passion / aspiration**

▶ His main ambition in life is to become rich and powerful.
他主要的人生抱負是變得富有和有權勢。

(95)

ambitious [æm'bɪʃ.əs] *adj.* 有野心的

搭 **ambitious project** 胸懷大志的專案

同 **earnest / aggressive**

▶ If you're just starting an exercise routine, don't be too ambitious or you may hurt yourself.
如果你才剛開始作一套新的運動動作，不要太有野心，否則會傷到自己。

amid / amidst [ə'mɪd ; ə-mɪdst] *prep.* 在⋯之中

▶ One lonely tree stood out amid a field of flowers.
一棵孤樹矗立在萬花叢裡。

amuse [ə'mjuːz] *v.* 逗人笑；使歡樂

同 **gratify / cheer**

實用片語
amuse with 以⋯取悅

▶ My classmate always tries to amuse us with her silly jokes.
我的同學老是講些很蠢的笑話來逗我們開心。

▶ I tried to amuse my son with this little toy.
我試著用這個小玩具逗我兒子開心。

amused [əˈmjuːzd] *adj.* 被逗樂的；頑皮的

同 **entertained / diverted**

▶ The child was amused by the dog chasing the cat.
小孩子看到狗追貓時，被逗得很開心。

---

amusement [əˈmjuːz.mənt] *n.* 娛樂；樂趣

搭 **amusement park** 遊樂園
同 **delight / pleasure**

▶ Movies and magazines are just two of the amusement options on the flight.
電影和雜誌只是飛機上的兩項娛樂選項。

97

amusing [əˈmjuː.zɪŋ]
adj. 好玩的；有趣的；引人發笑的

搭 **amusing incident** 有趣的事件
同 **engaging / entertaining**

▶ We spent an amusing day at the park.
我們在公園裡度過很好玩的一天。

---

analysis [əˈnæl.ə.sɪs] *n.* 分析；解析

同 **reasoning / investigation**
實用片語
in the final analysis 歸根究底

▶ The doctor conducted a thorough analysis of his patient's problem.
醫生針對他的病人的問題進行了一項澈底的分析。

▶ In the final analysis, the only people who will benefit from the new plan are managers.
歸根究底，唯一在新計畫中受益的人會是高層經理們。

---

analyze [ˈæn.əl.aɪz] *v.* 分析

搭 **analyze problem** 分析問題
同 **evaluate / inspect**

▶ Let's analyze the situation before we try to solve the problem.
在我們解決問題之前，先好好地分析狀況吧。

97

ancestor [ˈæn.ses.tɚ] *n.* 祖先

同 **forefather / ascendant**

▶ Many people in this country worship their ancestors.
這個國家有很多的民眾會祭祖。

---

angel [ˈeɪn.dʒəl] *n.* 天使

實用片語
guardian angel 守護神

▶ I believe we all have a guardian angel that watches over us.
我相信我們每個人都有一位守護天使看顧我們。

▶ You were lucky to avoid that accident. You must have a guardian angel.
你很幸運的躲過那場意外。你一定是有守護神。

98

angle [ˈæŋ.ɡəl] *n.* 角度

搭 **measure angle** 測量角度

同 **edge / aspect**

實用片語
know all the angles 瞭解所有眉角；在行

▶ We're practicing measuring angles in math class using a special tool.
在數學課，我們用一種特殊工具來練習測量角度。

▶ Ask Jerry about Math. He knows all the angles.
數學問題要問傑瑞。他對數學很在行。

104

anniversary [ˌæn.əˈvɝː.sɚ.i] *n.* 週年紀念日

同 **ceremony / festival**

▶ We'll be celebrating our fiftieth wedding anniversary next year!
我們明年將會慶祝結婚五十週年紀念。

---

announce [əˈnaʊns] *v.* 宣布

搭 **announce decision** 宣佈決定

同 **reveal / declare**

實用片語
announce to 宣佈

▶ He announced the top three winners of the speech contest.
他宣佈演講的前三名獲勝者。

▶ They will announce the news to the public.
他們將向大眾宣佈消息。

98

announcement [əˈnaʊns.mənt] *n.* 宣布

同 **publicity / broadcast**

▶ I have an announcement to make…I am pregnant!
我要宣佈一件事…我懷孕了！

---

announcer [əˈnaʊn.sɚ] *n.* 播報員；宣告者

同 **reporter / broadcaster**

▶ The announcer told the crowd that the concert was over.
播報員告知聽眾，演唱會已經結束了。

95

annoy [əˈnɔɪ] *v.* 令人惱怒；令人討厭

同 **disturb / trouble**

▶ The noise cicadas make annoys me.
我覺得蟬的叫聲真是討厭。

---

annoyed [əˈnɔɪd]
adj. 感到厭煩的；感到惱怒的；感到討厭的

同 **bothered / upset**

實用片語
annoyed about 被…惱火

▶ Everyone on the plane was annoyed by the crying baby.
飛機上的乘客對哭鬧不停的嬰兒，感到很厭煩。

▶ I was a bit annoyed about their argument.
我對於他們的爭吵有點惱火。

annoying [əˈnɔɪ.ɪŋ] *adj.* 惱人的；令人討厭的

搭 **somewhat annoying** 有點煩人

同 **irritating / disturbing**

▶ Her annoying cough kept her awake.
她被惱人的咳嗽弄得無法入睡。

---

annual [ˈæn.ju.əl] *adj.* 年度的

搭 **annual meeting** 年度會議

同 **yearly / once a year**

▶ Spring Scream is an annual event that takes place in Kenting.
「春吶」是場每年在墾丁舉辦的活動。

---

anxiety [æŋˈzaɪ.ə.tj] *n.* 焦慮；掛念

同 **suffering / concern**

▶ I always experience a lot of anxiety before a big test.
我慣性在大考前會感到極度的焦慮。

Exercise 4

I. 中英對應

_____ 1. 角度　　(A) angel　　　　　(B) anger

　　　　　　　　(C) angle　　　　　(D) analyze

_____ 2. 大使　　(A) ambition　　　(B) ambassador

　　　　　　　　(C) amateur　　　　(D) ambulance

_____ 3. 播報員　(A) annoyed　　　(B) announce

　　　　　　　　(C) announcement　(D) announcer

_____ 4. 在…之中　(A) amidst　　　(B) amount

　　　　　　　　(C) ambitious　　　(D) amuse

_____ 5. 祖先　　(A) accent　　　　(B) account

　　　　　　　　(C) ancestor　　　　(D) ancient

II. Derivatives

1. It was _____ (amaze) how well the airport handled the situation after it was hit by flooding twice in a month.

2. According to the latest _____ (analyze), the bus driver should be held responsible for the accident in which tourists burned to death.

3. Helen often draws pictures for her own _____ (amuse) in her leisure time.

4. Qin Shi Huang was an _____ (ambition) king who wanted too much. He was the first emperor of the Qin dynasty.

5. It is really _____ (annoy) that he is always late for our appointments.

102 99 98 95

anxious [ˈæŋk.ʃəs] *adj.* 焦急的；憂心的

搭 **anxious parents** 焦慮的父母

同 **afraid / fearful**

實用片語
anxious for 渴望，擔憂

▶ I'm glad the test is over, but now I'm anxious about the results.
我很高興考試已經結束了，但是現在另我焦急的是考試的結果。

▶ We are all very anxious for their safety.
我們都很擔憂他們的安全。

101

apart [əˈpɑːrt] *adv.* 分開地

同 **aside / by itself**

實用片語
apart from 除了⋯之外

▶ My sister and I are identical twins, but we were born fifteen hours apart.
我跟我的姊妹是雙胞胎，但是我們出生時間相隔 15 個小時。

▶ Apart from practicing yoga, she gets no exercise.
除了練習瑜珈，她沒有其他運動。

---

apologize [əˈpɑː.lə.dʒaɪz] *v.* 道歉；認錯

搭 **apologize profusely** 不斷地道歉

同 **confess / ask pardon**

實用片語
apologize for 為⋯道歉

▶ I apologize for breaking your vase; will you forgive me?
我為打破你的花瓶向你道歉。你願意原諒我嗎？

▶ You need to apologize for your past mistakes.
你需要為你過去的錯誤道歉。

---

apology [əˈpɑː.lə.dʒi] *n.* 道歉；賠罪

搭 **sincere apology** 誠心道歉

同 **regret / concession**

實用片語
apology for 為⋯道歉

▶ I accept your apology; of course I forgive you!
我接受你的道歉。我當然會原諒你啊！

▶ Jack offered an apology for losing the case.
傑克因為失去案子而道歉。

101

apparent [əˈper.ənt] *adj.* 明顯的

同 **obvious / clear**

▶ It was becoming very apparent that their relationship was not going to last.
他們的關係越來越明顯不會持續下去。

apparently [əˈper.ənt.li] *adv.* 顯然地；明顯地

搭 **apparently unrelated** 明顯地不相關

同 **clearly / obviously**

▶ A tree in the forest apparently fell down.
顯然森林中有一棵樹倒了。

---

appeal [əˈpiːl]

① *n.* 吸引力；感染力

搭 **strong appeal** 強烈吸引力

同 **allure / charm**

實用片語
street appeal 街景，視野

② *v.* 呼籲；請求

同 **request / claim**

▶ Steven Spielberg movies seem to have a lot of appeal.
史蒂夫 · 史匹柏的電影似乎有很大的吸引力。

▶ We bought this house because of its wonderful street appeal.
我們因為房子亮麗的街景而買下它。

▶ They're appealing for food and clothes to send to the victims of the tsunami disaster.
他們正呼籲把食物和衣服送去給海嘯災害的受害者。

---

appliance [əˈplaɪ.əns]

n. 電器用品；器具；設備

搭 **heating appliance** 暖氣設備

同 **device / gadget**

▶ My house lacks important appliances like microwaves and toasters.
我的家裡缺少像微波爐及烤麵包機這些重要的電器用品。

---

applicant [ˈæp.lə.kənt] *n.* 應徵者；申請人

同 **candidate / seeker**

▶ It's hard for the boss to decide which applicants to hire.
老闆很難決定要錄用哪一位應徵者。

---

application [ˌæp.ləˈkeɪ.ʃən] *n.* 申請；應用

搭 **job application** 工作申請

同 **request / petition**

實用片語
make an application 提出申請

▶ Please fill out the application form on that table over there.
麻煩請填寫放在那張桌子上面的申請表格。

▶ I'd like to make an application for a scholarship.
我想要申請獎學金。

appoint [ə'pɔɪnt]

① v. 指派；任命

同 **assign / designate**

實用片語
appoint to 指派

② v. 委任；任命

▶ I appoint you to be my assistant.
我指派你當我的助理。

▶ I will appoint you to the position of Sales Director.
我將指派你擔任銷售總監的職位。

▶ The CEO appointed a new marketing manager yesterday.
執行長昨天委任了一位新的行銷經理。

---

appointment [ə'pɔɪnt.mənt]

① n. 任命；委派的任務

同 **selection / assignment**

② n. 預約；約會

搭 **arrange an appointment** 安排會議

同 **meeting / interview**

實用片語
make an appointment 預約會議

▶ Shirley's appointment as manager surprised me; I didn't think she was good enough for the job.
雪莉被任命為經理這件事令我吃驚；我不覺得她配得上那個職位。

▶ You can't just walk in here and ask to see the doctor; you need to make an appointment.
你不能直接走進來就要給醫生看診；你必須要先預約。

▶ I've made an appointment with the doctor for today.
我已經預約今天看醫生的時間。

---

appreciate [ə'pri:.ʃi.eɪt] v. 欣賞

同 **adore / admire**

▶ As a painter, I really appreciate the work of Leonardo da Vinci.
身為一位畫家，我真的很欣賞達文西的作品。

---

appreciation [ə.pri:.ʃi'eɪ.ʃə] n. 欣賞；賞識

搭 **express appreciation** 表達感謝

同 **gratitude / thankfulness**

▶ The boss has always had an appreciation for his assistant's work.
那位老闆對他助理的工作表現相當賞識。

---

approach [ə'proʊtʃ]

① v. 接近

搭 **approach the problem** 迎向問題

同 **reach / go forwards**

實用片語
approach someone about
接近，找某人…談某事

▶ Summer is approaching fast, so be sure to find that perfect swimsuit soon.
夏季將近，務必儘快找到那件最好看的泳衣。

▶ I will approach Judy about the lost case.
我將會跟茱蒂商量那件搞砸的案子。

② *n.* 接近；靠近

搭 **propose approach** 提出方法

同 **access / nearing**

▶ The plane is now making its final approach into JFK airport.
飛機現在正向甘乃迪機場最後進場。

98

appropriate [əˈproʊ.pri.ət]

adj. 恰當的；適當的

搭 **appropriate language** 適當的用語

同 **relevant / proper**

▶ Your slippers are not appropriate for this fancy dinner.
你穿的拖鞋非常不適合這麼高級的晚宴。

---

approval [əˈpruː.vəl] *n.* 認同；認可

同 **agreement / permission**

▶ Casey cares too much about other peoples' approval.
凱西太在乎別人對他是否認同。

104

approve [əˈpruːv] *v.* 贊成；同意

搭 **approve the scheme** 確定主題

同 **accept / respect**

實用片語

approve of 准許，認可

▶ My father doesn't approve of my boyfriend because he is a smoker.
我爸爸不贊成我跟男友交往，因為他是一個菸槍。

▶ My teacher doesn't approve of using cellphones in class.
我的老師不准我們在班上使用手機。

---

aquarium [əˈkwer.i.əm] *n.* 水族箱

▶ Paul wants to put an aquarium in his house so he can enjoy looking at his fish.
保羅想在他家放一個水族箱，這樣就可以享受賞魚的樂趣。

---

arch [ɑːrtʃ]

① *n.* 拱門

② *v.* 拱起；形成弧形

同 **curve / bend**

▶ The city hall has beautiful arches in its entrance way.
市政府的入口處有幾座非常漂亮的拱門。

▶ My cat only arches her back when she's scared.
我的貓只有害怕的時候才會拱起背部。

98

arise [əˈraɪz] *v.* 起立；上升

搭 **trouble arise** 問題產生

同 **increase / soar**

▶ When the president enters, please arise and give him a warm round of applause.
當總統進來的時候，請大家起立並且給他熱烈的掌聲。

arithmetic / arithmetical

[əˈrɪθ.mə.tɪk ; ˌær.ɪθ.ˈmet.ɪ.kəl]

① *n.* 算術
② *adj.* 算術的

---

armed [ɑːrmd] *adj.* 攜帶槍械的；武裝的

同 equipped / loaded

---

arms [ɑːmz] *n.* 武器

---

arouse [əˈraʊz] *v.* 喚起；發憤

搭 **arouse passion** 喚起熱情

同 **awaken / provoke**

實用片語
arouse someone from 叫醒某人

▶ Do the arithmetic to find out how much we owe exactly.
算看看我們究竟欠多少錢。

▶ I am having a difficult time solving this arithmetical problem.
我不知道如何解決這個算數問題。

▶ The police officer stopped the armed robber.
警官制伏了攜帶槍械的強匪。

▶ The soldiers need more arms to protect the little town.
士兵們需要更多的武器來保護這座小城鎮。

▶ Sleeping Beauty was aroused from sleep when Prince Charming kissed her.
當白馬王子親吻睡美人時，她就從睡夢中被喚醒過來。

▶ I couldn't arouse her from her deep sleep.
我無法將熟睡的她叫醒。

Exercise 5

I. Derivatives

1. My boss showed his _____ (appreciate) for my work by raising my end of year bonus.
2. The salesman has an _____ (appoint) with my supervisor to introduce his products.
3. Steve finally submitted his job _____ (applicant) to the company last Friday.
4. I _____ (apology) for taking so long to reply to your Line message.
5. The student was late for school this morning, _____ (apparent) because the bus he was on had an accident.

II. Vocabulary Choice

(A) aquarium　(B) anxious　(C) appreciate　(D) apart　(E) announce
(F) anniversary　(G) appeal　(H) apology　(I) appliances　(J) approach

1. The _____ of summer means it is time to start using sunscreen to protect your skin.
2. Baseball has popular _____ in our country and every young boy wants to become a famous player.
3. Deborah likes to keep fish as pets, so she has an _____ in her office filled with colorful fish and cute decorations.
4. My mom's kitchen is equipped with modern _____ , such as the dishwasher, refrigerator and an oven.
5. I really _____ movies made by Pixar such as Finding Nemo, The Incredibles and Toy Story, etc because they teach valuable lessons.

103

arrival [əˈraɪ.vəl] *n.* 到達

同 **landing / return**

實用片語
dead on arrival 到達已死，上線就壞

▶ Due to his late arrival, the meeting had to be rescheduled.
因為他遲到，所以這個會議必須重新安排時間召開。

▶ Healthcare reform was dead on arrival, because too many people opposed it.
因為許多人反對，醫療改革已胎死腹中。

---

article [ˈɑːr.ţɪ.kəl] *n.* 一件；物品

同 **piece / commodity**

實用片語
genuine article 正品，真貨

▶ This colorful shirt is my favorite article of clothing.
這件色彩豐富的襯衫是我最喜歡的一件衣服。

▶ Is this a genuine article or a fake knock off?
這是真品還是假貨？

97

artificial [ˌɑːr.ţəˈfɪʃ.əl] *adj.* 人造的；人工的

搭 **artificial intelligence** 人工智慧
同 **unreal / fake**

▶ Sandy's jacket is made of artificial leather.
珊蒂的夾克是人造皮革製成的。

---

artistic [ɑːrˈtɪs.tɪk] *adj.* 藝術的

同 **creative / dramatic**

▶ We want the students to develop their artistic skills.
我們希望學生能夠提升他們的藝術技能。

104

ascending [əˈsen.dɪŋ] *adj.* 上升的

同 **climb / soar**

▶ The ascending trail takes you to the top of the mountain.
這條上坡的小徑會引領你到達山頂。

---

ash [ˈæʃ] *n.* 灰燼

▶ The building that was on fire yesterday has completely burned to ashes.
昨天失火的那棟建築物已經完全燒成灰燼。

104

ashamed [əˈʃeɪmd] *adj.* 羞愧的

搭 **deeply ashamed** 極度羞愧
同 **bashful / embarrassed**

▶ You should be ashamed of yourself for stealing that puppy.
你應該為自己偷小狗的那件事感到羞愧。

aside [əˈsaɪd] *adv.* 在旁邊

實用片語
put aside 放一邊，保留

▶ Step aside please so these people can pass.
請站到一邊，好讓這些人通過。

▶ Let's put aside the idea until the next meeting.
我們保留這個點子到下次會議討論。

aspect [ˈæs.pekt] *n.* 層面；方面；觀點

搭 **stress aspect** 強調觀點
同 **facet / viewpoint**

▶ One aspect of teaching is preparing the lessons.
教學的一個層面就是預備課程。

aspirin [ˈæs.prɪn] *n.* 阿斯匹林

▶ Take an aspirin after a stroke; it will help thin your blood.
在中風之後吃顆阿斯匹靈；它可以幫助稀釋你的血液。

 102

assemble [əˈsem.bəl] *v.* 召集；聚集

同 **compile / gather**

▶ Assemble the staff for a meeting.
召集員工們開會。

assembly [əˈsem.bli] *n.* 聚會；集合

搭 **assembly line** 生產線
同 **association / rally**

▶ Only twenty people out of a hundred showed up for the assembly.
一百人當中只有二十個人出席那個聚會。

102

assign [əˈsaɪn] *v.* 分派

同 **appoint / authorize**

實用片語
assign ... to 派⋯給

▶ Since you are the best at washing dishes, I'll assign that task to you.
既然你最會洗碗盤，我就把那項任務分派給你。

▶ They assigned the responsibility of planning the trip to Jack.
他們把規劃行程的責任派給傑克。

assignment [əˈsaɪn.mənt] *n.* 任務

搭 **homework assignment** 家庭作業
同 **duty / mission**

▶ The manager's newest assignment seemed strange to everybody.
經理最近指派的任務，在大家看來都感到很奇怪。

assist [əˈsɪst] *v.* 協助

同 **aid / support**

實用片語
assist in 協助

▶ The nurse assisted the patient to her room.
護士協助病人去她的病房。

▶ You have to assist the engineers in testing the product.
你必須協助工程師測試產品。

---

assistance [əˈsɪs.təns] *n.* 協助;幫助

搭 **provide assistance** 提供服務

同 **backing / service**

實用片語
come to someone's assistance
前來援助,即時解救

▶ I need your assistance in the office today.
我今天在公司裡需要你的協助。

▶ I am sure someone will come to our assistance soon.
我很確定很快就會有人趕來協助我們。

---

104 102 100

associate [əˈsoʊ.ʃi.ˌeɪt] *v.* 聯想

同 **correlate / link**

實用片語
associate with 聯想,產生關連

▶ I always associate pop music with Michael Jackson.
我總是把流行音樂和麥可傑克森聯想在一起。

▶ I always associate story books with my mother.
我總是把故事書跟媽媽聯想在一起。

associate [əˈsoʊ.ʃi.ˌət]

① *n.* 同事;合夥人

搭 **associate professor** 副教授

同 **colleague / coworker**

② *adj.* 副的;準的

▶ My associate will show you the way to the restroom.
我的同事會指引你洗手間怎麼走。

▶ The associate editor at our magazine company is sometimes busier than the managing editor.
我們雜誌出版社的副主編有時候比主編還要忙。

104

association [əˌsoʊ.siˈeɪ.ʃən] *n.* 協會

同 **organization / partnership**

▶ The Chinese Christian Relief Association helps people in need all over the country.
華人基督教救助協會在國內各地幫助有需要的人。

101

assume [əˈsuːm] *v.* 以為;假定為…

搭 **immediately assume** 馬上就認為

同 **consider / expect**

▶ Greg assumed mom wouldn't mind if he ate a cookie. He was wrong; mom was angry.
葛雷格以為媽媽不會介意他吃塊餅乾。結果他錯了,媽媽非常的生氣。

assurance [əˈʃʊr.əns] *n.* 保證

同 **pledge / promise**

▶ I can give you full assurance that our plan will succeed.

我可以給你百分之百的保證，我們的計畫一定會成功。

---

104 99 95

assure [əˈʃʊr] *v.* 向…保證

搭 **assure success** 確保成功

同 **convince / persuade**

實用片語
assure of 確定，保證

▶ Tony assured Tina that she would be safe while bungee jumping.

東尼向緹娜保證，她做高空彈跳絕對是安全的。

▶ I want to assure you of our good intentions.

我想跟您保證我們的意圖良善。

---

astonished [əˈstɑː.nɪʃt] *adj.* 感到驚訝的

同 **surprised / stunned**

▶ The children were astonished by the circus performers.

小朋友們對馬戲團的團員們讚嘆不已。

---

astonishing [əˈstɑː.nɪ.ʃɪŋ]

adj. 驚人的；令人驚訝的

搭 **astonishing speed** 驚人的速度

同 **surprising / amazing**

▶ He could eat an astonishing amount of noodles.

他可以吃下份量極驚人的麵食。

---

athlete [ˈæθ.liːt] *n.* 運動員

▶ Michael Jordan is one of the greatest athletes of all time.

麥克 · 喬登是史上最偉大的運動員之一。

---

athletic [æθˈlet.ɪk] *adj.* 運動的

同 **energetic / strong**

▶ The athletic team will attend more competitions this year.

這支體育團隊今年會參加更多的比賽。

Exercise 6

I. Derivatives

1. The students need to go into the stadium for _____ (assemble) every morning where the principal will talk about important things for the day.

2. John has many reading _____ (assign) to finish before the end of semester.

3. The fans waited through the night for the _____ (arrive) of the movie stars.

4. China Airlines is one of the members of the International Air Transport _____ (associate).

5. The presidential candidate gave her _____ (assure) that she will draft policies to reduce the unemployment rate if she wins the election.

II. Vocabulary Choice

(A) article   (B) artificial   (C) assistance   (D) ash   (E) ascending

(F) aspect   (G) aspirin   (H) ashamed   (I) astonished   (J) artistic

1. The birth of Robert's son affects almost every _____ of his life, from his sleep to his plans for the future.

2. Grace needs her brother's _____ to prepare for the final exams as she is not good at Math or English.

3. This juice contains no _____ colors or flavors.

4. The public was _____ over the news of the TransAsia Airways crash in Taipei, especially after the plane hit a taxi before crashing into the river.

5. He should be _____ of himself for using bad language at his teacher. It is a very rude thing to do.

Unit 7

ATM / automatic teller machine
[ˌeɪ.tiˈem] *n.* 自動櫃員機

▶ Carrie went to the ATM to withdraw some cash.
凱瑞到自動櫃員機去提取現金。

---

(95)

atmosphere [ˈæt.mə.sfɪr] *n.* 氣氛

搭 **learning atmosphere** 學習氛圍

同 **ambience / climate**

實用片語
clear the atmosphere 消除誤會

▶ The atmosphere in the theater was very tense during auditions.
在試鏡時，整個戲院的氣氛都令人緊張。

▶ I am not sure if Mr. Chen is still mad, but you can try to clear the atmosphere by apologizing first.
我不確定陳先生是否還在生氣，但你可以試著先道歉來消除誤會。

---

atom [ˈæt̬.əm] *n.* 原子

▶ There are millions of atoms just on the tip of your pencil.
單是你的筆尖就有數百萬顆的原子。

---

atomic [əˈtɑː.mɪk] *adj.* 原子的

▶ Atomic bombs are terrible weapons.
原子彈是非常可怕的武器。

---

attach [əˈtætʃ] *v.* 附上；裝上；貼上

同 **connect / unite**

實用片語
attach oneself to 參與，加入

▶ Grandma attached a sweet card to my Christmas gift.
祖母在我的聖誕禮物上附上了一張貼心的卡片。

▶ Sam attached himself to the tree, so that he doesn't fall.
山姆把身體貼著樹，所以他才沒有跌倒。

---

(101)

attachment [əˈtætʃ.mənt] *n.* 附件

同 **addition / supplement**

▶ The stereo comes with an attachment that allows you to access Wi-Fi.
這套音響還附贈一個附加裝置，讓你可以連接無線網路。

---

attempt [əˈtempt]

① *v.* 企圖；試圖

同 **try / make effort**

實用片語
attempt to 試圖

▶ Jon attempted to read the novel in three days, but it took him over a week to finish it.
喬恩試圖在三天內讀完這本小說，但實際上卻花了一個多禮拜才看完。

▶ Mary attempted to reach the drowning child, but did not succeed.
瑪莉試圖救起溺水的兒童，但失敗了。

② *n.* 企圖；試圖

搭 **desperate attempt** 強烈企圖

同 **effort / pursuit**

► To everyone's surprise, she caught a shark on her first attempt at fishing.
令大家意外的是，她第一次嘗試釣魚，就釣到一條鯊魚。

---

attitude [ˈæt̬.ə.tuːd] *n.* 態度

搭 **positive attitude** 正面的態度

同 **demeanor / position**

實用片語
wait-and-see attitude 再看看之態度

► The key to a happy life is to keep a positive attitude.
快樂生活的秘訣是保持正面積極的態度。

► Jenny thought Tom couldn't make it, but she took a wait-and-see attitude.
珍妮認為湯姆辦不到，但她抱持觀望態度。

---

attract [əˈtrækt] *v.* 吸引

搭 **attract attention** 吸引注意

同 **draw / allure**

實用片語
attract ... to 吸引

► Rats are attracted to the smell of peanut butter, so be sure not to leave any out.
花生醬的味道會引來老鼠，所以絕對不能把花生醬放在外面。

► The advertisement attracted a lot of people to the concert.
廣告吸引了許多人來參加音樂會。

---

attraction [əˈtræk.ʃən] *n.* 吸引力

同 **allure / appeal**

實用片語
center of attraction 焦點

► Yolanda feels a deep attraction to Henry and wants to marry him.
尤蘭深深被亨利吸引，並且想要嫁給他。

► Jack is always the center of attraction wherever he goes.
傑克不論走到哪裡都是目光焦點。

---

attractive [əˈtræk.tɪv] *adj.* 迷人的；吸引人的

搭 **attractive appearance** 吸引人的外表

同 **charming / appealing**

► The woman in the red dress is very attractive.
那位穿紅色洋裝的女子非常迷人。

---

audience [ˈɑː.di.əns] *n.* 觀眾

同 **public / crowd**

實用片語
captive audience 受限（不離開）之觀眾

► Speaking in front of a large audience can be quite terrifying.
在廣大觀眾的面前演講頗嚇人的。

► The key to maintaining a captive audience is to make sure your presentation is interesting.
維持聽眾不想離開的關鍵在於，要確認你的簡報內容很有趣。

audio [ˈɑː.di.oʊ] *adj.* 聲音的

▶ The audio quality of these speakers is the best I've ever heard.
這些喇叭的音質是我所聽過中最棒的。

---

author [ˈɑː.θɚ]

① *n.* 作者
搭 **famous author** 名作家
同 **editor / novelist**
② *v.* 寫作

▶ She is an American author who has written over thirty children's books.
她是一位美國作家，已著有超過三十本童書。

▶ She has authored over 20 magazine articles.
她已為雜誌寫了超過二十篇文章了。

103
authority [əˈθɔːr.ə.tj] *n.* 權力；職權
同 **force / government**
實用片語
have it on good authority 有可靠根據

▶ You don't have the authority to tell my students what to do.
你沒有權力來告訴我的學生他們該做什麼。

▶ I have it on good authority that their business is not doing well.
根據可靠資料顯示，他們的生意不大好。

---

autobiography [ˌɑː.tə.baɪˈɑː.grə.fi] *n.* 自傳
同 **biography / diary**

▶ Steve likes to write books about other people, but he's never written an autobiography.
史提夫很喜歡寫有關他人的書，但是自己卻沒有寫過自傳。

104
automatic [ˌɑː.təˈmæt̬.ɪk]
adj. 不自覺的；不假思索的；自動的
搭 **automatic system** 自動化系統
同 **electronic / self-moving**

▶ I didn't know the answer, but for some reason I gave an automatic reply.
我不知道答案，但不知怎麼地，我不假思索就給了一個答案。

---

automobile / auto [ˈɑː.tə.moʊ.biːl ; ˈɑː.t̬oʊ]
n. 汽車

▶ Last year, he was in a terrible automobile accident.
去年他遇上一場嚴重的車禍。

---

103 99 97
available [əˈveɪ.lə.bəl] *adj.* 可獲得的；可用的
同 **accessible / feasible**
實用片語
make available to 可取得

▶ Are there any more tickets available for the Christmas concert?
還有聖誕音樂會的票嗎？

▶ I make myself available to my family on weekends.
每個週末我都空出時間陪伴我的家人。

avenue [ˈæv.ə.nuː] *n.* 大道

> ► If you walk down this avenue you can see many beautiful cherry blossoms.
> 如果你沿著這條大道走，就會看見許多美麗盛開的櫻花。

---

 average [ˈæv.ə.ɪdʒ]

① *adj.* 平均的

搭 **average income** 平均收入

同 **median / middle**

② *n.* 平均數；平均

實用片語
a cut above average 高於平均水準

③ *v.* 平均數是；平均為

同 **balance / even out**

> ► The average height of American men is one hundred seventy-eight centimeters.
> 美國男性的平均身高是 178 公分。

> ► The class average for our history test was 84%.
> 我們班上歷史考試的平均分數是 84 分。

> ► The quality of this bag isn't the best, but it's a cut above average.
> 這個包包的品質不是最好的，但高於平均。

> ► Last year he averaged thirteen hours of exercise a week.
> 去年他平均每週運動 13 個小時。

---

await [əˈweɪt] *v.* 等待

搭 **await the outcome** 等待結果

同 **anticipate / stay**

> ► After writing Melissa my love letter, I patiently awaited her reply.
> 在寫了情書給瑪莉莎之後，我就耐心地等待她的回音。

---

awake [əˈweɪk]

① *adj.* 醒著的

同 **attentive / alive**

② *v.* 醒來；喚醒

同 **get up / wake up**

實用片語
awake to 醒來

> ► Drinking a cup of coffee every morning will help you stay awake for the rest of the day.
> 每天早上喝一杯咖啡會幫助你整天都保持清醒。

> ► I awoke several times during the night because the baby wouldn't stop crying.
> 我晚上醒來好幾次，因為小嬰兒一直哭個不停。

> ► I always awake to the smell of fresh coffee.
> 我總是被剛煮好的咖啡香味為喚醒。

---

awaken [əˈweɪ.kən] *v.* 喚醒；醒來

> ► My wife was awakened by the sound of the ambulance.
> 我太太被救護車的聲音吵醒。

95

award [əˈwɔːrd]

① n. 獎項；獎勵

搭 **award ceremony** 頒獎典禮

同 **endowment / grant**

② v. 授與（獎項等）

同 **grant / present**

實用片語
award to 頒予

▶ She won an award for her role in the movie.
她在電影中的角色為她贏得一座獎項。

▶ The children are awarded candy after they finish their homework.
孩子們在寫完家庭作業後得到糖果當作獎賞。

▶ The CEO awarded a plaque to Linda for her good sales performance.
因為琳達優良的銷售績效，執行長頒給她一個獎牌。

Exercise 7

I. Derivatives

1. My mobile phone has a special _____ (attach) for taking pictures remotely.

2. Many students think that Steven is the most _____ (attract) teacher in this school.

3. Teachers should have _____ (authorize) over their students to discipline them.

4. I was _____ (awake) early this morning by the noise of people fighting.

5. In the Germany's _____ (auto) industry, BMW is one of the three major German automotive companies.

II. Vocabulary Choice

(A) attempt   (B) awarded   (C) assign   (D) assure   (E) atmosphere
(F) atomic   (G) author   (H) attach   (I) attitude   (J) astonishing

1. The restaurant is popular for it not only serves good food but has a warm and comfortable _____ too.

2. My favorite _____ is C. S. Lewis.

3. Charlotte was _____ first prize in the national speech competition.

4. According to Christian author Joyce Meyer, "A positive _____ gives you power over your circumstances, instead of your circumstances having power over you."

5. The athlete made an _____ on the world record in Olympic Games but he failed as his time for the event was too slow.

aware [əˈwɛr] *adj.* 知道的

同 **mindful / informed**

▶ I wasn't aware that he was married to her.
我不知道他跟她結婚了。

---

awful [ˈɔːfəl] *adj.* 可怕的

搭 **awful idea** 很糟的意見
同 **terrible / horrible**

▶ The pasta I ate last night was so awful I couldn't take a second bite!
我昨晚吃的通心麵很難吃，才吃一口，我就吃不下去了！

101
awkward [ˈɔːkwərd] *adj.* 尷尬的；笨拙的

同 **stiff / strange**

實用片語
put someone in an awkward position
使某人處境尷尬

▶ Junior high school boys and girls tend to be awkward around each other.
國中男、女生們在一起時，常常感到有些尷尬。

▶ Mr. Chen's decision puts me in an awkward position.
陳先生的決定讓我陷入兩難困境。

---

ax [ˈæks] *n.* 斧頭

▶ Use a sharp ax to chop down the oak tree.
用尖銳的斧頭來砍橡樹。

---

axe [ˈæks] *v.* 用斧劈；解雇

▶ The firemen axed down the door to get to the fire.
消防員把門劈開，進入火場中。

---

background [ˈbæk‚graʊnd] *n.* 背景

搭 **educational background** 教育背景
同 **upbringing / education**

▶ If you look carefully, you can see a rainbow in the background of the photo.
你如果仔細看，就會看到照片的背景有一道彩虹。

---

backpack [ˈbæk‚pæk]

① *n.* 背包
② *v.* 當背包客爬山、旅行

▶ Tom's backpack was too heavy, so he took some things out.
湯姆的背包太重了，所以他只好把一些東西拿出來。

▶ We backpacked through the mountains of China for two weeks.
我們花了兩個星期在中國的山區裡當背包客。

bacon [ˈbeɪ.kən] *n.* 培根；燻豬肉

實用片語
bring home the bacon 養家活口

▶ Mary likes to eat crispy bacon with scrambled eggs.
瑪麗喜歡吃香酥的培根肉配上炒蛋。

▶ Get a job so you can bring home the bacon.
找個工作你就可以養家活口。

---

97 96

bacteria [bækˈtɪr.i.ə] *n.* 病菌（複數形）

▶ Bacteria found in food can cause food poisoning.
食物中的病菌能引起食物中毒。

---

badly [ˈbæd.li] *adj.* 嚴重地；不好地；非常

搭 **badly injured** 傷勢嚴重

同 **poorly / carelessly**

實用片語
badly off 境況不佳

▶ Albert can't play in the soccer game tomorrow because he hurt his knee badly.
亞伯特明天不能參加足球比賽，因為膝蓋傷得很嚴重。

▶ She's been badly off since she was laid off last year.
自她去年被裁員後就一直境況不佳。

---

badminton [ˈbæd.mɪn.tən] *n.* 羽球

▶ In my opinion, badminton is a lot more enjoyable than tennis.
我認為羽球比網球更好玩。

---

baggage [ˈbæg.ɪdʒ] *n.* 行李

搭 **carry baggage** 手提行李

同 **luggage / bags**

實用片語
bag and baggage 家當，行李

▶ Please contact the service office if your baggage does not arrive at your destination.
如果你的行李沒有抵達目的地，請聯絡服務辦公室。

▶ If you won't pay the rent, get bag and baggage out of here.
如果你不想付租金，那就收好全部家當離開這裡。

---

baggy [ˈbæg.i] *adj.* 寬鬆的；膨脹的；袋狀的

同 **roomy / droopy**

▶ Those baggy pants look like they are too big on you!
這條鬆垮垮的褲子對你來說似乎太大了！

bait [beɪt]

① *n.* （誘）餌
② *v.* 用餌引誘
同 **lure / snare**

▶ Worms are usually used as bait for catching fish.
蟲通常被用來作釣魚的魚餌。

▶ If we bait the trap with chicken, we can catch the crabs.
如果我們把雞肉放在捕捉器上當誘餌，就能捕到螃蟹。

---

balance [ˈbæl.əns]

① *n.* 平衡
搭 **maintain balance** 維持平衡
同 **equity / harmony**

實用片語
strike a balance 取得平衡

② *v.* 保持平衡；使平衡
搭 **balance the books** 平衡收支
同 **make equal / adjust**

▶ Try not to lose your balance when you walk across that narrow bridge.
當你走過那座狹長的橋時，盡量不要失去平衡。

▶ We have to strike a balance between what we want and what we can afford.
我們必須在我們想要以及可負擔的狀況間取得平衡。

▶ She can balance a basket of fruit on her head.
她可以在頭頂上放一籃水果而且保持平衡。

---

bald [bɑːld] *adj.* 禿頭的
同 **barren / uncovered**

▶ Trevor mainly wears a hat to cover his bald spot.
崔弗大部分的時候戴著帽子是為了遮掩他的禿頭。

---

ballet [bælˈeɪ] *n.* 芭蕾舞

▶ I'm going to a ballet performance this Friday night.
我這個星期五晚上要去看一場芭蕾舞表演。

---

bandage [ˈbæn.dɪdʒ]

① *n.* 繃帶
同 **plaster / compress**
② *v.* 用繃帶包紮
同 **wrap / bind**

▶ The doctor sent me home with pain medicine and clean bandages.
醫生給了我止痛藥，幫我換了乾淨的繃帶，就讓我回家了。

▶ You should bandage that cut on your finger before it gets worse.
你應該在手指割傷變得更嚴重前，用繃帶包紮起來。

---

bang [bæŋ]

① *n.* 砰砰作響
② *v.* 砰地敲

▶ She heard a loud bang coming from the basement.
她聽到從地下室傳來一聲巨響。

▶ He banged his fist into the wall.
他用拳頭打牆壁。

③ *adv.* 正好；砰地

> ▶ The hunter fired a shot, and it was bang on his target.
> 獵人開了一槍，正中他的目標。

---

bankrupt [ˈbæŋ.krʌpt]

① *adj.* 破產的
同 **broke / lacking**
② *n.* 破產者
③ *v.* 使破產

> ▶ Gina was bankrupt after making poor financial decisions for her company.
> 吉娜為了公司做出不明智的理財決定後，而宣告破產。

> ▶ The bankrupt went around asking his friends for money.
> 那位破產的人到處去跟他的朋友要錢。

> ▶ It's not nice to bankrupt your neighbors.
> 害你的鄰居破產實在是沒良心。

103

bare [ber]

① *adj.* 空的；赤裸的
搭 **bare hand** 徒手
同 **undressed / naked**

實用片語
bare one's teeth 呲牙咧嘴

② *v.* 使暴露；使赤裸
同 **expose / uncover**

> ▶ She caught a fish with her bare hands!
> 她徒手抓到一條魚！

> ▶ Mary bared her teeth when we talked about religion.
> 當我們論及宗教問題時，瑪莉馬上變臉呲牙咧嘴。

> ▶ The lion bared its teeth as it ran towards the zebra.
> 這隻獅子齜牙咧嘴著朝斑馬追過去。

104

barely [ˈber.li] *adv.* 幾乎沒有；僅；剛好

同 **almost / hardly**

實用片語
to barely make it 低空飛過

> ▶ We barely had time to take the test.
> 我們幾乎沒有時間考試。

> ▶ I barely made it through English class this term.
> 這學期我的英文課低空飛過。

---

bargain [ˈbɑːr.gɪn]

① *n.* 買賣；交易
搭 **real bargain** 的確很划算
同 **negotiation / transaction**
② *v.* 討價還價
同 **deal / negotiate**

實用片語
bargain over 討價還價

> ▶ The businessman got a good bargain and was very happy with the price.
> 那位生意人完成了一項很好的買賣，他對於價錢非常的滿意。

> ▶ If you don't like the price, you can bargain with the clerk.
> 如果你對那個價錢不滿意，你可以再跟店員討價還價。

> ▶ We need to bargain with vendors over prices.
> 價錢上我們需要跟供應商再討價還價。

barn [bɑːrn] *n.* 穀倉

B

▶ Most of the animals in the barn are chickens and pigs.
穀倉裡大部分的動物是雞和豬。

barrel [ˈber.əl] *n.* 大桶

▶ My grandmother uses wooded barrels to store wine.
我的祖母用木桶來儲存酒。

45

Exercise 8

I. Vocabulary Choice

(A) axe   (B) bang   (C) bacteria   (D) background   (E) bandage

(F) bait   (G) ballet   (H) awkward   (I) bald   (J) baggage

1. The girl felt _____ whenever she entered a room full of strangers.

2. Before you travel, it's better to make sure you check your _____ allowance with the airline you are flying with.

3. The nurse wrapped a _____ around my injured leg to stop it from bleeding.

4. I heard someone _____ at the door, but I pretended not to be home.

5. There are many types of _____ , some cause diseases but some can also be used for good purposes such as making cleaning products.

II. Multiple Choice

(   ) 1. My sister and I _____ around Italy for a month.

     (A) back (B) background (C) backpacked (D) backward

(   ) 2. _____ is a game which is played by two or four players.

     (A) basketball (B) badminton (C) baseball (D) football

(   ) 3. His parents don't like him to wear _____ pants.

     (A) baggage (B) badly (C) bandage (D) baggy

(   ) 4. She lost her _____ and tumbled down the stairs.

     (A) bald (B) balance (C) ballet (D) balcony

(   ) 5. Without his father's help, his company would have gone _____ after only a year in business.

     (A) bankrupt (B) bank (C) banking (D) bandage

Unit 9

101 **99**

barrier [ˈberiɚ] *n.* 障礙物

搭 **language barrier** 語言隔閡

同 **hurdle / roadblock**

▶ Language barriers are common when you visit other countries.
當你到其他國家時，語言障礙是很常見的。

based [beɪs] *adj.* 有根基的；基礎的

同 **located / placed**

▶ The new program is family based.
新的節目是以家庭為主要訴求。

basin [ˈbeɪsən] *n.* 水盆

▶ Take this basin of water outside, please.
請把這一盆水拿到外面去。

99

battery [ˈbætʃɚi] *n.* 電池

實用片語
recharge your batteries 養精蓄銳

▶ My toy car won't run because it needs new batteries.
我的玩具汽車跑不動了，因為它需要新的電池。

▶ We took a short vacation to recharge our batteries.
我們渡了個短的假期充電（養精蓄銳）。

bay [beɪ] *n.* （海或湖）灣

實用片語
keep at bay 牽制住，不逼近

▶ The bay near my house is excellent for swimming and sunbathing.
我家附近的海灣是游泳和日光浴的絕佳地點。

▶ She tried very hard to keep her unhappiness at bay.
她努力試著讓自己遠離不幸。

beak [biːk] *n.* 鳥嘴

▶ Magpies are birds known for their sharp beaks.
喜鵲以他們尖銳的鳥嘴而出名。

beam [biːm]

① *v.* 照耀

同 **glare / emit**

▶ When I woke up, the sun was beaming down on my face.
我醒來時，太陽照在我的臉上。

② *n.* 光線；光束

搭 **light beam** 光束

同 **ray / glow**

實用片語
on the beam 行事正確，抓到要領

▶ A beam of sunshine shone through the window.
一道陽光穿透玻璃窗。

▶ Now you get the idea; you are on the beam.
就是這樣；現在你懂了；你抓到要領了。

---

beast [biːst] *n.* 野獸

▶ The angry beast roared loudly as its prey ran away.
當獵物跑掉時，憤怒的野獸大聲咆哮。

---

bedtime [ˈbed.taɪm] *n.* 就寢時間

實用片語
bedtime story 動聽但不可信的說法

▶ She tried not to go to sleep past her bedtime.
她嘗試在平日上床時間過後才去睡覺。

▶ I don't want to hear a bedtime story, just the facts.
我不想聽動聽的話，只要事實。

---

beggar [ˈbeg.ɚ] *n.* 乞丐

▶ A beggar stopped a woman and asked her for some money.
乞丐攔下一個婦女，向她要一些錢。

99

behave [bɪˈheɪv] *v.* 守規矩；表現

搭 **behave properly** 適當地表現

同 **manage / control**

▶ Students are sent to the principal's office if they don't behave.
學生如果不守規矩就會被送到校長辦公室。

---

behavior [bɪˈheɪ.vjɚ] *n.* 行為

同 **manner / action**

實用片語
on someone's best behavior 最佳表現

▶ The students all laughed because the teacher's behavior was so funny.
因為老師的舉止實在太有趣，學生們都被逗笑了！

▶ The kids try to be on their best behavior all the time.
這些孩子們總是試著表現出最好的自己。

---

being [ˈbiː.ɪŋ] *n.* 存在；生命

▶ Dinosaurs came into being millions of years ago.
恐龍在幾百萬年前存在過。

---

belly [ˈbel.i] *n.* 腹部；胃

▶ My belly hurts from laughing too much.
我笑到肚子都痛了。

beneath [bɪˈniːθ] *prep.* 在…之下

▶ The soap is right beneath the kitchen sink.
肥皂就在廚房水槽的下方。

benefit [ˈben.ɪ.fɪt]

① *n.* 好處;益處;利益

搭 **medical benefit** 醫療津貼

同 **advantage / profit**

實用片語
benefit from 從…得到好處

② *v.* 有益於…

同 **enhance / aid**

實用片語
for the benefit of 為了…好

▶ There are many benefits to eating green vegetables.
吃綠色蔬菜有許多的好處。

▶ Both of us will benefit from the steady partnership.
我們雙方都因穩定的夥伴關係而受益。

▶ Receiving a college degree will most likely benefit you in the future.
取得大學學位對你的未來多半會有益處。

▶ Teachers assign homework for the benefit of students.
老師指派作業是為了學生好呀。

berry [ˈber.i] *n.* 莓果

▶ Tomorrow afternoon Riley will go berry picking.
萊利明天下午會去採草莓。

Bible / bible [ˈbaɪ.bəl] *n.* 聖經

▶ Todd reads his bible every morning and every night.
陶得每天早晚都讀聖經。

billion [ˈbɪl.jən] *n.* 十億

實用片語
one in a billion 萬中選一

▶ Every year billions of fish are killed for food.
每年上億的魚隻會被捕作為食物。

▶ This necklace is one in a billion.
這條項鍊可是萬中選一,獨一無二的。

bin [bɪn] *n.* 儲藏箱;容器

▶ Please throw that bottle into a recycling bin.
請把那個空瓶子丟入回收桶。

bingo [ˈbɪŋ.goʊ] *n.* 賓果遊戲

▶ Let's play bingo this Friday night at Jack's house.
我們這星期五晚上在傑克家玩賓果吧。

biography [baɪˈɑː.grə.fi] *n.* 傳記

同 **profile / life story**

▶ Before I write Bill Gates' biography, I need to research his life.
在我寫比爾蓋茲的傳記之前,我需要研究一下他的一生。

biology [baɪˈɑː.lə.dʒi] *n.* 生物學

▶ I love biology because I am interested in animals and plants.
我熱愛生物學因為我對動植物都很感興趣。

---

biscuit [ˈbɪs.kɪt] *n.* 餅乾；小麵包

▶ After baking the biscuits, let them cool for five minutes before eating them.
餅乾烤好之後，讓它冷卻五分鐘後再吃。

---

blade [bleɪd] *n.* 刀刃；刀片

▶ I can't cut with this knife because the blade needs to be sharpened.
我沒辦法用這把刀切東西，因為它的刀刃需要再磨得銳利些。

Exercise 9

I. 中英對應

_____ 1. 傳記   (A) biological   (B) bingo   (C) biology   (D) biography

_____ 2. 鳥嘴   (A) beak   (B) beam   (C) bear   (D) beat

_____ 3. 乞丐   (A) beginner   (B) begin   (C) beg   (D) beggar

_____ 4. 腹部   (A) belly   (B) bell   (C) below   (D) bellboy

_____ 5. 水盆   (A) basic   (B) base   (C) basin   (D) basis

II. Vocabulary Choice

(A) beneath   (B) Beasts   (C) bare(s)   (D) barrel   (E) behave(s)

(F) beam(s)   (G) benefits   (H) behavior   (I) batteries   (J) bedtime

1. He needs to buy some new _____ for his camera.

2. The lion is known to be the King of _____ .

3. New Zealand is still reaping the financial _____ years after the release of "The Lord of the Rings" trilogy.

4. The Wang children always _____ badly when their parents are away.

5. We used to stay in the cabin that was _____ this big tree whenever we went hiking in this mountain.

bless [bles] *v.* 祝福

同 **praise / honor**

實用片語
bless with 保佑

▶ I am blessed to have such great friends in my life.
我是有福的，因為生命中有很棒的朋友。

▶ God has blessed us with a fruitful year.
上帝保佑我們有個豐碩的一年。

---

blessing [ˈbles.ɪŋ] *n.* 祝福

搭 **blessing in disguise** 塞翁失馬焉知非福

同 **consent / regard**

實用片語
mixed blessing 喜憂參半

▶ I want to give you a blessing before you go on your trip.
在你啟程之前，我要為你祝福。

▶ Being accepted by MIT was a mixed blessing because I couldn't afford the tuition.
被 MIT 接受是喜憂參半，因為我負擔不起學費。

---

blink [ˈblɪŋk]

① *v.* 眨眼睛

搭 **blink her eyes** 眨動雙眼

同 **flash / bat**

實用片語
blink with 閃爍著…

② *n.* 眨眼睛；一瞬間

▶ Howie blinked his eyes a couple times as he woke up.
豪伊起床時眨了眨幾次眼睛。

▶ Mary blinked with great surprise.
瑪莉眼中閃爍著驚訝。

▶ When you see my blink, that's your signal to go on stage.
當你看到我眨眼睛，那就是你上台的訊號。

---

bloom [blu:m]

① *n.* （花）盛開；全部花朵（一棵樹）

搭 **flower bloom** 花開

同 **flower / bud**

② *v.* 開花

同 **thrive / prosper**

實用片語
come into bloom 開花

▶ The Japanese Cherry Blossom trees are in bloom.
日本的櫻花樹正在盛開中。

▶ I can't wait for the flowers to bloom this spring!
我等不及看到今年春天的百花盛開。

▶ The roses come into bloom in June.
玫瑰在六月盛開。

---

blossom [ˈblɑː.səm]

① *n.* 花

② *v.* 長成；變得更有魅力；開花

同 **grow / unfold**

實用片語
blossom into 綻放，開花

▶ The trees are full of blossoms.
這些樹上開滿了花。

▶ Dora has blossomed into quite a sweet young lady.
朵拉已經長成為一位非常甜美的少女。

▶ Jack's food delivery idea blossomed into a profitable business.
傑克的食物外送點子已發展成可獲利模式。

B

blouse [blaʊs] *n.* 女襯衫

▶ Amy spilled grape juice all over her new white blouse.
艾咪把葡萄汁灑到整件的新洋裝上。

blush [blʌʃ]

① *v.* 臉紅

實用片語
blush with 滿臉通紅

② *n.* 腮紅;臉紅

▶ Terry blushed as his prettiest classmate smiled at him.
當泰瑞最漂亮的同學對他微笑時,他滿臉通紅。

▶ Mary blushed with anger.
瑪莉因為生氣脹紅了臉。

▶ Kimmie's blush is as red as a rose.
秦蜜的腮紅簡直像玫瑰花一樣的紅。

 102 101

boast [boʊst]

① *v.* 自誇

同 **brag / exaggerate**

實用片語
boast about 吹牛,誇耀

② *n.* 自誇;大話

▶ Don't boast too much about your accomplishments; try to be humble.
不要過度誇口你的成就;請盡量謙卑一點。

▶ They always boast about their grandchild.
他們總是誇耀他們的孫兒。

▶ The class got tired of listening to Harry's boasts.
全班都聽膩了哈利的自誇。

bold [boʊld] *adj.* 大膽的

搭 **bold decision** 大膽的決定

同 **brave / fearless**

實用片語
bold-faced liar 說謊不眨眼,厚臉皮

▶ Harry finally grew bold enough to ask Amanda out on a dinner date.
哈利終於放膽邀請亞曼達出去吃晚餐。

▶ Everyone knows that John is a bold-faced liar.
大家都知道約翰是個厚顏無恥的騙子。

bond [bɑːnd]

① *n.* 聯結;結合力

同 **relationship / hookup**

② *v.* 使…黏合;聯結

同 **bind / glue**

實用片語
one's word is one's bond 一言九鼎

▶ The bond between a mother and her newborn is very strong.
母親和新生兒之間的聯結是非常緊密的。

▶ This new cement does a great job of bonding bricks together.
新的水泥把所有的磚塊緊緊地黏合在一起。

▶ You can trust me. My word is my bond.
你可以相信我。我一言九鼎。

booklet ['bʊk.lət] *n.* 小冊子

▶ The museum provides guests with a short booklet.
博物館提供給遊客們一本簡短的小冊子。

bookshelf [ˈbʊk.ʃelf]　*n.* 書架；書櫃

▶ He has read all the books on the bookshelf.
他已經讀遍書架上所有的書籍。

---

bookstore [ˈbʊk.stɔːr]　*n.* 書店

▶ I would like to go to the bookstore to buy a book.
我想去書店買一本書。

---

boot [buːt]
① *n.* 靴子
② *v.* 使穿靴

▶ My brother received black shiny boots for Christmas.
我的兄弟收到閃亮的黑靴子作為聖誕禮物。

▶ If you want to play in the snow, you should get booted up.
如果你想在雪地裡玩，就應該穿上靴子。

---

border [ˈbɔːr.dɚ]
① *n.* 邊界
搭 **cross border**　越過邊界
同 **outskirt / line**

實用片語
border on　接近，靠近邊界
② *v.* 毗鄰
同 **adjoin / surround**

▶ Jamie decorated the picture frame with a lace border to make it more beautiful.
傑米用蕾絲花邊裝飾相框，讓它看起來更漂亮。

▶ His house borders on a small lake.
她的房子接近一個小湖。

▶ There are several countries that border France.
有幾個國家與法國毗鄰。

---

bore [bɔːr]
① *v.* 鑽（洞）；鑿（洞）
搭 **bore hole**　鑽洞
同 **tunnel / mine**
② *n.* 令人討厭的人
同 **bummer / creep**

▶ The victim bored through the door to escape.
受害者把門鑿了個洞，逃脫出去。

▶ It's such a bore to sit and listen to her talk for hours.
坐著聽她講數個小時，實在是一件無趣的事。

---

bounce [baʊns]
① *v.* 彈回
搭 **bounce back**　彈回
同 **rebound / leap**
實用片語
bounce back　彈回，恢復
② *n.* 彈性；反彈
同 **rebound / animation**

▶ The ball bounced across the room.
這顆球彈回到教室的另一端。

▶ Mary bounced back from her illness quickly.
瑪莉在生病後恢復迅速。

▶ Pump more air into the basketball so it has a better bounce.
多灌一些氣到籃球裡，這樣它的彈性才會比較好。

bracelet ['breɪ.slət] *n.* 手鐲

▶ Julie bought a bracelet to match her necklace and earrings.
茱莉買了一條手鍊來搭配她的項鍊和耳環。

---

brake [breɪk]

① *n.* 煞車
② *v.* 煞住（車）
同 **impede / stop**

實用片語
put the brakes on 踩煞車，停止

▶ How often should I check my car brakes?
我應該多久檢查一次剎車？

▶ When driving in rain or snow, brake lightly.
當你在雨中或雪中開車時，要輕踩剎車。

▶ We need to put brakes on any further spending.
我們需要停止任何額外開銷。

---

brass [bræs]

① *n.* 黃銅
② *adj.* 黃銅色的

▶ My grandfather's trumpet is made of brass.
我祖父的喇叭是銅做的。

▶ David collects brass instruments from around the world.
大衛收集來自世界各地的銅製樂器。

---

brassiere / bra [brəˈzɪr ; brɑː] *n.* 胸罩

▶ Susie's mom took her to buy some bras.
蘇西的媽媽帶她去買一些胸罩。

Exercise 10

I. Vocabulary Choice

(A) blessings   (B) bleed   (C) bookstore   (D) boast   (E) bloom

(F) blossomed   (G) blend   (H) bore   (I) bond   (J) blouse

1. My youngest sister has really _____ into a very beautiful woman.

2. The Eslite Dunnan Store was listed on CNN's list of the "world's coolest _____ " last August.

3. "More _____ come from giving than from receiving" is my favorite Bible verse.

4. Our team was offended by the opposition's _____ that they could easily beat us.

5. American food is a _____ of foods, including Chinese, African American and European foods.

II. Multiple Choice

(   ) 1. Joy accompanied her sister to buy some _____ last Sunday.

   (A) brakes (B) brasses (C) barns (D) bras

(   ) 2. Alan _____ the ball over the wall.

   (A) bonded (B) bored (C) bounced (D) bordered

(   ) 3. Mary put on a little lipstick and _____ before she went out on a date.

   (A) blouse (B) blush (C) blue (D) blur

(   ) 4. The car's _____ failed and it crashed into an electric pole.

   (A) brake (B) brave (C) brain (D) brass

(   ) 5. TGV (Train à Grande Vitesse, i.e. "high-speed train") crosses the _____ between France and Germany.

   (A) board (B) border (C) broad (D) bore

① **accept** [ək'sɛpt] *v.* 接受、贊同
例 Most researchers have accepted the new theory.
多數研究人員已接受新理論了。

except [ɪk'sɛpt] *prep.* 除外、不包括
例 She didn't open her mouth except to complain.
她一開口就是抱怨而已。

② **access** ['æk.sɛs] *n.* 通路、門路、使用或參加的權力
例 Nowadays people have access to all kinds of information on the Internet.
現今人們可以自網路上取得各式的資訊。

excess [ɪk'sɛs / 'ɛk.sɛs] *n.* 過量、過多
例 I try to avoid excess sugar in my diet.
我試著減少飲食中的過量糖類攝取。

③ **addition** [ə'dɪʃ.ən] *n.* 加、附加
例 I'm sure that Mr. Smith is a worthy addition to our team.
我相信史密斯的加入對我們團隊來說是有助益的。

edition [ɪ'dɪʃ.ən] *n.* 版本
例 Mary is a small edition of her mother.
瑪莉是她媽媽小一號的翻版。

④ **advice** [əd'vaɪs] *n.* 勸告、忠告
例 I'd like to provide you one last piece of advice.
我要給你最後一個忠告。

advise [əd'vaɪz] *v.* 通知、告知
例 Mr. Smith advised her to make proper decisions.
史密斯先生建議她要做適當的決定。

⑤ **affect** [ə'fɛkt] *v.* 影響、對⋯發生作用
例 Both dancing and music affect me greatly.
舞蹈與音樂都影響我非常大。

effect [ə'fɛkt] *v.* 引起、促成、達到、完成
例 The new policies will have a significant effect on our business.
新的規定對我們的生意有重大的影響。

bravery [ˈbreɪ.və.i] *n.* 勇敢

同 **courage / daring**

▶ My son will always be remembered for his bravery.
我兒子勇敢的行為將會一直被紀念。

breast [brest] *n.* 胸；乳房

▶ Unfortunately, my grandmother died from breast cancer.
很不幸地，我的祖母死於乳癌。

103
breath [breθ] *n.* 呼吸；氣息

▶ She took a deep breath then jumped into the ocean.
她深深地吸一口氣，然後跳入海中。

breathe [briːð] *v.* 呼吸

搭 **breathe properly** 正確地呼吸

同 **exhale / inhale**

實用片語
breathe down one's neck 東窺西探

▶ My puppy makes weird noises when he breathes.
我的小狗呼吸時，發出奇怪的聲音。

▶ I can't work with you breathing down my neck.
你這樣東窺西探，我無法工作。

103
breed [briːd]

① *v.* 交配繁殖

② *n.* 品種

▶ This dog breeds beautiful puppies.
這隻狗繁殖出漂亮的幼犬。

▶ Himalayan cats are my favorite breed of cats.
喜馬拉雅貓是我最喜歡的貓品種。

104
breeze [briːz]

① *n.* 微風

搭 **gentle breeze** 微風

② *v.* 吹著微風

同 **sweep / sail**

實用片語
breeze along 輕鬆以對，不費力地完成

▶ The flowers are gently blowing in the breeze.
花兒在微風中被吹來吹去。

▶ Dan breezed past his sister and ran out the door.
丹泰然自若地從他的姊妹旁邊經過，並衝出了門。

▶ Don't just breeze along through life.
不要只是輕鬆過生活。

bride [braɪd] *n.* 新娘

▶ The groom smiled as the bride walked down the aisle.
當新娘走到座位中間的走道時，新郎笑了。

---

bridegroom [ˈbraɪd.gruːm] *n.* 新郎

▶ The bridegroom was extremely busy on his wedding day.
新郎在他的婚禮當天非常地忙碌。

98

brilliant [ˈbrɪl.jənt] *adj.* 卓越的；明亮的

搭 **brilliant performance** 卓越的表現
同 **vivid / bright**

▶ His brilliant sparkling blue eyes left her speechless.
他閃閃發亮的藍眼睛讓她啞口無言。

---

broil [brɔɪl] *v.* 烤

同 **roast / boil**

▶ I'm broiling some fish for dinner.
我正在烤一些魚當晚餐吃。

---

broke [broʊk] *adj.* 破產的；一無所有的

同 **bust / insolvent**

實用片語
dead broke 破產

▶ Gina is not broke yet, but she's almost out of money.
吉娜雖然還沒破產，但她的錢也快要花光了。

▶ He's been dead broke for a month now.
現在他已經破產一個月了（他這個月身無分文）。

---

brook [brʊk] *n.* 小溪

▶ She sat on a rock near the brook watching the water flow.
她坐在小溪附近的一塊石頭上看著水流。

---

broom [bruːm / brʊm] *n.* 掃帚

實用片語
a new broom 新上任有衝勁的人

▶ Use a broom to sweep up the broken glass.
用掃帚把碎玻璃掃起來。

▶ I think the company needs a new broom to improve customer service.
我認為公司要有具衝勁的新人來加強客戶服務。

---

brow [braʊ]

① *n.* 前額
② *n.* 眉毛

▶ Here's a towel for you to wipe your brow.
這裡有一條毛巾給你擦額頭。

▶ Lance raised his brow when he heard the surprising news.
藍斯聽到消息時，皺起了眉頭。

brownie [ˈbraʊ.ni] *n.* 布朗尼（果仁巧克力蛋糕）

▶ She baked brownies for the party.
她為派對烤了布朗尼。

98

brutal [ˈbruː.t̬əl] *adj.* 殘忍的；野蠻的

搭 **brutal attack** 無情地攻擊

同 **harsh / ruthless**

▶ The bully was very brutal to his classmates.
那位霸凌者對待自己的同學非常地殘忍。

bubble [ˈbʌb.əl]

① *n.* （水或氣）泡

② *v.* 冒泡；沸騰

同 **boil / stir**

實用片語
burst bubble 打破幻想，煞風景

▶ The children are at the park blowing bubbles.
孩子們在公園吹泡泡。

▶ Why is the water in my toilet bubbling?
為什麼我的馬桶在冒泡？

▶ I hate to burst your bubble, but you probably won't get the job offer.
我無意打破你的幻想，但其實你可能不會得到這份工作。

bucket [ˈbʌk.ɪt] *n.* 桶

實用片語
a drop in the bucket 杯水車薪

▶ To build a sandcastle, fill the bucket with wet sand.
要蓋一座沙堡，先要把潮濕的沙裝滿在桶子裡。

▶ What we were paid for our work was a drop in the bucket.
我們工作得到的報酬只是杯水車薪。

bud [bʌd]

① *n.* 花蕾；芽

② *v.* 發芽；開始生長

同 **shoot / bloom**

▶ By April the flower buds should be in full bloom.
到四月，花苞應該會全開。

▶ It's been a very long and cold winter, so the plants will bud late this year.
這是一個漫長又寒冷的冬天，所以植物將會晚點發芽。

99 96

budget [ˈbʌdʒ.ɪt]

① *n.* 預算

搭 **allocate budget** 分配預算

同 **allowance / allocation**

② *v.* 編列預算

同 **allocate / estimate**

實用片語
budget for 編預算

▶ My average monthly shopping budget is four-hundred dollars.
我每個月的平均購物預算是四百美元。

▶ If we carefully budget our money, we can buy the car.
我們如果小心計畫我們的錢，就能購買汽車。

▶ We budgeted $5,000 for food for this party.
我們為派對的食物預算編為五千元。

buffalo [ˈbʌf.ə.loʊ] *n.* 水牛

▶ The farmer and his buffalo were in the field.
農夫和他的水牛都在田中。

---

buffet [bəˈfeɪ] *n.* 自助餐

搭 **buffet restaurant** 自助餐廳
同 **cafeteria / salad bar**

▶ We celebrated his birthday at the Chinese buffet.
我們在中式自助餐廳慶祝他的生日。

---

bulb [ˈbʌlb] *n.* 球莖

▶ Kathy planted tulip bulbs in her garden.
凱蒂在她的花園栽種鬱金香球莖。

---

bull [bʊl] *n.* 公牛

實用片語
bull session 閒談，自由討論

▶ The bull was put in a cage after the attack.
這隻公牛在攻擊人之後被關進籠子裡。

▶ College students love late-night bull sessions.
大學生喜歡深夜閒聊。

---

bullet [ˈbʊl.ɪt] *n.* 子彈

實用片語
magic bullet 神丹妙藥

▶ Thankfully, the bullet missed the police officer's head.
幸好子彈沒有射進這位警員的頭。

▶ There is no magic bullet that will solve the problem.
沒有可以解決問題的神丹妙藥。

Exercise 11

I. 中英對應

_____ 1. 微風　(A) breed　(B) breeze　(C) bread　(D) break

_____ 2. 桶　(A) basket　(B) blanket　(C) button　(D) bucket

_____ 3. 眉毛　(A) brown　(B) browse　(C) brow　(D) brownie

_____ 4. 小溪　(A) brook　(B) broke　(C) brownie　(D) broom

_____ 5. 新郎　(A) bride　(B) bridesmaid　(C) bridegroom　(D) bridesman

II. Vocabulary Choice

(A) broil　(B) bride　(C) bubble　(D) brutal　(E) breath

(F) budget　(G) brilliant　(H) buffet　(I) bulb　(J) breed

1. Albert Einstein was one of the most _____ men and one of the 10 most influential scientists of the 20th century.

2. The girl had to stop running for a while to catch her _____ .

3. The Golden Retriever is a very popular dog _____ in the U.S. and many other countries.

4. Ben tries to live on a _____ of less than NT$10,000 a month.

5. The man was imprisoned for the _____ murder of a four-year-old girl.

Unit 12

97

bulletin [ˈbʊl.ə.tɪn] *n.* 公告

搭 **publish bulletin** 貼出公告

同 **announcement / message**

▶ You can find the information on the latest bulletin.
你可以在最新發佈的公告上找到資訊。

---

bump [bʌmp]

① *v.* 碰；撞

同 **crash / punch**

實用片語
bump into 遇見，巧遇

② *n.* 撞擊

▶ She bumped her elbow on the table and screamed.
她的手肘撞到桌子，就大叫。

▶ Can you believe it? I bumped into John Smith downtown today.
你相信嗎？我今天在城裡遇見約翰史密斯。

▶ Alice heard a loud bump when she entered the haunted house.
愛麗絲進入鬼屋時，聽到一個很大的撞擊。

---

bunch [bʌntʃ] *n.* 一串；一群

同 **cluster / flock**

▶ That is the largest bunch of bananas I have ever seen!
那是我見過最大一串的香蕉！

103

burden [ˈbɝː.dən]

① *n.* 負擔

搭 **carry burden** 承擔壓力

同 **hardship / duty**

實用片語
bear the burden 扛起責任

② *v.* 使負重擔

同 **hamper / hinder**

▶ The burden was too heavy for the horse to carry.
這個負擔對這匹馬來說太重。

▶ I have to bear the burden of earning enough to support the family.
我必須要扛起支撐家庭的責任。

▶ Please don't burden me with your problems.
請不要拿你的問題來煩我。

---

burglar [ˈbɝː.glɚ] *n.* 小偷；破門盜竊者

同 **robber / thief**

▶ Two burglars stole one million dollars in cash from the bank.
兩個竊賊從銀行偷了一百萬美元的現金。

bury [ˈber.i] *v.* 埋葬

實用片語
bury one's head in the sand 駝鳥心態

▶ The dog secretly buried the bone in the backyard.
這隻狗悄悄地把骨頭埋在後院裡。

▶ Jack, you can't bury your head in the sand about your health.
傑克，你不能對你的健康問題抱持駝鳥心態。

---

bush [bʊʃ] *n.* 灌木叢

▶ The rabbit hid in the bushes until the fox left.
這隻兔子躲在草叢中，直到狐狸離開。

---

buzz [bʌz]

① *v.* 嗡嗡叫

實用片語
buzz along 過來過往，匆促行過

② *n.* 嗡嗡聲

▶ Is there a bee buzzing by my ear?
有一隻蜜蜂在我耳邊嗡嗡叫嗎？

▶ Traffic is buzzing along.
路上交通過往迎來。

▶ She heard a buzz and then saw a helicopter fly by.
她聽見一個嗡嗡聲，然後看到一架直升機飛過。

---

cabin [ˈkæb.ɪn] *n.* 小屋

▶ Every summer we stay at our cabin in the mountains.
每年夏天我們都待在山上的小屋裡。

100
cabinet [ˈkæb.ən.ət] *n.* 櫥；櫃

▶ The plates are in the cabinet on the right; we keep mugs in left cabinet.
盤子在右邊的櫃子裡；我們把馬克杯放在左邊的櫃子裡。

98
calculate [ˈkæl.kjə.leɪt] *v.* 計算

搭 **calculate percentage** 計算比率

同 **count / measure**

實用片語
calculate on 盤算，規劃

▶ Can you calculate how much all this food will cost?
你能不能計算一下，這些食物合計多少錢？

▶ He is calculating on a serious problem.
他正為嚴重的問題做盤算。

---

calculating [ˈkæl.kjə.leɪ.tʃɪŋ]
adj. 計算的；慎重的

同 **artful / manipulative**

▶ The calcuating machine performs many tasks.
這個計算機能夠執行多項的工作。

calculation [ˌkæl.kjəˈleɪ.ʃən] *n.* 計算結果

同 **computation / forecast**

▶ Our calculations were not correct, so we need to start over.
我們的計算結果有誤，所以必須要重新計算。

---

calculator [ˈkæl.kjə.leɪ.tɚ] *n.* 計算機

▶ This math problem is too difficult to figure out without a calculator.
這道數學題目太難了，如果不用計算機是無法算出來的。

---

calorie [ˈkæl.ə.i] *n.* 卡路里

▶ I need to eat about 1700 calories per day.
我每天需要攝取大約一千七百卡的卡路里。

104

campaign [kæmˈpeɪn]

① *n.* （軍事）行動、計畫

搭 **election campaign** 選舉活動

同 **operation / movement**

② *v.* 發起運動；從事活動

同 **stump / contest**

實用片語
campaign for 競選

▶ The king's military campaigns were successful and his kingdom grew.
國王的軍事行動非常的成功，他的王國也隨之擴大。

▶ Many celebrities joined together to campaign to fight AIDS.
很多的名人聚集發起對抗愛滋病的運動。

▶ I want to campaign for the winning candidate.
我想參加當選者的競選活動。

---

camping [ˈkæm.pɪŋ] *n.* 露營

▶ Camping is a fun thing to do!
露營是一件有趣的事！

---

campus [ˈkæm.pəs] *n.* 校園；校區

搭 **university campus** 大學校園

同 **grounds / yard**

實用片語
on campus 住校

▶ Her daughter will be living in the dorms on campus.
她的女兒將會住在學校的宿舍。

▶ Do you live on campus or off campus?
你住校還是外面？

100

candidate [ˈkæn.dɪ.dət / ˈkæn.dɪ.deɪt] *n.* 候選人

搭 **potential candidate** 潛在候選人

同 **applicant / contender**

▶ Which presidential candidate will you vote for?
你會投給哪位總統候選人呢？

cane [keɪn] *n.* 手杖

▶ The old woman hit him across the head with her cane.
那位老婦人用手杖打他的頭。

---

canoe [kəˈnuː]

① *n.* 獨木舟
② *v.* 划或乘獨木舟

實用片語
paddle one's own canoe 獨立自主

▶ This canoe can only hold two adults or three children.
這個獨木舟只能容納兩個大人或三個小孩子。

▶ We went canoeing along Sweden's longest river.
我們沿著瑞典最長的一條河划獨木舟。

▶ Joe is learning to paddle his own canoe.
喬伊正在學習獨立自主。

---

canyon [ˈkæn.jən] *n.* 峽谷

同 **gorge / gully**

▶ The Grand Canyon is one of the largest canyons in the world.
美國大峽谷是世界最大的峽谷之一。

---

capable [ˈkeɪ.pə.bəl] *adj.* 能夠的；有能力的

搭 **fully capable** 完全可以
同 **able / adept**

實用片語
capable of 能夠，有能力

▶ She is a well educated and capable lawyer.
她是一位受過高等教育和能幹的律師。

▶ Do you think Jack is capable of closing this deal?
你認為傑克有能力結下這個案子嗎？

---

capacity [kəˈpæs.ə.tʃ] *n.* 容量

搭 **exceed capacity** 超出可容範圍
同 **quantity / scope**

▶ This elevator is already at full capacity and can't hold any more people.
這部電梯已經到達最高的乘載量，不能再容納更多人了。

---

cape [keɪp] *n.* 披肩；斗篷

同 **wrap / cloak**

▶ Superman has a cooler cape than Batman.
超人的披肩比蝙蝠俠的還要酷。

Exercise 12

I. Vocabulary Choice

(A) buried   (B) burglar   (C) cabin   (D) bush   (E) canoe

(F) calculate   (G) burden   (H) buzz   (I) canyon   (J) bunch

1. Golden Grotto, located in Taroko National Park is famous for its crystal blue stream and skyline _____ .
2. Our ancestors are _____ in the family cemetery.
3. Helen received a _____ of flowers from her husband on their wedding anniversary.
4. The new assistant took on the _____ of the director's work.
5. Daniel likes to travel in a _____ .

II. Multiple Choice

1. Hillary Clinton and Donald Trump were the final two _____ (candid) standing in the 2016 United States presidential election, 2016.
2. Taipei Arena has a seating _____ (capable) of 15,000.
3. The mayor is planning to draft a law and launch a _____ (camp) against drunk driving.
4. Mark kept his Avengers toy doll collection in a glass fronted _____ (cabin) to keep them safe.
5. The student needs a _____ (calculate) to cross-check his answers.

capital [ˈkæp.ə.ţəl]

① *n.* 首都

搭 **capital city** 首都

同 **county seat / metropolis**

實用片語
short of capital 缺錢

② *adj.* 首要的；資本的

同 **central / leading**

▶ Sacramento is the capital of California.
沙加緬度是加州的首府。

▶ I'm a bit short of capital this month.
我這個月有點資金短缺。

▶ Let's focus on the capital information and not waste time on unnecessary details.
讓我們聚焦在重要的資訊上，不要浪費時間在一些不必要的枝節上。

---

capitalism [ˈkæp.ə.ţəl.ɪ.zəm] *n.* 資本（主義）

▶ Some believe capitalism is responsible for healthy economies.
有些人相信資本主是經濟繁榮的原因。

---

capitalist [ˈkæp.ə.ţəl.ɪst] *n.* 資本家

同 **banker / investor**

▶ The capitalists discussed new business opportunities.
資本家們在討論一些新的商機。

---

103 97

capture [ˈkæp.tʃɚ]

① *v.* 捕獲；俘虜

搭 **capture the attention** 抓住注意力

同 **hook / grab**

② *n.* 捕獲；俘虜

同 **arrest / grasping**

▶ The five girls that were captured last year were found alive.
去年被俘擄的五位女孩被發現還活著。

▶ The capture of the murderer made worldwide news.
那兇手被捕造成了世界性的新聞。

---

102 101

career [kəˈrɪr] *n.* 職業

搭 **career span** 職業生涯

同 **progress / path**

實用片語
checkered career 變化無常的職涯

▶ Shelly is interested in starting her own career as a teacher.
雪莉有意開創自己的教師生涯。

▶ I had a checkered career after high school.
高中畢業後我的事業幾經波折。

---

cargo [ˈkɑːr.goʊ] *n.* 貨物

▶ This plane carries only cargo, not people.
這班飛機只載貨物，不載乘客。

carpenter [ˈkɑːr.pɪn.tə-] *n.* 木匠

同 **artisan / builder**

▶ Joe quit his desk job to become a carpenter.
喬辭去辦公室工作，成為一個木匠。

---

carriage [ˈker.ɪdʒ] *n.* 馬車；嬰兒車

▶ The queen stepped out of the carriage and waved her hand.
皇后踏出馬車，揮了揮手。

---

carrier [ˈker.i.ə-] *n.* 運送者

同 **courier / shipper**

▶ The mail carrier comes every afternoon.
郵差每天下午都會來。

---

carve [kɑːrv] *v.* 雕刻

同 **hack / shape**

實用片語
carve something from 將… 雕刻成…

▶ At Halloween every year, the Smith family carves pumpkins into jack-o-lanterns.
每年的萬聖節，史密斯一家人都會把南瓜雕刻成「傑克南瓜燈」。

▶ Can you carve a flower from a bar of soap?
你可以用這條肥皂雕出一朵花嗎？

---

cast [kæst]

① *v.* 投；拋；擲

搭 **cast spells** 下咒語

同 **toss / pitch**

② *n.* 投擲

同 **pitch / toss**

③ *n.* 演員陣容

④ *v.* 選派演員

實用片語
cast about for 設想方法

▶ Jamie cast the wreath into the sea.
傑米把花圈拋入海中。

▶ The boy's first cast sent the ball over the fence.
這男孩的第一投，擲過了圍欄。

▶ Many famous actors have agreed to join the cast.
許多著名的演員都同意加入聯合演出的陣容。

▶ Everyone was surprised when an unknown actor was cast as the hero of the story.
當一位默默無名的演員飾演故事中的英雄時，每個人都感到意外。

▶ We need to cast about for creative ideas.
我們需要設想出有創意的想法。

99

casual [ˈkæʒ.u.əl] *adj.* 偶然的

搭 **casual clothes** 輕便服裝

同 **by chance / informal**

實用片語
casual dress 輕鬆打扮

▶ Let's not plan anything and keep everything casual.
我們不要計畫任何事，讓每件事都隨意好了。

▶ You can come to the party in casual dress.
你可以穿著輕鬆的裝扮來派對。

---

catalog / catalogue [ˈkæṭ.əl.ɑːg]

① *n.* 目錄

搭 **product catalogue** 產品型錄

同 **flyer / directory**

② *v.* 將…編入目錄

▶ If you don't know where something is, check the catalog.
如果你不知道東西在哪裡，那就查一下目錄吧。

▶ Can you help me catalog all of these items?
你能不能幫我將這些品項編入目錄？

---

caterpillar [ˈkæṭ.ɚ.pɪl.ɚ] *n.* 毛毛蟲

▶ The caterpillar will eventually become a butterfly.
毛毛蟲遲早會變成一隻蝴蝶。

---

cattle [ˈkæṭ.əl] *n.* 牛

▶ My uncle raises cattle for meat.
我叔叔養牛是為了賣牛肉。

100

cease [siːs]

① *v.* 停止

同 **quit / end**

② *n.* 停息

▶ Let's cease working for a while and take a break.
讓我們暫停工作，休息一下吧。

▶ There was a cease in the shooting for an hour.
開槍射擊停息約一小時。

97

celebrate [ˈsel.ə.breɪt] *v.* 慶祝

同 **praise / proclaim**

實用片語
celebrate for 為…慶祝

▶ Christmas is celebrated differently around the world.
世界各地用不同的方式來慶祝聖誕節。

▶ The team celebrated John for his successful sales performance.
團隊為約翰慶祝他成功的銷售績效。

---

celebration [ˌsel.əˈbreɪ.ʃən] *n.* 慶祝

搭 **birthday celebration** 生日慶祝

同 **festival / ceremony**

▶ My parents had a big celebration for their fiftieth anniversary.
我的父母在五十週年結婚紀念日舉辦大型慶祝會。

C

cement [sə'ment]

① *n.* 水泥

② *v.* 黏緊

同 **seal / bond**

實用片語
cement something together 黏著，黏合

▶ If you want to build a house, you will need a lot of cement.
如果你想要蓋一間房子，你就需要很多的水泥。

▶ Building this house involved cementing bricks together.
建造這棟房子需要用水泥將磚塊黏起來。

▶ Can you cement the vase together before mom gets home?
你能在媽媽到家前把花瓶修好嗎？

---

centimeter ['sen.tə.miː.tə] *n.* 公分

▶ My hair grew about six centimeters this month.
這個月我的頭髮長長了六公分。

---

ceramic [sə'ræm.ıks]

① *adj.* 陶器的

② *n.* 陶器

同 **brick / tile**

▶ Kelly bought a beautiful ceramic vase for her flowers.
凱莉為了她的花買了一只陶瓷花瓶。

▶ Linda can make jewelry, ceramics and wooden furniture with her hand.
琳達會製作首飾、陶器和木製家具。

---

certainly ['sɝː.tən.li] *adv.* 無疑地；確實

同 **exactly / surely**

▶ Monica certainly knows a lot about history.
莫尼卡確實熟知歷史。

102

chain [tʃeın]

① *n.* 鎖鏈

② *v.* 用鎖鏈拴住

同 **attach / confine**

▶ We locked the pool door with a chain.
我們用鎖鏈把游泳池的門鎖起來。

▶ The dog was chained to a tree in the backyard.
這隻狗被拴在後院的一棵樹上。

98

challenge ['tʃæl.ındʒ]

① *n.* 挑戰

搭 **welcome challenge** 不畏挑戰

同 **protest / threat**

② *v.* 挑戰

同 **dispute / question**

實用片語
challenge on 對…挑戰

▶ The team that finishes first wins the challenge.
先完成的隊伍就會贏得這個挑戰。

▶ I am challenging myself to exercise three times a week.
我挑戰自己一週運動三次。

▶ I don't think Mr. Wang is right, but I won't challenge him on his idea.
我不認為王先生是對的，但我不會對他的想法提出挑戰。

chamber [ˈtʃeɪm.bə] *n.* 房間；寢室

搭 **chamber music** 室內音樂

同 **cubicle / apartment**

實用片語
chamber of commerce 商會

▶ The old castle has many chambers.
老舊的城堡裡有許多的房間。

▶ The chamber of commerce helps companies to promote their business.
商會協助企業推展業務。

Exercise 13

I. 中英對應

_____ 1. 陶器　　(A) cement　　(B) cease　　(C) ceramic　　(D) centimeter

_____ 2. 房間　　(A) champion　(B) chamber　(C) champagne　(D) campaign

_____ 3. 偶然的　(A) cast　　　(B) castle　　(C) cashier　　(D) casual

_____ 4. 鎖鏈　　(A) chain　　(B) charge　　(C) chair　　(D) chief

_____ 5. 停息　　(A) certain　　(B) cereal　　(C) cease　　(D) center

II. Vocabulary Choice

(A) caterpillar　　(B) catalog　　(C) celebrate　　(D) captured　　(E) cattle

(F) carriages　　(G) champion　　(H) carpenter　　(I) changeable　　(J) cast

1. The transformation from _____ to butterfly is one of the most exquisite works of God's creation.

2. Before Jesus began His ministry, he was employed as a _____ .

3. Two bank robbers were _____ by the police and sent to prison.

4. Horse-drawn _____ riding through New York Central Park are one of the most popular ways to see the Park.

5. Emma Watson was _____ in the lead role of Beauty and the Beast.

Unit 14

(104)

champion [ˈtʃæm.pi.ən] *n.* 冠軍；優勝者

搭 **world champion** 世界冠軍

同 **winner / champ**

▶ Not only is she a world champion in tennis, she is also a mother of three children.
她不僅是一位世界網球冠軍，還是三個孩子的母親。

championship [ˈtʃæmpɪənˌʃɪp]
n. 冠軍的地位

同 **tournament / victor**

▶ The championship game will be between the Red Sox and the Blue Jays.
冠軍賽將是紅襪和多倫多藍鳥的對決。

(100) (99)

changeable [ˈtʃendʒəbəl] *adj.* 易變的

同 **unsettled / varying**

▶ The changeable weather makes it difficult to know what to wear.
多變的天氣讓人不知道要穿什麼衣服。

(97)

channel [ˈtʃæn.əl]

① *n.* 水道；頻道

搭 **distribution channel** （產品）銷售通路

同 **route / pathway**

② *v.* 開水道；輸送

實用片語
change the channel 岔開話題，離題

▶ The water channel is wide enough for boats to pass through.
水道夠寬，能讓船隻通過。

▶ To avoid floods, the government decided to channel the area.
為避免洪災，政府決定在這個地區開水道。

▶ You changed the channel. Let's go back to the main topic.
你離題了。我們回到主題吧。

chapter [ˈtʃæptɚ] *n.* 章

▶ Did you finish reading chapter six?
你看完第六章了嗎？

characteristic [ˌker.ək.təˈrɪs.tɪk]

① *adj.* 特有的

同 **unique / specific**

② *n.* 特色；特性

搭 **personal characteristic** 個人特質

同 **trait / virtue**

▶ Dancing before a speech is very characteristic of Tanya.
在演講之前先手舞足蹈就是譚雅獨特的地方。

▶ A cool characteristic of our team is that we all like to sing.
我們的團隊有一個很酷的特色，那就是我們都喜歡唱歌。

charity [ˈtʃer.ə.tʃi] *n.* 慈善團體；善舉

同 **goodwill / mercy**

▶ The rich man has started many charities to help people in need.
那位富翁創辦很多慈善機構來幫助窮人。

---

charm [tʃɑːrm]

① *n.* 魅力；吸引力

搭 **personal charm** 個人魅力

同 **appeal / grace**

② *v.* 迷住；吸引；使著迷

同 **enchant / attract**

實用片語
charm with 吸引

▶ Your apartment has a lot of charm.
你的公寓深具魅力。

▶ It's a charming city on the hills.
那是座落在山坡上的迷人城市。

▶ He charmed everyone with his bright smile.
他用他燦爛的微笑迷倒大家。

---

charming [ˈtʃɑːr.mɪŋ] *adj.* 有魅力的；迷人的

搭 **charming personality** 迷人的個性

同 **alluring / elegant**

▶ The charming lady made the guests feel welcome.
這位迷人的女士讓客人們感到非常受歡迎。

---

chat [tʃæt]

① *v.* 聊天

同 **talk / converse**

實用片語
chat about 談話，討論

② *n.* 聊天

▶ Stop chatting and get back to work!
不要再聊天了，回去工作！

▶ We need to chat about your goals.
我們需要談一下你的目標。

▶ Sit next to me and let's have a chat.
來坐在我旁邊，我們來聊天。

---

cheek [tʃiːk] *n.* 臉頰

▶ On their first date, Jay kissed Kerri on the cheek.
在他們第一次約會中，傑吻了凱芮的臉頰。

---

cheer [ˈtʃɪr]

① *n.* 歡呼；喝采

同 **joy / delight**

② *v.* 歡呼；喝采

同 **inspirit / delight**

實用片語
cheer up 振作

▶ The crowd welcomed the king with cheers and flowers.
群眾用歡呼和花朵來歡迎國王。

▶ As the ball went into the net, everyone cheered loudly.
當球進網時，大家都大聲歡呼。

▶ We tried to cheer Jack up by singing to him.
我們唱歌給傑克聽，試著讓他振作。

cheerful [ˈtʃɪr.fəl]

adj. 愉快的；高興的；興高采烈的

搭 **cheerful voice** 高興的聲音

同 **lively / joyful**

實用片語
cheap and cheerful 便宜又大碗

▶ You look happy and cheerful today!
你今天看起來開心又愉快！

▶ We specialize in cheap and cheerful package holidays to Japan.
我們專長於便宜又大碗的日本假日套裝行程。

---

cheese [tʃiːz] *n.* 起司；乳酪

實用片語
big cheese 大老闆

▶ We are having ham and cheese sandwiches for lunch.
我們的午餐是火腿和起司三明治。

▶ Jason thought he was the big cheese here, but then he got fired.
傑生認為他是這裡的大老闆，但他卻被辭退了。

---

chemistry [ˈkem.ɪ.stri] *n.* 化學

▶ Harry's favorite science class is chemistry.
哈利最喜歡的科學類課程是化學。

---

cherish [ˈtʃer.ɪʃ] *v.* 珍惜

同 **treasure / worship**

▶ Mothers cherish all of the time they have with their kids.
母親們非常珍惜和孩子們在一起的任何時刻。

---

cherry [ˈtʃer.i]

① *n.* 櫻桃

② *adj.* 櫻桃紅的；鮮紅色的

搭 **cherry blossoms** 櫻花

同 **blushing / dark red**

▶ Steve gave Ann a bowl of beautiful ripe cherries.
史提夫給了安一碗賞心悅目而且熟了的櫻桃。

▶ Abby wore a cherry dress to the party.
亞比穿著櫻桃紅色的洋裝參加派對。

---

chest [tʃest] *n.* 胸膛

實用片語
get something off one's chest
宣洩情緒，一吐為快

▶ Chest pain is not something you should ignore.
你不應該忽視胸口的疼痛。

▶ You need to get your problems off your chest.
你需要宣洩一下你的問題。

chew [tʃuː]

① *v.* 咀嚼

同 **nibble / bite**

② *n.* 咀嚼

---

childbirth [ˈtʃaɪld.bɝːθ] *n.* 分娩；生孩子

---

childhood [ˈtʃaɪld‚hʊd] *n.* 童年

實用片語
in one's second childhood 重回童年

---

chill [tʃɪl]

① *n.* 寒冷

搭 **feel chill** 感覺冷

同 **coldness / rigor**

實用片語
chill out 放鬆

② *v.* （使）變冷；（使）冷卻

同 **freeze / frost**

③ *adj.* 冷的

同 **freezing / frigid**

---

chilly [ˈtʃɪl.i] *adj.* 冷颼颼的

搭 **chilly night** 寒冷的夜晚

同 **icy / brisk**

▶ Teach your children to chew with their mouths closed.
教導你的孩子在咀嚼時，把嘴巴閉上。

▶ The child's first chew of peppers made him cry.
這小孩第一次吃到胡椒時就哭了起來。

▶ The process of going through childbirth was tough on her.
她的分娩過程很難受。

▶ During my childhood, I spent most of my time drawing and reading books.
在孩童時期，我大部分的時間都花在繪畫和讀書上。

▶ When I play with my son's toys, I feel as if I'm in my second childhood.
當我玩我兒子的玩具時，感覺好像重回童年了。

▶ As the wind blew, Harry felt a cold chill going through his body.
起風時，哈利感受到一陣寒意吹進他的身子骨。

▶ I'd like to go home, have dinner, and chill out tonight.
今晚我想回家，吃個晚餐，放鬆一下。

▶ Pour some syrup on the fruit, then let it chill for twenty minutes.
把糖漿淋在水果上面，然後讓它冷卻二十分鐘。

▶ This chill weather is making me really uncomfortable.
這種寒冷的天氣讓我很不舒服。

▶ It's chilly in here. Please close the windows.
這裡很冷，請關上窗戶。

chimney [ˈtʃɪm.ni] *n.* 煙囪

實用片語

smoke like a chimney 煙一根接一根地抽

---

chip [tʃɪp]

① *n.* 炸薯條；炸洋芋片

② *v.* 弄缺口；使碎掉

同 **chop / crack**

▶ I can see black smoke rising from the chimney.

我可以看到黑煙從煙囪裡冒出來。

▶ My grandfather smoked like a chimney when he was alive.

我的祖父在世時菸一根接著一根抽。

▶ One popular British food is fish and chips.

一種受歡迎的英式食物是魚搭配炸薯條。

▶ My ten year old son chipped his two front teeth.

我十歲的兒子把兩顆門牙都撞出缺口了。

Exercise 14

I. Vocabulary Choice

(A) charming   (B) channel   (C) chapter   (D) cherish   (E) cheek

(F) characteristic   (G) charity   (H) cheese   (I) childbirth   (J) chest

1. _____ includes both labor and delivery, and the process usually is very painful.

2. The coastguard cutter often cruises near the entrance of the _____ .

3. Flexibility, communication and honesty are some of the most common traits in the _____ of a leader.

4. Brad Pitt, Keanu Reeves and Chris Hemsworth have been chosen as the most _____ actors on the 2015 IMDb list.

5. We should _____ the time with our family and friends because once they are gone, it is too late.

II. Multiple Choice

(   ) 1. I had a long ___ with my supervisor this afternoon about my future promotion.

      (A) chapter (B) chart (C) chat (D) change

(   ) 2. Everyone ___ loudly when they heard the news of Hsu winning Taiwan's first gold medal at the Rio 2016 Olympics.

      (A) cheered (B) cheeked (C) cheesed (D) cheated

(   ) 3. Marie Curie is the only person who has ever won Nobel Prizes in both physics and ___ .

      (A) characteristic (B) charity (C) chemical (D) chemistry

(   ) 4. Eating or ___ gum or betel nut is not allowed on the MRT system.

      (A) biting (B) chewing (C) drinking (D) licking

(   ) 5. Charlotte is good at making apple and ___ pie.

      (A) cheer (B) cheek (C) cherry (D) chest

Unit 15

chirp [tʃɜːp]

① *v.* （小鳥）發唧啾聲

② *n.* 唧啾聲

▶ You can hear the birds chirping in the trees.
你可以聽得到小鳥在樹上吱吱喳喳地叫。

▶ That bird must be from somewhere else; I haven't heard that chirp before.
那隻鳥一定是從別處飛來的；我以前從來沒聽過牠的叫聲。

---

choke [tʃoʊk]

① *v.* 噎住；窒息

同 **clog / block**

② *n.* 窒息；噎住

實用片語
choke someone up 令人哽咽

▶ Children can easily choke on fish bones.
小孩子很容易被魚刺噎住。

▶ That sounded like a choke.
那聲音聽起來像是噎住了。

▶ The sad story choked up most of the audience.
這悲傷的故事讓大多數的聽眾哽咽。

---

chop [tʃɑːp]

① *v.* 切碎；砍；劈

同 **axe / slash**

實用片語
chop someone off 打斷某人

② *n.* 砍；劈；排骨

▶ I'm going to chop up some broccoli for the salad.
我要切些花椰菜，放在沙拉裡。

▶ I'm not finished. Don't chop me off.
我還沒講完。不要打斷我。

▶ The man was skilled with the axe and gave the tree a quick chop.
這個人很會用斧頭，他快速地砍下這棵樹。

---

chore [tʃɔːr] *n.* 家庭雜務

搭 **domestic chore** 家事

同 **errand / duty**

▶ Cleaning my room is just one of the chores I must do every Saturday.
打掃我的房間只是我每週六必做的家庭雜務之一。

---

chorus [ˈkɔːrəs] *n.* 合唱團

▶ Johnny joined the chorus at school because he loves to sing.
強尼參加了學校的合唱團因為他熱愛唱歌。

cigar [sə'gɑːr] *n.* 雪茄

實用片語
close but no cigar 接近但還是沒成功

▶ You can't buy Cuban cigars in the United States.
你在美國買不到古巴的雪茄。

▶ We almost won the contest. Close but no cigar.
我們差一點就贏得競賽。功敗垂成。

---

cigarette ['sɪg.ə.ret] *n.* 菸

▶ Smoking cigarettes can increase a person's chance of getting cancer.
抽菸可能會增加罹患癌症的機率。

---

cinema ['sɪn.ə.mə] *n.* 電影院

▶ We went to the cinema to see which movies are playing.
我們到電影院去看看有哪些電影正在上映。

100
circular ['sɝː.kjə.lə] *adj.* 圓形的

▶ Most cups have a circular shape so that they're easier to drink from.
大部份的杯子是圓形的,所以喝東西時比較方便。

---

98 95
circulate ['sɝː.kjə.leɪt] *v.* 流傳;循環

搭 **circulate freely** 充分流通
同 **rotate / fly about**
實用片語
circulate among 周旋於…

▶ The news is circulating that Lois is leaving the company.
魯伊斯要離職的消息正在到處流傳。

▶ The host circulated among the guests.
主人周旋於賓客之間。

---

103 96
circulation [ˌsɝː.kjəˈleɪ.ʃən] *n.* 循環;運行

搭 **blood circulation** 血液循環
同 **currency / spread**

▶ Regular exercise is good for your blood circulation.
規律的運動對你的血液循環很有幫助。

101
circumstance ['sɝː.kəm.stæns] *n.* 情況

同 **situation / condition**

▶ I can't work well in stressful circumstances.
我在有壓力的情況下無法好好工作。

---

circus ['sɝː.kəs] *n.* 馬戲團

實用片語
three-ring circus 場面熱鬧,鬧哄哄

▶ Before Fred joined the circus, he was a clown for children's birthday parties.
弗萊德在加入馬戲團之前,曾在兒童生日派對上擔任小丑。

▶ The class is like a three-ring circus.
這課堂內熱哄哄地。

civil [ˈsɪv.əl] *adj.* 公民的

同 **local / public**

實用片語
keep a civil tongue 出言客氣，說話有禮

▶ Some civil responsibilities include paying taxes and respecting others.
部份公民的義務包括繳稅和尊重別人。

▶ Joe seems unable to keep a civil tongue.
喬伊似乎無法彬彬有禮地說話。

104
civilian [səˈvɪl.jən]

① *n.* 平民；百姓
② *adj.* 平民的；百姓的

同 **private / public**

▶ No civilians were killed in the war, only soldiers.
在這場戰爭中沒有平民百姓被殺死，只有士兵。

▶ This court deals with all civilian matters.
這個法庭處理的都是民事的案件。

---

civilization [ˌsɪv.əl.əˈzeɪ.ʃən] *n.* 文明

搭 **civilization process** 文明化過程
同 **culture / progress**

▶ Steve loves history and learning about ancient civilizations.
史提夫熱愛歷史也喜歡研究古代文明。

100
clarify [ˈkler.ə.faɪ] *v.* 解釋清楚；得到澄清

搭 **clarify points** 闡明要點
同 **analyze / define**

▶ Please clarify what you mean because I don't understand.
請你解釋清楚你的意思，因為我聽不懂。

---

clash [klæʃ]

① *n.* 碰撞聲

實用片語
clash with 與⋯衝突

② *v.* 相碰撞
同 **collide / smash**

▶ I heard a clash and went to see what caused it.
我聽到了碰撞聲就過去看看是什麼造成的。

▶ This yellow sweater does not clash with the blue pants.
這黃色毛衣跟藍色褲子一點也不衝突。

▶ The child held a pan and a pot and clashed them against each other.
那個小孩抓起炒菜鍋和湯鍋，然後將它們互相敲敲撞撞。

---

classical [ˈklæs.ɪ.kəl] *adj.* 古典的；經典的

搭 **classical literature** 古典文學
同 **elegant / classic**

▶ Jenny is currently reading a book about classical Greek art and culture.
甄妮目前正在讀一本關於希臘古典藝術和文化的書。

classification [ˌklæs.ə.fəˈkeɪ.ʃən]

n. 歸類；將 ... 分類

同 **assortment / division**

▶ The scientist spent 10 years in the classification of butterflies.

這個科學家花了十年的時間將蝴蝶分類。

---

classify [ˈklæs.ə.faɪ] *v.* 歸類；將⋯分類

同 **tabulate / arrange**

▶ Vern classified the information as top secret.

芬恩將這個資料歸類為最高機密。

---

click [klɪk]

① *v.* 點擊（滑鼠）

② *n.* 喀嚓聲；點擊滑鼠

▶ Tom clicked the mouse, but it didn't work.

湯姆點擊了滑鼠，可是沒有任何反應。

▶ Ken slid his hotel key card in the door and heard the click of the lock.

肯恩把鑰匙卡插入旅館門上的鎖孔中，就聽見開啟的聲音。

---

client [ˈklaɪ.ənt] *n.* 顧客；客戶

搭 **deal with client** 應付客戶

同 **customer / shopper**

▶ Everyone knows Mr. Cho always puts his clients first.

大家都知道邱先生總是把顧客排在第一位。

---

cliff [klɪf] *n.* 懸崖；斷崖；峭壁

▶ Don't step too close to the edge of the cliff or you will fall over.

不要走的太靠近懸崖，否則你可能會摔下去。

---

climax [ˈklaɪ.mæks]

① *n.* 頂點

搭 **reach climax** 到達頂點

同 **summit / peak**

② *v.* （使）達到高潮；達到頂點

同 **succeed / achieve**

實用片語
bring something to a climax 推上台面

▶ We reached the climax of our hike; now let's go back down the mountain.

我們已經攻頂了；現在可以回頭下山了。

▶ The music climaxed with all of the instruments playing a beautiful melody before it ended.

這首曲子在結束之前，所有的樂器和奏出美妙的旋律而達到了最高潮。

▶ I think it's time to bring this matter to a climax.

我認為是時候把這件事搬到台面上討論了。

Exercise 15

I. 中英對應

_____ 1. 噎住   (A) chick   (B) choke

                     (C) chord   (D) chore

_____ 2. 圓形的   (A) circulate   (B) circus

                     (C) circuit   (D) circular

_____ 3. 歸類；分級   (A) classic   (B) classical

                     (C) classmate   (D) classification

_____ 4. 頂點   (A) climate   (B) climb

                     (C) climax   (D) climber

_____ 5. 平民百姓   (A) civilian   (B) civil

                     (C) civilize   (D) civic

II. Vocabulary Choice

(A) cliff   (B) chilly   (C) chimney   (D) clients   (E) chop

(F) cinemas   (G) chore   (H) cigarettes   (I) circulation   (J) cigar

1. After I started exercising daily, my blood _____ improved drastically.

2. She fell off a _____ in her nightmares last night, but before she hit the ground she woke up.

3. The Hollywood lawyer has a number of famous movies stars as _____ including Angelina Jolie and Matt Damon.

4. Although I have many DVDs at home, I still prefer watching movies at the _____ .

5. Secondhand smoke causes lung cancer in nonsmoking adults, and the source of most secondhand smoke is from _____ .

Unit 10

102

blame [bleɪm]

① *v.* 責怪;指責

同 **accuse / criticize**

實用片語
blame for 怪罪於…

② *n.* 責怪;指責

搭 **accept blame** 接受譴責

同 **criticism / attack**

▶ My wife blames me for everything!
我太太把每件事都怪在我身上!

▶ We should not blame Linda for this mistake.
我們不該為這個錯誤怪罪琳達。

▶ Mary took the blame for her brother even though she didn't do anything wrong.
瑪麗承擔她兄弟的過失,即使她沒有做錯任何事。

---

blanket [ˈblæŋ.kɪt]

① *n.* 毯子

② *v.* 用毯覆蓋

搭 **wet blanket** 掃興

同 **cover / throw**

實用片語
eyes like two burnt holes in a blanket
熊貓眼,黑眼圈

▶ In the winter, Eve uses a heavier blanket to keep her warm at night.
在冬天,伊芙晚上用厚毯子保暖。

▶ In September, colorful leaves blanket our front yard.
在九月,色彩繽紛的葉子覆蓋在我家的前院。

▶ You've got eyes like two burnt holes in a blanket.
你有黑眼圈。

---

bleed [bli:d] *v.* 流血

▶ The soccer ball hit my face so hard that my nose started to bleed.
我的臉被足球用力地打中,鼻子開始流血。

---

blend [blend]

① *v.* (用果汁機)打;混合

搭 **blend together** 混在一起

同 **mix / meld**

實用片語
blend in 混合

② *n.* 混合

同 **mixture / combination**

▶ Blend ice, guava, and apple together for a delicious drink.
將冰塊,番石榴以及蘋果加在一起,就可以打出好喝的飲料。

▶ The oil won't blend into the water at all.
油與水完全不相融。

▶ This shade of orange is a lighter blend of red and yellow.
這色調的橘色是亮度較高的紅黃混合色。

climber [ˈklaɪ.mɚ] *n.* 攀登者；登山者

搭 **social climber** 攀高枝者

同 **hiker / backpacker**

▶ A climber can easily climb up to the top of that rock!

攀登者能夠很輕易地登上那個岩石的頂端！

---

clinic [ˈklɪn.ɪk] *n.* 診所

▶ The pregnant woman entered the clinic to give birth.

孕婦進到診所生產。

---

(104)

clip [klɪp]

① *n.* 剪；剪下來的東西

② *v.* 剪；夾住

同 **prune / trim**

實用片語
clip from 剪自⋯

▶ She's really good with scissors. Just look at her clip work.

她真的很會使用剪刀，光看她的剪紙作品就知道了。

▶ She clipped her cat's claws because they were getting too sharp.

她幫她的貓咪修剪爪子，因為實在太尖銳了。

▶ I clipped the photo from that magazine.

我從那本雜誌上剪貼相片。

---

clothed [kloʊðd]

adj. 穿⋯衣服的；覆蓋⋯著的

同 **cloaked / covered**

▶ All the clothed people stayed near the dry area.

所有穿好衣服的人待在靠近乾的地方。

---

clue [kluː] *n.* 線索

搭 **vital clue** 重要線索

同 **cue / hint**

實用片語
not a clue 沒線索，不知情

▶ New clues could help the police solve the case.

新的線索可以幫助警察解決案情。

▶ Q: Where is John? A: Not a clue.

Q: 約翰在哪裡？A: 一無所知。

---

(101) (98) (97)

clumsy [ˈklʌm.zi] *adj.* 笨拙的；手腳不靈活的

同 **crude / bumbling**

▶ Katie is clumsy and often bumps into walls.

凱蒂笨手笨腳的，常常撞到牆壁。

---

coarse [kɔːrs] *adj.* 粗糙的

同 **raw / gruff**

▶ The surface of this table is too coarse to write on.

這張桌子的桌面太粗糙了，很難在上面寫字。

cocktail [ˈkɑːk.teɪl] *n.* 雞尾酒

> ▶ My sister enjoys sweet cocktails with lots fruit juice and ice.
> 我的姊妹喜歡裡面有很多果汁和冰塊的甜雞尾酒。

---

coconut [ˈkoʊ.kə.nʌt] *n.* 椰子

> ▶ She's relaxing on the beach drinking from a coconut shell.
> 她正悠閒地在海灘上喝著新鮮的椰子汁。

---

code [koʊd]

① *n.* 密碼；代碼

同 **cipher / system**

② *v.* 為⋯編碼

> ▶ What's the code for your phone?
> 你電話的密碼是什麼？

> ▶ We need to organize all the samples and code them.
> 我們需要把所有的樣品都整理好，然後再編碼。

---

103 102 99

collapse [kəˈlæps]

① *v.* 崩塌

同 **crumple / break**

實用片語
collapse into 潰散

② *n.* 瓦解；倒塌

搭 **economic collapse** 經濟崩盤

同 **crash / disruption**

> ▶ The building was too weak and collapsed after the earthquake.
> 這棟建築物太不穩固，所以地震過後就倒塌了。

> ▶ After work I just collapsed into the sofa.
> 下班後我只能癱在沙發上。

> ▶ The Great Depression is known for the collapse of the economy.
> 「經濟大蕭條」以經濟瓦解而聞名。

---

collar [ˈkɑː.lə] *n.* 衣領

實用片語
blue collar 藍領階級

> ▶ Don't forget to fix your collar before you leave the house.
> 你離開房子前，別忘了要先把衣領整理好。

> ▶ My parents are both blue collar workers.
> 我的父母都是藍領階級的勞工。

99

collection [kəˈlek.ʃən] *n.* 收集

搭 **stamp collection** 集郵

同 **selection / assortment**

> ▶ She has a collection of stamps that dates back to the 1800's.
> 她收集的郵票，最早可追溯到 1800 年代。

---

college [ˈkɑː.lɪdʒ] *n.* 大專；學院

搭 **business college** 商業學院

同 **university / school**

> ▶ Betty got accepted to the college of her dreams!
> 貝蒂被她心目中的理想大學接受入學了！

colony [ˈkɑː.lə.ni] *n.* 殖民地

▶ The first colonies in America were located on the east coast.
美國的最早的殖民地位於東岸。

---

colored [ˈkʌl.ɚd] *adj.* 有顏色的；彩色的

同 **flushed / glowing**

實用片語
see through rose-colored glasses
樂觀地看待事物

▶ Noah used colored paper for the art project.
諾亞用色紙來創作藝術作品。

▶ Sara sees the world through rose-colored glasses.
莎拉以樂觀的態度看待世界。

---

column [ˈkɑː.ləm] *n.* 圓柱；專欄

搭 **monthly column** 每月專欄
同 **procession / file**

▶ The building has many beautiful columns.
那棟建築擁有很多美麗的圓柱。

---

combination [ˌkɑːm.bəˈneɪ.ʃən] *n.* 組合；結合（體）

同 **merger / consolidation**

▶ That fruit bowl has a nice combination of apples, oranges and pears.
這個水果盅有蘋果，橘子和水梨，是個很棒的組合。

---

(98)
combine [kəmˈbaɪn] *v.* 混合；合併；結合

搭 **combine elements** 綜合條件
同 **integrate / conjoin**

實用片語
combine with 綜合

▶ In a large bowl, combine eggs, milk, and flour.
在一個大碗中，把雞蛋、牛奶和麵粉混在一起。

▶ First you should combine the eggs with the sugar.
首先你應該先將蛋與糖混在一起。

---

combined [kəmˈbaɪnd] *adj.* 聯合的；結合的

同 **mixed / joined**

▶ It took the combined efforts of both departments to get the job done.
這項工作圓滿完成就在於兩個部門共同的努力。

---

comedy [ˈkɑː.mə.di] *n.* 喜劇

實用片語
cut the comedy 不要再鬧

▶ I really need to laugh; let's watch a comedy tonight!
我需要好好地開懷大笑；那我們今晚就來看部喜劇好了。

▶ Guys, cut the comedy and get to work.
各位，現在別胡鬧，開始工作吧。

comfort [ˈkʌm.fət] *n.* 舒適

搭 **comfort zone** 舒適圈

同 **amenity / well-being**

▶ Cindy didn't want to leave the comfort of her father's arms.
辛蒂不想離開爸爸舒適的膀臂。

---

comfortably [ˈkʌmf.tə.bli] *adv.* 舒服地

同 **restfully / cozily**

▶ He is able to comfortably wear his new hat.
他戴的新帽子很舒服。

---

comic [ˈkɑː.mɪk] *adj.* 滑稽的；喜劇的

搭 **comic books** 漫畫書

同 **clown / funny**

▶ The comedian has a very funny comic routine.
那位喜劇演員有一套很好笑的滑稽表演。

---

comic(s) [ˈkɑː.mɪk(s)] *n.* 連環漫畫

▶ Jerry's favorite comic book is One Piece.
傑瑞最喜歡的連環漫畫是「One Piece 航海王」。

---

coming [ˈkʌm.ɪŋ] *adj.* 即將到來的；接著的

搭 **coming generation** 下一代

同 **foreseen / expected**

▶ Our company has big plans for the coming year.
我們的公司對即將到來的一年有很大的計畫。

Exercise 16

I. 中英對應

_____ 1. 診所　(A) clinic　　　(B) client　　　(C) clip　　　(D) clue

_____ 2. 笨拙的　(A) clarify　　(B) clash　　　(C) clumsy　　(D) coarse

_____ 3. 瓦解　(A) collaborate　(B) college　　(C) collar　　(D) collapse

_____ 4. 結合的　(A) combine　(B) combined　(C) combination　(D) combat

_____ 5. 舒適　(A) comics　　(B) coming　　(C) comfort　　(D) colored

II. Vocabulary Choice

(A) collection　(B) cocktail　(C) colony　(D) coconut　(E) clip

(F) code　(G) clue　(H) comedy　(I) clothed　(J) columns

1. The lobby bar of the hotel that we stayed at offers creative _____ and soft drinks.

2. Australia is a former British _____ .

3. Amanda has a very good _____ of perfumes and perfume bottles.

4. Jim Carrey and Ben Stiller are two of the funniest _____ actors in Hollywood.

5. The ancient Greeks designed three types of stylish _____ to support their large buildings.

90

C

comma [ˈkɑː.mə] *n.* 逗號

▶ Tim often forgets to put in commas when he writes emails.
提姆寫電子郵件時，常常忘記加上逗號。

95

command [kəˈmænd] *n.* 命令

同 direction / instruction

實用片語
have a good command of 精通於⋯

▶ Soldiers must obey their captain's commands.
士兵們必須服從長官的命令。

▶ Mr. Jones has a good command of his emotions.
瓊斯先生很能駕馭管理他的情緒。

commander [kəˈmæn.dɚ] *n.* 指揮官

搭 **chief commander** 指揮官
同 director / leader

▶ I'm the master and commander of this ship, so you listen to me!
我是這艘船的艦長及指揮官，所以你要聽我的！

103 102

comment [ˈkɑː.ment] *n.* 留言；意見；註解

同 judgment / opinion

實用片語
address comments 發表意見

▶ Did you leave a comment on my Facebook wall? Please comment on my post.
你有沒有在我的臉書牆上留言？請在我的貼文留言。

▶ Mr. Chen addressed his comments to all employees.
陳先生向所有員工發表意見。

commerce [ˈkɑː.mɝːs] *n.* 貿易；商業

同 business / trade

▶ There is a lot of commerce within Toronto because it is a port city.
在多倫多有很多的貿易往來，因為它是一個海港城市。

104 103

commercial [kəˈmɝː.ʃəl] *adj.* 商業的

搭 **commercial development** 商業發展
同 profitable / wholesale

▶ This product will not go into commercial production until next year.
這個產品明年才會商業量產。

commit [kəˈmɪt] *v.* 犯（罪）

同 violate / sin

實用片語
commit oneself to 承諾

▶ Benjamin spent twenty years in prison for committing murder.
班傑明因為犯了謀殺罪而坐了二十年的牢。

▶ I commit myself to finishing this report on time.
我承諾準時完成這份報告。

---

(103)
committee [kəˈmɪt̮.i] *n.* 委員會

▶ Our school committee meets every month.
我們學校的委員會每個月開一次會。

---

(96)
communicate [kəˈmjuː.nə.keɪt] *v.* 溝通

同 confer / correspond

實用片語
communicate with 溝通，告知

▶ Thanks to the internet, we can communicate with people across the world.
拜網際網路科技之賜，我們才能與世界各地的人溝通。

▶ Regarding that issue, I have to communicate with my mom first.
關於這個問題，我必須先跟我媽媽溝通

---

communication [kəˌmjuː.nəˈkeɪ.ʃən]
n. 溝通；傳達；交流

搭 **communication skill** 溝通技巧

同 interaction / conversation

▶ Many people say that communication is the most important thing in a relationship.
很多人都說溝通是人際關係中最重要的一環。

---

community [kəˈmjuː.nə.tj] *n.* 社區

同 society / group

▶ People from my town like to spend time at the community center.
我們鎮上的人都很喜歡聚在社區中心。

---

compact disk (CD) [ˌkɑːm.pækt ˈdɪsk]
n. 光碟

▶ I listen to most of my music on my MP3 player, but my brother still listens to CDs.
我幾乎都用 MP3 播放器在聽我的音樂，但是我的哥哥還在聽光碟片。

---

(96)
companion [kəmˈpæn.jən] *n.* 同伴

同 friend / co-worker

實用片語
boon companion 知心伴侶

▶ It's really helpful to have a companion.
有個同伴真的幫助很大。

▶ Sandra and I are boon companions.
珊卓和我是知心伴侶。

compared [kəmˈper] *adj.* 比較的；對照的

同 **correlated / related**

▶ The two compared paintings are similar in price.
被拿來相互比較的兩幅畫價格差不多。

---

comparison [kəmˈper.ɪ.sən] *n.* 比較；對照

搭 **meaningful comparison** 有意義的比較

同 **relation / analogy**

實用片語
no comparison 無可比擬

▶ Our boss will do a brief comparison and then decide.
我們的老闆會做簡短的比較，然後做出決定。

▶ This is the best restaurant in town, no comparison.
這是鎮上最好的餐廳，無人可比。

98

compete [kəmˈpiːt] *v.* 參加比賽；競爭

同 **contend / battle**

實用片語
compete with 與…競爭

▶ Ellen will compete in the gymnastics competition this weekend.
艾倫這個週末會參加體操比賽。

▶ We have to compete with other major vendors.
我們必須與其他主要的供應商競爭。

---

competition [ˌkɑːm.pəˈtɪʃ.ən] *n.* 比賽；競爭

同 **contest / rivalry**

▶ Kelly won the singing competition and Laura came in second place.
凱莉在歌唱比賽得勝，而蘿拉得了第二名。

---

competitive [kəmˈpet̬.ə.t̬ɪv]

adj. 好競爭的；競爭的

搭 **competitive edge** 競爭優勢

同 **ambitious / aggressive**

▶ Katrina isn't a competitive person; she just likes to play games for fun.
柯菊娜不是個好競爭的人；她只是喜歡玩遊戲消遣一下。

---

competitor [kəmˈpet̬.ə.t̬ɚ] *n.* 參賽者；競爭者

搭 **chief competitor** 主要對手

同 **rival / participant**

▶ The competitors are ready to begin the race.
這些參賽者準備好要開始比賽了。

---

complaint [kəmˈpleɪnt] *n.* 投訴；抱怨

搭 **customer complaint** 客戶抱怨

同 **protest / accusation**

▶ If you need to make a complaint, contact your local council.
如果你需要投訴，請與當地市議會聯絡。

complex [kɑːmˈpleks] *adj.* 複雜的

搭 **complex structure**　複雜的結構

同 **elaborate / complicated**

▶ I can't comprehend all these complex issues.
我不理解這些複雜的問題。

complex [ˈkɑːm.pleks]

n. 綜合大樓；綜合物；複合體

▶ Burglaries occur often in this apartment complex.
這棟公寓綜合大樓經常發生竊盜案。

97 96 95

complicate [ˈkɑːm.plə.keɪt]

v. 使複雜；使更麻煩

▶ The weather complicates our picnic plans.
這種天氣把我們的野餐計畫變得很麻煩。

complicated [ˈkɑːm.plə.keɪ.t̬ɪd]

adj. 複雜的；難懂的

搭 **complicated situation**　複雜的狀況

同 **complex / intricate**

▶ The complicated math problem took many hours to solve.
這題複雜的數學題目是花了好幾個小時才解答出來的。

101

compose [kəmˈpoʊz] *v.* 由⋯組成；由⋯構成

同 **comprise / construct**

▶ The country is composed of 31 states.
這個國家是由三十一個州所組成的。

composer [kəmˈpoʊ.zɚ] *n.* 作曲家

▶ Mozart is one of the most famous composers in history.
莫扎特是史上最有名的作曲家之一。

Exercise 17

I. Derivatives

1. Adele's first _____ (commerce) and debut album, "19" was released in 2008.

2. Susie plans to take a course on _____ (communicate) skills.

3. The army will go into action as soon as their _____ (command) gives the order.

4. The prices of our products are _____ (compete) in world markets.

5. The public transit system in Frankfurt is so _____ (complicate) that we had to ask people several times to find the right platform.

II. Vocabulary Choice

(A) comment   (B) committee   (C) companion   (D) complaints   (E) compared

(F) competition   (G) complicate   (H) complex   (I) compose   (J) comparison

1. My cat has been my constant _____ these past sixteen years.

2. Many artists and celebrities like to check the _____ on their Facebook wall and even respond to their fans.

3. Sport is generally good for a person's health. By _____ too much exercise can be bad for your body and cause permanent injury.

4. The police station has received a number of _____ about the noise.

5. Miramar Entertainment Park, which is located in Taipei City, is a _____ shopping mall and it is easy to get lost there.

Unit 18

composition [ˌkɑːm.pəˈzɪʃ.ən]

n. （音樂）作品；樂曲

搭 **musical composition** 寫音樂

同 **harmony / design**

▶ Mozart wrote hundreds of compositions during his lifetime.
莫札特一生寫了幾百首樂曲。

96
concentrate [ˈkɑːn.sən.treɪt]

v. 全神貫注；集中

搭 **concentrate entirely** 完全專心

同 **focus / sharpen**

實用片語
concentrate on 專注於

▶ With only two months left before school is out, Steven wants to concentrate on his research.
還有兩個月學校就要放假了，所以史提夫要全神專注在他的研究報告。

▶ He concentrated on studying and didn't go out much.
他專注於念書，很少出去。

---

concentration [ˌkɑːn.sənˈtreɪ.ʃən]

n. 注意力；集中；專注

搭 **demand concentration** 需集中注意力

同 **focusing / centering**

▶ With so much noise around him, Max shows amazing concentration.
即使周遭有這麼多的噪音，麥克斯仍展現驚人的注意力。

---

concept [ˈkɑːn.sept] *n.* 概念

搭 **business concept** 商業概念

同 **theory / approach**

▶ Theo likes his philosophy class even though some of the concepts are hard to understand.
西歐很喜歡哲學課，即使有些概念很難理解。

---

100 96 95
concern [kənˈsɜːn]

① *v.* 擔心；憂慮

同 **worry / trouble**

實用片語
concern about 擔憂

② *n.* 擔心；憂慮

同 **burden / anxiety**

▶ Parents are concerned about their children's online privacy.
家長們很關心他們子女的線上隱私。

▶ Please don't concern yourself about me. I'm fine.
請不要擔心我。我很好。

▶ My concern is that you are not getting enough sleep.
我擔心你睡眠不足。

concerning [kənˈsɝːnɪŋ] *prep.* 關於

▶ I need to speak to you concerning your son's behavior at school.
我必須要跟你談談有關你兒子在校的行為。

---

concert [ˈkɑːnsət] *n.* 音樂會

搭 **gala concert** 節慶演唱會
同 **performance / recital**

實用片語
in concert 一致

▶ The musicians will arrive early to rehearse for the concert.
樂手們會提早抵達,為音樂會排練。

▶ We worked in concert on the project.
我們在專案上合作一致。

---

⑨⑤
conclude [kənˈkluːd] *v.* 結束;作出結論

同 **wrap up / terminate**

▶ The funeral concluded with a prayer.
喪禮以禱告作為結束。

101
conclusion [kənˈkluːʒən] *n.* 結論

搭 **jump to conclusion** 做出結論
同 **decision / agreement**

▶ You need to write a conclusion to your essay.
你需要為你的短文下一個結論。

---

103 102 100
concrete [ˈkɑːnkriːt]

① *adj.* 確實的;具體的
搭 **concrete example** 具體的例子
同 **solid / definite**

實用片語
written in concrete 具體寫下

② *n.* 混凝土

③ *v.* 用混凝土覆蓋

▶ The judge wanted to see concrete evidence that the man on trial was guilty.
法官想要看到受審人有罪的確實證據。

▶ Everything is written in concrete, so we can't make changes.
所有事情皆已具體寫下,所以我們不能進行變更。

▶ This building is made of concrete.
這棟大樓是用混凝土蓋的。

▶ The construction workers concreted the building.
這些建築工人用混凝土來蓋大樓。

---

104 99
condition [kənˈdɪʃən]

① *n.* 情況
搭 **standard condition** 標準狀態
同 **situation / status**

② *v.* 使習慣於;使適應

實用片語
in good condition 狀況良好

▶ It may be old, but it's in perfect condition.
它也許舊了,但是狀況仍十分良好。

▶ Patients can become conditioned to certain medical treatments.
病人會漸漸習慣於某些醫療方式。

▶ His health is in good condition now.
他現在的健康狀況良好。

conductor [kənˈdʌk.tɚ] *n.* 指揮；領導者

同 **director / leader**

▶ I really admire the way our conductor leads our orchestra.
我非常佩服我們的指揮帶領我們管弦樂團的方式。

---

cone [koʊn] *n.* 圓錐形

▶ Today in math class, we will learn about the volume of a cone.
在今天的數學課，我們要來學習圓錐體的體積。

---

conference [ˈkɑːn.fɚ.əns] *n.* 大會；討論會

搭 **management conference** 管理研討會

同 **seminar / convention**

▶ Twenty of our company's staff went to the leadership conference last weekend.
上個週末我們公司有二十位員工去參加領袖研習會。

---

confess [kənˈfes] *v.* 坦承；供認

同 **assert / disclose**

實用片語
confess to 坦白

▶ George confessed to stealing the necklace after we told the police.
在我們報警之後，喬治坦承他偷了項鍊。

▶ Tom eventually confessed to the police.
湯姆最後向警察坦白。

---

confidence [ˈkɑːn.fə.dəns] *n.* 自信；信心

搭 **boost confidence** 提升信心

同 **assurance / certainty**

實用片語
confidence in 有信心

▶ Nelly feels that she needs more confidence before she can sing in public.
娜莉覺得她需要有更多的自信才能夠公開演唱。

▶ We have confidence in you.
我們對你有信心。

---

confident [ˈkɑːn.fə.dənt]
adj. 有信心的；自信的

同 **morale / spirit**

▶ We are confident she will be successful in her future career.
我們都相信她未來的職業生涯會很成功。

---

confine [kənˈfaɪn] *v.* 把…侷限在；限制

同 **detain / limit**

實用片語
confine to 限制

▶ Please confine your statements to this issue.
請你針對這項議題來發表聲明。

▶ Please confine the dog to the backyard.
請把狗栓在後院。

100

confuse [kənˈfjuːz] *v.* 使困惑

同 distract / perplex

實用片語
confuse with 與⋯混淆

▶ Most of the questions on the test were very confusing.
測卷上大部分的考題都很不清楚。

▶ I am afraid you have confused me with my twin sister.
我想你是把我跟我的孿生姊妹混淆了。

102
confusion [kənˈfjuː.ʒən] *n.* 困惑；混亂狀況

搭 cause confusion 引起困惑
同 turmoil / abashment

▶ When the students saw the math problem on the board, they all had a look of confusion on their faces.
當學生們看到黑板上的數學題目時，所有人的臉上都露出了困惑的表情。

---

congratulate [kənˈgrætʃ.ə.leɪt] *v.* 祝賀

同 applaud / salute

實用片語
congratulate on 恭喜

▶ I wish to congratulate you on having your first baby!
我要祝賀你生了第一個寶寶。

▶ I want to congratulate you on your recent success.
我想向您恭賀您近來的成就。

---

congress [ˈkɑːŋ.gres] *n.* 代表大會

▶ I agree with Mr. Smith's values and so I hope he becomes a member of congress.
我非常認同史密斯先生的價值觀，所以我希望他能成為大會成員。

---

conjunction [kənˈdʒʌŋk.ʃən]
n. 結合；連接詞

▶ The conjunction of the temperature and the wind made us extremely cold.
是氣溫和風力兩個因素加起來才讓我們覺得特別冷。

---

 103 102 101 98
connect [kəˈnekt] *v.* 連接

同 associate / attach

實用片語
connect to 連結，接上

▶ Is the cable connected to the computer?
電線接上電腦了嗎？

▶ I need to connect to the internet first.
我需要先連上網路。

102
connection [kəˈnek.ʃən] *n.* 連接

搭 establish connection 建立關係
同 network / relation

▶ I felt a connection with her because we both enjoy playing tennis.
我好像跟她有關係，因為我們兩人都喜歡打網球。

Exercise 18

I. Derivatives

1. The St Matthew Passion is one of Bach's best-known _____ (compose).

2. After many experiments, the scientist came to the _____ (conclude) that there is no cure for Ebola.

3. Confidence, _____ (concentrate), control and commitment are considered some of the main qualities important for successful performance in most sports.

4. Our company has _____ (connect) with many European enterprises.

5. I have _____ (confident) in my sister. I believe that she will do a great job.

II. Vocabulary Choice

(A) congratulated   (B) confused   (C) confessed   (D) congress   (E) concern

(F) concrete   (G) conjunction   (H) condition   (I) confusion   (J) confine

1. General public _____ about food safety has shown a marked increase over the past three years following several food scandals.

2. We plan to travel around Europe next year, but no _____ plans have been made yet.

3. She _____ me warmly on my new job and wished me luck for my first day.

4. The doctor told the anxious family that their son's _____ was improving.

5. The student _____ to cheating on the exam after the teacher challenged his unusually high score.

conquer [ˈkɑːŋ.kɚ] *v.* 征服；得勝

搭 **conquer disease** 戰勝病魔

同 **crush / overcome**

▶ Alexander the Great conquered many countries in the ancient world.
亞歷山大大帝在古代世界征服了許多的國家。

---

conscience [ˈkɑːn.ʃəns] *n.* 良心

同 **morals / sense**

▶ Many people feel that modern shows negatively affect the consciences of the youth.
許多人認為現代表演對年輕人的良知產生了負面影響。

---

conscious [ˈkɑːn.ʃəs] *adj.* 有知覺的

搭 **environmentally conscious**
有環保意識的

同 **sensible / informed**

▶ The students are conscious of the amount of time they have to finish the test.
學生們都知道考試的時間有多長。

---

98 95

consequence [ˈkɑːn.sə.kwəns] *n.* 結果

同 **result / outcome**

實用片語
in consequence of 後果

▶ Harriet suffered the consequences of stealing her roommate's boyfriend.
海瑞特為搶走室友的男朋友而承擔了後果。

▶ In consequence of the typhoon, there was no electricity.
颱風所帶來的後果是停電。

---

consequent [ˈkɑːn.sə.kwənt]
adj. 隨之而來的；由此引起的

同 **ensuing / following**

▶ The typhoon and consequent destruction left a lasting impression on Bernice.
颱風以及它所造成的災害在伯尼斯的心中留下深刻的印象。

103

consequently [ˈkɑːn.sə.kwənt.li]
adv. 結果；因此；必然地

同 **therefore / as a result**

▶ The problem was consequently fixed after being found.
這問題被發現之後獲得了解決。

conservative [kənˈsɝː.və.t̬ɪv]

① *adj.* 保守的

搭 **conservative view** 保守的觀念

同 **traditional / timid**

② *n.* 守舊者

同 **preserver / conserver**

▶ I was surprised to see your conservative sister wearing a short skirt.
看到你那位保守的妹妹穿著短裙，讓我很驚訝。

▶ Mr. Smith is a conservative, which is why I want him in congress.
史密斯先生是位保守派人士，這就是我希望他加入大會的原因。

---

considerable [kənˈsɪd.ɚ.ə.bəl]

adj. 相當多的；相當大的

同 **noticeable / major**

▶ I spend a considerable amount of time with my children.
我花相當多的時間陪伴我的孩子。

---

consideration [kənˌsɪd.əˈreɪ.ʃən] *n.* 考慮

搭 **thorough consideration** 全盤考量

同 **thought / judgment**

▶ We have given great consideration about hiring you to work for our company.
我們很慎重地考慮是否雇用你為我們公司工作。

96
consist [kənˈsɪst] *v.* 包含；組成

同 **exist / include**

實用片語
consist of 組成

▶ This soup consists of onions and apples.
這碗湯裡面含有洋蔥和蘋果。

▶ The English exam consisted of two essays.
此英語測驗包括要寫兩篇論說文。

100
consistent [kənˈsɪs.tənt] *adj.* 前後一致的

搭 **consistent performance** 穩定的表現

同 **steady / logical**

▶ Please be consistent; don't keep changing things every day.
請你保持前後一致；不要每天都改來改去的。

---

consonant [ˈkɑːn.sə.nənt] *n.* 子音

▶ A lot of rap music relies on its use of consonants.
很多的饒舌音樂是在於子音的運用。

102
constant [ˈkɑːn.stənt]

① *adj.* 不變的

同 **nonstop / stable**

實用片語
constant dropping wears away a stone
水滴石穿

▶ She needs constant attention from her boyfriend or else she will get upset.
她需要男朋友不停地關注，不然就不開心。

② *n.* 常數

▶ His relationship with his Mom is the only constant in his life.
他跟他母親的關係是他生命中唯一不會改變的事實。

constitute [ˈkɑːn.stə.tuːt] *v.* 構成
同 create / establish

▶ Loyalty and honesty constitute our company's foreign affairs policy.
忠誠以及誠實構成我們公司的外交政策。

constitution [ˌkɑːn.stəˈtuː.ʃən] *n.* 憲法

▶ Many feel that some parts of the constitution need to be changed.
有些人認為部分的憲法需要修改。

96
construct [kənˈstrʌkt] *v.* 建造；構成
同 compose / organize
實用片語
construct from 以⋯建造

▶ The farmer is looking for some workers to help him construct a barn.
那位農夫正在找些工人幫他搭建間穀倉。

▶ We constructed this house from wood.
我們用木頭建造這間房子。

100 96
construction [kənˈstrʌk.ʃən] *n.* 工程；建設
搭 road construction 道路施工
同 development / system

▶ Construction on the tall building is almost finished.
那棟高樓的工程已經快要結束了。

constructive [kənˈstrʌk.tɪv]
adj. 建設性的；積極的
搭 constructive feedback 有建設性的回饋
同 useful / practical

▶ If you're going to say something to the performers, make sure it's constructive.
如果你想要對演出者說些什麼，請確定是有建設性的。

104 103
consult [kənˈsʌlt] *v.* 請教；商議
同 consider / discuss
實用片語
consult with 向⋯諮詢

▶ You should consult the professor about your questions.
你應該跟專家諮詢你的問題。

▶ Why didn't you consult with your boss before proceeding?
你在執行之間為什麼沒有先請教你的老闆呢？

consultant [kənˈsʌl.tənt] *n.* 顧問；諮詢者

同 **advisor / mentor**

▶ I think you should talk to a consultant before buying that property.
我覺得你在購買那塊土地之前，最好先找個顧問談談。

---

 consume [kənˈsuːm] *v.* 耗盡；揮霍

同 **deplete / expend**

▶ Jack's job consumes a lot of time and energy; no wonder he's always tired.
捷克的工作消耗掉他很多的時間和精力，怪不得他總是那麼疲憊。

---

consumer [kənˈsuː.mɚ] *n.* 消費者

搭 **consumer protection** 消費者保護
同 **client / shopper**

▶ Most companies are concerned about their consumers' needs.
大部份的公司都很在意消費者的需求。

100

container [kənˈteɪ.nɚ] *n.* 容器

▶ This container isn't big enough for all of the food.
這個容器不夠大，裝不下所有的食物。

100

content [kənˈtent]

① *adj.* 滿足的
同 **willing / fulfilled**

實用片語
content with 以…為滿足

② *v.* 使滿意；使滿足
同 **gratify / satisfy**

▶ Not content with his salary, John looked for other ways to make money.
約翰不滿意他的薪水，只好找其他賺錢的管道。

▶ I had to content myself with fewer vacations after I had kids.
有了小孩後，我不得不滿足於較少的假期。

▶ Hungry, Sally contented herself with a hamburger.
肚子餓了，莎莉吃了個漢堡來滿足自己。

---

content [ˈkɑːn.tent]

① *n.* 內容；含量
搭 **reveal content** 揭發內容
同 **measure / load**

② *n.* 內容物；含量

▶ The contents of my drawer include magazines and papers.
我抽屜裡面的東西包括雜誌和報告。

▶ I can't eat the contents in this sandwich.
我不能吃這個三明治裡面的東西。

98

contentment [kənˈtent.mənt] *n.* 知足

同 **pleasure / fulfillment**

▶ Contentment is a choice.
知足是一項選擇。

Exercise 19

I. 中英對應

_____ 1. 子音   (A) constant   (B) consonant

                       (C) consent   (D) consist

_____ 2. 有知覺的   (A) congress   (B) consequence

                       (C) conscience   (D) conscious

_____ 3. 容器   (A) container   (B) contain

                       (C) contained   (D) contact

_____ 4. 保守的   (A) consequent   (B) constitution

                       (C) conservative   (D) constant

_____ 5. 常數   (A) content   (B) consult

                       (C) constant   (D) consist

II. Derivatives

1. Tom spent most of the time during summer vacation to play and _____ (consequent) he has to stay up late to finish his summer homework before school begins.

2. The lying politician's behavior is not _____ (consist) with his political views before he was elected to congress.

3. Luke has a good command of English because he spent a _____ (consider) time learning the language.

4. She offered me a very _____ (construct) suggestion – to listen to some English programs every day to improve my listening.

5. Sharon serves as a _____ (consult) in a law firm where she gives advice to improve communication skills.

Unit 20

(100)(99)

contest [ˈkɑːn.test] *n.* 比賽

搭 **withdraw from contest** 退出比賽

同 **competition / match**

▶ Let's have a contest and see who wins!
我們來場比賽，看看誰贏！

contest [kənˈtest] *v.* 爭奪；競爭

同 **compete / oppose**

▶ Three fishermen contested for one giant fish near their boats.
三位漁夫為了他們船邊的一條大魚而互相爭奪。

context [ˈkɑːn.tekst] *n.* 上下文

同 **background / relation**

▶ If you're not sure what a word means, look at it in context.
如果你不太確定某個字的意思，那就參考它的上下文。

continent [ˈkɑːn.tən.ənt] *n.* 大陸

▶ Will you tour the continent of Europe this summer?
你這個暑假會去歐洲旅行嗎？

continual [kənˈtɪn.ju.əl] *adj.* 頻頻的；再三的

同 **enduring / recurrent**

▶ Phone companies give us continual upgrades.
電信公司給我們一而再，再而三的升等。

continuous [kənˈtɪn.ju.əs]
adj. 不斷的；連續的

同 **uninterrupted / endless**

▶ I couldn't concentrate with the continuous noise in the background.
由於現場的噪音不斷，使我無法專心。

(100)

contract [ˈkɑːn.trækt] *n.* 契約

搭 **commercial contract** 商業合約

同 **agreement / settlement**

實用片語
contract with 與…訂約，承包

▶ I signed a one year contract today for a school I will be teaching at.
我今天和將會任教的學校簽約一年。

▶ We need to contract with an expert for that part of the project.
我們需要專案的某部份外包給專家做。

(100)

contract [kənˈtrækt] *v.* 訂契約

同 **negotiate / undertake**

▶ The company is contracted to write a series of novels for children by next year.
這間公司簽約明年要寫一系列兒童小說。

102

contrary [ˈkɑːn.trə.i / kənˈtrer.i]

adj. 相反的；對立的

同 **opposed / adverse**

▶ Bob's views on politics seem contrary to Tom's, but they are best friends.
鮑伯的政治理念似乎和湯姆的是對立的，但是他們是最好的朋友。

contrary [ˈkɑːn.tre.ri] *n.* 相反的事物

搭 **contrary to expectations** 事與願違

 實用片語
contrary to 與…對立，相反

▶ Light and dark may seem like contraries, but we often see them in action together.
光明和黑暗看起來似乎是相反的東西，但是我們常常看到他們同時出現。

▶ Contrary to what the teacher might think, Jack studies very hard.
跟老師想的相反，傑克其實唸書十分認真。

103

contrast [ˈkɑːn.træst] *n.* 對比

同 **difference / variation**

▶ Molly's warm voice is a nice contrast to Harry's gruff one.
茉莉溫暖的聲音和哈利粗啞的聲音成了一個很好的對比。

contrast [kənˈtræst] *v.* 形成對照

同 **contradict / deviate**

▶ This evening's professional performance greatly contrasted the children's show we saw this morning.
今天晚上的職業表演和今天早上的兒童表演真是極大的對比。

104 103 102 96

contribute [kənˈtrɪb.juːt] *v.* 提供；捐獻

搭 **contribute significantly** 做很大的貢獻
同 **devote / provide**

實用片語
contribute to 貢獻，捐出

▶ Jennifer contributed a delicious salad to the potluck.
珍妮佛在一家一菜的餐會上提供一道美味的沙拉。

▶ I contributed to the fund for the needy.
我捐出資金給有需要的人。

99

contribution [ˌkɑːn.trɪˈbjuː.ʃən] *n.* 貢獻

搭 **make contribution** 做出貢獻
同 **addition / offering**

▶ Jack made several contributions to the brainstorming meeting.
傑克在腦力激盪會議提出了好多點子。

102

convenience [kənˈviː.ni.əns] *n.* 便利性；方便

搭 **convenience store** 便利商店

▶ I like the convenience of living in the city.
我喜歡住在大都市的便利性。

同 benefit / facility

實用片語
at one's earliest convenience 最方便時

▶ Call me back at your earliest convenience.
你最方便時請回我電話。

101

convention [kən'ven.ʃən] *n.* 大會；會議

搭 convention center 會議中心
同 seminar / conference

▶ I learned a lot about computers at the computer convention.
我在電腦大會裡學到很多關於電腦的知識。

conventional [kən'ven.ʃən.əl]
adj. 傳統的；常規的

同 traditional / typical

▶ "Do unto others as you would have them do unto you" is conventional wisdom.
「己所欲則施於人」是大家認同的智慧。

converse ['kɑːn.vɜːs / kən'vɜːs] *v.* 交談

同 communicate / discuss

實用片語
converse with 談話，聊起

▶ My friend and I always enjoy conversing about different issues.
我和我的朋友很喜歡針對不同主題對話。

▶ Please converse with Mr. Chen about that issue.
請跟陳先生談談那個問題。

104 103 99 95

convey [kən'veɪ] *v.* 傳達；運送

同 transfer / transmit

實用片語
convey from... to... 運輸至…

▶ I can give a speech in English, but trying to convey my thoughts in another language is very difficult.
我可以用英文演講，但是要用其他語言來表達我的想法就很困難。

▶ Please convey these boxes from here to the meeting room.
請將箱子運送到會議室。

102 101 99 98 96

convince [kən'vɪns] *v.* 說服

搭 firmly convince 堅定地說服
同 persuade / sway

實用片語
convince someone of 說服某人…

▶ Dan convinced his dad to buy him an ice cream cone.
丁恩說服他的爸爸買甜筒冰淇淋給他吃。

▶ I need to convince Mr. Chen of the need to allocate more budget.
我需要說服陳先生關於分配更多預算的事情。

98

cooperate [koʊˈɑː.pə.reɪt] *v.* 合作

同 **collaborate / coordinate**

實用片語
cooperate with 與…合作

▶ If you're doing a group project, it's important to cooperate with the others in your group.
如果你正在執行小組方案，那麼和小組裡面其他成員共同合作是很重要的。

▶ Please cooperate with me on this assignment.
請與我合作此任務。

99

cooperation [koʊˌɑː.pəˈreɪ.ʃən] *n.* 合作

搭 **encourage cooperation** 促進合作關係
同 **unity / partnership**

▶ We'll need everyone's cooperation if we want to finish successfully.
如果我們想要順利的完工，就需要每一個人的合作。

97

cooperative [koʊˈɑː.pə.ə.t̬ɪv]

① *adj.* 合作的

同 **coefficient / coactive**

② *n.* 合作企業；合作商店

▶ Tommy wasn't very cooperative with his mother, so he was punished.
湯米不太配合他的媽媽，因此被處罰了！

▶ We are all invested in the cooperative.
我們也共同投資了這家合作社。

---

cope [koʊp] *v.* 應付；對付

同 **endure / deal**

實用片語
cope with 處理，應付

▶ It was difficult for Megan to cope with all the pressure from work and school.
梅根很難應付所有來自工作和學校方面的壓力。

▶ I can't cope with any more difficult customers.
我無法再應付任何棘手難纏的客戶了。

---

copper [ˈkɑː.pɚ]

① *n.* 銅

② *adj.* 銅製的

▶ The copper from the mine was used to make coins.
礦區裡的銅被用來製成銅幣。

▶ Rachel's hair turned from a bright shade of red to a dark copper color.
瑞秋的頭髮從亮紅色變成深銅色。

---

cord [kɔːrd] *n.* 細繩；電線

▶ We secured our pile of firewood by tying two thick cords around it.
我們用兩條粗繩將木材牢牢地捆綁住。

cork [kɔːrk]

① *n.* 軟木塞
② *v.* 用軟木塞塞住

▶ Tim could not pull the cork out of the wine bottle.
提姆無法將酒瓶的軟木塞拔出來。

▶ The sailor corked the bottle containing his message and threw it out to sea.
水手用軟木塞塞住裝有他的紙條的瓶子，然後丟入海中。

---

correspond [ˌkɔːr.əˈspɑːnd]

v. 相符合；相類似

同 conform / correlate

實用片語
correspond with 與…溝通，討論

▶ The police believed us since our accounts of seeing the robbery corresponded with each other.
由於我們對於親眼目睹的搶劫案的描述相符合，警察就相信我們。

▶ I will have to correspond with my manager about the budget issue.
我會與我的經理討論預算問題。

---

costume [ˈkɑː.stuːm] *n.* 服裝（戲服、制服）

▶ What kind of costume are you going to wear this Halloween?
今年的萬聖節你打算穿什麼服裝來打扮？

Exercise 20

I. 中英對應

_____ 1. 上下文   (A) contest   (B) context   (C) content   (D) contact

_____ 2. 交談   (A) converse   (B) convert   (C) convey   (D) convince

_____ 3. 相反的   (A) control   (B) contrast   (C) contract   (D) contrary

_____ 4. 服裝   (A) costume   (B) customer   (C) custom   (D) consume

_____ 5. 軟木塞   (A) cork   (B) cook   (C) cope   (D) cord

II. Derivatives

1. The man assures his fiancée that his actions will _____ (respond) with his words even after their marriage.

2. The president's visit further promoted the _____ (cooperate) between the two countries.

3. Alan Turing is famous for his _____ (contribute) to computer science.

4. Sherry's views on dating are more _____ (convention) than those of some of her friends and colleagues so they argue often.

5. The air conditioner in my room makes a _____ (continue) low buzzing noise, so I can't sleep well.

⑥ **ambiguous** [æmˈbɪg.ju.əs] *adj.* 含糊不清的
例 Mr. Jones gave me an ambiguous answer.
瓊斯先生給我了個模糊不清的答案。

ambivalent [æmˈbɪv.ə.lənt] *adj.* （對同一人或事物）有矛盾情緒的
例 He holds ambivalent feelings towards life.
他對生命抱持猶疑的感覺。

⑦ **amiable** [ˈeɪ.mi.ə.bəl] *adj.* 和藹可親、親切的
例 I was surprised at how amiable and polite Jack seemed.
我對傑克看來如此親切又有禮感到驚訝。

amicable [ˈæm.ɪ.kə.bəl] *adj.* 友善的、友好的、和平的
例 The two parties eventually reached an amicable settlement.
雙方最後達成友好協定了。

⑧ **angel** [ˈeɪn.dʒəl] *n.* 天使；天使般的人
例 Thank you for your assistance. You're my angel.
謝謝你的協助，你是我的天使。

angle [ˈæŋ.gəl] *n.* 角；角度
例 Let's analyze this issue from a different angle.
讓我們從不同角度來分析此議題。

⑨ **ballet** [bælˈeɪ] *n.* 芭蕾舞
例 Her goal is to be a top ballet dancer.
她的目標是想成為頂尖的芭蕾舞者。

ballot [ˈbæl.ət] *n.* 投票用紙、選票
例 We need to hold a ballot to select a new representative.
我們要辦一場投票來選出新的代表。

⑩ **bath** [bæθ] *n.* 沐浴、洗澡
例 I'm going to run a bath before going to bed.
睡覺之前我要來洗個澡。

bathe [beɪð] *v.* 為…洗澡、把…浸入、浸洗
例 You should go back to your room and bathe first.
你應該回房間並先洗個澡。

cottage [ˈkɑtɪdʒ] *n.* 小屋；農舍

▶ For the summer, my family rented a cottage in the countryside.
為這個夏天，我們家人在鄉下租了一間小屋。

couch [ˈkaʊtʃ]

① *n.* 沙發
② *v.* 躺著

▶ Let's sit on the couch and watch a romantic movie.
我們來沙發上坐，看一部浪漫的電影吧。

▶ The writing is couched in vocabulary I am unfamiliar with.
這份寫作是使用我所不熟悉的詞彙。

council [ˈkaʊn.səl]

n. 地方議會；政務會；協調會
同 **board / committee**

▶ Tom brought his proposition to the city council so they could vote on it.
湯姆將這項提議帶到市議會，以便他們投票決定。

countable [ˈkaʊntəbəl] *adj.* 可數的
同 **computable / estimable**

▶ Is "bread" countable or not?
「麵包」這個生字是可數，還是不可數？

counter [ˈkaʊntɚ]

① *n.* 檯面
② *v.* 反駁；反對
同 **counteract / resist**
③ *adv.* 相反地
同 **versus / against**
④ *adj.* 相反的
同 **conflicting / contrary**

▶ Carrie took the groceries inside and placed them on the kitchen counter.
凱芮將品雜貨帶進屋內，並且把它們放在廚房的流理台上。

▶ Jerry countered Sarah's argument with plenty of information that he had researched.
傑瑞用許多他所收集的資料來反駁莎拉的論點。

▶ Ben ran counter to his teammates and scored in the wrong goal.
班恩朝隊友們的反方向跑，結果射錯到對手的球門。

▶ Jeff's opinion was counter to the rest of the group's.
傑夫的意見和其他所有組員的意見相反。

98

courageous [kəˈreɪ.dʒəs]

adj. 有膽量的;英勇的;勇敢的

搭 **exceptionally courageous** 相當地勇敢

同 **daring / fearless**

▶ Paul was very courageous when he defended his opinion in front of the whole class.

當保羅在全班同學的面前為自己辯解時,他的表現非常有膽量。

103

courteous [ˈkɝ·tiəs] *adj.* 有禮貌的

搭 **courteous gentleman** 彬彬有禮的紳士

同 **polite / respectful**

▶ Please be courteous and give up your chair for someone who needs it.

請你有禮貌一點,把你的椅子讓給有需要的人。

96

courtesy [ˈkɝ·təsi] *n.* 禮貌

同 **respect / refinement**

實用片語
out of courtesy 出自禮貌

▶ Holding the door for someone is a common courtesy.

幫別人開門是一種基本的禮貌。

▶ We invited the boss' wife to attend the party out of courtesy.

我出於禮貌邀請老闆的太太參加派對。

---

coward [ˈkaʊ.ɚd] *n.* 懦夫;膽怯者

同 **chicken / shirker**

▶ Many bullies are cowards on the inside.

許多霸凌者內心是個膽小鬼。

---

crack [ˈkræk]

① *n.* 裂縫;破裂

② *v.* 使破裂

同 **break / burst**

▶ There is a crack in the pipe and water is leaking everywhere!

水管有個裂縫,所以水漏的到處都是。

▶ I accidentally dropped my phone and cracked the screen.

我不小心掉了手機,把螢幕給摔裂了。

---

cradle [ˈkreɪ.dəl]

① *n.* 搖籃

② *v.* 輕搖;輕托;輕抱

同 **nestle / support**

▶ The baby fell asleep in its cradle.

小嬰孩在搖籃中睡著了。

▶ The mother gently cradled her newborn baby.

母親輕柔地搖著剛出生的嬰孩。

---

craft [ˈkræft] *n.* 手藝;工藝

搭 **ancient craft** 古法工藝

同 **expertise / artistry**

▶ Steven has spent many years developing his craft of carpentry.

史提芬花了許多年來培養他的木工手藝。

cram [ˈkræm] *v.* 把⋯塞進，把⋯塞滿

同 **pack / choke**

實用片語
cram for a test 抱佛腳

▶ I crammed all my clothes into this tiny suitcase.
我把所有的衣服都塞進這個小皮箱。

▶ I have to go cram for my English test now.
我要為英文考試抱佛腳了。

---

crash [ˈkræʃ]

① *n.* 撞擊（聲）；砸碎（聲）

搭 **airplane crash** 飛機失事

同 **bang / boom**

實用片語
crash around 跑來跑去

② *v.* 碰撞；墜落

同 **smash / dash**

▶ Witnesses told news reporters they heard a loud crash.
目擊者告訴新聞記者他們聽到很大的撞擊聲。

▶ Please ask the kids to stop crashing around.
請要求小孩停止跑來跑去了。

▶ The vase fell to the floor and crashed into pieces.
花瓶掉落到地板上，摔成碎片。

---

crawl [krɑːl]

① *v.* 爬行

同 **creep / drag**

② *n.* 爬行

▶ He desperately crawled through the desert until he reached a road.
他拼命地爬過沙漠，直到抵達一條公路。

▶ The baby's crawl was so cute to watch.
小嬰兒爬行看起來實在太可愛了。

---

creation [kriˈeɪʃən] *n.* 作品；創造

同 **production / formation**

▶ The artist took a step back to admire his latest creation.
這位藝術家往後退了一步，來欣賞他的最新創作。

---

creative [kriˈeɪtɪv] *adj.* 創造的；有創意的

搭 **creative approach** 有創意的方式

同 **inventive / original**

▶ Encourage your students to become creative thinkers.
要鼓勵你的學生成為創意的思考者。

102

creativity [ˌkriˈeɪˈtɪv·ɪ·tɪ] *n.* 創造力

同 **genius / cleverness**

▶ It takes a lot of creativity to write an entertaining story.
寫一篇有趣的故事必須要有很多的創造力。

---

creator [kriˈeɪtɚ] *n.* 創造者；創作者

同 **inventor / producer**

▶ Jon is the founder and creator of this company.
瓊恩是這間公司的創辦人和創建人。

C

creature [ˈkritʃɚ]　*n.* 生物

實用片語

creature comforts　物質享受

► All creatures have the right to live.
所有生物都有生存的權利。

► The hotel room is small, but all the creature comforts are there.
飯店房間雖然很小，但已有所有的物質享受了。

98

credit [ˈkred.ɪt]

① *n.* 信賴；信用；讚揚

搭 **credit abuser**　卡奴

同 **approval / status**

實用片語

give credit to　歸功於…

② *v.* 讚揚；把功勞歸因於…

同 **ascribe to / attribute to**

實用片語

get credit for　正面居功

► He's known to be such a liar, so I wouldn't give him any credit.
大家都知道他很會說謊，我一點都不信任他。

► We must give credit to Joe for finishing the project on time.
我們必須歸功於喬伊準時完成專案。

► The discovery was never properly credited.
這項發現從未受到適當地讚揚。

► It's wonderful to see Jack get credit for his hard work.
看到傑克因為辛勤工作而得到此功勞真是太好了。

---

creep [ˈkrip]　*v.* 躡手躡腳地走

同 **snake / crawl**

► The thief creeped around the room looking for a place to hide.
小偷躡手躡腳地在屋內走著，想要找一個藏身之地。

---

crew [ˈkru]　*n.* 全體工作人員

同 **team / troop**

► A crew of painters were painting a building red and blue.
全體油漆工把一棟建築物漆上紅色與藍色。

---

cricket [ˈkrɪk.ɪt]　*n.* 蟋蟀

► Two crickets leaped into my lap.
兩隻蟋蟀跳到我的大腿上。

---

criminal [ˈkrɪm.ə.nəl]

① *adj.* 犯罪的

搭 **criminal evidence**　犯罪證據

同 **illegal / unlawful**

② *n.* 罪犯

► In college, I studied criminal behavior.
我在大學研究犯罪行為。

► The criminal will be put in jail for murdering the old woman.
這位罪犯將因謀殺一位老婦人而入獄。

Exercise 21

I. 中英對應

_____ 1. 有創意的　(A) creative　　(B) creation　　(C) creativity　　(D) creator

_____ 2. 裂縫　　　(A) crash　　　(B) crazy　　　(C) crack　　　　(D) crab

_____ 3. 爬行　　　(A) crammed　　(B) crawled　　(C) crowed　　　(D) creep

_____ 4. 相反的　　(A) count　　　(B) country　　(C) county　　　(D) counter

_____ 5. 碰撞　　　(A) crashed　　(B) crafted　　(C) cracked　　　(D) crammed

II. Vocabulary Choice

(A) criminal　　(B) courtesy　　(C) courteous　　(D) cradle　　(E) craft

(F) couch　　(G) council　　(H) crew　　(I) credit　　(J) cricket

1. It is a common _____ to thank someone when they help you.

2. My father becomes a _____ potato during NBA basketball season.

3. Chinese people refer to the Yellow River as the _____ of Chinese civilization.

4. The police found that the gangster has been involved in some kind of _____ activity since he was in high-school.

5. The _____ for this award-winning book goes to the writer and his innovative literary agent.

cripple [ˈkrɪp.əl]

① *n.* 跛子

② *v.* 使受傷致殘；使成為跛子

同 **disable / debilitate**

▶ Jim was a cripple from birth, but after undergoing surgery, he can now walk normally.

吉姆天生是個跛子，但在接受手術之後，他現在已經可以正常的走路了。

▶ Danny tripped and fell down the stairs which crippled him for a whole week.

丹尼絆到東西而從樓上摔了下來，使他跛了一整個星期。

---

crispy / crisp [ˈkrɪs.pi / krɪsp] *adj.* 脆的

同 **fragile / weak**

▶ These potato chips are very crispy.

這些洋芋片很脆。

---

critic [ˈkrɪtɪk] *n.* 評論家；批評家

同 **expert / judge**

▶ Business has increased since a famous food critic gave our restaurant a good rating.

自從一位美食評論家給予我們餐廳很好的評價後，生意就變得很好。

---

critical [ˈkrɪt̬.ɪ.kəl] *adj.* 吹毛求疵的；挑剔的

搭 **critical thinking** 批判思考能力

同 **fault-finding / demanding**

▶ Hannah is too critical of herself and needs more self-confidence.

漢娜對自己太吹毛求疵了，她需要多一些自信心。

---

criticism [ˈkrɪt̬.ɪ.sɪ.zəm] *n.* 批評；評論

搭 **accept criticism** 接受批評

同 **judgment / review**

▶ To be a famous singer, you have to be able to accept criticism.

為了要成為一位出名的歌手，你必須能夠接受他人的批評。

99

criticize [ˈkrɪt̬.ɪ.saɪz] *v.* 批評；苛求

同 **blame / censure**

實用片語

criticize for 批評

▶ The news article strongly criticized the singer on his poor television performance.

這篇新聞報導強烈地批評那位歌手在電視上的演出。

▶ Jack criticized Mary for not finishing the report on time.

傑克因為瑪莉沒有準時完成報告而批評她。

crossroad [ˈkrɒs.rəʊd / ˈkrɑːs.roʊd] *n.* 十字路口

同 **intersection / byroad**

實用片語
at a crossroads 在十字路口上

▶ Please turn left when you get to the crossroad.
到十字路口時請左轉。

▶ I am at a crossroads in my career.
我現在正在職業生涯中的十字路口上。

---

crown [ˈkraʊn]

① *n.* 王冠
② *v.* 為…加冕；立…為王
同 **reward / induct**

▶ The princess wore a crown made of real diamonds.
公主戴了一頂用真的鑽石做的皇冠。

▶ Megan Young was crowned Miss Universe in 2013.
梅根 · 楊被加冕為 2013 年環球小姐。

---

cruelty [ˈkruː.əl.tj] *n.* 殘忍

同 **inhumanity / brutality**

▶ We started a movement to end any cruelty shown to animals.
我們發起一項運動來制止虐待動物的殘忍行為。

---

crunchy [ˈkrʌntʃi] *adj.* 脆的

同 **crusty / crispy**

▶ These peanut cookies are crunchy.
這些花生餅乾很脆。

---

crush [ˈkrʌʃ]

① *v.* 壓碎
同 **smash / compress**
② *n.* 壓扁；壓碎；搗碎

▶ Seeing the approaching thunderstorm crushed our hopes of going to the water park today.
看到逐漸逼近的暴風雨，粉碎了我們今天去水上樂園玩的希望。

▶ The crush of the ice made a loud sound.
壓碎冰塊發出很大的聲音。

---

crutch [ˈkrʌtʃ] *n.* 丁形拐杖

▶ Dan is using crutches because he broke his leg.
丹拄著拐杖，因為他跌斷了腿。

---

cube [ˈkjub]

① *n.* 立方體
② *v.* 將…切成小方塊

▶ Look at this delicious stinky tofu, served in perfectly shaped cubes.
看看這盤美味的臭豆腐，切成完美的小方塊。

▶ The chef cubed the melons and tossed them into the salad.
廚師把哈密瓜切丁，然後丟進沙拉裡面。

cucumber [ˈkjuː.kʌm.bə-] *n.* 黃瓜

cool as a cucumber 淡定

▶ A cool cucumber salad makes a great snack for a hot summer day.
在炎熱的夏季理，清涼的黃瓜沙拉是道很棒的點心。

▶ Linda is as cool as a cucumber when she gives presentation.
琳達在做簡報時泰然自若。

---

cue [ˈkju]

① *n.* 提示
同 **clue / hint**

cue someone in 告知，通知某人

② *v.* 給…暗示

▶ When Mark gives us the cue, we will jump out and yell "surprise!"
當馬克給我們提示時，我們就要跳出來大喊「驚喜」！

▶ I want to know what's going on. Cue me in.
我想知道目前的情形。請通知我。

▶ The director cued each actor to tell them when to come on stage.
導演給每位演員提示，讓他們知道什麼時候該上台。

---

cultural [ˈkʌl.tʃə.əl] *adj.* 文化的

搭 **cultural difference** 文化差異
同 **civilizing / educative**

▶ Being an exchange student taught me a lot about cultural differences.
當交換學生讓我認識了許多文化差異之處。

95

cunning [ˈkʌnɪŋ]

① *adj.* 狡猾的；熟練的
同 **skillful / canny**

② *n.* 狡猾奸詐

▶ Frank carefully planned out his cunning plan of revenge.
法蘭克小心翼翼地規劃他狡猾的復仇計畫。

▶ Irene seemed like a nice girl. Her cunning surprised us.
艾琳看起來像個好女孩，但是她的狡猾奸詐讓我們很詫異。

---

cupboard [ˈkʌb.ə-d] *n.* 碗櫃

▶ Becky cleaned all the tea cups that were in the cupboard.
貝琪把碗櫃裡所有的茶杯都洗乾淨了。

---

curiosity [ˌkjʊr.iˈɑː.sə.tʃi] *n.* 好奇心

同 **interest / inquisitiveness**

die of curiosity 非常好奇，極想知道

▶ The little boy was filled with curiosity as to what was in his birthday present.
小男孩充滿了好奇心，想要知道他的生日禮物裡裝了什麼。

▶ Linda was dying of curiosity to meet her sister's new boyfriend.
琳達超想見她姐姐的新男友。

curl [kɝːl]

① *v.* 使…捲曲

搭 **curl finger** 手指交纏

同 **bend / loop**

② *n.* 捲髮

同 **twist / curve**

▶ My mom curled the ribbons wrapped around the package to make it look extra special.
媽媽把綁包裹的彩帶捲了一捲，讓禮物看起來更特別。

▶ My curls always get tangled in my hair brush.
我的捲髮常常打結卡在梳子上。

current [ˈkɝːənt]

① *adj.* 目前的

同 **modern / present**

實用片語
swim against the current
逆勢而為，逆向操作

② *n.* 氣流；水流

搭 **electric current** 電流

同 **flood / stream**

▶ Our current teacher is pregnant and will leave next month.
我們現在的老師懷孕了，她下個月會離開。

▶ You are swimming against the current if you refuse to use a mobile phone.
如果你拒絕使用手機，就是跟不上潮流。

▶ Strong currents of wind made the trees fall to the ground.
強烈氣流造成樹木倒塌。

curse [ˈkɝːs]

① *n.* 詛咒

同 **jinx / evil eye**

② *v.* 咒罵；求上帝降禍於…

▶ For years we believed a curse was on our family.
多年以來我們相信我們一家人受了詛咒。

▶ The elderly woman cursed the young boy for stealing from her.
那位老太太因為小男孩偷了她的東西而咒罵他。

curve [ˈkɝːv]

① *n.* 弧形；曲線

同 **arc / bend**

② *v.* 彎曲

▶ The little girl drew a curve inside the circle to represent a friendly smile.
小女孩在圈圈裡面畫了一道弧形來表示親切的笑容。

▶ The road twisted and curved its way through the mountains.
這條道路彎彎曲曲地繞著這座山。

cushion [ˈkʊʃən]

① *n.* 墊子

▶ Mom nervously rearranged the cushions on the couch while waiting for guests to arrive.
媽媽一邊等待客人的到來，一邊緊張地重新擺設靠墊。

② *v.* 給…安上墊子

▶ My grandma cushioned her china dishes with towels as she packed them into boxes.
祖母用毛巾墊著她的瓷器，然後將它們打包入箱。

---

cycle [ˈsaɪkəl]

① *n.* 週期；循環

回 **orbit / period**

② *v.* 循環

▶ In the museum, you can watch the life cycle of a butterfly.
你可以在這家博物館看到蝴蝶生命的週期。

▶ That piece of paper will cycle its way through every department.
這張紙會傳至每一個部門。

Exercise 22

I. 中英對應

_____ 1. 曲線   (A) curve   (B) curl   (C) curse   (D) cure

_____ 2. 週期   (A) cyber   (B) cycle   (C) circle   (D) circus

_____ 3. 碗櫃   (A) cup   (B) cupcake   (C) cupboard   (D) cupid

_____ 4. 十字路口   (A) cross   (B) crossover   (C) crossword   (D) crossroad

_____ 5. 氣流   (A) cunning   (B) current   (C) currency   (D) curse

II. Vocabulary Choice

(A) crunchy   (B) cucumber   (C) curiosity   (D) cushion   (E) cruelty

(F) cultural   (G) crippled   (H) critical   (I) crutch   (J) crushing

1. Although Australians and the British speak the same language, there has always been a history of _____ differences between the two countries.

2. "_____ killed the cat" is a proverb used to warn of the dangers of unnecessary investigation or experimentation.

3. The Gospel of John describes a miracle in which Jesus heals a man who had been _____ for 38 years.

4. There were so many passengers on the MRT that passangers were _____ against each other.

5. The public was shocked at the man's _____ to cats and they wanted him to go to jail.

cyclist [ˈsaɪ.klɪst] *n.* 騎腳踏車的人

▶ The bus avoided hitting the cyclist.
那輛公車避免撞上腳踏車騎士。

---

dairy [ˈder.i] *n.* 乳品；製酪業

搭 **dairy product** 奶製品

▶ Eating too much dairy, such as milk and cheese, is not healthy.
吃太多乳製品，像是牛奶和起司，對身體健康不太好。

---

dam [ˈdæm]

① *n.* 水壩

同 **dike / wall**

② *v.* 築壩於…

▶ The beavers built a dam to protect against animals that might harm him.
水狸築了一道壩來保護自己不受到其他動物的傷害。

▶ The beavers dammed up the river again.
河狸又在河上築壩了。

---

damn [ˈdæm] *v.* 定罪；罵…該死

▶ The judge damned the man to ten years in jail.
法官定了那個男人十年的罪。

---

damp [ˈdæmp]

① *adj.* 潮濕的

搭 **damp air** 空氣潮濕

同 **soggy / moist**

② *n.* 濕氣

③ *v.* 使潮濕

實用片語
damp something down 噴濕

▶ I placed a cool, damp cloth on Lisa's forehead to bring down her fever.
我把一條濕冷的毛巾放在麗莎的額頭幫她降溫。

▶ The old boxes were left out there in the damp.
那些老舊箱子被丟在外面潮濕的地方。

▶ Can you damp the handkerchief with a little water?
你能不能用一點點水把手帕弄濕？

▶ Please damp down the clothes first.
請先噴溼布料。

---

dare [der]

① *v.* 激；向…挑戰；膽敢

搭 **hardly dare** 顯少害怕

同 **provoke / taunt**

實用片語
I dare say 我敢說

▶ Ava dared Jenny to dance in the middle of the store.
艾娃挑戰珍妮，要她在商店中央跳舞。

▶ I dare say my proposal will be accepted.
我敢說我的提案一定會被接受。

② *aux v.* 竟敢

► How dare she sneak out of her room in the middle of the night!
她竟敢在午夜偷溜出她的房間！

darling [ˈdɑrlɪŋ]

① *n.* 心愛的人
② *adj.* 親愛的
同 **sweetheart / beloved**

► Darling, would you please cook dinner for us tonight?
親愛的，請你今晚為我們準備晚餐好嗎？

► That's my darling husband standing over there!
站在那邊的是我親愛的丈夫！

dash [ˈdæʃ]

① *v.* 猛衝；跑
同 **hurry / bolt**
② *n.* 猛衝；跑

► The children dashed down the hallways after the bell rang.
鈴聲響了之後，孩童們都衝到走廊上。

► Emily made a dash for the door, hoping her parents wouldn't see her.
愛莫莉朝大門跑去，希望她的父母沒看見她。

daylight [ˈdeɪ.laɪt] *n.* 日光；白晝；黎明

► It was nice to see the daylight shine through the clouds.
看到日光穿透雲層真的很美。

deadline [ˈded.laɪn] *n.* 截止期限

搭 **project deadline** 專案期限
同 **target date / time limit**

► The deadline for our writing project is this Friday.
這個星期五是我的寫作作業的截稿日期。

deafen [ˈdef.ən] *v.* 使聾

► I was deafened by the music in the cafe that I had to leave.
咖啡店中的音樂震耳欲聾，我不得不離開那裡。

dealer [ˈdilɚ] *n.* 商人

► The car dealer gave us a great price on the van we wanted.
我們想要這台廂型車，車商給我們開了很棒的價格。

decade [ˈdek.eɪd / dekˈeɪd] *n.* 十年

► Wow, I graduated from college a decade ago!
哇，我從大學畢業已經十年了！

deck [dek] *n.* 甲板

▶ The cruise ship has a pool located on the top deck.
遊輪上有游泳池，設在最上層的甲板上。

---

¹⁰⁴

declare [dɪˈkler] *v.* 宣告；聲明

搭 **officially declare** 官方說明

同 **claim / announce**

實用片語
declare war against 對…宣戰

▶ The President has declared that he will serve the country well.
總統發表聲明他將會好好的服務這個國家。

▶ The president declared war against crime and drugs.
總統向犯罪與毒品宣戰。

---

¹⁰⁰

decoration [ˌdek.əˈreɪ.ʃən] *n.* 裝飾

同 **ornament / adornment**

▶ The home designer completes the room decorations with some final details.
室內設計師運用一些小細節來完成他的房間設計。

---

¹⁰⁰

decrease [ˈdiː.kriːs]

① *v.* 下降；減小
同 **drop / decline**

② *n.* 減少
搭 **price decrease** 價格下降
同 **downturn / cutback**

▶ Her weight decreased after starting the exercise program.
她開始運動課程後，體重就下降了。

▶ There have been a decrease in violent crimes over the past few years.
過去幾年來的暴力犯罪已經減少了。

---

deed [ˈdid] *n.* 行為

同 **behavior / manner**

▶ Your good deeds will never be forgotten by the victims of the hurricane.
颶風的受難者將對你的善行永誌不忘。

---

deepen [ˈdipən] *v.* 加深；使變深

同 **dig / extend**

▶ Tom wants to deepen his understanding about outer space.
湯姆想要加深自己對外太空知識的理解。

---

⁹⁹ ⁹⁶

defeat [dɪˈfit]

① *v.* 擊敗；戰勝
搭 **defeat enemy** 擊敗敵人
同 **overpower / overthrow**

實用片語
admit defeat 承認失敗

▶ Michael defeated Jason in yesterday's table tennis competition.
麥可在昨天的桌球比賽中擊敗了傑生。

▶ They admitted defeat in this election.
他們承認此次選舉失利。

② *n.* 失敗；落敗
同 **beating / breakdown**

---

102 97

defend [dɪˈfɛnd] *v.* 防禦；保衛
同 **contend / guard**

實用片語
defend against 抵禦，防備

---

defense [dɪˈfɛns] *n.* 防禦
同 **protection / security**

---

defensible [dɪˈfɛn.sə.bəl]
adj. 合乎情理的；有防禦能力的
同 **tenable / logical**

---

103 96

defensive [dɪˈfɛn.sɪv] *adj.* 防禦性的；自衛的
同 **protecting / withstanding**

---

deficit [ˈdɛf.ə.sɪt] *n.* 不足額；赤字
搭 **budget deficit** 預算赤字
同 **shortfall / loss**

▶ Our swim team partied all night to celebrate the defeat of our strongest competitor.
我們的游泳隊整夜通宵地開派對慶祝我們最強勁的對手落敗了。

▶ Your body needs vitamins to defend itself from germs.
你的身體需要維他命來防禦病菌入侵。

▶ The lawyer defended the company against the suit.
律師為公司防備這項訴訟。

▶ This plant has a natural defense against caterpillars.
這棵植物對於毛毛蟲有天然防禦力。

▶ He gave a defensible account of what happened last night.
他對昨晚發生的事提出合情合理的說明。

▶ The government refuses to provide defensive weapons to that country.
政府拒絕提供防禦性的武器給那個國家。

▶ The deficit in rain caused the crops to fail.
雨量的不足導致農作物無法收成。

Exercise 23

I. Vocabulary Choice

(A) cycle   (B) cyclists   (C) dealer   (D) dared   (E) damp

(F) dash   (G) deafen   (H) deadline   (I) darling   (J) daylight

1. Persons engaged in cycling or biking are referred to as " _____ " or "bikers".

2. The _____ for my job application is this Friday.

3. Amy _____ her boyfriend to propose to her on the MRT in front of all the people.

4. Jesus says, "What you say in the dark will be heard in the _____ , and what you whisper in the ear in the inner rooms will be proclaimed from the roofs."

5. The girl was kept busy by her teacher after school, so she had to make a _____ for cram school so as not to be late.

II. Multiple Choice

(   ) 1. The soldiers carved some tunnels in the mountains for __ purposes.

     (A) defensible (B) defensive (C) defense   (D) decoration

(   ) 2. My brother is a very competitive person and he hates to admit __ .

     (A) deficit   (B) define   (C) defend   (D) defeat

(   ) 3. The number of births in Taiwan has __ over the past decade.

     (A) deepened (B) declared   (C) decreased (D) demanded

(   ) 4. Israel __ its independence on May 14, 1948.

     (A) declared   (B) declined   (C) decided   (D) described

(   ) 5. The student's interest in history __ after watching Chinese Period Dramas.

     (A) deep   (B) deepened (C) deemed   (D) deer

D

(97)

define [dɪˈfaɪn] *v.* 下定義

(同) **specify / describe**

實用片語
define as 將… 定義為

▶ According to the dictionary, the word "reality" is defined as "the state or quality of being real".
根據字典，「reality」這個字的定義是「真實的狀態或性質」。

▶ We define that comment as unthinking.
我們將此評論定義為思慮不周。

---

(103) (98)

definite [ˈdef.ən.ət] *adj.* 明確的

(搭) **definite evidence** 明確的證據

(同) **exact / precise**

▶ John needs more information before he can give a definite answer.
約翰需要更多的資訊才能夠給出一個明確的答案。

---

(104)

definition [ˌdef.ɪˈnɪʃ.ən] *n.* 定義

(同) **description / interpretation**

▶ What is the definition of "tough"?
「tough」這個字的定義是什麼？

---

(104)

delicate [ˈdel.ə.kət]

adj. 嬌弱的；易碎的；纖細的

(同) **fragile / gentle**

▶ Please handle the delicate flowers carefully.
請小心處理那些嬌弱的花朵。

---

(100) (96)

delight [dɪˈlaɪt]

① *n.* 欣喜

(搭) **express delight** 表達欣喜之意

(同) **enjoyment / joy**

② *v.* 喜愛；使高興

(同) **gratify / enchant**

實用片語
delight by 使…欣喜

▶ The crowd screamed in delight when the famous singer came out onto the stage.
當那位有名的歌星出場時，觀眾們都欣喜尖叫。

▶ My father delights in taking long walks with my mother.
我的爸爸很喜愛和媽媽散長步。

▶ The children were delighted by the magician's tricks.
孩子們很高興看到魔術師表演。

delighted [dɪˈlaɪtɪd] *adj.* 高興的；欣喜的

同 **overjoyed / pleased**

實用片語
delighted with 感到高興

▶ The children were delighted to eat the cake.
小朋友們很高興能夠吃到蛋糕。

▶ Rosa's parents are delighted with her new baby.
蘿莎的父母為了她剛出生的孩子感到高興。

---

delightful [dɪˈlaɪtfəl]
adj. 令人愉快的；令人欣喜的

同 **enjoyable / lovely**

▶ Everyone enjoyed the delightful play.
大家都很享受那場令人愉快的表演。

---

delivery [dɪˈlɪv.ə.i] *n.* 遞送

搭 **delivery schedule** 遞送時程

同 **shipment / conveyance**

▶ The pizza will be delivered shortly.
披薩很快就會送到。

---

103 102 100 99

demand [dɪˈmænd]

① *n.* 需求；請求

同 **request / claim**

② *v.* 要求

同 **require / expect**

▶ There was a huge demand for face masks when SARS hit Asia.
當 SARS 疫情在亞洲肆虐時，口罩有了大量的需求。

▶ The customer demanded to see the manager because she found a hair in her soup.
那位顧客要求見經理，因為她在她的湯裡發現了一根頭髮。

98

demanding [dɪˈmændɪŋ]
adj. 苛求的；使人吃力的

搭 **a demanding manager** 要求高的老闆

同 **tough / difficult**

▶ May's job was very demanding.
梅的工作真是勞神費力。

---

democracy [dɪˈmɑkrəsi] *n.* 民主

▶ Both Canada and the United States are democracies.
加拿大和美國都是民主國家。

---

democratic [ˌdɛməˈkrætɪk] *adj.* 民主的

同 **self-governing / popular**

▶ Today, there are over one hundred democratic countries in the world.
現今全世界有一百多個民主國家。

demonstrate [ˈdem.ən.streɪt] *v.* 表示；示範

同 **present / show**

▶ The father demonstrates his love for his son by giving him a hug.
那位父親給了他兒子一個擁抱來表達對他的愛。

 95

demonstration [ˌdem.ənˈstreɪ.ʃən]
n. 表示；示範；證明

搭 **software demonstration** 軟體展示

同 **presentation / display**

▶ Brandon quit smoking as a demonstration of his love for his family.
布蘭登戒了菸，作為他愛家人的表示。

 103 102 99

dense [dens] *adj.* 濃厚的；密集的

同 **compressed / thick**

▶ The dense fog is making it dangerous to drive.
這樣的濃霧導致開車時非常的危險。

 95

depart [dɪˈpɑrt] *v.* 離開；啟程

同 **leave / retreat**

實用片語
depart from this world 死亡

▶ Do you know where you are going when you depart from this world?
你知道在你離開這個世上後，你將會去哪裡嗎？

▶ We need to contribute something positive to others before we depart from this world.
在死前，我們需要為其他人做些正面的貢獻。

 104

departure [dɪˈpɑrtʃɚ] *n.* 離去；出發

搭 **departure date** 出發日期

同 **farewell / leave**

▶ Please remember to check your departure time before you go to the airport.
在你出發前往機場前，請記得查詢一下你的班機的起飛時間。

dependable [dɪˈpen.də.bəl] *adj.* 可靠的

同 **reliable / trustworthy**

▶ Dan is a dependable person whom you can always count on to complete a task.
但恩是個很可靠的人，你可以信任他去完成任務。

dependent [dɪˈpen.dənt]

① *adj.* 依賴的

同 **reliant / clinging**

② *n.* 受撫養者

▶ In all her relationships, Lydia is the dependent type.
在莉蒂亞所有的人際關係中，她都是屬於依賴型的。

▶ My younger sister is listed as a dependent on my parents' tax return form.
我的妹妹在父母的報稅退額表格上被列為是受撫養人。

deposit [dɪˈpɑː.zɪt]

① *n.* 存款

搭 **initial deposit** 初期押金

同 **down payment / installment**

實用片語
deposit in 存於

② *v.* 存放；存款於⋯

同 **collect / installment**

▶ To open a bank account, you need to make a deposit of $200.
若要開一個銀行戶頭，你需要存入 200 美元。

▶ I deposited my money in the bank.
我把錢存在銀行。

▶ The pirate deposited his treasure on the island.
海盜將他的財寶存放在島嶼上。

---

depress [dɪˈpres] *v.* 使沮喪

同 **bother / discourage**

▶ The rainy weather depresses me terribly.
下雨天使我非常沮喪。

---

depressed [dɪˈprest] *adj.* 沮喪的；抑鬱的

搭 **depressed market** 市場不景氣

同 **pessimistic / melancholic**

▶ The depressed man over there just lost his job.
那邊那個沮喪的男子剛剛失業。

---

depressing [dɪˈpresɪŋ]
adj. 令人消沉的；令人沮喪的

同 **gloomy / dreary**

▶ I felt sad after listening to that depressing story.
聽完那個令人消沈的故事後，我感到難過。

---

depression [dɪˈpreʃ.ən] *n.* 憂鬱症；沮喪

▶ Anyone suffering from depression should receive help as soon as possible.
所有的憂鬱患者都應該儘早尋求協助。

---

description [dɪˈskrɪpʃən] *n.* 描述

同 **picture / statement**

▶ Can you give me a description of the robber?
你可以形容一下強盜的長相嗎？

Exercise 24

I. 中英對應

_____ 1. 示範 (n.)   (A) democracy   (B) demonstrate

                          (C) demonstration   (D) demand

_____ 2. 嬌弱的   (A) delight   (B) delicate

                          (C) definite   (D) define

_____ 3. 濃厚的   (A) dance   (B) deny

                          (C) dentist   (D) dense

_____ 4. 令人欣喜的   (A) diligent   (B) delighted

                          (C) delivery   (D) delicious

_____ 5. 描述 (n.)   (A) definition   (B) describe

                          (C) departure   (D) description

II. Derivatives

1. The Bahamas' economy is _____ (depend) on tourism.

2. India, Japan and the Philippines are _____ (democracy) countries in Asia and they have regular elections.

3. Lynn suffered a lot from _____ (depress) after the death of her grandson.

4. The concept and _____ (define) of 'family' has changed over the past 100 years.

5. Being a software engineer is one of the most _____ (demand) jobs in technology.

95

deserve [dɪˈzɝv] *v.* 應受；該得

同 **earn / merit**

實用片語
deserve credit for 值得功勞，讚許

▶ Sally deserves a good break after spending so much time on the project.
莎莉在那個案子上花了那麼多時間，她應該得到一個足夠的休息。

▶ He deserves credit for the work he did on the project.
他絕對值得受到讚許，因為他為專案貢獻良多。

---

designer [dɪˈzaɪnɚ] *n.* 設計者

▶ Giorgio Armani is a very famous Italian fashion designer.
喬治・亞曼尼是一位非常著名的義大利時尚設計師。

100

desirable [dɪˈzaɪr.ə.bəl]
adj. 有魅力的；渴望獲得的；值得擁有的

搭 **desirable quality** 賣點
同 **despairing / dejected**

▶ Scarlett Johansson is one of the most desirable women in Hollywood.
史嘉蕾・喬韓森是好萊塢最有魅力的女人之一。

---

desperate [ˈdes.pɚ.ət]
adj. 絕望的；極度渴望的

同 **daring / bold**

▶ Hunger and cold made the villagers desperate.
飢寒交迫使得村民們非常的絕望。

---

102 **99** **95**

despite [dɪˈspaɪt] *prep.* 儘管；不管

同 **although / even though**

▶ The team managed to reach the mountain top despite the bad weather conditions.
儘管天氣狀況是如此的惡劣，登山隊還是盡全力的攻到山頂。

---

104 **100**

destroy [dɪˈstrɔɪ] *v.* 摧毀

搭 **destroy evidence** 破壞證據
同 **damage / ruin**

▶ Some homes were completely destroyed after the earthquake.
有些房子在地震後完全被摧毀。

destruction [dɪˈstrʌkʃən] *n.* 毀損；破壞

同 **ruin / downfall**

▶ He stood by the injured woman, unaffected by the destruction around him.
他陪在這位受傷的女士身邊，完全不受周遭毀損的影響。

---

detail [dɪˈteɪl]

① *n.* 細節

實用片語
go into details 深入細節

② *v.* 詳述

▶ Honey, let's discuss the final details for the wedding.
親愛的，我們來討論一下婚禮最後的細節吧。

▶ Just give me a simple answer. Don't go into details.
只要給我簡單的答案。不用深入細節。

▶ The lawyer detailed charges against the criminals.
這位律師詳述對罪犯的控訴。

---

detailed [dɪˈteɪld] *adj.* 詳細的

搭 **detailed procedure** 詳細的步驟

同 **specific / thorough**

▶ Here is a detailed list of what to find at the night market.
這是去夜市要找的東西的詳細清單。

102
detective [dɪˈtek.tɪv]

① *n.* 偵探

② *adj.* 偵探的

同 **spy / investigator**

▶ The detective solved the difficult murder case within a week.
那位偵探在一星期之內就破了那件棘手的謀殺案件。

▶ Brandon loves to read detective novels during his free time.
布蘭登在空閒的時候很喜歡閱讀偵探小說。

95
determination [dɪˌtɜː.mɪˈneɪ.ʃən] *n.* 決心

搭 **sheer determination** 下定決心

同 **resolution / perseverance**

▶ In order to complete the race, you need physical strength and determination.
為了要完成競賽，你需要體力及毅力。

96
determine [dɪˈtɜː.mɪn] *v.* 決定

同 **resolve / settle**

▶ Emily is determined to finish medical school and become a doctor.
愛茉莉決心完成醫學院學業，成為一位醫生。

---

determined [dɪˈtɜːmɪnd]
adj. 已下決心的；堅定的

同 **decisive / persistent**

▶ No one was able to change the determined boy's mind.
沒有人能改變這位意志堅定的男孩的心意。

device [dɪˈvaɪs] *n.* 設備;裝置

搭 **electronic device** 電子設備

同 **tool / equipment**

實用片語
leave to one's own devices 自由活動

► A smart phone is a device with multiple functions.
智慧型手機是擁有很多功能的設備。

► I left my children to their own devices for an hour.
我讓小孩自由活動一小時。

- -

devil [ˈdev.əl] *n.* 魔鬼

► Do you believe that the devil exists?
你認為魔鬼存在嗎?

- -

devise [dɪˈvaɪz] *v.* 設計

同 **design / engineer**

► The teenagers devised a plan to build a treehouse.
那些年輕人設計了一個蓋樹屋的計畫。

- -

devote [dɪˈvoʊt] *v.* 將…奉獻給…

搭 **devote effort** 貢獻己力

同 **contribute / donate**

實用片語
devote to 獻身於

► Tim devotes too much time to his work.
提姆貢獻了太多的時間在工作上。

► Tom devoted himself entirely to working.
湯姆完全獻身於工作中。

- -

devoted [dɪˈvoʊ.tɪd]
adj. 盡心盡力的;專心致志的;忠實的

同 **dedicated / faithful**

► The devoted musician was in love with his music.
這位盡心盡力的音樂家熱愛自己的音樂。

- -

dialogue [ˈdaɪ.ə.lɑːg] *n.* 對話

同 **conversation / discussion**

實用片語
dialogue with 談話,聊聊

► The play began with a dialogue between mother and daughter.
這齣舞台劇是以母親和女兒的一段對話來拉開序幕。

► I look forward to dialoguing with you next week.
我很期待下週與您的談話。

- -

diaper [ˈdaɪpɚ] *n.* 尿布

► Whenever the baby cries, the mother will always check his diaper first.
只要小嬰兒一哭,媽媽總是會先檢查他的尿布。

diet [ˈdaɪət]

① *n.* 飲食

實用片語
on a diet 節食

② *v.* 限制飲食；節食

▶ It's important to eat a healthy diet full of fruits and vegetables.
吃含有豐富蔬果的健康飲食是很重要的。

▶ I don't eat much because I am on a diet.
因為我在節食所以沒吃太多。

▶ Are you dieting to lose weight or for health reasons?
你現在限制飲食是為了減重，還是為了健康？

---

differ [ˈdɪfə] *v.* 不同

同 **vary / diverge**

實用片語
differ from 與…不同

▶ My style greatly differs from yours.
我的型和你相差很大。

▶ How do you differ from other candidates?
你跟其他候選人有何不同？

---

103 97

digest [daɪˈdʒest] *v.* 消化

搭 **digest food** 消化食物

同 **grasp / absorb**

digest [ˈdaɪˌdʒest] *n.* 文摘

▶ You should let your food digest before going for a run.
你應該等到食物消化後再去跑步。

▶ Summaries of recent articles were collected and made into a digest.
最近文章的總結都被收集，做成文摘。

---

digestion [daɪˈdʒes.tʃən] *n.* 消化作用

搭 **digestion system** 消化系統

同 **metabolism / absorption**

▶ According to my mother, eating yogurt can help with my digestion.
依據我媽媽的說法，吃優格可以幫助我腸胃的消化。

---

digital [ˈdɪdʒ.ə.təl] *adj.* 數字的；數位顯示的

同 **analog / numeral**

▶ All digital recordings are stored in this library.
所有數位的錄音都被儲存在這個圖書館裡。

Exercise 25

I. 中英對應

_____ 1. 尿布   (A) diabetes   (B) diaper   (C) dialogue   (D) diagram

_____ 2. 摧毀   (A) despite   (B) destroy   (C) destiny   (D) destination

_____ 3. 裝置   (A) devise   (B) devote   (C) device   (D) develop

_____ 4. 對話   (A) dialogue   (B) diet   (C) digital   (D) differ

_____ 5. 絕望的   (A) description   (B) despair   (C) despite   (D) desperate

II. Derivatives

1. Super typhoon Nepartak caused severe _____ (destruct) to the east coast of Taiwan in July, 2016.

2. Eating late-night snacks is not good for our _____ (digest).

3. Matthew has managed to overcome his difficulties with courage and _____ (determine).

4. The couple is so _____ (devote) to each other, they will probably get married soon.

5. Lucy is trying to transfer _____ (digit) images from her cellphone to her computer, but she is having some difficulty.

Unit 26

dignity [ˈdɪɡ.ə.tɪ] *n.* 尊嚴；高尚

同 **grace / virtue**

實用片語
stand on one's dignity 保持尊嚴

▶ In competitive sports, it is important to learn to win or lose with dignity.
在體育競賽中，很重要的是要學習不管輸贏都要有尊嚴。

▶ We should stand on our dignity to the end.
我們應該保持尊嚴到底。

---

diligence [ˈdɪlɪdʒəns] *n.* 勤奮

同 **briskness / intensity**

▶ With passion and diligence, Steve's career is on the road to success.
史提夫憑著熱情和勤奮，他的事業已邁向成功之路。

---

diligent [ˈdɪlədʒənt] *adj.* 勤奮的

同 **hard-working / tireless**

▶ Tammy is a very diligent student. She is always prepared for class.
譚米是很勤奮的學生，她總是為課堂做好準備。

---

dim [ˈdɪm]

① *adj.* 暗淡的

搭 **dim light** 昏暗的燈光

同 **darkish / gloomy**

② *v.* 使變暗

同 **blur / dull**

實用片語
dim down 變暗

▶ The room was too dim to take pictures in.
這房間太暗，不能拍照。

▶ The stage lights dimmed, and the ballerina started to dance.
舞台的燈暗了下來，女芭蕾舞者開始起舞。

▶ Let me dim down the light.
讓我把燈光調暗。

---

dime [ˈdaɪm] *n.* 一角硬幣

▶ Your piggy bank contains $21.60 in dimes and quarters.
你的小豬撲滿裡的 21.60 美元都是一角和 25 分的硬幣。

---

dine [ˈdaɪn] *v.* 用餐

▶ His father once dined with the President of Russia.
他的父親曾經和蘇俄總統吃過飯。

dip [ˈdɪp]

① v. 浸;泡

搭 **dip finger** 以指輕沾

同 **immerse / drench**

實用片語
dip into 下降

② n. 浸;泡

同 **dabble / browse**

▶ **Dip** the strawberries in chocolate, then put it on the tray.
把草莓沾上巧克力,然後放在盤子裡。

▶ The temperature dipped to 10°C last night.
昨晚溫度下降到 10°C。

▶ Let's take a dip in the pool before dinner.
晚餐前,讓我們先在游泳池小游一會兒。

---

(103)

diploma [dɪˈploʊ.mə] n. 畢業文憑

▶ Jane received her diploma after four years of college.
珍恩在上完四年大學後拿到了文憑。

---

diplomat [ˈdɪplə͵mæt] n. 外交官

▶ George has worked as a diplomat for many years.
喬治多年來是美國的外交官。

---

(100)

dirt [ˈdɝt] n. 灰塵;汙物

▶ Why is your shirt covered in dirt?
為什麼你的襯衫上沾滿灰塵?

---

disabled [dɪˈseɪ.bəld]

adj. 故障的;殘廢的;有缺陷的

同 **challenged / handicapped**

▶ You can't make any calls with that disabled cell phone.
你那支故障的手機無法用來打電話。

---

(101)

disadvantage [͵dɪsədˈvæntɪdʒ]

① n. 不利條件

搭 **social disadvantage** 社會弱勢

同 **harm / damage**

② v. 使處於不利地位

▶ Peter's basketball team is at a disadvantage because the players are only five feet tall!
彼得的籃球隊處於劣勢,因為隊員們都只有五呎高。

▶ Kids whose parents don't have money to put them in school are disadvantaged.
孩子的父母親沒錢送他們去學校,就處於劣勢。

---

disadvantaged [͵dɪsədˈvæntɪdʒd]

adj. 弱勢的;社會地位低下的;不利的

同 **deprived / impaired**

▶ The disadvantaged family was forced to work extra hard.
這個弱勢家庭被迫加倍努力工作。

96

disappoint [ˌdɪsəˈpɔɪnt] *v.* 使失望

搭 **bitterly disappoint** 極度失望

同 **displeased / let down**

實用片語
disappoint at 對…失望

---

disappointed [ˌdɪsəˈpɔɪntɪd] *adj.* 失望的

同 **frustrated / upset**

---

disappointing [ˌdɪsəˈpɔɪntɪŋ]
adj. 令人失望的

同 **depressing / unpleasant**

---

disappointment [ˌdɪsəˈpɔɪntmənt] *n.* 失望

同 **failure / blow**

---

disapproval [ˌdɪsəˈpruvəl] *n.* 不贊成

搭 **accept disapproval** 接受反對意見

同 **objection / censure**

99

disaster [dɪˈzæstə] *n.* 災害；災難

搭 **natural disaster** 天然災害

同 **mishap / hazard**

實用片語
a walking disaster 災難王，麻煩製造者

---

discipline [ˈdɪsəplɪn]

① *n.* 紀律

搭 **enforce discipline** 實施紀律

同 **control / regulation**

② *v.* 訓練

同 **drill / exercise**

▶ I'm sorry to disappoint you, but I can't come to your wedding.
我很抱歉讓你失望，但是我不能參加你的婚禮。

▶ We are very disappointed at what you said.
我們對你說的話相當失望。

▶ She had a disappointed look on her face after the exam.
考試完畢，她臉上露出失望的表情。

▶ Nobody was happy with the disappointing ending to the film.
大家都不滿意這部結局令人失望的電影。

▶ It will be a huge disappointment if they don't win the game tonight.
如果他們今晚不能贏得比賽，將會令人非常失望。

▶ She gave him a look of disapproval.
她給他一個不贊成的眼神。

▶ Last year's earthquake was the worst natural disaster recorded in history.
去年的地震是所有史以來最嚴重的天然災害。

▶ John is a walking disaster. He causes trouble everywhere he goes.
約翰是麻煩製造者。他走到哪都闖禍。

▶ The discipline received in military training helps to develop strength and character.
在軍事訓練中所學到的紀律能夠幫助你培養力量及品格。

▶ The boxing instructor disciplines his students to become professional boxers.
拳擊教練訓練他的學生成為職業拳擊手。

disco / discotheque [ˈdɪs.koʊ / ˈdɪs.kə.tek]

n. 迪斯可舞廳

▶ My friends agreed to meet at the disco.
我的朋友同意在迪斯可舞廳碰面。

---

disconnect [ˌdɪs.kəˈnekt]

v. （電腦）連結中斷；使分離；分開

同 **detach / cut off**

▶ Simon's computer was disconnected from the server for no reason.
賽門的電腦無緣無故與伺服器連結中斷。

---

discount [ˈdɪsˌkaʊnt]

① *n.* 折扣

搭 **offer discount** 提供優惠

同 **concession / rebate**

實用片語
at a discount 折扣

② *v.* 打折

同 **deduct / exempt**

▶ All store employees receive a 10% discount on clothes.
店裡所有員工買衣服可以打九折。

▶ I'm holding off on buying a new bag until I can get one at a discount.
我一直忍著沒買新的包包，直到有折扣才要買。

▶ The travel agency offers discounted rates on flights and hotels.
旅行社提供機票和旅館住宿的折扣。

---

discourage [dɪsˈkɝ.ɪdʒ] *v.* 使洩氣

同 **dispirit / depress**

實用片語
discourage from 勸阻，阻礙

▶ Our team felt discouraged after spending so much effort but making no progress.
我們小組在盡了全力卻沒有任何進步，感到非常洩氣。

▶ Please discourage Jones from leaving the company.
請勸阻約翰離開公司。

---

discouragement [dɪsˈkɝ.ɪdʒmənt]

n. 氣餒

同 **hopelessness / despair**

▶ His negative comment towards her work performance is a source of discouragement.
他對她工作表現的負面評語，就是她氣餒的原因。

Exercise 26

I. Vocabulary Choice

(A) discount   (B) disaster   (C) diligent   (D) diligence   (E) diplomat
(F) disconnect   (G) discipline   (H) dip   (I) diploma   (J) disabled

1. Janet received her _____ in Business Administration from the Chinese Cultural University.

2. Our government has declared a state of emergency due to the natural _____ .

3. Employees of this publisher can buy books at a 30% _____ .

4. In addition to excellent reading and comprehension skills in your source languages, _____ is one of the skills that you must have to succeed as a freelance translator.

5. Doris is a _____ student and she always finishes her homework before the deadline.

II. Multiple Choice

(   ) 1. Adam's father served his country as a ____ abroad for seven years.
   (A) diploma   (B) diplomat   (C) dealer   (D) detective

(   ) 2. The farewell party turned out to be a ____ .
   (A) disappoint   (B) disappointed   (C) disappointment   (D) disappointing

(   ) 3. John was from a ____ family because his parents both lacked higher education.
   (A) disadvantaged   (B) disabled   (C) dirty   (D) distinguished

(   ) 4. My father shook his head in ____ of my brother's sudden marriage to Joyce.
   (A) disappearance   (B) disappear   (C) disapprove   (D) disapproval

(   ) 5. Our teacher's negative comments on my assignment were such a ____ to me that I don't care about it anymore.
   (A) discourage   (B) discover   (C) discouragement   (D) discouragement

(104) (102)

discovery [dɪˈskʌv.ə.i] *n.* 發現

同 **detection / encounter**

▶ The discovery of the missing girl's body closed the case.
失蹤女孩的屍體被找到，讓案子得以結案。

disease [dɪˈziz] *n.* 疾病

同 **illness / malady**

實用片語
foot-in-mouth disease 口沒遮攔

▶ I'm sorry, but there is no cure for this disease.
很抱歉，這個疾病無藥可治。

▶ Tim's kids have foot-in-mouth disease again.
提姆的孩子們又口無遮攔了。

(104) (101)

disguise [dɪsˈgaɪz]

① *v.* 偽裝；把…假裝起來

搭 **disguise feeling** 隱藏心情

同 **cloak / conceal**

實用片語
a blessing in disguise 塞翁失馬焉知非福

② *n.* 喬裝

同 **veil / covering**

▶ Ellen disguised herself using a wig and a false beard.
艾倫戴了假髮，假鬍子，把自己偽裝起來。

▶ Losing my job turned out to be a blessing in disguise.
失去我的工作真是塞翁失馬焉知非福。

▶ The detective believes that the robber is using different disguises to fool the police.
偵探相信那位強盜使用不同的偽裝來騙過警察。

disgust [dɪsˈgʌst]

① *n.* 厭惡；憎惡；反感

同 **dislike / hatred**

實用片語
be disgusted at 感到反感

② *v.* 使厭惡

同 **displease / offend**

▶ The principal expressed his disgust at the boys who attacked the helpless old lady.
校長對那些攻擊無助的老婦人的男孩表示憎惡。

▶ Kim is disgusted at Eva's cheating husband.
金對伊娃不忠的老公感到反感。

▶ His inappropriate behavior disgusts everyone in that meeting.
他不恰當的行為使得會議中所有的人感到厭惡。

disk / disc [ˈdɪsk] *n.* 磁碟片；圓盤；唱片

▶ Put the disk into the computer to see the photos.
把磁碟片放進電腦來看照片。

dislike [dɪˈslaɪk]

① v. 不喜歡；厭惡
- 同 **hate / distaste**

② n. 不喜歡；厭惡
- 同 **disapproval / enmity**

▶ My five year old daughter dislikes all vegetables.
我五歲的女兒不喜歡所有蔬菜。

▶ My cat took an instant dislike to the new kitten.
我的貓咪一見到新來的小貓就不喜歡。

---

(103) (102) (97)

dismiss [dɪsˈmɪs] v. 解散；讓⋯離開

- 同 **decline / reject**

實用片語
dismiss someone 解僱某人

▶ Leo was dismissed from his job because he was caught in a dishonest act.
李奧被逮到不誠實的行為，因而被遣職。

▶ The boss dismissed John, because he was always late.
老闆解僱了約翰，因為他常遲到。

---

disorder [dɪˈsɔːr.dɚ]

① n. 無秩序
- 搭 **political disorder** 無政府狀態
- 同 **disarray / mess**

② v. 使擾亂
- 同 **clutter / disjoint**

▶ When the school teacher walked into the classroom, it was in a state of disorder.
當學校老師走進教室時，全班亂成一團。

▶ Stop disordering the public with false claims like these!
不要再提出這種錯誤的主張來擾亂公眾。

---

(99)

dispute [dɪˈspjuːt]

① v. 對⋯提出質疑；爭論
- 同 **argue / contest**

實用片語
in dispute 有爭議

② n. 爭端
- 同 **quarrel / debate**

▶ The scientists disputed the researcher's claim about the existence of aliens.
科學家們對於外星人存在的研究報告提出了質疑。

▶ The answer to this question is still in dispute.
這個問題的答案仍有爭議。

▶ There is a constant dispute over the presence of a monster in this lake.
大家對於湖裡妖怪存在的問題不斷地有爭端。

---

dissatisfaction [ˌdɪsˈsæt̬.əs.faɪd]

n. 不滿
- 同 **unhappiness / dismay**

▶ Mom couldn't hide her dissatisfaction with the meal.
媽媽無法隱藏對餐飲的不滿。

distinct [dɪˈstɪŋkt] *adj.* 明顯的；有區別的

搭 **distinct impression** 顯著的印象

同 **apparent / obvious**

▶ This dish has a distinct flavor of lemon.
這道菜有明顯的檸檬味。

---

104 101 95

distinguish [dɪˈstɪŋ.gwɪʃ] *v.* 區別；分辨

同 **identify / recognize**

▶ It is often difficult for a child to distinguish between a truth and a lie.
要一個小孩區別實話和謊言通常是很困難的。

---

distinguished [dɪˈstɪŋgwɪʃt]
adj. 著名的；卓越的

同 **famous / notable**

▶ The school has invited a distinguished guest to speak at the graduation ceremony.
學校請了一位著名的講員在畢業典禮上致詞。

---

103 102

distribute [dɪˈstrɪb.juːt] *v.* 分配

同 **allocate / assign**

實用片語
distribute to 貢獻給

▶ The teacher asked a student to distribute the handouts to the rest of the class.
老師請一位學生把講義分發給班上其他同學。

▶ The volunteers distributed food to the needy.
志工們捐獻了食物給貧困的人。

---

104 96

distribution [ˌdɪs.trɪˈbjuː.ʃən]
n. 銷售；配給物；分發

同 **marketing / sharing**

▶ Knowing the right distribution channel is important in managing a business.
在經營事業時，知道正確的銷售管道是非常重要的。

---

district [ˈdɪs.trɪkt] *n.* 轄區；行政區

同 **neighborhood / region**

▶ This city has been divided into ten administrative districts.
這個城市被規劃分成十個行政區域。

104

disturb [dɪˈstɝb] *v.* 打擾

同 **annoy / bother**

▶ My sleep was disturbed by someone playing the drums at midnight.
我的睡眠被一位在半夜十二點打鼓的人給打斷了。

---

ditch [ˈdɪtʃ]
① *n.* 溝渠

▶ They lost control of the car and fell into a ditch.
他們的汽車失控，掉進了溝渠裡。

② *v.* 掘溝渠

▶ Nobody understood why the farmer wanted to ditch the area around his barn.
沒人知道為什麼這農夫要在他穀倉周圍挖溝渠。

dive ['daɪv]

① *v.* 潛水；跳水

同 **dip / plunge**

實用片語
dive into 潛入

② *n.* 跳水；潛水

▶ The divers dove headfirst into the ocean.
潛水夫頭朝前地跳入海中。

▶ All the swimmers dived into the pool.
所有的游泳選手都潛入池中。

▶ So far, that was the best dive I've seen in this competition.
到目前為止，那是這次競賽中我看到最棒的跳水。

divine [də'vaɪn] *adj.* 天賜的；神祇的

▶ Esther prayed for divine help when she got lost in the forest.
當艾絲特在樹林裡迷路時，她禱告祈求上天的幫助。

95
divorce [dɪ'vɔːrs]

① *n.* 離婚

② *v.* 與…離婚

▶ Divorce affects an entire family, not just the couple alone.
離婚會影響整個的家庭，而不只是夫妻兩人而已。

▶ The counselor advises Mr. Smith not to divorce his wife of ten years.
那位律師建議史密斯先生不要和結婚十年的妻子離婚。

dock ['dɑk] *n.* 碼頭

▶ No one knew how soon the ferry would return to the dock.
沒有人知道渡輪多久會回到碼頭。

dodge ['dɑdʒ]

① *v.* 躲避

同 **avoid / evade**

② *n.* 迴避

▶ As the boy was crossing the street, he had to dodge a few cars.
男孩在穿越馬路時不得不閃躲幾輛汽車。

▶ Andrew made a dodge to the left, so the ball wouldn't hit him.
安得烈往左邊閃躲，這樣球就不會打到他。

102 101
domestic [də'mes.tɪk] *adj.* 家庭的；國內的

同 **household / home-like**

▶ Domestic violence and abuse is a serious crime.
家庭暴力和虐待是嚴重的罪行。（註：主詞雖以 and 連接，但被視為一個群組，所以動詞用單數）

dominant [ˈdɑmənənt]

adj. 主要的；佔優勢的；支配的

同 **leading / ruling**

▶ The dominant nations worked together to end World War II.

那些佔優勢的國家聯合起來結束了第二次世界大戰。

I. 中英對應

_____ 1. 解散　　(A) dismiss　　(B) dismay　　(C) disorder　　(D) dispute

_____ 2. 天賜的　(A) device　　(B) division　(C) divide　　(D) divine

_____ 3. 碼頭　　(A) duck　　(B) dock　　(C) dodge　　(D) dove

_____ 4. 爭端　　(A) display　　(B) dispatch　(C) dispose　　(D) dispute

_____ 5. 喬裝　　(A) disguise　(B) disgust　(C) disgrace　(D) disgusting

II. Derivatives

1. The whole classroom was in a state of _____ (order).

2. World Vision Taiwan organized the _____ (distribute) of food and clothing in the earthquake disaster area.

3. The _____ (discover) of oil in Dubai seriously impacted the entire economy of the United Arab Emirates.

4. Harper Lee was a _____ (distinguish) American writer.

5. Sixty percent of customers expressed their _____ (dissatisfy) with the quality of service and food at the restaurant.

dominate [ˈdɑː.mə.neɪt] *v.* 主導；支配

同 **govern / control**

▶ The manager dominates the discussion of the meeting.
那位經理在整場會議裡主導了討論。

---

dormitory / dorm [ˈdɔːr.mə.tɔːr.i / dɔːm / dɔːrm]

n. 學生宿舍

▶ Students need to return to their dormitories before midnight.
學生們必須在半夜十二點前回到宿舍。

---

dose [doʊs]

① *n.* 一劑藥

同 **catnap / snooze**

② *v.* 給藥；服藥

實用片語
a dose of medicine 一劑藥

▶ I took a large dose of vitamin C and I feel so much better.
我吃了一顆劑量很高的維他命 C，感覺好多了。

▶ The nurse accidentally dosed the patient with too much medicine.
護士不小心給病人服下過多的藥物。

▶ The doctor gave Ken a dose of medicine.
醫生給肯尼一劑藥。

---

doubtful [ˈdaʊtfəl] *adj.* 懷疑的

同 **questionable / unsettled**

▶ She is doubtful about hiring a nanny to take care of her children.
她對雇用一位保姆來照顧小孩存有疑慮。

---

download [ˈdaʊn.loʊd] *v.* 下載

搭 **download application** 下載應用程式
同 **input / load**

▶ Jason accidentally downloaded a computer virus from the gaming website.
傑生不小心從動玩網站上下載了電腦病毒。

---

doze [doʊz]

① *v.* 打瞌睡

同 **nod off / sleep**

實用片語
doze off 打瞌睡

② *n.* 小睡；打盹

同 **nap / snooze**

▶ Deborah is content to rest and doze in the comfortable couch.
黛博拉非常滿足地在舒適的沙發上休息，打瞌睡。

▶ My mom dozed off in front of the TV.
我媽媽在電視前打起瞌睡。

▶ Linda was awakened from her doze by a loud bang.
琳達小睡時被一聲巨響給吵醒。

draft [ˈdræft]

① *n.* 冷空氣

② *v.* 徵集

搭 **draft players** 招募球員

同 **recruit / enlist**

實用片語
draft for 選擇，挑選

▶ A cool draft came in through the open window.
一股冷空氣從敞開的窗戶吹進來。

▶ My brother was drafted into the navy special division.
我的哥哥被徵招入海軍特種部隊。

▶ We drafted some boys for moving textbooks.
我挑選一些男生去搬課本。

---

drain [dreɪn]

① *v.* 使排出

同 **exhaust / consume**

實用片語
go down the drain 破產，每況愈下

② *n.* 下水道；排水管

同 **pipe / sink**

▶ After washing the dishes, make sure to drain the sink.
洗完餐具後，務必把水槽的水放掉。

▶ That company is going down the drain because of poor management.
因為經營不善，這間公司的狀況每況愈下。

▶ My wedding ring accidentally went down the drain!
我的結婚戒子不小心掉落到排水管裡。

97

dramatic [drəˈmætɪk] *adj.* 戲劇性的

同 **powerful / striking**

▶ In my opinion, the movie was overly dramatic and unrealistic.
我的看法是，這部電影過度戲劇化，並且不真實。

---

dread [dred]

① *v.* 感到恐懼，害怕

同 **fear / tremble**

② *n.* 畏懼

同 **horror / terror**

▶ What I most dreaded as a child was the sound of loud footsteps.
我小時候最懼怕的就是大聲的腳步聲。

▶ The farmer was filled with dread when he saw that all his chickens were dead.
當農夫看到他的雞群都死了後，他感到萬分恐懼。

---

drift [ˈdrɪft]

① *n.* 漂流

② *v.* 使漂流

同 **float / flow**

實用片語
drift along 隨波逐流

▶ A drift of logs is flowing down the river towards a sawmill.
一批伐木順著河流流到鋸木廠。

▶ The strong current caused the boat to drift to the other side of the river.
急流使得船隻漂流到河流的另一端。

▶ The boat drifted along with the current.
這艘船隨波逐流。

99

drill [ˈdrɪl]

① *n.* 電鑽;鑽頭
② *v.* 在…上鑽孔
搭 **drill wells** 挖井
同 **dig / pierce**

▶ A drill is a very useful tool for making holes in the wall.
電鑽是可以用來在牆上鑽洞的利器。

▶ You need to drill a hole in the wall to put up this frame.
你必須要在牆上鑽個洞才能掛起這個相框。

drip [ˈdrɪp]

① *v.* 滴下
同 **drizzle / trickle**
② *n.* 滴下之液體;滴下

▶ Why is the ceiling dripping water?
為什麼天花板在滴水?

▶ We need a bucket to catch the drips from the ceiling.
我們需要一個桶子來接從天花板滴下來的水。

96

drown [ˈdraʊn] *v.* 溺水

同 **immerse / soak**

實用片語
drown in something 淹沒在…之中

▶ He would drown his victims then bury them in the woods.
他會把受害者淹死,然後把他們埋在樹林中。

▶ I am drowning in bills.
我被淹沒在帳單之中。

drowsy [ˈdraʊ.zi] *adj.* 昏昏欲睡的

同 **restful / sluggish**

▶ Every time I leave the sauna, I feel relaxed and drowsy.
每次離開蒸氣室,我都覺得很放鬆,且昏昏欲睡。

drunk [drʌŋk]

① *adj.* 喝醉酒的
② *n.* 醉酒者

▶ The man was fined for drunk driving.
那名男子因為酒醉駕駛而被罰款。

▶ He used to be a drunk, but now he only drinks non-alcoholic drinks.
他從前是一個酒鬼,但是現在只喝不含酒精的飲料。

due [ˈdu]

① *adj.* 應支付的;欠債的;由於
同 **payable / outstanding**
② *n.* 別人應付的款項或欠的錢
③ *adv.* 正對著的

▶ The rent money is due at the end of every month.
租金應在每個月月底支付。

▶ Were you able to receive your due?
你收到錢了嗎?

▶ Go due north until you see the bridge.
正對著北邊走,直到看到橋為止。

dump [ˈdʌmp]

① *v.* 傾倒

搭 **dump toxic waste** 傾倒有害廢料

同 **drop / throw away**

實用片語
dump on 傾倒，丟

② *n.* 垃圾場

▶ Three kittens have been rescued after being dumped in a garbage bag.
之前被丟棄在垃圾袋中的三隻小貓獲救。

▶ She dumped all her troubles on her family.
她向家人傾訴了所有的煩惱。

▶ Terri carried two trash bags and threw them into a garbage dump.
泰利提著兩袋垃圾，把它們丟進垃圾場。

---

durable [ˈdʊr.ə.bəl] *adj.* 耐穿的；耐用的

同 **lasting / reliable**

▶ These shoes from the night market are very durable.
這雙在夜市買的鞋子非常地耐穿。

---

dust [ˈdʌst]

① *n.* 灰塵

② *v.* 擦去…的灰塵；給…除塵

同 **sweep / wipe**

實用片語
dust off 掃灰塵，撢塵

▶ There is too much dust in the air.
空氣中的灰塵太多了。

▶ Keep your furniture clean by dusting at least once a week.
每週至少清理一次家具上的灰塵，以保持清潔。

▶ Please dust off this vase.
請撢掃這花瓶上的灰塵。

---

dusty [ˈdʌs.ti] *adj.* 滿是灰塵的

同 **dirty / sandy**

▶ The dusty grand piano needs some serious cleaning.
這台佈滿塵埃的鋼琴需要好好的清理一番。

DVD / digital video disk / digital versatile disk

[ˈdɪdʒ.ə.ţəl ; ˈvɪd.i.oʊ ; dɪsk / ˈdɪdʒ.ə.ţəl ; ˈvɚ-ː.sə.ţəl ; dɪsk]

n. 數位視訊影碟

▶ The DVD player in my computer is broken.
我電腦裡的光碟機壞掉了。

---

dye [ˈdaɪ]

① *n.* 染料

② *v.* 把…染上顏色

搭 **dye hair** 染髮

同 **stain / tint**

▶ People in the past used special snails to make a purple dye.
人們在古時曾使用特別的蝸牛來做出紫色的染料。

▶ Tom was sent home by the discipline master because he dyed his hair blue.
湯姆因為把頭髮染成藍色而被教官趕回家。

dynamic [daɪˈnæm.ɪk] *adj.* 有活力的
搭 **dynamic atmosphere** 活躍的氣氛
同 **energetic / compelling**

---

dynasty [ˈdaɪ.nə.sti] *n.* 王朝

▶ The dynamic trio band will be performing in town tonight.
那個有活力的三重奏樂團今晚將在鎮上演出。

- -

▶ Every dynasty has its own story of power and passion.
每一個朝代都有它自己的權利與慾望的故事。

Exercise 28

I. 中英對應

_____ 1. 冷空氣　(A) draw　　(B) draft　　(C) drawer　　(D) drawback

_____ 2. 下水道　(A) drain　　(B) drawn　　(C) drama　　(D) drag

_____ 3. 醉酒者　(A) drown　　(B) draft　　(C) drunk　　(D) drink

_____ 4. 畏懼　　(A) dream　　(B) drain　　(C) dress　　(D) dread

_____ 5. 耐用的　(A) during　　(B) durable　(C) duration　(D) durian

II. Vocabulary Choice

(A) dynamic　(B) drifted　　(C) drowned　(D) drowsy　(E) dyed

(F) doubtful　(G) download　(H) draft　　(I) dominate　(J) dramatic

1. A small boat slowly _____ out to sea.

2. Ginny _____ her hair purple.

3. According to the UN refugee agency, hundreds of migrants _____ in
   three days when their boats overturned off southern Italy in May, 2016.

4. It is _____ that the missing airplane will ever be found.

5. The change in Paul's attitude was _____ after he was called in by the
   manager.

e-mail / email [ˈiː.meɪl]

① *n.* 電子郵件

② *v.* 寄電子郵件給⋯

▶ I received an email from an unknown sender, asking me out on a date.
我收到一封來自未知寄件者的電子郵件，邀請我赴約會。

▶ Can you email the latest meeting schedule to Jonathan?
你能不能把最新的開會時間用電子郵件傳給強那生？

---

eager [ˈiː.gɚ] *adj.* 渴望的；熱心的

同 **ambitious / keen**

實用片語
eager beaver 雄心壯志

▶ After living abroad for two years, Ben was eager to go back home.
在國外住了兩年之後，班渴望回家。

▶ She gets to work very early. She's an eager beaver.
她很早開始工作。她有雄心壯志。

104

earnest [ˈɝː.nɪst]

① *adj.* 認真的；誠摯的

同 **diligent / ardent**

② *n.* 保證金；誠摯

實用片語
in earnest 認真

▶ His earnest confession of his love for her is beyond description.
他對她真心的愛的告白真是無法形容。

▶ The couple put down $1000 of earnest money for their new home.
那對夫妻拿出一千元作為新房子的保證金。

▶ I spent the day doing research in earnest.
我整天認真做研究。

---

earnings [ˈɝː.nɪŋz] *n.* 收入

搭 **annual earnings** 年收入

同 **income / salary**

▶ After I got paid, I put half of my earnings in a jar.
我收到薪水後，把一半收入放進罐子裡。

---

earphone [ˈɪr.foʊn] *n.* 耳機

▶ It is dangerous to put on earphones while driving.
在開車時戴著耳機是非常危險的，

---

earring [ˈɪr.ɪŋ] *n.* 耳環

▶ The girls wore earrings to the formal event.
這些女生戴耳環參加正式活動。

99 **97**

easily [ˈiː.zəl.i] *adv.* 容易地；輕易地

搭 **easily available** 容易取得

同 **readily / handily**

實用片語
breathe easily 安心，鬆一口氣

▶ I can easily catch the fish with a large net!
我用很大的魚網就可以輕易釣到魚！

▶ I can finally breathe easily now that I've finished my project.
完成專案後，我可以鬆一口氣了。

---

echo [ˈek.oʊ]

① *n.* 回聲；仿效

同 **repeat / copy**

② *v.* 發出回聲

▶ Echoes are often heard in houses with large open rooms.
在大而寬敞房間的房子裡經常會聽到回音。

▶ My voice echoed as I shouted from the mountain top.
我從山頂上大叫而產生了回聲。

101

economic [iː.kəˈnɑː.mɪk / ek.əˈnɑː.mɪk]

adj. 經濟上的

同 **budgetary / fiscal**

▶ The economic factors surrounding the slow growth of a country should not be overlooked.
一個國家緩慢成長的經濟因素不容忽視。

---

economical [ˌiː.kəˈnɑː.mɪ.kəl / ek.əˈnɑː.mɪ.kəl]

adj. 節約的；經濟的

搭 **economical solution** 省錢 / 划算的解決方案

同 **prudent / cost-effective**

▶ An economical heating system is introduced by the government which can help to save money.
政府推出了節約的加熱取暖系統，將會幫助人省錢。

---

economics [ˌiː.kəˈnɑː.mɪks / ek.əˈnɑː.mɪks]

n. 經濟學

▶ Daniel was more interested in economics than political science when he was in college.
丹尼爾在大學時期，對經濟學比對政治學更有興趣。

---

economist [iˈkɑː.nə.mɪst] *n.* 經濟學家

▶ The man on the front cover of the magazine is a famous economist.
在雜誌封面的這位男士是位有名的經濟學家。

96

economy [iˈkɑː.nə.mi] *n.* 節約

搭 **booming economy** 經濟繁榮

▶ Many families are learning to practice economy in planning their household budgets.
很多家庭都在學習在制定家計預算時節省開銷。

101

edit [ˈed.ɪt] *v.* 校訂;編輯

同 **arrange / revise**

▶ I edited your paper and found very few mistakes.
我校訂了你的論文,發現錯誤不多。

---

edition [ɪˈdɪʃ.ən] *n.* 版本

實用片語
dead-tree edition 紙本書

▶ Usually, first editions are the most expensive books.
通常初版的書籍最貴。

▶ This book is also available online, so few people bought the dead-tree edition.
此書也可在線上看,所以很少人付錢買紙本書。

---

editor [ˈed.ɪ.t̬ə] *n.* 主編;編輯

搭 **chief editor** 總編輯
同 **copyreader / reviser**

▶ Pam has just been hired as the new editor of the magazine.
潘剛被聘為雜誌的新主編。

---

educate [ˈedʒ.ə.keɪt] *v.* 教育

同 **train / teach**

實用片語
educate someone for 教育某人做某事

▶ Not many children are educated at home.
接受在家教育的孩子並不多。

▶ The company educated the workers for doing the new project.
我們會在新員工到工廠前進行職前訓練。

---

educational [ˌedʒ.əˈkeɪ.ʃən.əl] *adj.* 教育的

同 **instructive / informational**

▶ We watched a very educational video in science class today.
我們今天在科學課看了一部很有教育意義的影片。

---

efficiency [ɪˈfɪʃ.ən.si] *n.* 效率

搭 **increase efficiency** 增加效率
同 **readiness / performance**

▶ I'm sure we can improve our efficiency by re-evaluating our work process.
我相信只要重新評估我們的工作流程,就可以增進我們的效率。

101

efficient [ɪˈfɪʃ.ənt] *adj.* 效率高的;有效率的

搭 **efficient method** 有效率的方式
同 **productive / competent**

▶ Subways are an inexpensive and efficient form of transportation.
地鐵是便宜且效率高的一種交通工具。

elastic [iˈlæs.tɪk]

① *adj.* 有彈性的

同 **flexible / plastic**

② *n.* 鬆緊帶

▶ Kim tied up her hair with an elastic band before going for a run.
琴在出門跑步之前，先用橡皮筋綁好頭髮。

▶ The letters were held together by elastics.
這些信件是用鬆緊帶套在一起。

---

elbow [ˈel.boʊ]

① *n.* 手肘

② *v.* 用手肘推

▶ She banged her elbow on the table.
她用手肘敲桌子。

▶ The bully elbowed him in the stomach.
霸凌者用手肘推他的腹部。

---

elderly [ˈel.də.li] *adj.* 年長的

同 **retired / aging**

▶ It is polite to offer your seat to an elderly person.
讓坐給年長者是有禮貌的行為。

---

election [iˈlek.ʃən] *n.* 選舉

搭 **election pledge** 選舉支票

同 **poll / selection**

▶ I voted for Obama in the last election.
我在上次的選舉中投給歐巴馬。

---

electric / electrical [iˈlek.trɪk / iˈlek.trɪ.kəl]

adj. 電的

▶ Use this electric blanket to keep yourself warm.
用這條電毯來讓自己保暖。

Exercise 29

I. Derivatives

1. Mandy worked as a book _____ (edit) in a well-known publishing house for years.
2. Josh handed half of his _____ (earn) to his wife every month.
3. Paul Krugman is a world famous _____ (economy), and also a winner of the 2008 Nobel Prize for Economics.
4. Karen works for an _____ (educate) institution in Taipei.
5. The new facilities we purchased are aimed at improving _____ (efficient) and customer service at our restaurant.

II. Vocabulary Choice

(A) easily   (B) elections   (C) elderly   (D) eager   (E) economical

(F) earnest   (G) elbow   (H) elastic   (I) electric   (J) echoes

1. The tight running pants is made of a highly _____ material.
2. My father is _____ to see the Olympic medal results, so he stays up late every evening.
3. According to research, only about 45% of the citizens voted in the local government _____ .
4. Andrew is a very _____ worker and he might be promoted soon.
5. The _____ of my shouts sounded in the tunnel for several seconds.

Unit 30

electrician [ˌɪl.ek'trɪʃ.ən] *n.* 電工；電氣技師

▶ The electrician managed to fix the lights in our house.
電工把我們家裡的電燈給修好了。

---

electricity [iˌlek'trɪs.ə.tj] *n.* 電力

▶ Leaving the light on wastes a lot of electricity.
讓電燈一直開著會浪費許多電力。

---

electronic [iˌlek'trɑː.nɪk] *adj.* 電子的
搭 **electronic devices** 電子設備

▶ My parents bought me an electronic keyboard for Christmas.
我爸媽買了一架電子琴給我，作為聖誕禮物。

---

electronics [iˌlek'trɑː.nɪks] *n.* 電子學

▶ You can find books about electronics on the third shelf to your right.
你可以在右手邊第三層的書架上找到有關電子學的書籍。

---

elegant ['el.ə.gənt] *adj.* 優雅的
搭 **elegant look** 優雅的外表
同 **graceful / stylish**

▶ Sophie put on an elegant dress for the ball tonight.
蘇菲亞今晚出席晚宴時穿了一件非常優雅的洋裝。

---

elementary [ˌel.ə'men.tə.i] *adj.* 基本的
搭 **elementary school** 小學
同 **basic / fundamental**

▶ Love and tender care are the elementary needs of a newborn baby.
愛和溫柔的照顧是每位新生兒的基本需求。

103
eliminate [i'lɪm.ə.neɪt] *v.* 排除；消除
同 **delete / get rid of**
實用片語
eliminate from 自…刪除

▶ To eliminate homelessness, a special fund is set up to help those in need.
為了要減少無業遊民的問題，我們設定了一個特別的基金來幫助有需要的人。

▶ The team was eliminated from the competition.
這支隊伍在競賽中被淘汰。

---

elsewhere ['els.wer] *adv.* 別處

▶ The rich man has bought mansions by the coast and elsewhere.
那個有錢人在海岸邊以及其他地方，買了好幾棟別墅。

embarrass [ɪmˈber.əs] *v.* 使尷尬;使困窘

同 **annoy / bother**

實用片語
embarrass with 感到尷尬

▶ Carolyn felt embarrassed after Peter made a remark about her dress.
凱洛琳聽到彼得對她的洋裝做的評論,感到非常的尷尬。

▶ Please don't embarrass me with that old story again.
請不要再用那個老掉牙的故事讓我尷尬了。

---

embarrassment [ɪmˈber.əs.mənt] *n.* 難堪

同 **disgrace / meanness**

▶ Jason was an embarrassment to his father when the police found drugs on him.
當警察在傑生身上找到毒品時,他讓他的爸爸的感到很難堪。

---

embassy [ˈem.bə.si] *n.* 大使館

▶ She had to go to the embassy to report her stolen passport.
她必須到大使館去報備護照遭竊。

---

emerge [ɪˈmɝːdʒ] *v.* 浮現

同 **develop / appear**

▶ The whale emerges from the water to breathe.
大鯨魚從水裡浮出來呼吸。

102
emergency [ɪˈmɝː.dʒən.si]
n. 緊急;緊急事件

搭 **emergency landing** 緊急迫降

同 **difficulty / tension**

▶ The airplane was forced to make an emergency landing on the beach.
這架飛機被緊急迫降在海灘上。

---

emotional [ɪˈmoʊ.ʃən.əl]
adj. 使人動容的;情感的

搭 **highly emotional** 很情緒化

同 **touching / moving**

▶ It was an emotional moment when the mother found her long-lost daughter.
當母親找到她失散多年的女兒時,那真是令人動容的一刻。

95
emperor [ˈem.pɚ.ɚ] *n.* 皇帝

▶ Augustus was Rome's first emperor.
奧古斯都屋大維是羅馬帝國第一位皇帝。

---

103 102
emphasis [ˈem.fə.sɪs] *n.* 重視;重點

同 **attention / strength**

▶ Tomorrow's lecture is about business administration with emphasis on financial management.
明天的演講是關於企業行政,而重點是在財務管理。

實用片語
lay emphasis on 強調某事

▶ When you present, lay emphasis on the matter of budgeting.
當你報告時,請強調預算的事宜。

 99 97 96

emphasize [ˈem.fə.saɪz] *v.* 強調

搭 **emphasize rightly** 肯定地強調
同 **highlight / underline**

▶ She emphasized the importance of exercise.
她強調運動的重要。

102
empire [ˈem.paɪr] *n.* 帝國

▶ It does not take one person to build an empire.
一個帝國不是一個人就可以建造起來的。

employ [ɪmˈplɔɪ] *v.* 雇用

搭 **employ helpers** 雇用幫手
同 **hire / recruit**
實用片語
employ... as 雇某人為⋯

▶ Our company needs to employ more staff.
我們公司需要雇用更多的員工。

▶ The boss employed Mary as an assistant.
老闆雇用瑪莉當助理。

employee [ɪmˈplɔɪ.i: / ˌem.plɔɪˈi:] *n.* 員工

▶ We treat our employees like family.
我們待員工有如家人一般。

employer [ɪmˈplɔɪ.ə] *n.* 雇主

▶ If you want more vacation time, discuss it with your employer.
如果你想要更多的休假時間,就和你的雇主討論。

employment [ɪmˈplɔɪ.mənt] *n.* 工作;雇用

▶ Are you looking for employment?
你在找工作嗎?

empty [ˈemp.ti]

① *adj.* 空的
搭 **empty office** 空辦公室
同 **vacant / devoid**
② *v.* 倒空;使成為空的
同 **clear / remove**
實用片語
empty suit 虛有其表,不學無術

▶ The school was empty except for a couple of students.
除了幾個學生以外,學校空盪盪的。

▶ She emptied her purse to find her credit card.
她把皮包倒空來找信用卡。

▶ She acted as if she knew everything, but she was really an empty suit.
她表現得好像什麼都知道,但她真的是虛有其表。

E

enable [ɪˈneɪ.bəl] v. 使能夠

同 allow / empower

實用片語
enable... to 使…能夠

---

enclose [ɪnˈkloʊz] v. 包住；圍住

同 encompass / wrap

實用片語
enclose in 圍起，圈起

▶ The class enables students to think for themselves.
這個課程讓學生可以學習自己思考。

▶ This budget will enable me to run my own restaurant.
這個預算將讓我可以營運我自己的餐廳。

▶ The mirror is entirely enclosed in bubble wrap to prevent it from breaking.
這面鏡子已被用泡泡綿完全包住，以避免破裂。

▶ The police enclosed the people in a safe area.
警察把民眾圍在安全區域。

Exercise 30

I. Derivatives

1. Candy felt her face burning with _____ (embarrass) when she sneezed loudly during the concert.

2. My mother called an _____ (electric) to repair our air conditioner.

3. Our boss _____ (emphasis) that all the staff should attend the meeting.

4. The pilot was forced to make an _____ (emergent) landing on New York's Hudson River after the engine failed.

5. Kylie found _____ (employ) with a foreign company right after graduation.

II. 中英對應

_____ 1. 皇帝   (A) embassy   (B) empire

       (C) emperor   (D) embrace

_____ 2. 圍住   (A) enable   (B) enlarge

       (C) enhance   (D) enclose

_____ 3. 排除   (A) eliminate   (B) elementary

       (C) election   (D) elderly

_____ 4. 優雅的   (A) electric   (B) eligible

       (C) elder   (D) elegant

_____ 5. 電子學   (A) electrician   (B) electronics

       (C) electronic   (D) electrical

⑪ **biennial** [baɪˈen.i.əl] *adj.* 兩年一度的

例 BT World Briefing is a biennial conference held by Best Tech Company.
BT 全球簡報是 Best Tech 公司舉辦兩年一次的研討會。

biannual [ˌbaɪˈænjəwəl] *adj.* 每年兩次的、每半年的

例 The company's biannual recruitments are conducted in May and November.
公司半年一次的招募會是在五月和十一月。

⑫ **broil** [brɔɪl] *v.* 烤、炙

例 Mary was assigned by her mother to broil the chicken.
瑪莉的媽媽請他烤雞。

boil [bɔɪl] *v.* 沸騰、開、滾

例 Don't let the vegetables boil for too long.
請不要將蔬菜煮得過久。

⑬ **clothes** [klˈoðz] *n.* 衣服、服裝

例 During the weekend, I like to wear casual clothes.
我在週末都穿輕便的服裝。

cloth [ˈklɔθ] *n.* 布、織物、衣料

例 She covered her bike with a piece of cloth.
她用一條布將單車蓋起來。

⑭ **college** [ˈkɑlɪdʒ] *n.* 大學、學院

例 Mary took some business courses offered at a community college.
瑪莉在一所社區大學修過一些商務課程。

collage [kəˈlɑʒ] *n.* 美術拼貼

例 Nowadays people use various applications to create photo collages.
現在人們使用各式應用程式來做照片拼貼。

⑮ **comma** [ˈkɑmə] *n.* 逗號

例 Mary has trouble understanding when a comma should be used.
瑪莉不瞭解何時要使用逗號。

coma [ˈkomə] *n.* 昏睡、昏迷

例 Jack was in a coma for a couple of days after the accident.
傑克在意外發生之後昏迷了兩天。

Unit 31

enclosed [ɪnˈkloʊzd]

adj. 被…圍住的;封閉的;附上的

同 **confined / immured**

▶ We felt enclosed by the crowd of people.
我們感覺像是被人群團團圍住。

---

encounter [ɪnˈkaʊn.tɚ]

① *v.* (意外)遇見

搭 **encounter difficulties** 遭致困難

同 **confront / detect**

② *n.* 偶然碰見

同 **concurrence / appointment**

▶ James encountered an old friend when he went fishing by the lake.
詹姆士在湖邊垂釣時,意外遇到一位老朋友。

▶ I had a strange encounter with a magician in the park the other day.
我前幾天在公園裡很奇妙地遇見了一位魔術師。

---

100 96

endanger [ɪnˈdeɪn.dʒɚ] *v.* 危及;使陷入危險

搭 **seriously endanger** 身處險境

同 **menace / expose**

▶ The man's careless driving has endangered the lives of those in his car.
那個男人的粗心駕駛危及了他車上乘客的生命安全。

---

endure [ɪnˈdʊr] *v.* 忍受;忍耐

同 **undergo / suffer**

▶ The trapped climber endured great pain when he cut off his arm to free himself.
那位被困的登山客忍受了劇痛,因為他必須自行斷臂才能脫困。

---

energetic [ˌen.ɚˈdʒeɽ.ɪk]

adj. 精力旺盛的;充滿活力的

搭 **remarkably energetic** 精力非常旺盛

同 **powerful / strong**

▶ Kelly drank three cups of coffee and became very energetic.
凱莉喝完三杯咖啡,就變得精力旺盛。

---

enforce [ɪnˈfɔːrs] *v.* 實施;施行

搭 **strictly enforce** 嚴格地執行

同 **carry out / invoke**

▶ A speed limit is enforced along this stretch of road because of frequent accidents.
由於這段道路經常出車禍,所以速限是強制執行的。

enforcement [ɪnˈfɔːrsmənt] *n.* 執行；強制

同 **imposition / execution**

▶ Law enforcement is only a temporary solution to hate crimes in the city.
強致執行法律對都市裡的仇恨犯罪只不過是臨時的解決方法。

103

engage [ɪnˈgeɪdʒ] *v.* 聘請；雇用；從事；訂婚

搭 **actively engage** 積極參與

同 **enlist / contract**

實用片語
engage in small talk 寒暄閒聊

▶ Tom engaged a detective to help him with the case.
湯姆聘了一個偵探來協助他辦案。

▶ All the attendees at the reception are engaging in small talk.
所有接待處的與會者都在寒暄閒聊。

104

engagement [ɪnˈgeɪdʒ.mənt] *n.* 訂婚

▶ Kate is very excited about her upcoming engagement.
凱特對快要訂婚感到非常興奮。

---

engine [ˈen.dʒɪn] *n.* 引擎

▶ Both airplane engines failed and the plane crashed into the river.
飛機兩邊的引擎都壞了，就墜入到河裡。

104

engineer [ˌen.dʒɪˈnɪr] *n.* 工程師

▶ The engineer repaired my laptop.
工程師修理了我的筆記型電腦。

---

engineering [ˌen.dʒɪˈnɪr.ɪŋ] *n.* 工程學

▶ Engineering is a popular major among students in India.
工程學在印度是一科很受到學生歡迎的主修。

100

enjoyable [ɪnˈdʒɔɪ.ə.bəl]
adj. 快樂的；令人愉快的

搭 **enjoyable trip** 愉快的旅途

同 **gratifying / pleasing**

▶ Watching the children dance on stage was a very enjoyable experience.
看小孩子在台上跳舞是一種愉悅的經驗。

---

enlarge [ɪnˈlɑːrdʒ] *v.* 放大；擴大；擴張

同 **broaden / extend**

實用片語
enlarge on 詳述

▶ You need to enlarge the photo in order to fit it into the frame.
你必須要把照片放大，才能放進這個相框。

▶ Please enlarge on the details of the plan.
請詳述此計劃的細節。

enlargement [ɪnˈlɑːrdʒ.mənt]
n. （建築物）增建；（照片）放大
同 **growth / spread**

▶ The enlargement of the science building is expected to cost more than $1 million.
科學大樓的擴建預期會花掉超過一百萬的經費。

enormous [əˈnɔːr.məs] *adj.* 巨大的
同 **huge / excessive**

▶ Supporting the ancient structures were enormous pillars carved out from rocks.
支撐這座古代建築物的是一些由岩石所挖鑿出來的巨大柱子。

entertain [en.t̬ɚˈteɪn] *v.* 使歡樂
同 **inspire / cheer**
實用片語
entertain with 取悅，款待

▶ The guests are entertained by the popular comedians from Canada.
來自加拿大一些受歡迎的諧星把賓客們逗得很開心。

▶ We tried to entertain the children with fun games.
我們試著用有趣的遊戲讓兒童開心。

entertainer [en.t̬ɚˈteɪ.nɚ]
n. 表演者；演藝人員
同 **artist / player**

▶ We hired an entertainer for the birthday party.
我們聘了一位餘興節目表演者到慶生會表演。

entertainment [en.t̬ɚˈteɪn.mənt] *n.* 娛樂
搭 **entertainment business** 娛樂事業
同 **treat / pastime**

▶ There is not a lot to do for entertainment in that small town.
在那個小鎮上根本沒什麼娛樂活動可言。

enthusiasm [ɪnˈθuzi.æzəm] *n.* 熱心；熱衷
搭 **maintain enthusiasm** 保有熱情
同 **keenness / zeal**

▶ Can you show a little more enthusiasm for the upcoming trip?
你能不能對將要出發的旅遊多表現一點熱情呢？

entry [ˈen.tri] *n.* 進入
同 **access / passage**

▶ The bride and groom made their entry into the ballroom.
新娘和新郎走進舞廳。

envious [ˈen.vi.əs] *adj.* 羨慕的
同 **jealous / craving**

▶ My niece looks in an envious way at the little girl holding a doll.
我的姪女用羨慕的眼光看著那位抱著洋娃娃的小女孩。

environmental [ɪnˌvaɪ.rənˈmen.t̬əl]

adj. 環境的

搭 **environmental problems** 環境問題

同 **ecological / biodegradable**

▶ People are becoming more aware of environmental issues.
人們開始更意識到環境的議題。

---

envy [ˈen.vi]

① *n.* 羨慕；忌妒

搭 **extreme envy** 極度羨慕

同 **jealousy / ill will**

② *v.* 羨慕；忌妒

同 **crave / yearn**

實用片語
green with envy 眼紅羨慕，妒忌

▶ I watched with envy as the boy kissed the girl.
當男孩親吻女孩時，我帶著羨慕的眼神。

▶ She envied her sister's big blue eyes.
她羨慕自己姊妹大大的藍眼睛。

▶ My friend turned green with envy when they saw my new house.
我的新房讓我的朋友眼紅了。

---

equality [ɪˈkwɑləti] *n.* 平等

搭 **racial equality** 種族平等

同 **fairness / similarity**

▶ Many countries are pushing for equality in opportunities for all people.
很多國家正為全民爭取機會平等。

Exercise 31

I. 中英對應

_____ 1. 熱心   (A) entertain   (B) enthrone

                    (C) enthusiasm   (D) entrepreneur

_____ 2. 忍受   (A) endure   (B) endorse

                    (C) endeavor   (D) energy

_____ 3. 巨大的   (A) enough   (B) environment

                    (C) enormous   (D) entire

_____ 4. 偶然碰見   (A) encompass   (B) encore

                    (C) encounter   (D) encourage

_____ 5. 平等   (A) equity   (B) equality

                    (C) equip   (D) equivalent

II. Derivatives

1. The National Police Agency is one of several law _____ (enforce) agencies in our country.

2. The proprietor is working on the _____ (enlarge) of his business to also include exports.

3. If we continue to ignore the _____ (environment) problems, we will reap what we sow.

4. Daniel studied _____ (engineer) at National Taiwan University.

5. Gabriel and Annie invited many friends to their _____ (engage) party.

Unit 32

(102) (95)

equip [ɪˈkwɪp] *v.* 具備；配備；裝備

同 **gear / supply**

實用片語
equip with 配備有…

▶ You must be equipped with the right tools before climbing the mountain.
登山之前，你必須具備好正確的裝備。

▶ This van is equipped with GPS.
這輛貨車配備有 GPS。

---

equipment [ɪˈkwɪp.mənt] *n.* 設備

搭 **modern equipment** 現代化設備
同 **apparatus / material**

▶ They load the equipment needed for the concert onto the van.
他們將演唱會所需的設備裝上廂型車。

---

era [ˈɪr.ə] *n.* 時代

▶ In today's computer era, it is so easy to keep in touch with people.
在現今這個電腦時代，與人聯繫變得非常容易。

---

erase [ɪˈreɪs] *v.* 擦掉

同 **abolish / wipe out**

實用片語
erase from 自…刪除

▶ Diane, did you erase the white board?
黛安，你擦白板了嗎？

▶ Please erase the writing from the wall.
請將牆上的字除去（擦乾淨）。

---

(100)

errand [ˈer.ənd] *n.* 差事

同 **duty / mission**

實用片語
run an errand 處理雜務

▶ My mother asked me to run an errand for her at the grocery store.
媽媽請我去食品雜貨店幫她跑腿。

▶ I've got to run an errand after work.
我下班後必須處理雜務。

---

escalator [ˈes.kə.leɪ.tɚ] *n.* 電扶梯

▶ The old man is afraid to take the escalator because it is moving so fast.
那位老人家不敢搭電扶梯，因為它移動的速度太快了。

---

(104) (97)

escape [ɪˈskeɪp]

① *v.* 逃跑
同 **flee / leave**

▶ Julie was able to escape from the burning building.
茱莉順利從失火的大樓中逃了出來。

escape from 自⋯脫逃

② *n.* 逃跑

搭 **prevent escape** 預防脫逃

同 **getaway / flee**

▶ The monkey escaped from the zoo.
猴子從動物園逃脫。

▶ She planned to make her escape while he was sleeping.
她計畫趁著他在睡覺時逃走。

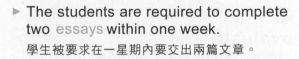

---

essay [ˈes.eɪ] *n.* 文章；散文；小品文

▶ The students are required to complete two essays within one week.
學生被要求在一星期內要交出兩篇文章。

---

104 99 96

essential [ɪˈsen.ʃəl]

① *adj.* 必要的

搭 **essential element** 重要的因素

同 **crucial / necessary**

② *n.* 必需品；不可或缺的東西

同 **necessity / element**

▶ Salt is one of the essential minerals to our human body.
鹽巴是我們人體所必要的礦物質之一。

▶ If money is spent unnecessarily, there will be little left to buy the essentials.
如果花了不必花的錢，就沒剩多少去買必需品了。

103

essentially [ɪˈsen.ʃəl.i] *adv.* 基本上；實質上

同 **virtually / actually**

▶ The banquet is essentially over. We only have dessert left.
這頓宴席基本上已經結束了。我們只剩下甜點要吃。

103

establish [ɪˈstæb.lɪʃ] *v.* 建立

搭 **establish company** 創辦公司

同 **authorize / settle**

establish someone in 將⋯安排，使立足

▶ It took many years to establish a school in the rural village.
要在鄉下村莊建立一所學校要花好多年的時間。

▶ My father established me in the software business.
我父親安排我到軟體業。

---

establishment [ɪˈstæb.lɪʃ.mənt] *n.* 建立的機構

同 **installation / formation**

▶ The eating establishment has been in the same location for 34 years.
這個美食機構已經在同個據點營業三十四年了。

---

104 102 99 98 95

estimate [ˈes.tə.meɪt]

① *n.* 估價單；評估

搭 **official estimate** 正式估算

同 **evaluation / measure**

▶ The insurance company gave me an estimate of the damage caused by the accident.
保險公司給我一份車禍損傷的維修報價單。

② *v.* 估計

同 **assess / examine**

實用片語
ballpark estimate 約略估算

▶ How much do you estimate it will cost to fix my car?
你估計把我的車修好需要花多少錢？

▶ Just give me a ballpark estimate please.
請指給我約略估算的數字就好。

101

evaluate [ɪˈvæl.ju.eɪt]
v. 評估；對⋯的評價；估⋯的價

搭 **evaluate performance** 評估表現

同 **grade / classify**

▶ The insurance company will evaluate the amount of damage caused by the earthquake.
保險公司會先評估一下地震造成的毀損程度。

---

evaluation [ɪˌvælju'eɪʃən]
n. 評估；估算；評價

同 **rating / judgment**

▶ The teacher will give us an evaluation of the students' English levels.
老師會給我們一個學生英文程度的評估。

---

eve [iːv] *n.* 前夕

實用片語
on the eve of 前夕

▶ On the eve of our wedding, we had a special dinner with our family.
在我們結婚的前夕，我們和家人有個特別的晚餐。

▶ On the eve of the conference, Mr. Chen backed out.
會議前夕，陳先生退出了。

---

eventual [ɪˈven.tʃu.əl] *adj.* 最後的

同 **final / ultimate**

▶ The eventual release of the movie may take longer than the book's fans had hoped.
那部電影最後的上映日期可能會比書迷們所期待的更晚。

---

104 95

eventually [ɪˈven.tʃu.ə.li] *adv.* 最後；終於

同 **ultimately / finally**

▶ After being friends for years, Bob and Sue eventually decided to get married.
鮑伯和蘇在作朋友多年之後，最後終於決定要結婚了。

---

evidence [ˈev.ə.dəns]

① *n.* 證據

搭 **reveal evidence** 揭露證據

同 **proof / reason**

▶ The police don't have enough evidence to charge Kim with robbery.
警察沒有足夠的證據來指控金恩搶劫的行為。

② *v.* 證明；清楚指出

同 **confirmation / indication**

實用片語
much in evidence 揭露證據

▶ Your bad eating habits are evidenced by all the junk food in your refrigerator.
你冰箱裡所有的垃圾食物都證明了你不好的飲食習慣。

▶ His influence is much in evidence.
他的影響顯而易見。

evident [ˈev.ə.dənt] *adj.* 明顯的

搭 **clearly evident** 非常明顯

同 **visible / obvious**

▶ It was evident to the dentist that Paul takes good care of his teeth.
以牙醫來看，保羅很明顯地是非常用心在照顧自己的牙齒。

evil [ˈiː.vəl]

① *adj.* 邪惡的

搭 **evil power** 邪惡的力量

同 **hateful / foul**

實用片語
evil eye 惡毒眼光

② *n.* 邪惡

▶ The evil ruler took over all the land.
邪惡的統治者奪取了所有土地。

▶ I arrived late and my boss gave me the evil eye.
我來遲了，而我的老闆射來惡毒的眼光。

▶ There is much evil in the world today.
今日世上有很多邪惡的情事。

exactly [ɪgˈzækt.li] *adv.* 準切地；恰好地

搭 **remember exactly** 確實記得

同 **completely / precisely**

實用片語
does exactly what it says on the tin
表現恰如其分

▶ Those two people jumped at exactly the same time.
這兩個人同時間一起跳起來。

▶ This software is straightforward and does exactly what it says on the tin.
此款軟體的功能呈現恰如其分。

102
exaggerate [ɪgˈzædʒ.ə.reɪt] *v.* 誇大

搭 **deliberately exaggerate** 刻意誇大

同 **fudge / overdo**

▶ Don't exaggerate the details in your stories. Just stick to the facts.
請不要誇大你故事的細節。只要按照事實陳述就好。

examinee [ɪgˌzæməˈni] *n.* 應試者

▶ Each examinee should be prepared for a three-hour test and interview.
每位應試者都應該為三個小時的考試及面談做好準備。

examiner [ɪgˈzæm.ɪ.nɚ] *n.* 主考人

▶ The examiner will read a list of instructions before the test begins.
主考人會在考試之前先唸出一系列的指令。

Exercise 32

I. Derivatives

1. Robert has worked in the educational _____ (establish) for over ten years.

2. Michael went to an outdoor supplies store to rent a tent and buy other camping _____ (equip) for his trip to the mountains.

3. The company asked its employees to do a self- _____ (evaluate) in order to review their own performance.

4. Water, light and air are _____ (essence) for all living things to survive.

5. Five of the fifty _____ (exam) failed in the final test.

II. 中英對應

_____ 1. 估計　(A) estate　(B) estimate　(C) esteem　(D) escape

_____ 2. 散文　(A) estate　(B) essentially　(C) essay　(D) escape

_____ 3. 電扶梯　(A) escalate　(B) essay　(C) elevator　(D) escalator

_____ 4. 誇大　(A) exaggerate　(B) exactly　(C) examination　(D) example

_____ 5. 差事　(A) error　(B) errand　(C) era　(D) erase

excellence [ˈek.səl.əns] *n.* 傑出；卓越

搭 **academic excellence** 學業成就

同 **brilliance / greatness**

▶ Excellence has been shown in this work of art.
這個藝術作品相當傑出。

---

exception [ɪkˈsep.ʃən] *n.* 例外

同 **exclusion / passing over**

實用片語
make an exception 例外，開恩

▶ I have cleaned all of the rooms, with the exception of the kitchen.
我已經把所有的房間都打掃乾淨了，除了廚房以外。

▶ My boss made an exception and let me work from home.
我老闆破例讓我在家工作。

---

103 98 95

exchange [ɪksˈtʃeɪndʒ]

① *n.* 交換

② *v.* 交換

搭 **exchange viewpoints** 交換意見

同 **swap / barter**

實用片語
exchange for 交換

▶ We crossed the road and we all exchanged a friendly greeting.
我們穿越馬路，互相交換了友善的問候。

▶ Please exchange the dollars into pound sterling.
請把美金換成英鎊。

▶ I will need to exchange this T-shirt for a larger size.
我需要將這件上衣換成大尺寸的。

---

excitedly [ɪkˈsaɪ.tɪd·li] *adv.* 興奮地

同 **eagerly / wildly**

▶ The puppies excitedly ran over to their mother.
這些小狗興奮地跑向母狗。

---

excursion [ɪkˈskɜː.ʃən]
n. 遠足；（集體）短途旅行

搭 **sightseeing excursion** 觀光遊覽

同 **trip / journey**

▶ We took an excursion to the countryside.
我們去了一趟鄉下旅遊。

---

exhaust [ɪgˈzɑːst]

① *n.* （引擎排出的）廢氣；排出的氣；排氣管

② *v.* 使精疲力盡；排出氣體

同 **drain / consume**

▶ Inside the city, the exhaust from the cars causes the air to be very polluted.
在都市裡面，汽車的廢氣造成了嚴重的空氣污染。

▶ Working all day in the hot sun exhausted me.
一整天曝露在酷熱的陽光下工作讓我精疲力盡。

99

exhibit [ɪɡˈzɪb.ɪt]

① v. 展示
同 **display / showcase**
② n. 展覽；展示品
同 **viewing / fair**

▶ Stella will exhibit her paintings this weekend.
思緹拉在這個週末會展示她的畫作。

▶ The Titanic exhibit will be here next month. We should go to see it.
鐵達尼號的展示會將於下週在此舉行。我們應該去參觀一下。

 98

exhibition [ˌek.səˈbɪʃ.ən] n. 展覽

搭 **art exhibition** 藝術展覽
同 **performance / show**

▶ The exhibition will be held in the back of the building.
展覽將在大樓的後面舉行。

 102

existence [ɪɡˈzɪs.təns] n. 存在

搭 **independent existence** 獨立存在
同 **presence / reality**

實用片語
have a charmed existence
有護身符，冥冥之中似有保護

▶ Some people question the existence of heaven.
有些人質疑天堂的存在。

▶ Mania seems to have a charmed existence.
曼尼亞好像冥冥之中似有保護。

103

exit [ˈek.sɪt / ˈeg.zɪt]

① n. 出口
② v. 出去
同 **depart / retire**

實用片語
exit stage left 偷溜，靜靜離開

▶ I see the exit we want in the distance.
我看見我們要找的出口就在遠處。

▶ I need to exit immediately.
我得馬上出去。

▶ He suggested Amy exits stage left to avoid trouble.
他建議艾咪靜靜離開避免麻煩。

104 **103** **96**

expand [ɪkˈspænd] v. 擴大；展開

搭 **expand product line** 拓展產品線
同 **broaden / spread**

實用片語
expand into 拓展至…

▶ If my waist continues to expand, I'll need bigger pants.
如果我的腰圍一直擴大，我就需要更大號的褲子了。

▶ Mr. Chen expanded his business into other industries.
陳先生拓展他的事業進入其他產業。

expansion [ɪkˈspæn.ʃən] *n.* 擴張

搭 **market expansion** 市場拓展

同 **extension / growth**

▶ Our company has been able to increase its global expansion faster than we thought possible.
我們的公司一直在進行全球性的擴張；速度比我們原先所想的還要快。

---

expectation [ˌek.spekˈteɪ.ʃən] *n.* 期待；預期

同 **promise / belief**

實用片語
live up to someone's expectations
符合某人期望

▶ The expectation of reading her next novel is overwhelming.
非常期待想讀她的下一本小說。

▶ I hope this movie lives up to my expectations.
我希望這部電影符合我的期望。

---

expense [ɪkˈspens] *n.* 花費；支出

搭 **extra expense** 額外花費

同 **charge / cost**

實用片語
spare no expense 毫不保留

▶ I certainly went to great expense to finish the preparations for my daughter's wedding.
我花了很多錢來完成籌備女兒的婚禮。

▶ We spared no expense in making the guests feel comfortable.
我在讓賓客感到舒適上毫無保留。

97

experiment [ɪkˈsper.ə.mənt]

① *n.* 實驗

搭 **conduct an experiment** 處理實驗

同 **attempt / trial**

② *v.* 進行實驗

同 **investigate / analyze**

實用片語
experiment in 做實驗

▶ I will conduct an experiment to satisfy my curiosity.
我會做一個實驗來滿足我的好奇心。

▶ We will experiment with two compounds in this class.
我們會在班上用兩個化合物來做實驗。

▶ We plan to experiment in new drugs.
我們計劃做實驗在開發新藥上。

---

experimental [ɪkˌsper.əˈmen.təl] *adj.* 實驗性的

搭 **experimental model** 實驗模型

同 **pilot / unproved**

▶ The experimental drug won't be on the market for about 10 years.
那個實驗性的藥品大約十年後才會上市。

---

explanation [ˌek.spləˈneɪ.ʃən] *n.* 解釋

搭 **reasonable explanation** 合理的解釋

同 **comment / description**

▶ Do you have an explanation for why you arrived so late?
你能不能給我們一個解釋，為什麼你這麼晚才到達？

explode [ɪkˈsploʊd] *v.* 爆炸

同 **erupt / blast**

實用片語
explode with 爆發出⋯

▶ The tire will explode if you don't stop filling it with air.
如果你不停止打氣進去的話，這個輪胎會爆掉。

▶ Tom told a joke and the audience exploded with laughter.
湯姆說了個笑話然後觀眾爆出笑聲。

explore [ɪkˈsplɔːr] *v.* 探索；探查；探險

搭 **explore new opportunity** 開拓新機會
同 **research / seek**

▶ Let's arrive early and explore the area before our meeting begins.
讓我們早點抵達，並且在會議開始之前好好地探索一下那個區域。

104

explorer [ɪkˈsplɔːrɚ] *n.* 探險家；勘探者

同 **pioneer / pathfinder**

▶ Early American explorers encountered many dangers.
早期到美洲的探險家遇到很多的危險。

explosion [ɪkˈsploʊʒən] *n.* 爆炸

同 **burst / blast**

▶ The gas explosion left 56 people injured.
氣體爆炸造成五十六個人受傷。

102

explosive [ɪkˈsploʊsɪv]

① *adj.* 爆炸性的
同 **unstable / forceful**

② *n.* 爆炸物；炸藥

▶ The group placed an explosive device on the train.
那群人把一個具爆炸性的裝置安裝在火車上。

▶ The soldiers carefully moved the wagon filled with explosives.
士兵們小心翼翼地移動那部裝滿爆炸物的馬車。

export [ˈek.spɔːrt]

① *v.* 出口

搭 **export textiles** 出口布料
同 **ship / convey**

實用片語
export to 出口到⋯

② *n.* 出口（物資）
同 **freight / transport**

▶ I want to export my new candy line.
我想要出口我的糖果新系列。

▶ We export our products to the US.
我們出口產品到美國。

▶ Bananas and pineapples are the island's main exports.
香蕉和鳳梨是該島的主要出口品。

expose [ɪkˈspoʊz] *v.* 使暴露於⋯

同 disclose / uncover

實用片語
expose to 暴露於⋯

---

exposure [ɪkˈspoʊ.ʒɚ] *n.* 接觸；暴露

同 hazard / uncovering

▶ Wayne became sick after he was exposed to the cold winter weather.
偉恩因接觸了寒冷的冬季氣候而生病。

▶ I never expose my children to violent video games.
我從未讓我的小孩暴露在暴力電玩遊戲中。

▶ The trip to Spain was Celeste's first exposure to a foreign culture.
西班牙之旅是思樂絲特首次接觸異國的文化。

Exercise 33

I. Derivatives

1. According to the news, 25 people were injured in the _____ (explode) on Train 1258 operated by the Taiwan Railway Administration on July 7th.

2. Joy and I went to an interesting _____ (exhibit) called "Terracotta: The Rise and Legacy of Qin Culture" at the National Palace Museum.

3. The treatment is still considered risky and _____ (experiment), so it is too early to tell whether it works.

4. The _____ (expand) of our department will mean the employment of an additional five employees.

5. The movie star's new film has had a lot of _____ (expose) on TV and radio recently.

II. Vocabulary Choice

(A) explanation (B) excellence (C) existence (D) exception (E) exhibit
(F) expectation (G) exhaust (H) exit (I) explosive (J) exchange

1. The designer won a prize for _____ in book design.

2. Debbie went to a bank to _____ some New Taiwan Dollars for Japanese Yen.

3. Joy was expecting an _____ and an apology from James because he stood her up last night.

4. My brother questions the _____ of God and is a believer in evolution.

5. Car and motorcycle _____ fume is the main reason for the city's pollution.

E

98

expression [ɪkˈspreʃ.ən] *n.* 表達；表情

搭 **facial expression** 面部表情

同 **character / remark**

▶ The expression on her face made the whole audience laugh.

她臉上的表情讓所有觀眾都笑了。

---

104 **96**

expressive [ɪkˈspres.ɪv] *adj.* 表現的；表達的

同 **vivid / striking**

▶ Jill's expressive eyes cast a spell on her boyfriend.

吉兒表情豐富的眼神迷住了她的男友。

---

extend [ɪkˈstend] *v.* 延長；伸展

同 **stretch / expand**

實用片語
extend to 延伸，延期

▶ Our teacher extended the deadline for our paper. We have two more weeks.

我們老師延長了我們交作業的最後期限。所以我們又多了兩個星期。

▶ We need to extend the deadline to next week.

我需要延伸截止日期到下週。

---

104 **95**

extent [ɪkˈstent] *n.* 程度；廣度；寬度；長度

同 **degree / matter**

實用片語
to a great extent 大幅，很大程度

▶ We still don't know the full extent of the earthquake's damage.

我們仍然不知道地震所造成的全面損害程度。

▶ We've finished the project to a great extent.

我已經完成大部份的專案了。

96

extreme [ɪkˈstriːm]

① *adj.* 末端的；盡頭的；極度的

同 **utmost / intense**

② *n.* 極端；極度

搭 **climatic extreme** 極端氣候

同 **ultimate / acme**

實用片語
go from one extreme to the other
從一極端到另一極端

▶ Kara is an extreme fitness lover. She exercises 3 hours a day.

卡拉極度愛好健身。她每天運動三小時之多。

▶ Who would do something like? That's an extreme.

誰會做出那種事？真的太極端了。

▶ Kent is unpredictable. He goes from one extreme to the other.

肯特不按牌理出牌，行為極端。

extremely [ɪkˈstriːm.li] *adv.* 極端地；非常

搭 **extremely busy** 相當忙碌

同 **utterly / overly**

▶ Winter in China can be extremely cold.
在中國大陸，冬天可能會非常冷。

---

fable [ˈfeɪ.bəl] *n.* 寓言

實用片語
have a fable for 有故事

▶ I enjoy a good fable from time to time.
我偶而會喜歡讀一則好的寓言故事。

▶ She always had a fable for children.
她總是有適合小孩的寓言。

---

facial [ˈfeɪ.ʃəl] *adj.* 臉的

▶ Brent has too much facial hair. I wish he would shave.
布蘭特臉上的鬍鬚實在是太多了。我希望他能剃一剃。

98
facility [fəˈsɪl.ə.tj]

n. （特定用途的）場所；設備；能力

同 **tact / ability**

▶ The new medical facility is close to your apartment.
新的醫療中心離你的公寓很近。

95
factor [ˈfæk.tə] *n.* 因素

搭 **decisive factor** 決定因素

同 **aspect / element**

實用片語
x factor 獨具特色

▶ Respect is the greatest factor in a marriage.
尊重是婚姻中最大的要素。

▶ In this competitive market, our products have to have an x factor.
在這競爭激烈的市場中，我們的產品必須獨具特色。

100
fade [feɪd] *v.* 褪色；消逝

同 **dim / vanish**

實用片語
fade away 褪色，淡忘

▶ The sun will fade the photo if you display it there.
如果你把照片放在那邊，太陽會讓它褪色。

▶ His memories faded away.
他的記憶逐漸褪色。

---

faint [feɪnt]

① *adj.* 虛弱的；頭暈的

同 **weak / hazy**

▶ The old woman had a faint grip of my arm.
老婦人虛弱地扶著我的手臂。

② *v.* 昏厥；暈倒

搭 **nearly faint**　幾乎昏厥

同 **black out / pass out**

實用片語
faint from　因…昏倒

③ *n.* 昏厥

同 **knockout / dizziness**

---

fairly [ˈfer.li] *adv.* 公平地

同 **resonably / moderately**

---

fairy [ˈfer.i]

① *n.* 精靈；仙子

② *adj.* 仙子的

---

faith [feɪθ] *n.* 信念；信仰

搭 **unshakeable faith**　穩固的信念

同 **belief / truth**

實用片語
lose faith in　對…失去信心

---

faithful [ˈfeɪθ.fəl] *adj.* 忠心的；忠誠的

同 **devoted / loyal**

---

fake [feɪk]

① *adj.* 冒充的

搭 **fake fur**　假的皮毛

同 **counterfeit / bogus**

② *n.* 冒牌貨

③ *v.* 假冒

同 **pretend / fabricate**

實用片語
fake on someone　騙過某人

▶ The boy hadn't eaten all day and almost fainted.
這個男孩一整天都沒吃東西，幾乎昏倒。

▶ She nearly fainted from fear.
她幾乎因為恐懼而昏倒。

▶ No one knew why the woman fell into a faint.
沒人知道這女人為什麼會昏倒。

▶ Everyone had hoped the teacher would judge more fairly.
大家原本都希望老師能更公平的評分。

▶ The fairy buzzed here and there and everywhere.
小精靈一下飛到這裡和那裏，到處飛來飛去。

▶ The child had heard about a mysterious fairy kingdom.
這個小孩曾聽說過有個神祕的精靈王國。

▶ The doctor had a lot of faith and knew everything would be fine.
醫生深信，並且知道一切都會沒事。

▶ I lost my faith in my friends when they turned their backs on me.
當朋友們背棄我時，我對我的朋友失去信心。

▶ The faithful dog waited by the door for his owner to return home each day.
那隻忠心的小狗每天都在門邊等著他的主人回家。

▶ I have been receiving fake checks for over six months.
我六個月以來一直收到假支票。

▶ You are a fake, and the whole community knows it.
你是一個冒牌貨，而整個社區都知道。

▶ You might not know what you're doing, but you can still fake it.
你也許知道自己在做什麼，但你還是有可能是假裝的。

▶ If you fake on me again, I will never speak to you again.
如果你再騙我，我就不會再和你說話了。

185

fame [feɪm] *n.* 名聲

搭 **international fame** 國際知名

同 **acclaim / honor**

實用片語
someone's claim to fame 賴以成名之原因

▶ Randy hopes to someday achieve fame and fortune.
藍帝希望有一天能夠贏得名聲和財富。

▶ His claim to fame is that he composed that popular song.
他賴以成名之原因是他作的那首熱門歌曲。

---

familiar [fəˈmɪl.i.jɚ] *adj.* 熟悉的

同 **routine / usual**

實用片語
familiar with 對⋯熟悉

▶ That historic church looks very familiar to me.
那座深具歷史意義的教堂看起來很眼熟。

▶ I am not familiar with his artwork.
我對他的藝術作品不太熟悉。

---

fan [ˈfæn] *n.* ⋯迷

搭 **devoted fan** 鐵粉

▶ Paul is the singer's biggest fan.
保羅是這位歌手的頭號粉絲。

---

fanatic [fəˈnæt.ɪk] *n.* 狂熱者

同 **devotee / activist**

▶ You truly are a fanatic when it comes to this celebrity.
談到這個名人時，你就變得很狂熱。

---

fancy [ˈfæn.si]

① *n.* 幻想；想像

同 **fantasy / inclination**

② *adj.* 花俏的；豪華的；昂貴的

搭 **fancy restaurant** 高檔餐廳

同 **deluxe / elegant**

③ *v.* 想像

同 **visualize / feature**

▶ These strange ideas all appeared in a fancy.
這些奇怪的想法全都是在一次幻想中產生的。

▶ That is such a fancy cake.
這個蛋糕很花俏。

▶ I fancy myself driving that car.
我想像自己在開那部車。

---

fantastic [fænˈtæs.tɪk] *adj.* 很棒的；想像中的

搭 **fantastic vacation** 極棒的假期

同 **exotic / incredible**

▶ Lauren did a fantastic job in her performance at the concert.
蘿倫在音樂會上有很棒的表現。

---

fantasy [ˈfæn.tə.si] *n.* 幻想；空想

同 **illusion / vision**

▶ The famous movie is a fantasy about a little girl who travels over a rainbow.
這部有名的電影是有關一位小女孩跨過彩虹的幻想片。

fare [fer] *n.* 票價

搭 **bus fare** 公車票價

同 **price / ticket**

► The fare on this coach bus is quite expensive.

這長途客運的票價蠻貴的。

Exercise 34

I. Derivatives

1. Her boss gave her an _____ (express) look when asked about a promotion, and she could see that he was not happy.

2. The local government plans to improve the public toilet _____ (facile) at the metro stations.

3. Inside Out is a _____ (fantasy) animation movie.

4. Dr. Albert Schweitzer was a great humanitarian and a _____ (faith) servant of God.

5. It is _____ (extreme) difficult and tiring to look after the twins alone, so I hired a nanny to help.

II. Vocabulary Choice

(A) fairly   (B) fare   (C) fairy   (D) factor   (E) familiar

(F) extend   (G) fake   (H) extent   (I) faint   (J) fade

1. Upon receiving the shocking news, the woman fell into a dead _____ and had to be taken to hospital for treatment.

2. The teacher tries her best to treat her students _____ but it is not always possible.

3. Price of a product is the single most important _____ for this company's decision to buy it or not.

4. We're planning to _____ our publishing of children's books.

5. The wanted criminal tried to go through immigration at the airport with a _____ passport, but the police arrested him.

Unit 35

farewell [ˌfɛrˈwɛl] *n.* 告別

搭 **farewell party** 送別派對

同 **departure / sendoff**

▶ It was hard to say farewell to my friends, knowing I would miss them terribly.
我很難跟我的朋友們告別，因為我知道我會非常想念他們。

95

farther [ˈfɑːr.ðɚ]

① *adv.* 更遠地

同 **beyond / further**

② *adj.* 更遠的

同 **beyond / longer**

▶ I think the girl ran farther than the boy.
我認為女生跑得比男生更遠。

▶ The farther the shore, the safer we will be.
我們離岸邊越遠，就越安全。

---

fascinated [ˈfæs.ən.eɪ.tɪd] *adj.* 著迷的

同 **spellbound / absorbed**

▶ The children were fascinated by the aquarium.
小朋友們被水族館給迷住了！

---

fascinating [ˈfæs.ən.eɪ.tɪŋ]
adj. 非常精彩的；迷人的；令人神魂顛倒的

同 **interesting / appealing**

▶ The TV show about space was fascinating.
有關太空的電視節目實在是太精彩了！

101

fashion [ˈfæʃ.ən]

① *n.* 時尚

搭 **fashion industry** 流行產業

同 **fad / trend**

② *v.* 製作

實用片語
come into fashion 帶起流行

▶ The secretary knew everything about fashion.
這個秘書對時尚無所不知。

▶ You may want to fashion a table runner from scraps of material.
你也許會想要用碎布製作出一張桌旗。

▶ I really think this kind of design will come into fashion.
我真的認為這種設計會帶起流行。

---

fashionable [ˈfæʃ.ən.ə.bəl]
adj. 時髦的；流行的

搭 **no longer fashionable** 退流行

同 **stylish / trendy**

▶ A fashionable wardrobe is an asset to a business woman.
時髦的服裝是職場女性的資產。

fasten [ˈfæs.ən]   *n.*   繫緊

搭 **fasten seatbelt**   繫上安全帶

同 **tighten / affix**

實用片語
fasten up   扣起，弄緊

► Please fasten your seatbelt before the flight takes off.
請在飛機起飛前繫上安全帶。

► Please fasten up your jacket. It's cold outside.
外面很冷。請拉上你的夾克。

---

fatal [ˈfeɪ.təl]   *adj.*   致命的；命運的

同 **fateful / mortal**

► Dennis suffered from a fatal disease and wasn't able to recover.
丹尼斯得到了致命的疾病，且沒有復原。

---

fate [feɪt]   *n.*   命運

搭 **tragic fate**   悲慘命運

同 **chance / outcome**

實用片語
seal one's fate   決定自身的命運（負面）

► Fate did not play a positive role in his life.
命運沒在他的生命中成為助力。

► Jack's cheating sealed his fate.
傑克的欺騙決定他自身的命運。

---

faucet [ˈfɑː.sət]   *n.*   水龍頭

► The faucet is quite rusted.
水龍頭鏽得蠻厲害的。

---

faulty [ˈfɑːl.tʃi]   *adj.*   有毛病的；有缺點的

同 **defective / invalid**

► This faulty remote-control does not work anymore.
這個有毛病的遙控器不能用了。

---

favorable [ˈfeɪ.vər.ə.bəl]

adj. 適合的；有幫助的；贊成的

同 **positive / agreeable**

► Driving home was easy due to the favorable weather.
由於氣候怡人，所以開車回家很舒服。

---

fax [ˈfæks]

① *n.* 傳真

實用片語
junk fax   垃圾傳真

② *v.* 發傳真

► I need a new fax machine.
我需要一台新的傳真機。

► We've got a pile of junk faxes today.
我們今天收到一堆垃圾傳真。

► Please fax me the documents immediately.
請立刻把文件傳真給我。

feast [fiːst]

① *n.* 盛宴

搭 **wedding feast** 婚宴

同 **festival / gala**

實用片語

a feast for the eyes 大飽眼福

② *v.* 盡情地吃；參加盛宴

同 **dine / entertain**

---

feather [ˈfeð.ɚ] *n.* 羽毛

---

feature [ˈfiː.tʃɚ]

① *n.* 五官；特徵；特色

搭 **notable feature** 特殊特色

同 **quality / component**

② *v.* 以⋯為特色

同 **headline / spotlight**

實用片語

feature someone in 想像某人穿⋯

---

ferry [ˈfer.i]

① *n.* 渡輪；渡船

② *v.* （乘渡船）渡過

同 **shuttle / carry**

實用片語

ferry someone around 接來送去

---

fertile [ˈfɝː.təl]

adj. （土地）肥沃的；（動植物）多產的

搭 **fertile soil** 肥沃的土壤

同 **arable / abundant**

► The school provided a feast for all of the graduates and their parents.
學校為了畢業生們以及他們的家長舉辦了一個盛宴。

► His new film is truly a feast for the eyes.
他的新片真是讓人大飽眼福。

► At the restaurant, we feasted on steak and lobster.
在餐廳裡，我們盡情地享用牛排和龍蝦。

► Look at the variety of colors in that one feather.
你看那片羽毛上面的五顏六色。

► Your facial features are very delicate.
你的五官很細緻。

► We will feature your article in our next magazine.
我們會在下一本雜誌上以你的文章作為專題報導。

► I can feature you in that funny hat.
我可以想像你戴那頂好笑的帽子。

► The ferry from Hong Kong to Macau is quite convenient.
從香港到澳門的渡輪相當的便利。

► We ferried from Cozumel, Mexico to see the ancient ruins of Tulum.
我們從墨西哥的寇如梅爾小島搭渡輪去看古代的圖倫遺跡。

► I spent the whole day ferrying children around.
我花了一整天把小孩接來送去。

► Land near the river is expensive because the ground is very fertile.
靠近河流的土地非常昂貴，因為那裡的土壤十分肥沃。

fetch [fetʃ]

① v. （去）拿來

同 **yield / obtain**

實用片語
fetch in 帶進，拉進

② n. 拿取

▶ Stan taught his dog Fido to fetch the ball.
史丹教他的小狗肥嘟去撿球。

▶ Can you fetch in more firewood, please?
可以請你拿更多柴火進來嗎？

▶ The puppy is too young to understand how to play fetch.
那隻幼犬太小，牠根本不懂得怎麼玩『你丟我撿』。

---

fiction [ˈfɪk.ʃən] n. 小說

搭 **fiction novel** 科幻小說

同 **drama / novel**

▶ John Grisham is a very popular writer of fiction.
約翰·葛里遜是一名很受歡迎的小說家。

---

fierce [ˈfɪrs] adj. 兇猛的；猛烈的

同 **stormy / furious**

▶ The Mongols were recognized as fierce fighters.
蒙古人被認為是最兇猛的戰士。

---

file [faɪl]

① n. 檔案

② v. 把…歸檔

搭 **file a lawsuit** 提出告訴

同 **register / arrange**

實用片語
file away 歸檔

▶ The file cabinet should be moved against the wall.
這個檔案櫃應該移到靠牆的位置。

▶ Please file this legal form in the bottom drawer.
請把這份法律表格歸到最下層的抽屜。

▶ Please file away this report.
請將此報告歸檔。

96

finance [ˈfaɪ.næns]

① n. 財務狀況；財政

同 **banking / investment**

② v. 籌措資金

同 **fund / underwrite**

▶ The company's finances are a mess. We need an accountant.
公司的財務狀況一團糟。我們需要一位會計師。

▶ The bank will finance my new car.
那家銀行讓我貸款購買新車。

---

financial [faɪˈnæn.ʃəl / fəˈnæn.ʃəl] adj. 財政的

搭 **financial management** 財務管理

同 **monetary / commercial**

▶ The financial advisor gave us some good suggestions.
那位財務顧問給了我們一些很好的建議。

---

finished [ˈfɪn.ɪʃt] adj. 已完成的；結束了的

同 **complete / done**

▶ We finally delivered the finished project to the boss.
我們終於把完成的專案交給老闆了。

Exercise 35

I. 中英對應

_____ 1. 盛宴   (A) feast   (B) feature   (C) fast   (D) fasten

_____ 2. 小說   (A) fitness   (B) fierce   (C) fiction   (D) fetch

_____ 3. 告別   (A) faith   (B) farewell   (C) fairytale   (D) farther

_____ 4. 羽毛   (A) feather   (B) feature   (C) farther   (D) father

_____ 5. 水龍頭   (A) faulty   (B) facial   (C) fault   (D) faucet

II. Vocabulary Choice

(A) fascinated   (B) farther   (C) financial   (D) fashion   (E) favor

(F) favorable   (G) fetch   (H) feather   (I) finance   (J) fascinating

1. Florence is a _____ city, full of impressive historical sights and attractions.

2. The new film received _____ reviews from critics and I recommend that you see it.

3. Harry lost his job last month so he is in _____ difficulties.

4. The elders were too tired to walk any _____ , so they took a taxi home.

5. Her supervisor asked her to _____ the guest a cup of coffee.

Unit 36

firecracker [ˈfaɪrˌkræk.ə] *n.* 鞭炮

▶ Timmy was hurt when a firecracker exploded in his hand.
當鞭炮在提米手中爆開時，他受傷了。

---

fireplace [ˈfaɪr.pleɪs] *n.* 壁爐

▶ Let's go warm up by the fireplace.
讓我們到壁爐旁取暖一下吧。

---

firework [ˈfaɪr.wɝːk] *n.* 爆竹；煙火

▶ Where do people buy fireworks?
大家都到哪裡買爆竹？

---

fist [ˈfɪst]

① *n.* 拳頭

② *v.* 握拳

實用片語
hand over fist 快速穩當地

▶ Show me your fist.
給我看你的拳頭。

▶ The little boy fisted his hands to show he was angry.
這小男孩雙手握拳來表示他生氣了。

▶ The company is making money hand over fist.
公司快速穩當地賺錢。

---

flame [fleɪm]

① *n.* 火焰

搭 **Olympic flame** 奧運火把

同 **flash / flare**

② *v.* 點燃

同 **blaze / fire**

實用片語
flame with anger 怒火中燒

▶ The flame of the candle is about to be snuffed out.
蠟燭的火焰就快要被吹熄了。

▶ The fire flamed in the fireplace as guests came in from the snow.
賓客從雪地裡進到屋內時，壁爐中的火燃了起來。

▶ His eyes flamed with anger.
他的眼睛內燃燒著怒火。

---

flatter [ˈflæt̬.ə] *v.* 奉承；討好；諂媚

同 **complement / sweet-talk**

▶ You flattered my mother when you complimented her cooking.
當你稱讚我媽媽烹飪的好手藝時，就是在討好她。

---

flavor [ˈfleɪ.vər / ˈfleɪ.və]

① *n.* 味道

同 **seasoning / aroma**

▶ I truly enjoy the flavor of steak.
我真的很喜歡牛排的味道。

② *v.* 給…調味
同 **spice / lace**

▶ Add some flavor to that dish you are making.
多加些調味料在你正在煮的菜裡面。

---

flea [ˈfli] *n.* 跳蚤

實用片語
flea market 跳蚤市場

▶ The flea jumped from my cat to the back of my leg.
一隻跳蚤從我的貓咪身上跳到我的腿後面。

▶ I like our town's flea market.
我喜歡我們鎮上的跳蚤市場。

---

flee [ˈfli] *v.* 逃走

搭 **flee abroad** 逃到國外
同 **escape / take off**
實用片語
flee from 自…逃脫

▶ At the first sign of trouble, you should flee the scene.
你一看到有麻煩的跡象時，就應該要逃離現場。

▶ Sometimes, people want to flee from their busy lives in big cities.
有時候人們想從大都市的忙碌生活中逃脫。

---

flesh [fleʃ] *n.* 肉

▶ The tiger smelled flesh and became hungry.
老虎聞到肉味就餓了。

---

flexible [ˈflek.sə.bəl] *adj.* 有彈性的

搭 **flexible personality** 有彈性 / 溫和的個性
同 **elastic / formable**

▶ Some cellphone screens are flexible enough to bend, but not break.
有些手機的螢幕是有彈性的，你可以折彎它，但不會折斷它。

101
float [floʊt]

① *v.* 漂流
同 **glide / slide**
實用片語
float a loan 舉債
② *n.* 漂流物

▶ Our boat just floated on the lake.
我們的船只是在湖上漂浮著。

▶ We need money so we have to float a loan.
我們需要錢，所以舉債。

▶ Put the float between the dock and the side of the boat.
把漂流物放在甲板和船邊之間。

---

flock [flɑːk]

① *n.* 一群
同 **herd / colony**

▶ There's a flock of sheep on the hill.
山丘上有一群羊。

② v. 聚集；成群地來去

同 **gather / collect**

實用片語
flock into 湧進

▶ Let's flock together for our private meeting.
讓我們聚在一起開個私人會議吧。

▶ People flock into the shopping center every weekend.
每個週末人們湧進購物中心。

---

flooding [ˈflʌd.ɪŋ] *n.* 淹水；洪災；氾濫

▶ The flooding in the house ruined all the furniture.
淹到屋子裡的水破壞了所有的家具。

---

(98)

fluent [ˈfluː.ənt] *adj.* 流利的；流暢的

搭 **fluent English speaker** 英文流利的人

同 **smooth / flowing**

▶ Eleni was born in Singapore, grew up in Europe and is fluent in five languages.
伊蕾妮出生在新加坡，然後在歐洲長大，現在可以說五種流利的語言。

---

flunk [ˈflʌŋk]

① v. 不及格；使（某人）不及格

實用片語
flunk out 退學

② n. 失敗

同 **drop out / miss**

▶ Ron flunked the weekly test because he didn't study for it.
榮恩因為沒有準備，所以這次週考不及格。

▶ Cindy flunked out of the university after just one year.
辛蒂只待一年就從大學退學。

▶ Stewart felt like a flunk after he failed the entrance exam.
史都華在入學考試落榜時，感到自己是個失敗者。

---

flush [ˈflʌʃ]

① v. 沖洗

同 **cleanse / drench**

實用片語
flush out 沖掉，排出

② n. 沖洗

搭 **a flush toilet** 抽水馬桶

▶ Barb flushed the old medicine down the drain.
芭爾芭將舊的藥丸沖入排水管。

▶ Use water to flush the sand out of your eyes.
用水沖掉眼中的沙子。

▶ A flush of cool water washed away the dirt in my eye.
我用冷水沖洗眼睛裡的灰塵。

---

foam [foʊm]

① n. 泡沫

▶ Ben used so much soap when taking a shower that he had foam all over his body.
班恩沖澡的時候用了太多的肥皂，現在他全身都是泡沫。

② *v.* 起泡沫
同 **lather / bubble**

▶ The dog must be sick because he is foaming at the mouth.
那隻狗一定是生病了，因為牠口吐白沫。

---

fold [foʊld]

① *v.* 摺疊
搭 **fold in half** 折成兩半
同 **bend / tuck**
實用片語
fold up 折起，折疊
② *n.* 摺疊；摺痕
同 **pleat / tuck**

▶ Please fold your paper for the game.
請把紙折起來玩遊戲。

▶ Please fold up that box and put it away.
請折好那個箱子並放到旁邊。

▶ There should be a fold in that style of skirt.
那種樣式的裙子應該要有一個摺子。

---

folk [foʊk] *n.* 人們
實用片語
different strokes for different folks
品味不同，各有所好

▶ Folks need to understand that change doesn't happen immediately.
大家要明白改變不會立即發生。

▶ Just do whatever you like. Different strokes for different folks.
儘管做你喜歡的事。品味不同，各有所好。

---

follower [ˈfɑː.loʊ.ɚ] *n.* 追隨者；信徒
搭 **loyal follower** 忠誠信徒
同 **worshiper / backer**

▶ I am a follower of wise teachings.
我相信智慧的教導。

---

fond [fɑːnd] *adj.* 喜歡的
同 **amorous / lovesome**
實用片語
be fond of 喜愛

▶ I am very fond of pink tulips.
我很喜歡粉紅色的鬱金香。

▶ I'm fond of ice cream.
我喜歡冰淇淋。

---

forbid [fɚˈbɪd] *v.* 禁止
同 **ban / deny**

▶ I forbid you to go out tonight!
我今晚禁止你外出。

---

forecast [ˈfɔːr.kæst]

① *n.* 預測
搭 **weather forecast** 氣象預報
同 **prediction / foresight**

▶ I watched today's weather forecast to find out if it is going to rain.
我看了一下今天的天氣預報，看看是否會下雨。

② *v.* 作預測
同 **anticipate / foresee**

---

forehead [ˈfɑr·hed] *n.* 前額
搭 **smooth forehead** 光滑的額頭

▶ The price of gas is forecast to drop again this month.
這個月的油價預測將會再下降。

- -

▶ My forehead can become very itchy in extreme heat.
在極高的溫度下，我的額頭會變得很癢。

Exercise 36

I. 中英對應

_____ 1. 沖洗　(A) flash　(B) flush　(C) flesh　(D) flunk

_____ 2. 壁爐　(A) firecracker　(B) fireplace　(C) firework　(D) firefighter

_____ 3. 拳頭　(A) fist　(B) feast　(C) feet　(D) fit

_____ 4. 喜歡的　(A) fold　(B) found　(C) fond　(D) font

_____ 5. 奉承　(A) flatten　(B) flatter　(C) flatness　(D) flexible

II. Vocabulary Choice

(A) favor　(B) forbids　(C) flexible　(D) flock　(E) flow

(F) floats　(G) flavor　(H) flunk　(I) forecast　(J) flesh

1. Daniel likes his new job a lot for it offers _____ working hours.

2. My mother uses fresh herbs to _____ the soup and it is delicious.

3. The new law _____ smoking in public places, including even at bus stops.

4. According to the weather _____ , a typhoon is approaching and will impact Taiwan in 30 hours.

5. The tourists watched the colorful Carnival _____ as they moved through the streets of Rio.

forever [fərˈev·ər] *adv.* 永遠

同 **eternally / always**

實用片語
forever and a day 極長久，很久遠

▶ No pet can live forever.
寵物不會永遠活著。

▶ It's been forever and a day since I last saw you.
我上次看到你好像是很久以前的事了。

---

103 102 96

formation [fɔːrˈmeɪ.ʃən] *n.* 結構；形成

搭 **family formation** 家庭結構

同 **creation / arrangement**

▶ The unique rock formations look like works of art.
那些岩石的獨特造型看起來像是藝術品。

101

formula [ˈfɔːr.mjə.lə]

n. 方案；慣用語；公式；配方

搭 **scientific formula** 科學運算

同 **recipe / blueprint**

▶ The new formula for increasing the company's profits is working well.
那個提升公司獲利的新方案正在順利地進著。

---

fort [fɔːrt] *n.* 堡壘

同 **camp / castle**

實用片語
hold the fort 看門，看家

▶ The settlers found safety inside the fort.
殖民者進到堡壘內以求安全。

▶ You have to stay at home and hold the fort.
你必須待在家裡看家。

---

forth [fɔːrθ] *adv.* 向前

同 **away / forward**

▶ You will move forth in everything you do.
你會在所做的每件事上都往前行。

---

fortunate [ˈfɔːr.tʃən.ət] *adj.* 幸運的

同 **lucky / encouraging**

▶ We were fortunate to have passed through the tunnel an hour before the landslide.
我們很幸運地在土石流坍方之前的一小時通過了隧道。

---

96 95

fortunately [ˈfɔːr.tʃən.ət.li] *adv.* 幸運地；僥倖地

同 **luckily / successfully**

▶ My parents fortunately avoided the traffic accident.
我的父母很幸運地避開了那場車禍。

fortune [ˈfɔːr.tʃuːn] *n.* 財富

搭 **make a fortune** 賺很多錢

同 **capital / estate**

實用片語
make a fortune 賺很多錢

▶ Mary made a fortune selling products online.
瑪麗在網路上販售商品結果賺了一大筆財富。

▶ He made a fortune on the stock market.
他在股市賺了很多錢。

---

 fossil [ˈfɑː.səl]

① *n.* 化石
② *adj.* 化石的

▶ Beth and her class will take a trip to search for dinosaur fossils.
貝絲和她們全班會去一趟尋找恐龍化石之旅。

▶ The discovery of fossil insects provided important information about ancient environments.
那些已成化石的昆蟲的發現提供了有關古代環境的重要資訊。

---

 found [faʊnd] *v.* 建立

同 **begin / organize**

▶ John's father founded the company.
約翰的爸爸創立這家公司。

---

 foundation [faʊnˈdeɪ.ʃən] *n.* 地基；建立；創辦

同 **establish / start**

▶ Inspectors found a crack in the building's foundation.
勘察員在大樓的地基上發現了一道裂痕。

---

 founder [ˈfaʊn.dɚ] *n.* 創辦人；創立者

搭 **company founder** 公司創辦人

同 **builder / designer**

▶ The company's founder was born in Italy.
這家公司的創辦人出生於義大利。

---

fountain [ˈfaʊn.tɪn] *n.* 噴泉

▶ The ornate fountain on the front lawn is beautiful.
屋子前面草坪上裝飾華麗的噴泉好美。

---

 fragrance [ˈfreɪ.grəns] *n.* 芬芳；香氣

▶ A sweet fragrance reached us long before we entered the flower garden.
遠在我們進入花園之前，一陣陣的花香就飄向我們。

fragrant [ˈfreɪ.grənt] *adj.* 芳香的

搭 **mildly fragrant** 溫和香味

同 **aromatic / savory**

▶ The fragrant perfume smells like roses.
這瓶香氣十足的香水聞起來像玫瑰花。

---

frame [freɪm]

① *n.* 框架；骨架

搭 **picture frame** 畫框

同 **structure / framework**

② *v.* 給…裝框

同 **build / compose**

實用片語
frame in 為…裝框

▶ This picture frame is too small. You'll need something larger.
這個相框太小了。你需要一個再大一點的。

▶ Your paintings are beautiful! You should frame them and hang them in your apartment.
你的畫作好漂亮。你應該把它們都框起來，然後掛在你的公寓裡。

▶ We chose to frame the photo in a wooden frame.
我們選擇把相片裝在木頭框中。

---

freeway [ˈfriː.weɪ] *n.* 高速公路

▶ The freeway is very crowded at this time of day.
高速公路在這個時段會很擁擠。

100

freeze [friːz]

① *v.* 結冰；凍結

同 **frost / harden**

② *n.* 凍結；結冰

實用片語
freeze up 怯場，凍住

▶ We will watch the water freeze.
我們會看著水結冰。

▶ Our homemade ice cream didn't taste right because the freeze wasn't long enough.
我們自製的冰淇淋味道還沒到位，因為還未完全凍結。

▶ When I stood in front of the audience, I froze up.
當我站在觀眾前，我怯場了。

---

freezing [ˈfriː.zɪŋ] *adj.* 極冷的

搭 **freezing point** 結冰點

同 **icy / frigid**

▶ Why are you wearing so little in this freezing weather?
你為什麼在這麼冷的天氣穿那麼少？

---

frequency [ˈfriː.kwən.si] *n.* 頻繁；頻率

同 **commonness / density**

▶ Scott began missing work with increasing frequency.
史考特曠職的頻率越來越高了。

frequent [ˈfriː.kwənt]

① *adj.* 頻繁的；時常的

搭 **frequent visitor** 常來訪者

同 **constant / recurring**

② *v.* 常去

同 **attend / overrun**

▶ I enjoy making frequent visits to my grandmother's home.
我很喜歡經常去探望我的祖母。

▶ Bill frequents this Italian restaurant.
比爾常去這家義大利餐廳。

---

freshman [ˈfreʃ.mən] *n.* 新生

▶ Cecilia is a freshman in high school. She is learning many new things this year.
西西里雅是位高中的新生。她今年學了很多的東西。

---

friendship [ˈfrend.ʃɪp] *n.* 友誼

▶ Your friendship means a lot to me.
你的友誼對我很重要。

---

frightened [ˈfraɪ.tənd] *adj.* 受驚嚇的；害怕的

搭 **frightened to death** 嚇得半死

同 **afraid / fearful**

▶ The frightened child hid behind the door.
那個受到驚嚇的小孩躲在門的後面。

---

frightening [ˈfraɪ.tən.ɪŋ] *adj.* 令人恐懼的

同 **daunting / fearsome**

▶ The frightening thunderstorm caused the baby to cry.
那嚇人的暴雷雨把嬰兒給嚇哭了。

Exercise 37

I. Multiple Choice

(   ) 1. Both Mary and Joseph are __ of this college.

    (A) freshman   (B) fresh   (C) freshmen   (D) flesh

(   ) 2. There was a car accident on the __ .

    (A) freezer   (B) freeway   (C) foundation (D) fort

(   ) 3. This dinosaur __ may be over 70 million years old.

    (A) fossil   (B) fragrance   (C) forest   (D) facility

(   ) 4. Janelle likes to go skating on the lake after it __ in winter.

    (A) freezer   (B) freezes   (C) flee   (D) freely

(   ) 5. David's eyeglasses __ is broken, he needs to buy a new one.

    (A) flame   (B) formation   (C) fragrant   (D) frame

II. Derivatives

1. I can smell the _____ (fragrant) of the cut flowers in the living room.

2. There was a fire in our office, but _____ (fortunate) we discovered it soon after it started and we could put it out before it caused too much damage.

3. Getting stuck in the elevator alone after hours was the most _____ (frighten) experience of my life.

4. The pastor believes that Christianity is the _____ (found) of a civilized society.

5. Drunk-driving accidents have been occurring at this intersection with increasing _____ (frequent).

frisbee [ˈfrɪz.bi] *n.* 飛盤

▶ The children played frisbee in the park after school.
小朋友們放學之後到公園去玩飛盤。

frost [frɑːst]

① *n.* 霜
② *v.* 結霜
同 **blight / ice**

實用片語
frost over 結霜

▶ The frost on the windows formed some pretty designs.
窗戶上的霜結出很多漂亮的圖案。

▶ The ground frosted over. Now my strawberry plants are ruined.
土地都結霜了。現在我種的草莓也都毀了。

▶ The windows frosted over.
窗戶上都結霜了。

frosty [ˈfrɑː.sti] *adj.* 結霜的
同 **chilly / frigid**

▶ The frosty windows were difficult to see out of.
我們很難從結霜的窗戶看到外面。

frown [ˈfraʊn]

① *v.* 皺眉以表不滿
同 **glare / glower**

實用片語
frown upon 看不慣
② *n.* 皺眉

▶ My mom frowned at me when I called my sister a name.
我罵妹妹的時候，媽媽不滿地對著我皺了眉頭。

▶ My parents frowned upon my choice of boyfriend.
我的父母不滿意我選擇男友的標準。

▶ My dad's frown let me know that he wasn't happy with my behavior.
爸爸用皺眉頭讓我知道他對我的表現不太滿意。

frozen [ˈfroʊ.zən] *adj.* 冰凍的；凍結的
同 **chilled / ice-cold**

▶ It is easy to slip and fall on the frozen ground over there.
你很容易在那邊結冰的地上滑倒。

103 102 99
frustrate [ˈfrʌs.treɪt] *v.* 使氣餒；使灰心
同 **confront / depress**

▶ Ken was frustrated he couldn't exercise because of his injury.
肯恩因為受傷而不能運動，使他感到很氣餒。

96
frustration [frʌsˈtreɪ.ʃən] *n.* 挫折
搭 **experience frustration** 陷入低潮
同 **setback / obstacle**

▶ My frustration with this project is caused by a lack of progress.
我對這個計畫案很沮喪，因為根本沒有進展。

fry [ˈfraɪ]

① v. 煎；炒

② n. 油炸物

▶ I want to fry the fish on an open flame.
我想要在明火上煎魚。

▶ I'm just going to take one fry off your plate.
我只是想從你的盤子裡拿一片油炸物。

---

fuel [ˈfjuː.əl]

① n. 燃料

② v. 加燃料

同 **feed / incite**

實用片語
add fuel to the fire 火上加油

▶ Airline prices have gone up because fuel is so expensive.
機票票價全面上漲，因為燃料實在是太貴了。

▶ Solar cars are fueled by the power of the sun.
太陽能汽車是透過太陽能來供給燃料。

▶ His bad attitude just added fuel to the fire.
他的惡劣態度只是雪上加霜。

 101

fulfill [fʊlˈfɪl] v. 履行（諾言）；執行（命令等）

搭 **fulfill dream** 實現夢想

同 **achieve / finish**

▶ Stacie fulfilled her promise of being home for my birthday.
絲黛西履行了她會回家幫我慶生的諾言。

---

fulfillment [fʊlˈfɪl·mənt] n. 實現

同 **achievement / contentment**

▶ Becoming president of the university is the fulfillment of one of Nick's dreams.
當上大學校長實現了尼克其中一個夢想。

---

fully [ˈfʊl.i] adv. 完全地；充分地

同 **entirely / totally**

▶ My fully repaired computer works perfectly now.
我的電腦已完全修好，現在運作得非常好。

---

functional [ˈfʌŋk.ʃən.əl]

adj. 能正常運作的；有功能的；實用的

同 **practical / utilitarian**

▶ My car isn't great to look at, but it's very functional.
我的汽車看起來不怎麼樣，但它的性能非常好。

---

fund [ˈfʌnd]

① n. 資金

搭 **allocate fund** 撥款

同 **stock / supply**

② v. 資助；提供資金

同 **finance / endow**

▶ The new company needs funds to survive.
這間新公司需要資金才能營運下去。

▶ Angela's parents funded her college tuition.
安琪拉的父母資助了她的大學學費。

fundamental [ˌfʌn.dəˈmen.t̮əl]

97

① *adj.* 基本的；主要的

搭 **fundamental subjects** 基本科技

同 **elemental / crucial**

② *n.* 基本原則；根本要素

同 **component / cornerstone**

▶ Our company has certain fundamental principles that we cannot change.
我們公司有一些特定的基本原則是無法改變的。

▶ I didn't do well in algebra because I never understood the fundamentals.
我的代數修得不太好，因為我從來不懂得它的基本原則。

F

funeral [ˈfju:.nə.əl] *n.* 葬禮

▶ Hundreds attended our principal's funeral. He was greatly loved by many people.
數以百計的人來參加我們校長的喪禮。他深受大家的愛戴。

fur [ˈfɚ] *n.* 毛皮

▶ I love the feel of real fur.
我喜歡真皮毛的觸感。

101

furious [ˈfʊr.i.əs] *adj.* 狂怒的

搭 **furious customer** 憤怒的客戶

同 **angry / mad**

▶ Kevin became furious when he found out that I wrecked his car.
當凱文得知我撞壞了他的車時，他勃然大怒。

furnish [ˈfɚ:.nɪʃ]

v. 給（房間）配置（家具）；供給

同 **equip / fix up**

▶ My new apartment already has furniture in it, so I won't need to furnish it.
我的新公寓裡面已經附有家具了，所以我不需要再添家具。

furnished [ˈfɚ:.nɪʃt]

adj. （房間或房子）配置有家具的；供給的

同 **equipped / provided**

▶ They rented a furnished apartment.
他們租了一間配置好家具的公寓。

furniture [ˈfɚ:.nɪ.tʃə] *n.* 傢俱

搭 **antique furniture** 老骨董傢俱

同 **appliance / equipment**

▶ Your furniture gives the room a very comfortable feeling.
你的家具帶給房間一種很舒適的感覺。

103

furthermore [ˈfɚ:.ðə.mɔːr] *adv.* 此外；再者

同 **additionally / moreover**

▶ I don't know why my brothers are arguing, and furthermore, I refuse to get involved.
我不知道我的兄弟們為何爭吵，此外我也拒絕介入。

gallery [ˈɡæl.ə.i] *n.* 畫廊

> ► Let's go to the art gallery this weekend to see the new exhibit.
> 我們這星期去畫廊去看那個新展覽吧！

---

gallon [ˈɡæl.ən] *n.* 加侖（容量）

> ► That is not enough milk. I need at least a gallon.
> 這牛奶還不夠，我至少需要一加侖。

---

gamble [ˈɡæm.bəl]

① *v.* 賭博
同 **bet / speculate**
② *n.* 賭博

> ► Robert loves to gamble and has lost so much money already.
> 羅伯喜歡賭博，他已經輸掉許多錢。
>
> ► Ross made a gamble when he sold his house to start-up a new company.
> 羅斯把房子賣掉去開創一家新公司，可說是一場賭博。

Exercise 38

I. 中英對應

_____ 1. 葬禮　　(A) funny　　(B) funeral　　(C) fund　　(D) function

_____ 2. 畫廊　　(A) garage　　(B) gather　　(C) gallery　　(D) gateway

_____ 3. 實用的　(A) functional　(B) function　(C) functionally　(D) functionality

_____ 4. 狂怒的　(A) fierce　　(B) furnish　　(C) fury　　(D) furious

_____ 5. 皺眉　　(A) from　　(B) front　　(C) frown　　(D) frost

II. Derivatives

1. They bought some expensive _____ (furnish) after they moved into their new house.

2. The river is completely _____ (freeze) over, but be careful because the ice might break.

3. Her relationship with the writers is _____ (fundament) to her work as an editor.

4. After losing the game, there is a sense of _____ (frustrate) among players.

5. To become an animator was the _____ (fulfill) of my life's dream.

gambler [ˈgæm.blɚ] *n.* 賭徒

▶ The gamblers lost a lot of money on the race.
賭徒們在這場比賽中輸掉很多錢。

---

gambling [ˈgæm.blɪŋ] *n.* 賭博

▶ Gambling is not allowed in this city.
這個城市禁止賭博。

---

gang [ˈgæŋ]

① *n.* 一幫歹徒
② *v.* 集結；結夥

▶ The gang likes to terrorize the neighborhood.
這幫歹徒喜歡恐嚇鄰近地區的居民。

▶ We need to gang together to finish the job.
我們需要一起合作完成這個工作。

---

gangster [ˈgæŋ.stɚ]
n. 幫派份子；一幫歹徒；流氓

▶ That area is known for having many gangsters. I think we should avoid it.
那個地區是有名的幫派份子聚集處。我想我們應該避開。

---

gap [ˈgæp] *n.* 間隙；缺口

搭 **wealth gap** 貧富差距
同 **chasm / crack**

實用片語
mind the gap 注意空隙

▶ Please mind the gap when you step on the train.
上火車時請留意間隙。

▶ Your train is coming. Please mind the gap.
你的火車來了。請注意空隙。

---

garlic [ˈgɑːr.lɪk] *n.* 大蒜

▶ The garlic in this dish really makes it taste good.
這盤菜裡的大蒜讓這道菜很美味。

---

gasoline/gas [ˈgæs.əl.iːn / gæs] *n.* 汽油

▶ I am in desperate need of gasoline for my car.
我的車迫切需要汽油。

---

gaze [geɪz]

① *v.* 凝視

搭 **gaze unblinkingly** 凝視（眼睛不眨一下）
同 **peek / look**

▶ The mother gazed at her new baby lovingly.
那位母親充滿愛意地凝視著她的新生兒。

gaze at 凝視

② *v.* 讀取（電腦資訊）

同 **approach / admission**

▶ Jack stood there gazing at the sky.
傑克站在那裏凝視天空。

▶ Tim's gaze followed the pretty new student.
提姆的目光緊緊地跟隨著那位漂亮的新生。

---

gear [ˈgɪr]

① *n.* 齒輪

② *v.* 使⋯適合；加上裝備

同 **adapt / tailor**

▶ You need to clean the mud off your bicycle gears before you go riding.
在你出發騎車之前，需要把自行車齒輪上的泥巴先清洗掉。

▶ The car is geared for off-road racing.
這部車加添裝備使其適合越野比賽。

---

gene [dʒiːn] *n.* 基因

▶ Genes determine your hair and eye color.
基因決定你的頭髮和眼睛的顏色。

95

generally [ˈdʒen.ə r.əl.i]

adv. 一般地；廣泛地；概括地

同 **mainly / typically**

▶ Fishing is generally known to be a very relaxing activity.
釣魚一般被認為是種非常鬆弛身心的活動。

---

generation [ˌdʒen.əˈreɪ.ʃən] *n.* 世代

搭 **generation gap** 世代差異

同 **breed / time**

▶ Ron's family lived in the same town for generations.
榮恩的家人住在同一個鎮上已經有好幾代了。

102

generosity [ˌdʒen.əˈrɑː.sə.tj]

n. 慷慨；寬宏大量

同 **hospitality / kindness**

▶ Mason is known for his generosity. He always helps those in need.
梅森以慷慨出名。他總是在幫助有需要的人。

---

genius [ˈdʒiː.ni.əs] *n.* 天才；天賦

搭 **creative genius** 創意天才

同 **accomplishment / aptitude**

stroke of genius 神來一筆

▶ Mozart was a musical genius, who composed music from the age of 5.
莫札特是位音樂天才，他從五歲起就開始作曲了。

▶ Your idea was a stroke of genius.
你的想法真是神來一筆。

genuine [ˈdʒen.ju.ɪn] *adj.* 真誠的；真正的

▶ Daniel expressed genuine concern about my health and offered to take me to the doctor.
丹尼爾對我的健康表達真心的關切，並且主動要帶我去看醫生。

---

germ [dʒɝːm] *n.* 細菌；微生物

▶ Be sure to wash your hands before dinner to get rid of the germs.
在吃晚餐之前，請確定先洗手去除細菌。

---

gifted [ˈgɪf.tɪd] *adj.* 有天賦的
搭 **musically gifted** 有音樂天份
同 **talented / skilled**

▶ Lu Yang is a gifted student who will graduate from high school early.
盧彥是一位很有天賦的學生，他將提早從高中畢業。

---

gigantic [ˌdʒaɪˈgæn.tɪk] *adj.* 龐大的；巨人般的
同 **enormous / gargantuan**

▶ The gigantic whale jumped several feet up into the air.
這隻龐大的鯨魚跳出海面好幾英尺高。

101

giggle [ˈgɪg.əl]
① *v.* 咯咯地笑
② *n.* 格格笑；傻笑

▶ The baby giggles every time his dad makes a funny face.
小嬰兒每次看到爸爸做的鬼臉都會咯咯地笑。

▶ The movie star heard some nervous giggles as he walked into the room.
那位電影明星在走進房間時，聽到了略帶緊張的傻笑聲。

---

ginger [ˈdʒɪn.dʒɚ] *n.* 薑

▶ Ginger is used in many delicious Chinese dishes.
薑被使用在許多美味的中式菜餚裡。

---

girlfriend [ˈgɝːl.frend] *n.* 女朋友

▶ The man always treated his girlfriend like a lady.
這個男子總是對待他的女朋友如同淑女。

103

glide [ˈglaɪd]
① *v.* 使滑動
同 **skim / slide**
實用片語
glide across 滑過，飛越
② *n.* 滑動

▶ Shelly can glide easily across the snow on her skis.
雪莉穿著雪橇能夠輕鬆自在地在雪地上滑行。

▶ The jet glided across the sky.
一架噴射滑翔機滑過天際。

▶ The new dance move is called the "Glide" because you slide across the floor.
這個新的舞步叫做『滑行』，因為你要滑過地板。

glimpse [glɪmps]

① *n.* 一瞥；一見

搭 **fleeting glimpse** 匆匆一瞥

同 **flash / glance**

② *v.* 瞥見；看一眼

同 **check out / peek**

---

globe [gloʊb] *n.* 地球儀；地球；球狀物

搭 **global economy** 全球經濟

同 **world / planet**

95

glorious [ˈglɔːri.əs] *n.* 美好的；光榮的

同 **gorgeous / marvelous**

▶ I caught a glimpse of the singer before she left the building.
我在那位歌手離開大樓前，得以瞥見她一眼。

▶ I glimpsed the ocean one last time before we drove away.
在我們開車離開之前，我又再看海洋最後一眼。

G

▶ We are learning to identify many countries on the globe.
我們學習在地球儀上指認出許多國家。

▶ It was a glorious day, with the sun shining and birds singing.
那真是美好的一日，陽光普照，鳥兒鳴叫。

Exercise 39

I. Derivatives

1. Anne is a _____ (genus) to think of that solution.
2. Over ten _____ (gang) have been arrested by the police for the violence in the street.
3. I shall never forget the _____ (generous) shown by the people of our church when I was experiencing a difficult time.
4. The country won a _____ (glory) victory in battle.
5. Three _____ (genus) of this family live together in a big traditional Chinese residence.

II. 中英對應

_____ 1. 龐大的   (A) gigantic   (B) giggle   (C) google   (D) giant

_____ 2. 汽油   (A) gap   (B) garlic   (C) gallon   (D) gasoline

_____ 3. 細菌   (A) gene   (B) germ   (C) gear   (D) genius

_____ 4. 間隙   (A) gate   (B) gas   (C) gap   (D) gasp

_____ 5. 注視   (A) gaze   (B) gang   (C) garlic   (D) gear

99

goodness [ˈɡʊd.nəs] *n.* 善良;仁慈

同 **grace / mercy**

▶ Goodness is a virtue.
善良是一種美德。

goods [ɡʊdz] *n.* 商品

搭 **durable goods** 耐用品

同 **product / belongings**

▶ The shop sells sporting goods.
這家店賣的是運動用品。

grace [ɡreɪs]

① *n.* 優美

同 **beauty / style**

② *v.* 為…增色;使優美

同 **adorn / decorate**

實用片語
grace with 以…使優美

▶ The young woman moves with the grace of a dancer.
那位年輕女士舉手投足帶著舞者的優雅。

▶ Her beautiful face and pleasant personality have graced our company for 22 years.
她漂亮的臉孔以及宜人的個性在過去二十二年為公司增色不少。

▶ The stage was graced with flowers.
舞台用花來美化。

graceful [ˈɡreɪs.fəl] *adj.* 優雅的

同 **elegant / delicate**

實用片語
graceful as a swan 如天鵝般優雅

▶ Sandy isn't very graceful. In fact, she's very clumsy.
珊蒂一點也不優雅。事實上,她還真是笨手笨腳呢。

▶ Tina is graceful as a swan.
蒂娜如天鵝般優雅。

gracious [ˈɡreɪ.ʃəs] *adj.* 親切的;和藹的

同 **accommodating / affable**

▶ We enjoy eating dinner at Kimberly's house. She's always a gracious hostess.
我們很喜歡在金柏莉家吃晚餐。她永遠是個親切的女主人。

101 **100**

gradually [ˈɡrædʒ.u.ə.li] *adv.* 逐漸地

搭 **increase gradually** 逐漸地增加

同 **increasingly / gently**

▶ The waves gradually washed the sand castle away.
海浪逐漸地把沙堡給沖走了。

graduation [ˌɡrædʒ.uˈeɪ.ʃən]

n. 畢業典禮；畢業

▶ Many of Danny's family members will attend his graduation.
丹尼的多位家人都會出席他的畢業典禮。

---

grammar [ˈɡræm.ɚ] *n.* 文法

▶ Mark doesn't always use correct grammar, but he's not afraid to speak English.
馬克不見得總是用對文法，但是他不害怕開口說英文。

---

grammatical [ɡrəˈmæt.ɪ.kəl] *adj.* 文法的

▶ The article focuses on the 10 most common grammatical errors.
這篇文章著重在十個最常見的文法錯誤。

---

grandparent [ˈɡræn.per.ənt]

n. （外）祖父；（外）祖母

▶ My grandparents are always loving and caring to me.
我的祖父母一直很疼愛我。

---

grapefruit [ˈɡreɪp.fruːt] *n.* 葡萄柚

▶ The market has some nice pink grapefruit.
市場上有一些很漂亮的紅葡萄柚。

---

103 102 98

grateful [ˈɡreɪt.fəl] *adj.* 感激的

搭 **immensely grateful** 充滿感謝

同 **pleased / beholden**

實用片語
grateful for small blessings 享受小確幸

▶ We're grateful for your help while my father was sick.
我們非常感激你在爸爸生病時所提供的協助。

▶ The meeting ended early. I guess I should be grateful for small blessings.
會議很早結束。我想我應該要享受小確幸。

---

gratitude [ˈɡræt.ə.tuːd] *n.* 感激

搭 **profound gratitude** 充滿感謝

同 **acknowledgment / obligation**

▶ I want to develop the habit of showing gratitude to others.
我要養成一個對他人表達感激的習慣。

---

grave [ɡreɪv]

① *adj.* 重大的；嚴重的

同 **acute / heavy**

② *n.* 墳墓；墓穴

▶ Daniel's mom suffers from a grave illness.
丹尼兒的母親患了一個重大的疾病。

▶ Behind the church, you'll see some ancient graves with interesting things written on them.
在教會的後面，你會看到一些古老的墳墓，上面記載著一些有趣的事情。

greasy [ˈgriː.si] *adj.* 油膩的

同 **oily / fatty**

實用片語
greasy spoon 經濟小吃店

▶ The food at that restaurant is too greasy.
那家餐廳的食物太油膩了。

▶ Jim's parents ran a greasy spoon for many years.
吉姆的父母經營一間小吃店許多年。

---

greatly [ˈgreɪt.li] *adv.* 極其;非常

搭 **improve greatly** 進步很大
同 **notably / markedly**

▶ As a visitor, I greatly appreciated the warm welcome.
身為一位訪客,我非常感激自己所受到的熱誠歡迎。

---

greeting(s) [ˈgriː.tɪŋ] *n.* 問候

同 **reception / salutation**

▶ I'm sorry your parents couldn't join us. Please send them my greetings.
我很抱歉你的父母無法參加。請幫我跟他們問候。

---

grief [griːf] *n.* 悲傷

搭 **considerable grief** 極度悲傷
同 **despair / gloom**

▶ Each person works through the process of grief in their own way.
每一個人會用自己的方式來處理哀傷。

---

grieve [griːv] *v.* 悲痛;悲傷

同 **regret / weep**

▶ Jennifer is grieving for the loss of her husband.
珍妮佛正為去世的丈夫悲痛不已。

---

grind [ˈgraɪnd]

① *v.* 磨碎

搭 **grind into powder** 磨成粉
同 **crumble / reduce**
② *n.* 苦差事
同 **chore / labor**

實用片語
daily grind 日常工作,例行苦事

▶ You can watch them grind the coffee beans right in front of you.
你可以看他們在你面前研磨咖啡豆。

▶ After my vacation, I had to go back to the daily grind.
假期之後,我必須回到日常工作。

▶ I'm tired of the daily grind, and I'm ready for a vacation.
我非常厭煩每日的苦差事,我準備好要去度假了。

---

groom [gruːm / grʊm] *v.* 新郎

▶ The groom smiled as his bride walked down the aisle.
當新娘走上紅毯時,新郎微笑了。

---

104 103

guarantee [ˌger.ən'tiː]

① *n.* 保證;保證書

▶ The product came with a guarantee that if I am not pleased, I can return it.
那項產品有著一項『如果我不滿意,就可以退貨』的保證。

② *v.* 保證

搭 **lifetime guarantee**　永久保證

同 **maintain / insure**

▶ I can't guarantee that you'll like the newer version better than your current phone.

我不保證你會比你現在這隻手機更喜歡那個新款的手機。

---

guilt [ˈgɪlt]　*n.* 犯罪行為；有罪

搭 **admit guilt**　認罪

同 **culpability / disgrace**

▶ A great deal of evidence was discovered that all pointed to the man's guilt.

許多發掘出來的證據都指出那個男人的罪行。

99

guilty [ˈgɪl.ti]　*adj.* 有罪的

同 **convicted / remorseful**

▶ Timmy had a guilty look on his face after stealing a candy bar.

提米每次偷了一條糖果，臉上都會有罪惡感。

---

gulf [ˈgʌlf]　*n.* 海灣

▶ Some very pretty beaches can be found in the Gulf of Mexico.

在墨西哥灣可以找到一些非常漂亮的沙灘。

Exercise 40

I. Derivatives

1. Our teacher spent a lot of time explaining the _____ (grammar) structure of the sentence.

2. Grace Kelly and Audrey Hepburn were two of the most beautiful and _____ (grace) Hollywood actresses.

3. Phoebe hopes to get a good job in her hometown after _____ (graduate).

4. Nick felt _____ (guilt) about the things he said to his father when he was a teenager, but it was too late for him to apologize.

5. She wrote an email to express her _____ (grace) to the man who found her cat.

II. Multiple Choice

(　　) 1. Her face became very __ after she heard the bad news.
(A) glorious　(B) graceful　(C) greasy　(D) grave

(　　) 2. The bride and __ walked down the aisle together after the wedding ceremony was completed.
(A) bridesmaid　(B) groom　(C) bridesman　(D) grandparent

(　　) 3. My uncle sells electronic __ such as batteries, chargers and lights, etc.
(A) goods　(B) good　(C) goose　(D) goodness

(　　) 4. The computer has a one year __ .
(A) greasy　(B) guardian　(C) guarantee　(D) grind

(　　) 5. Alzheimer's disease is a progressive condition, which means the symptoms develop __ and become more severe over the course of several years.
(A) graduate　(B) gradually　(C) gradual　(D) graduation

⑯ **complacent** [kəmˈpleɪ.sənt] *adj.* 滿足的、自滿的

例 The booming economy has made people complacent.
經濟起飛讓人民感到滿足。

complaisant [kəmˈpleɪ.səns] *adj.* 彬彬有禮的、殷勤的

例 Jack is the most complaisant child I've ever met.
傑克是我看過最彬彬有禮的孩子。

---

⑰ **deprecate** [ˈdep.rə.keɪt] *v.* 非難、對唱反調

例 A good teacher should not deprecate her students' efforts.
一個好老師不應否定學生的努力。

depreciate [dɪˈpriː.ʃi.eɪt] *v.* 貶值、輕視、貶低

例 Inflation is rising quickly and the dollar is depreciating.
快速的通貨膨脹讓美元貶值。

---

⑱ **device** [dɪˈvaɪs] *n.* 設備、儀器、裝置

例 This device can be used to read people's mind.
此設備可以用來讀出人的心思。

devise [dɪˈvaɪz] *v.* 設計、發明、策劃、想出

例 We need to devise a system for handling online orders.
我們需要設計一套可以處理線上訂單的系統。

---

⑲ **discomfort** [dɪˈskʌm.fɚt] *v.* 使不舒服、使不安

例 People are greatly discomforted by these issues.
人們被這些問題搞得很不安。

discomfit [dɪˈskʌm.fɪt] *v.* 使困窘、挫敗、擾亂

例 His remarks had successfully discomfited his competitors.
他的評論成功地讓對手失色。

---

⑳ **eligible** [ˈel.ə.dʒə.bəl] *adj.* 有資格當選的、法律上合格的

例 Mark is eligible to join the national baseball team.
馬克夠資格進入國家棒球隊。

illegible [ɪˈledʒ.ə.bəl] *adj.* 難讀的、難認的

例 Please note that illegible applications will not be considered.
請注意難以辨讀的申請書將不被採納。

Unit 41

habitual [həˈbɪtʃ.u.əl] *adj.* 習慣性的
同 **addicted / chronic**

▶ Eric's habitual lateness is affecting his work.
艾瑞克習慣性的遲到已經影響到他的工作。

---

halfway [ˌhæfˈweɪ]
adj. 在中途；到一半；不徹底地
搭 **halfway correct** 不全然正確
同 **midway / between**

實用片語
go halfway 妥協，向…讓步

▶ I walked halfway home, then took a bus for the rest of the way.
我回家的途中走到半路，就改搭客運了。

▶ I'm willing to go halfway and pay for the electricity.
我想要妥協，並支付我的電費。

---

halt [hɑːlt]
① *v.* 停止行進
同 **pause / stop**
② *n.* 停止
搭 **abrupt halt** 驟然停止
同 **arrest / interruption**

實用片語
come to a halt 停下

▶ The engineer halted the train when he spotted a car on the tracks.
那位火車司機在看到鐵軌上有輛汽車時就馬上煞住火車。

▶ We brought the meeting to a halt until the protests ended.
我們暫停這個會議直到抗議結束。

▶ The bus slowly came to a halt.
公車緩緩停下。

---

handbag [ˈhænd.bæg] *n.* （女用）手提包

▶ My sister keeps a small handbag with all sorts of things.
我的姊妹把各樣的東西裝在一個小手提包裡。

---

handicapped [ˈhæn.dɪ.kæpt] *adj.* 殘障的
搭 **physically handicapped** 肢體殘障
同 **crippled / disadvantaged**

▶ The parking spot is for handicapped drivers.
這個停車位是專門給殘障駕駛們使用的。

---

handwriting [ˈhænd.raɪ.tɪŋ] *adj.* 筆跡；手寫

▶ My teacher has very nice handwriting.
我的老師寫一手漂亮的字。

---

happily [ˈhæp.əl.i] *adv.* 快樂地
同 **gladly / playfully**

▶ I happily accepted my red envelope during the new year.
我在新年期間開心地拿紅包。

harden [ˈhɑːr.dən] *v.* 變硬

同 **solidify / set**

實用片語
harden up 使變硬

▶ The glue on your mended plate will harden within an hour.
你用來修補破盤子的膠水在一小時內就會變硬。

▶ Please harden up the ice cream by putting it in the freezer.
請讓冰淇淋在冰箱中冷凍一下。

---

hardship [ˈhɑːrd.ʃɪp] *n.* 受苦；艱難

搭 **financial hardship** 財務困難

同 **disaster / suffering**

▶ Since James lost his job, he has experienced many hardships.
自從詹姆士失去工作之後，他就受到很多的苦。

---

hardware [ˈhɑːrd.wer]

n. 五金器具；（電腦）硬體

▶ I'm sorry. I don't have the right hardware to repair your broken doorknob.
對不起，我沒有合適的五金工具來修理你家壞掉的門把。

---

harmonica [hɑːrˈmɑː.nɪ.kə] *n.* 口琴

▶ Mike can play many different songs on the harmonica.
麥克能用口琴吹奏出許多不同的曲子。

---

(98)
harmony [ˈhɑːr.mə.ni] *n.* 和睦；融洽；一致

搭 **maintain harmony** 維持和平

同 **good will / kinship**

▶ The young child wished for all the nations to live in peace and harmony.
那位年幼的小孩希望所有的國家都能過著平安以及和睦的生活。

---

(103) (102)
harsh [hɑːrʃ] *adj.* 嚴酷的；過於強烈的

搭 **extremely harsh** 極度強烈

同 **severe / rigid**

▶ The harsh winter weather killed many of our trees and plants.
嚴酷的冬天氣候凍死了很多我們所種的樹木以及植物。

---

hassle [ˈhæs.əl] *n.* 口角；麻煩；困難

同 **commotion / wrangle**

▶ The brothers got into a hassle over the last piece of cake.
兄弟們為了最後一塊蛋糕而起了口角。

---

(100)
haste [heɪst] *n.* 急忙

同 **alacrity / urgency**

▶ Penny and her family left in haste to catch the train.
潘妮和她的家人匆忙離開去趕火車。

hasten [ˈheɪ.sən] *v.* 加速；趕忙
同 **precipitate / step up**

▶ Newspapers reported the politician's bad behavior, which hastened the end of his career.
報紙上報導了這位政客的不良行為，因而加速了結他的生涯。

hatred [ˈheɪ.trɪd] *n.* 怨恨
搭 **irrational hatred** 不理性的埋怨
同 **revenge / scorn**

▶ Marty still has hatred in her heart for the man who killed her parents.
瑪蒂心中對那位殺害她父母的男人仍舊充滿怨恨。

headmaster [ˈhedˌmæs.tə]
n. （私立學校的）校長

▶ The headmaster of our school punished the naughty boys.
我們校長處罰了那群調皮的學生。

headphones [ˈhed.foʊnz] *n.* 頭戴式耳機

▶ Donald gave me a very expensive set of headphones.
唐納給了我一組價錢昂貴的頭戴式耳機。

headsets [ˈhed.sets]
n. 頭戴式附有麥克風的耳機

▶ Our headsets were broken so we couldn't hear in the studio.
我們的耳機壞了，所以在錄音室裡什麼都聽不到。

healthful [ˈhelθ.fəl] *adj.* 有益健康的
同 **wholesome / healthy**

▶ My sister always serves delicious and healthful meals.
我的姊姊總是煮些既美味又有益健康的餐點。

heartbreak [ˈhɑːrt.breɪk] *n.* 心碎

▶ Kim's heartbreak over her father's death was unbearable.
金因為父親過世而心碎，令人難以承受。

helicopter [ˈhel.əˌkɑːp.tə] *n.* 直升機

▶ As we flew over the volcano, the scenery from the helicopter was beautiful.
當直升機飛過火山頭，我們從機內看出去的景色實在是太美了。

103 102

herd [ˈhɝːd]
① *n.* 畜群
② *v.* 把…趕在一起；聚在一起
同 **corral / round up**

▶ A herd of sheep ran down the middle of the road.
一群羊跑到馬路正中央。

▶ The farm dog does a great job of herding the cows.
牧場的狗很厲害地把牛群趕在一起。

實用片語
herd together 成群，趕成一組

▶ The teacher herded all the kids together.
老師把小孩趕成一組。

---

101 97

hesitation [ˌhɛz.əˈteɪ.ʃən] *n.* 猶豫

同 **mistrust / hesitancy**

▶ Rhonda had some hesitation when I asked her to speak at the conference.
當我邀請蓉姐在會議中致詞時，她有些猶豫。

Exercise 41

I. Derivatives

1. The doctor believes that his patient will recover better in a more
   _____ (health) environment where the air is fresher.
2. My work was brought to a sudden _____ (hold) when the
   computer crashed.
3. The downtown cinema is planning to improve access for people who
   are physically _____ (handicap) .
4. Jenny believed the relationship with her father was the reason for her
   _____ (hate) of men.
5. I have no _____ (hesitate) in recommending Ms. Hung for this
   job.

II. 中英對應

_____ 1. 口琴　　　　　(A) harmony　　　　(B) harmonica
　　　　　　　　　　　　(C) harmonic　　　　(D) harmonious

_____ 2.（電腦）硬體　(A) hardship　　　　(B) hardware
　　　　　　　　　　　　(C) hardworking　　(D) hardness

_____ 3. 口角　　　　　(A) harsh　　　　　(B) haste
　　　　　　　　　　　　(C) hassle　　　　　(D) hasten

_____ 4.（私立學校）校長　(A) headmaster　　(B) headsets
　　　　　　　　　　　　(C) headphones　　(D) headquarters

_____ 5. 畜群　　　　　(A) hero　　　　　(B) herb
　　　　　　　　　　　　(C) herbal　　　　　(D) herd

Unit 42

hidden [ˈhɪd.ən] *adj.* 隱藏的；隱密的

搭 **hidden costs** 隱性花費

同 **invisible / covered**

▶ The hidden clue was almost impossible to find.
隱藏的線索幾乎很難被找到。

---

highly [ˈhaɪ.li] *adv.* 非常；（評價）高地

搭 **highly recommend** 非常推薦

同 **greatly / vastly**

實用片語
speak highly 評價很高

▶ Rick does a great job and is highly valued at our company.
瑞克表現相當出色，在我們公司裡非常受好評。

▶ The boss always speaks highly of you.
老闆對你的評價總是很高。

---

hijacker [ˈhaɪˌdʒæk·ər] *n.* 劫持者；劫機者

同 **robber / kidnapper**

▶ The officer stopped the hijacker from taking over the airplane.
員警制止了劫機者，沒讓他們挾持飛機。

---

hijacking [ˈhaɪ.dʒækɪŋ] *n.* 劫持；強制；脅迫

▶ The hijacking took the bus passengers by surprise.
這件劫持事件讓公車乘客措手不及。

---

hiker [ˈhaɪ.kə] *n.* 健行者；徒步旅行者

同 **pedestrian / climber**

▶ The hiker traveled a long distance up the trail.
這位健行者在步道朝上走了很長一段路。

---

homeland [ˈhoʊm.lænd] *n.* 祖國

同 **country / nation**

▶ In Celia's homeland, French is a major language.
在希莉亞的祖國，法語是主要的語言。

---

honestly [ˈɑː.nɪst.li] *adv.* 誠實地；老實說

同 **fairly / justly**

▶ Please answer honestly - do you like my haircut?
請老實回答我，「你喜歡我新剪的髮型嗎？」

---

honeymoon [ˈhʌn.i.muːn]

① *n.* 蜜月

搭 **honeymoon period** 蜜月期

② *v.* 度蜜月

▶ Ron and Cindy took a 7-day honeymoon to Hawaii.
榮恩和辛蒂到夏威夷度過了七天的蜜月之旅。

▶ We honeymooned in Phuket and had a wonderful time.
我們在普吉島度蜜月，享受了美好的時光。

honorable [ˈɑn·ər·ə·bəl] *adj.* 正直的；可尊敬的
同 **conscientious / respectable**

▶ My father was a good man who lived an honorable life.
我的父親生前是個好人，他一生過著正直的生活。

---

hook [ˈhʊk]

① *n.* 鉤子
② *v.* 用鉤勾住
同 **fasten / fix**

▶ The hook you're using is too small to catch a big fish.
你用的魚鉤太小了，無法釣到大魚。

▶ The large fish was hooked on Jack's line for nearly two hours before he could pull it in.
那隻巨大的魚被傑克的釣線給勾住了，他花了快兩個小時才終於把魚給拉上來。

---

hopeful [ˈhoʊp.fəl] *adj.* 充滿希望的
同 **cheerful / eager**

▶ Janie is hopeful that she did well on yesterday's test.
珍妮對於她昨天考試能考好抱著很大的希望。

---

hopefully [ˈhoʊp.fəl.i] *adv.* 充滿希望地；但願
同 **positive / upbeat**

▶ I hopefully searched for clues to the correct answer.
我滿心希望能找到正確解答的線索。

---

horizon [həˈraɪ.zən] *n.* 地平線
同 **perspective / prospect**

▶ Far out to sea, we could see dolphins swimming against the horizon.
遠遠的海上，我們看到了許多海豚沿著地平線游泳。

---

horrify [ˈhɔːr.ə.faɪ] *v.* 震驚；使害怕
同 **shake / petrify**

▶ Ellie was horrified to see the damage caused by the earthquake.
愛爾麗看到了地震造成的毀損感到相當震驚。

---

hose [hoʊz]

① *n.* 水管
② *v.* 用軟管淋澆（或沖洗）

▶ This water hose is too heavy. We should buy one of the lighter ones.
這條水管太重了。我們應該買一條比較輕一點的。

▶ Please clean off the balcony and hose it down.
請把陽台打掃乾淨，再用水沖洗一下。

---

host [hoʊst] *v.* 以主人身份招待；主辦

▶ Mary hosted her college classmates for the weekend.
瑪麗這個週末會招待她的大學同學們。

---

hostel [ˈhɑː.stəl] *n.* 旅舍（尤指青年之家）

▶ We traveled cheaply through Europe by staying in hostels.
我們旅遊歐洲時，住廉價旅舍來省錢。

household [ˈhaʊs.hoʊld] *n.* 家庭；一家人
搭 **household chores** 家事

▶ My mom does a great job of running a household with five people.
媽媽把我們一家五口打理照顧得很好。

---

housewife [ˈhaʊsˌwaɪf] *n.* 家庭主婦

▶ A housewife has many things to take care of every day.
家庭主婦每天都有許多事情要處理。

---

housework [ˈhaʊs.wɜːk] *n.* 家事

▶ My father helps with the housework by washing the dishes every night.
我的父親也會幫忙做家事，他每天晚上都會洗碗筷。

98

humanity [hjuːˈmæn.ə.tj] *n.* 人性
搭 **common humanity** 一般人性
同 **humankind / mankind**

▶ The brutal leader was arrested for committing crimes against humanity.
那位殘忍的領導者因為犯了泯滅人性的罪行而被逮捕。

---

humidity [hjuːˈmɪd.ə.tj] *n.* 濕度
同 **evaporation / moisture**

▶ In my hometown, the humidity is very high during the summer months.
在我的家鄉，每到夏天那幾個月濕度都很高。

---

hurricane [ˈhɜː.ɪ.kən] *n.* 颶風

▶ Paul worries about living on the coast because of the possibility of hurricanes.
保羅有點擔心住在海岸邊，因為可能會遇到颶風襲擊。

---

hydrogen [ˈhaɪ.drə.dʒən] *n.* 氫

▶ Water is made up of hydrogen and oxygen.
水是由氫氣和氧氣所組合成的。

---

iceberg [ˈaɪs.bɜːg] *n.* 冰山

▶ It isn't safe to travel through those icy waters because of the possibility of icebergs.
在結冰的海面上航行不太安全，因為可能會遇到冰山。

Exercise 42

I. Derivatives

1. My father is an _____ (honor) man.

2. We should treat all living creatures with _____ (human).

3. The _____ (hijack) was overpowered by the passengers and the plane made it to the airport safely.

4. The thriller fiction author claims that the new book she is writing will absolutely _____ (horror) readers.

5. Families are classified by the occupation of the head of the _____ (house).

II. Multiple Choice

(   ) 1. The sun is rising above the ___ .
    (A) horse   (B) house   (C) horizon   (D) household

(   ) 2. The state of Louisiana was hit by ___ Katrina and caused serious damage.
    (A) typhoon   (B) hurricane   (C) tornado   (D) earthquake

(   ) 3. Most foreigners love to live in Taiwan, but many of them still struggle to accept the ___ and heat in summer, even after having lived here for many years.
    (A) humidity   (B) humanity   (C) humor   (D) humble

(   ) 4. ___ there will still be some seats available when we arrive at the theater.
    (A) healthfully   (B) hopeful   (C) hopeless   (D) hopefully

(   ) 5. May lived in a ___ when she was studying in Canada.
    (A) inn   (B) barn   (C) hostel   (D) iceberg

identical [aɪˈden.t̬ə.kəl]

adj. 完全相同的；極為相似的

搭 **exactly identical** 完全相同

同 **exact / look-alike**

▶ Sheila and Shelly are identical twins, and it is really hard to tell them apart.
席拉和雪莉是同卵雙胞胎，所以真的很難分辨出她們兩個人。

---

identification / ID [aɪˌden.t̬ə.fəˈkeɪ.ʃən]

n. 身分證明

搭 **personal ID** 個人證明

▶ Be sure to take your identification with you when you apply for a driver's license.
當你申請駕照時，一定要記得帶著身份證。

---

104 99 98

identify [aɪˈden.t̬ə.faɪ] *v.* 識別

同 **describe / determine**

identify as 視為，認為

▶ I was not able to identify the man in the stolen car.
我無法辨認在那部贓車裡面的男人是誰。

▶ Jones was identified as a risk taker.
瓊斯被視為是冒險家。

---

idiom [ˈɪd.i.əm] *n.* 成語；慣用語

▶ Idioms are fun to use but sometimes difficult to identify.
成語使用起來很好玩，但是有時候很難辨別。

---

idle [ˈaɪ.dəl]

① *adj.* 空閒的

同 **unproductive / empty**

實用片語
idle something away 荒廢，浪費

② *v.* 無所事事；閒逛

▶ The employees were idle most of the afternoon. They need more to do.
這些職員們大半個下午都很悠閒。他們需要有更多的工作。

▶ Don't idle away the whole morning.
不要浪費整個早晨。

▶ On Saturday, I just idled the day away eating and watching movies.
星期六我無所事事地吃東西、看電影度過了一整天。

---

idol [ˈaɪ.dəl] *n.* 偶像

▶ He has become the newest teen idol and attracts fans everywhere he goes.
他已經成為最新的青少年偶像，他所到之處都吸引了不少紛絲。

ignorant [ˈɪɡ·nər·ənt] *adj.* 無知的

同 **naïve / uneducated**

▶ I don't want to appear ignorant, but I don't know much about this subject.
我不希望我顯得無知，但是我對這個主題了解不多。

---

illegal [ɪˈliː.ɡəl]
adj. 違規的；不合法的；非法的

搭 **illegal act** 非法行為

同 **unlawful / wrongful**

▶ It is illegal to eat food or drink on the MRT.
在捷運上飲食是違規的。

104
illustrate [ˈɪl.ə.streɪt] *v.* 舉圖或實例說明

同 **lay out / portray**

實用片語
illustrate with 以⋯示範，展示

▶ The teacher illustrated the idea with an example.
老師舉例說明那個想法。

▶ She illustrated her points with photos.
她使用圖片示範她的觀點。

---

104 101
illustration [ˌɪl.əˈstreɪ.ʃən] *n.* 插畫；圖解

搭 **striking illustration** 引人注目的圖

同 **depiction / photograph**

▶ The illustration works perfectly with this article.
這插畫與這篇文章搭配得太完美了。

---

imaginable [ɪˈmædʒ.ə.nə.bəl]
adj. 可想像得到的

同 **plausible / conceivable**

▶ Lisa and Stephen had the most beautiful wedding imaginable!
莉莎和史提芬有個你所能想像最美的婚禮。

---

imaginary [ɪˈmædʒ.ə.ner.i] *adj.* 想像中的

同 **fanciful / imagined**

▶ Bobby has invented an imaginary friend.
鮑比創造出一位假想的朋友。

---

imaginative [ɪˈmædʒ.ə.nə.t̬ɪv]
adj. 富有想像力的；有創意的

搭 **imaginative idea** 有創意的點子

同 **extravagant / original**

▶ The new staff member had some imaginative ideas that hadn't been considered yet.
那位新來的職員有極富想像力點子，還未被考慮採用。

---

imitate [ˈɪm.ə.teɪt] *v.* 模仿

同 **mimic / copy**

▶ Anna's baby tries to imitate everything she says.
安娜的小嬰兒試著模仿媽媽說的每一句話。

imitation [ˌɪm.əˈteɪ.ʃən] *n.* 模仿；偽造

同 **clone / impression**

▶ Charley does great imitations of many well-known stars.
查理模仿一些有名的明星模仿得很棒。

---

102 99 96 95

immediately [ɪˈmiː.di.ət.li]

adv. 直接地；立即地

搭 **respond immediately** 立即回應

同 **urgently / rapidly**

▶ We ate dinner immediately after the movie.
我們一看完電影就直接去吃晚餐。

---

99 97

immigrant [ˈɪm.ɪ.grənt] *n.* （外來）移民

▶ In the 1940s, Pam's family arrived in the U.S. as immigrants from Italy.
在一九四零年代，潘的家人以義大利移民的身份抵達美國。

---

immigrate [ˈɪm.ə.greɪt] *v.* 移民；遷入

同 **arrive / migrate**

實用片語
immigrate to 移居到…

▶ My family immigrated to Australia three years ago.
我的家人在三年前移民到澳洲。

▶ They immigrated to the US.
他們移居到美國。

---

immigration [ˌɪm.əˈgreɪ.ʃən] *n.* 移居

同 **migration / travel**

實用片語
illegal immigration 非法居留

▶ Because of the war on the border, immigration into the neighboring country is increasing.
由於邊境戰亂的緣故，移居到鄰近國家的人數也逐漸增加。

---

impact [ɪmˈpækt]

① *n.* 撞擊（力）；影響

搭 **permit access to** 評估影響力

同 **evaluate impact**

② *v.* （對…）產生影響

同 **jolt / force**

實用片語
have an impact on 造成衝擊

▶ The impact of the car crash broke Leah's leg.
受到車禍的衝擊，麗雅的腿斷了。

▶ The movie's message impacted me in a powerful way.
這部電影裡的信息帶給我很大的影響。

▶ Your story really had an impact on us.
你的故事真的對我們造成衝擊。

---

impatient [ɪmˈpeɪ.ʃənt]

adj. 沒有耐心的；不耐煩的

同 **anxious / irritable**

▶ The traffic jam made my father impatient.
路上大塞車讓爸爸變得沒耐心。

impersonal [ɪmˈpɝː.sən.əl]

adj. 沒有人情味的；冷淡的

同 **indifferent / detached**

---

103 102

imply [ɪmˈplaɪ] *v.* 暗示

搭 **strongly imply** 強烈暗示

同 **indicate / hint**

---

impolite [ˌɪm.pəlˈaɪt] *adj.* 無禮的

同 **rude / boorish**

---

97 95

impression [ɪmˈpreʃ.ən] *n.* 印象

搭 **first impression** 留下印象

同 **feeling / response**

實用片語

leave an impression on 留下印象

▶ Chatting online can feel impersonal.
在網路上聊天沒什麼親切感。

▶ I didn't mean to imply that I'm too busy to talk with you.
我不是故意要暗示你我太忙而無法跟你聊天。

▶ Asking me my age is impolite.
問我年齡是非常不禮貌的。

▶ Meeting and talking with the successful businessman made a big impression on Paul.
和成功的生意人見面以及交談，為保羅留下了深刻的印象。

▶ She left a very good impression on us.
她讓我們留下好印象。

I

Exercise 43

I. 中英對應

_____ 1. 直接地 (A) immigrant   (B) immediately   (C) immigrate   (D) impatient

_____ 2. 無知的 (A) ignore   (B) idle   (C) impatient   (D) ignorant

_____ 3. 冷淡的 (A) impersonal (B) impatient   (C) imperfect   (D) impolite

_____ 4. 非法的 (A) legal   (B) impolite   (C) illegal   (D) imaginary

_____ 5. 影響   (A) improve   (B) impress   (C) imply   (D) impact

II. Derivatives

1. The police asked Tom to show his _____ (identify) when he was stopped for drunk driving check.

2. Ben can do a great _____ (imitate) of Robert De Niro.

3. The applicant tried to make a good _____ (impress) on everyone she met during her job interview.

4. Hong Kong International Airport is the winner of the 2016 Award for "Best Airport _____ (immigrate) Service".

5. C. S. Lewis, author of The Chronicles of Narnia and The Four Loves is not only a theologian, but also an _____ (imagine) writer.

(104)

inadequate [ɪˈnæd.ə.kwət]

adj. 不足夠的；不適當的

同 **incomplete / lacking**

▶ The amount of paper in the printer is inadequate.
印表機裡面的紙張已經不夠用了。

---

(99)

incident [ˈɪn.sɪ.dənt] *n.* 事件

搭 **unfortunate incident** 不幸的事件
同 **circumstance / episode**

▶ Last week's incident was minor; I wouldn't worry about it.
上星期的事件只是小事，我才不會擔心呢。

---

included [ɪnˈkludɪd] *adj.* 包含在內的

▶ You need to pay 3,025 dollars, tax included.
你必須付 3025 美元，含稅。

---

(101)

including [ɪnˈkludɪŋ] *perp.* 包含

▶ The entire family is going on vacation, including my Uncle Bill.
我們全家人都要去度假了，包括我叔叔比爾。

---

(96)

incomplete [ˌɪnkəmˈplit] *adj.* 不完整的

搭 **incomplete record** 不完整的記錄
同 **inadequate / insufficient**

▶ You didn't answer all the questions, so your assigment is incomplete.
你沒有回答所有的問題，所以你的任務不算達成。

---

inconvenient [ˌɪnkənˈvinjənt] *adj.* 不方便的

同 **annoying / troublesome**

▶ Parking can make driving a car inconvenient.
停車問題可能使得開車變得不方便。

---

increasingly [ɪnˈkrisɪŋli] *adv.* 越來越；漸增地

同 **progressively / gradually**

▶ It became increasingly harder for the man to find work.
這個男子越來越難找工作。

---

indication [ˌɪn.dəˈkeɪ.ʃən] *n.* 跡象；指示

搭 **reliable indication** 可靠的跡象
同 **reminder / inkling**

▶ There is no indication that this is a serious medical condition.
完全沒有跡象顯示出這是個嚴重的醫療狀況。

I

industrialize [ɪnˈdʌstrɪəˌlaɪz] v. 使工業化
同 **motorize / mechanize**

▶ The nation is the last in the region to industrialize.
這個國家是在這個區域裡最後一個邁向工業化的國家。

---

infant [ˈɪn.fənt] n. 嬰兒

▶ New parents can find good information about how to care for an infant.
新手爸媽可以找到一些有關於如何照顧新生兒的好資訊。

---

infect [ɪnˈfekt] v. 傳染；感染
同 **taint / blight**
實用片語
infect with 感染

▶ The passenger infected many on the plane with his disease.
這位乘客把他的疾病傳染給飛機上很多的人。

▶ The sick child infected his classmates with flu virus.
這生病的小孩把感冒傳染給他同學。

---

infection [ɪnˈfek.ʃən] n. 感染；傳染
搭 **bacterial infection** 細菌感染
同 **disease / epidemic**

▶ Jessica picked up a serious infection when she swam in the dirty water.
潔西卡在污水中游泳時受到了嚴重的感染。

99
inflation [ɪnˈfleɪ.ʃən] n. 通貨膨脹；膨脹
同 **boom / expansion**

▶ The economy is strong, and inflation has remained low this year.
今年的經濟景況良好，通貨膨脹率一直很低。

---

influential [ˌɪn.fluˈen.ʃəl] adj. 有影響力的
同 **authoritative / dominant**

▶ A few influential people helped Michael get a job with the government.
一些有影響力的人幫忙麥可在政府機關裡找到一份工作。

99
informal [ɪnˈfɔːr.məl]
adj. 非正式的；不拘禮節的
搭 **informal meeting** 非正式會議
同 **casual / relaxed**

▶ Ellen invited friends over for an informal dinner party.
艾倫邀請朋友到家裡參加一個隨性的晚餐聚會。

---

information [ˌɪn.fɚˈmeɪ.ʃən] n. 資訊

▶ You should gather plenty of information before you make a decision about a school overseas.
你在決定要到國外哪所大學就讀之前，應該要先收集大量的資訊。

informative [ɪnˈfɔːr.mə.t̬ɪv]

adj. 資料豐富的；情報的

搭 **informative seminar** 資訊豐富的會議

同 **instructional / explanatory**

▶ Cynthia's speech was interesting and informative.
辛西雅的演講非常有趣而且內容豐富。

---

informed [ɪnˈfɔːrmd]

adj. 消息靈通的；見多識廣的；有依據的

同 **knowledgeable / abreast**

▶ The secretary keeps the boss informed about company news.
祕書讓老闆隨時知道公司所有的消息。

---

ingredient [ɪnˈgriː.di.ənt]

n. 食材；（烹調）原料；組成部分

搭 **natural ingredient** 天然成份

同 **element / additive**

▶ Maybe we can find an easier recipe with fewer ingredients.
也許你可以找一個比較簡易的食譜，用少一點的食材。

---

initial [ɪˈnɪʃ.əl]

① *adj.* 最初的；開始的

同 **basic**

② *n.* （字的）起首字母

③ *v.* 刻印姓名首字母；簽章於⋯

▶ Sara's initial reaction to Jim's invitation was one of interest.
莎拉對於吉姆的邀請的最初反應是感到有些興趣。

▶ The first initial in the word is "N", but it isn't pronounced.
這個字的第一個字母是「N」，可是它不發音。

▶ We can initial the luggage for you, and it will make a nice gift.
我們可以將姓名的首字母刻在行李箱上，這樣就成了一個很棒的禮物。

---

injured [ˈɪn.dʒə-d] *adj.* 受傷的

搭 **injured patient** 受傷的病人

同 **damaged / wounded**

▶ The boy rested his injured arm on the desk.
男孩把受傷的手臂靠在桌上休息。

---

innocence [ˈɪn.ə.səns] *n.* 清白；無罪

同 **guiltlessness / inculpability**

▶ The man's lawyer was able to prove his innocence.
這位男士的律師證明了他的清白。

I

input [ˈɪnˌpʊt]

① n. （投入的）意見；投入

搭 **accept input** 接受意見

同 **feedback / opinion**

② v. 將（資料）輸入（電腦）

▶ We value Bart's input, so we hope he'll join us in the meeting.
我們很重視巴特的意見，所以希望他能夠參加我們的會議。

▶ Sarah input the wrong data into the computer, and now my chart has mistakes.
莎拉把錯誤的資料輸入電腦，現在我的圖表出現錯誤。

---

insert [ɪnˈsɝt]

① v. 插入

同 **enter / stick in**

實用片語
insert in 投入

② n. （插入的）宣傳廣告；插入物

▶ If you'll insert your card into the machine, the gate will open.
如果你把卡片插入機器裡，大門就會打開。

▶ You can just insert the coins in the machine.
你只需將硬幣投入機器中。

▶ I usually throw away all the inserts in the newspaper.
我通常會把夾在報紙裡的所有宣傳廣告都丟掉。

---

inspection [ɪnˈspɛkʃən] n. 檢查

搭 **car inspection** 車檢

同 **analysis / investigation**

▶ We'll have a house inspection today for insects.
我們今天會進行一個室內害蟲的檢查。

Exercise 44

I. 中英對應

_____ 1. 清白   (A) innocence   (B) innovation
                        (C) innovator   (D) innominate

_____ 2. 不方便的 (A) inconsistent   (B) inconsistency
                        (C) inconvenience   (D) inconvenient

_____ 3. 起首字母 (A) infant   (B) initial
                        (C) injured   (D) initiate

_____ 4. 事件   (A) included   (B) incentive
                        (C) incident   (D) increasingly

_____ 5. 食材   (A) incomplete   (B) indication
                        (C) infant   (D) ingredient

II. Derivatives

1. This is an interesting, entertaining and _____ (inform) film.
2. Some officers of the Taipei City Fire Department carried out a fire safety _____ (inspect) of the building.
3. We are now living in a highly _____ (industrial) commercial world where everything is made by machines in factories.
4. According to a survey by The Folio Society, the Bible has been voted as the most _____ (influence) and valuable book in history.
5. Breastfeeding helps babies defend against _____ (infect), prevents allergies and protects against a number of chronic conditions.

(98)

inspiration [ˌɪn.spəˈreɪ.ʃən] *n.* 靈感

搭 **seek inspiration** 尋找靈感

同 **encouragement / motivation**

▶ Her poetry has been a source of inspiration for me.
她寫的詩一直是我的靈感的源頭。

 (104) (103) (101) (97)

inspire [ɪnˈspaɪr] *v.* 激勵；啟發；鼓舞；激動

同 **arouse / motivate**

實用片語
inspire with 激勵，激發

▶ His music inspires me every time I hear it.
每次聽到他的音樂，我都會受到音樂的激勵。

▶ She inspired us all with her personal story.
她用她個人的故事激勵我們。

install [ɪnˈstɑːl] *v.* 安裝；任命

同 **build in / settle**

實用片語
install someone as 將某人任命為⋯

▶ After the workers installed the new stove, they demonstrated it for me.
工人們在安裝好新的爐子之後，就為我示範操作方式。

▶ My mother installed herself as the boss of the kitchen.
我的母親將自己任命為廚房的老大。

(99)

instinct [ˈɪn.stɪŋkt] *n.* 本能

搭 **follow instinct** 跟隨本能

同 **aptitude / intuition**

▶ My instinct tells me Anthony is not someone who can be trusted.
我的本能告訴我，安東尼不是一個值得信任的人。

instruct [ɪnˈstrʌkt] *n.* 教導；指示

同 **advise / guide**

實用片語
instruct in 給指示，教導

▶ I hope you will instruct me on how to play the guitar.
我希望你能夠教我如何彈吉他。

▶ Linda will instruct you in the way to operate this machine.
琳達將教導你操作此機器的方法。

instructor [ɪnˈstrʌk.tɚ] *n.* 教練；指導者

搭 **English instructor** 英文老師

同 **adviser / mentor**

▶ Lynn's swimming instructor is very patient with small children.
林恩的游泳教練對小小朋友們非常有耐心。

insult [ɪnˈsʌlt]

① *v.* 羞辱;侮辱
同 **abuse / offend**

② *n.* 羞辱
同 **slap / affront**

▶ Kathleen insulted my new haircut, but I like it.
凱瑟琳羞辱了我的新髮型,但是我卻很喜歡。

▶ Why do your comments always sound like insults? You need to be more positive.
為什麼你的意見聽起來都像是侮辱?你需要再正面一點。

---

insurance [ɪnˈʃʊərˑəns] *n.* 保險

搭 **compulsory insurance** 強制保險

▶ If you buy a car, you'll also need to get insurance.
如果你買了車,你還需要買保險。

---

intellectual [ˌɪn.t̬əlˈek.tʃu.əl]

① *adj.* 知性的;智力的
搭 **intellectual property** 智慧財產
同 **creative / mental**

② *n.* 知識份子;有高智力的人
同 **academician / intelligentsia**

▶ Each month, our book club has intellectual discussions about the books we've read.
我們的讀書社每個月會對我們閱讀書籍進行知性的討論。

▶ Some of the nation's leading intellectuals will attend the conference.
一些國家的主要知識份子將會參加這個大會。

---

intelligence [ɪnˈtel.ə.dʒəns] *n.* 智力;智慧
同 **brilliance / perception**

▶ All students will be given tests to measure their intelligence.
所有的學生都需要接受智力測驗的考試。

---

intelligent [ɪnˈtel.ə.dʒənt]

adj. 聰明的;有才智的
搭 **intelligent system** 智慧型系統
同 **knowledgeable / smart**

▶ Greg is a very intelligent little boy who loves to read.
格瑞格是一位非常聰明的小男孩,他熱愛閱讀。

---

intend [ɪnˈtend] *v.* 打算;想要
同 **expect / aim**

實用片語
intend as 意指,視為

▶ We intend to go to the beach this weekend if it doesn't rain.
如果這個週末沒下雨,我們打算去海灘。

▶ We intend this money as a gift.
我們把這筆錢視為禮物。

---

100 99

intense [ɪnˈtens] *adj.* 強烈的;極度的
搭 **intense competition** 競爭激烈
同 **extreme / extraordinary**

▶ The region's intense heat makes it difficult to work outside.
這個地區的酷熱使得在戶外工作變得相當辛苦。

intensify [ɪnˈtɛn.sə.faɪ]

① v. 加強
同 heighten / escalate
② n. 認真；強度

▶ The group has intensified its search for the missing child.
這個小組已經加強對這位失蹤小孩的搜尋工作。

▶ Mr. Chen teaches his classes with such intensity that his love of history is obvious.
陳老師在上課時是如此認真，很明顯的是他熱愛歷史。

---

intensive [ɪnˈtɛn.sɪv] adj. 密集的；加強的

搭 intensive course 密集課程
同 comprehensive / demanding

▶ We'll have a three-month intensive language class. Then we'll take a yearlong program.
我們將有一個為期三個月的語言密集班。接著就要參加一整年的課程。

---

intention [ɪnˈtɛn.ʃən] n. 打算；意圖

同 motive / objective

▶ Kenny's intention was to go to university right away. But he didn't have the money.
肯尼的打算是馬上上大學。但是他卻負擔不起學費。

104
interact [ˌɪn.tɚˈækt] v. 互動

搭 interact directly 直接互動
同 relate / interplay

實用片語
interact with 與…互動

▶ Martha enjoys interacting with the neighborhood kids, especially since her grandchildren live so far away.
瑪莎很喜歡和鄰居的小孩互動，主要是因為她的孫子女們都住得很遠。

▶ The game helped students interact with each other.
這個遊戲讓學生們能彼此互動。

---

interaction [ˌɪn.tɚˈræk.ʃən]
n. 互動；互相作用

搭 face-to-face interaction 面對面互動
同 synergy / communication

▶ The interaction between our older dog, Jake, and the new dog has not been positive.
我們的老狗傑克和我們的新狗沒有很好的互動。

103
interfere [ˌɪn.tɚˈfɪr] v. 介入；妨礙

同 hamper / obstruct

實用片語
interfere in 干預，涉及

▶ You shouldn't interfere when people are arguing. They will work it out.
你不應該介入別人的紛爭。他們自己會想辦法解決。

▶ Please don't interfere in my business.
請勿干預我的事。

intermediate [ˌɪn.tə.ˈmiː.di.ət]

① *adj.* 中級的；中間的

搭 **intermediate level** 中等程度

同 **transitional / median**

② *n.* 中間人；調解人

③ *v.* 充當調解人；干預

▶ The students have already progressed from the basic to the intermediate reading level.
學生們的閱讀已經從初級程度進步到中級的程度。

▶ The couple asked an intermediate to help them resolve their problems.
那對夫婦請了一位中間人來幫忙解決他們的問題。

▶ Edward was asked to intermediate for the two groups to try to find some resolution.
愛德華被找去充當這兩個團體的調解人，並且要試著找出解決方法。

Internet / internet [ˈɪn.tə.net] *n.* 網際網路

同 **online / world wide web**

▶ The Internet has made my job much easier.
網際網路使得我的工作輕鬆多了。

interpret [ɪn.ˈtɜː.prɪt] *v.* 解釋；口譯

同 **explain / translate**

實用片語
interpret for 翻譯

▶ We couldn't understand the Old English language, so our teacher interpreted the poem for us.
我們看不懂老式的英文，所以老師就為我們解釋這首詩。

▶ The tour guide interpreted for me at the market.
導遊在市場為我翻譯。

interruption [ˌɪn.tə.ˈrʌp.ʃən] *n.* 打岔；中斷

搭 **avoid interruption** 避免被打斷

同 **disruption / disturbance**

▶ When I am on the phone, your constant interruptions are annoying.
當我在講電話的時候，你不斷的打岔是很令人討厭的。

intimate [ˈɪn.tə.mət]

① *adj.* 親密的

同 **affectionate / confidential**

② *n.* 密友

搭 **intimate friendship** 密閨

同 **confidant / confidante**

▶ Bonnie and I are close, intimate friends, and I can trust her with my secrets.
邦妮和我是很親近、親密的朋友，我可以把我的秘密都告訴她。

▶ Elsa is one of the singer's intimates and travels with her everywhere.
愛紗是那位歌手的一位密友，經常陪著她到處旅行。

Exercise 45

I. Vocabulary Choice

(A) instruct (B) interfere (C) instinct (D) intermediate (E) interpreter

(F) interpret (G) insults (H) insurance (I) intensive (J) intimate

1. Ginny asked an _____ to help her to resolve the problems between her and her former employer.

2. Only family members and _____ friends were invited to their wedding.

3. We don't understand German, so we need someone to _____ for us.

4. Birds have the _____ to learn to fly.

5. The chef _____ the customers by ignoring their complaints.

II. Derivatives

1. Joshua is an _____ (intelligence) man and he has written several books on political systems.

2. Mandy tried very hard to work all morning without _____ (interrupt), but the phone kept ringing.

3. It was not my _____ (intend) to make you cry.

4. The _____ (interact) between the management and the workers of this company is not sufficient and it could lead to serious labor problems later on.

5. We could hear the sound of the explosion from a long distance away due to its _____ (intense).

intonation [ˌɪn.təˈneɪ.ʃən] *n.* 語調

同 **modulation / pitch**

▶ Kathy's statements usually end in a rising intonation.
凱西的聲明通常在句尾時提高語調。

---

100 97

invade [ɪnˈveɪd] *v.* 入侵；侵略

搭 **invade privacy** 侵犯隱私
同 **occupy / raid**

▶ Before the fighters invaded our area, this used to be a quiet, peaceful village.
在那些戰士入侵我們這個區域之前，這裡一直是個安靜，平安的小村莊。

---

101 100

invasion [ɪnˈveɪ.ʒən] *n.* 侵略；侵犯

同 **aggression / offensive**

▶ In what felt like an invasion, thousands of insects arrived and destroyed our crops.
數以計千的害蟲像大舉侵襲似地摧毀了我們的農作物。

97

invention [ɪnˈven.ʃən] *n.* 發明

同 **creativity / design**

▶ Benjamin Franklin is known for his many inventions.
班傑明富蘭克林以他的發明而出名。

103

invest [ɪnˈvest] *v.* 投資

搭 **invest time and effort** 投資時間和精神
同 **supply / devote**

實用片語
invest time in 投入時間做…

▶ Tim invested in some property on the coast.
提姆投資了一些海岸邊的房地產。

▶ Jack invests his time in social work.
傑克投入時間做社會工作。

98

investigation [ɪnˌves.təˈgeɪ.ʃən] *n.* 調查

同 **inspection / search**

▶ The police will perform an investigation into the robbery.
警察將會對這個搶劫案進行調查。

---

investment [ɪnˈvest.mənt] *n.* 投資；投資額

▶ The banker advised us against such a risky investment.
那位銀行家奉勸我們不要做這個高風險的投資。

I

investor [ɪnˈvɛs.tə] *n.* 投資者

搭 **overseas investor** 海外投資人
同 **banker / stockholder**

▶ The investors lost all their money when the company closed.
當公司一倒閉，所有投資人的錢都一去不回。

---

invisible [ɪnˈvɪz.ə.bəl] *adj.* 無形的；看不見的

同 **imperceptible / microscopic**

▶ The gas in the air was invisible, but we could smell it.
瀰漫在空氣中的瓦斯是肉眼看不見的，但是我們卻聞得到。

104

involve [ɪnˈvɑːlv] *v.* 需要；包含

搭 **emotionally involve** 放入情感
同 **entail / require**

實用片語
involve in 參與，涉及

▶ The recipe involves using an oven, but I don't have one.
這個食譜需要用到烤箱，但是我沒有烤箱。

▶ Tammy is involved in several charities.
譚美參與了多項公益活動。

---

involved [ɪnˈvɑːlvd] *adj.* 複雜的；牽扯在內的

同 **complicated / tangled**

▶ The process for joining the club was very involved.
加入俱樂部的程序非常的複雜。

97

involvement [ɪnˈvɑːlv.mənt]
n. 參與；連累；纏繞

同 **engagement / relationship**

▶ Philip's involvement with the project will give everyone more confidence.
這項計畫有了菲利浦的參與，它將會帶給大家更多的信心。

---

irregular [ɪˈrɛg.jə.lə]
adj. 不固定的；不規則的；非正規的

搭 **irregular shape** 不規則形狀
同 **inappropriate / unusual**

▶ The restaurant's irregular schedule frustrated customers.
這家餐廳不固定的營業時間讓顧客感到很受挫。

---

99 96

isolate [ˈaɪ.sə.leɪt] *v.* 隔離

同 **detach / remove**

實用片語
isolate from 自⋯脫離，獨立出

▶ The firefighters isolated the burning houses, hoping the fire wouldn't spread.
消防隊員將著火的房子隔離起來，希望大火不會蔓延。

▶ Tony's parents tried to isolated him from negative influences.
湯尼的父母試著讓他遠離負面的影響。

isolation [ˌaɪ.səlˈeɪ.ʃən] *n.* 隔離；孤立

搭 **social isolation** 社會孤立

同 **confinement / remoteness**

▶ Abby is in isolation and can't receive any visitors.
艾比正在隔離中，並且不准會客。

---

itch [ˈɪtʃ]

① *v.* 發癢；抓癢

② *n.* 癢

▶ These bug bites are making me itch.
這些蟲咬使得我全身發癢。

▶ I have an itch in the middle of my back that I can't reach.
我的背部中間很癢，但是我卻抓不到。

---

jealousy [ˈdʒel.ə.si] *n.* 嫉妒

搭 **feel jealousy** 感覺妒嫉

同 **grudge / resentment**

▶ You've been friends too long to let jealousy ruin your friendship.
你們已經是多年的好友了，不該讓嫉妒破壞你們的友情。

---

junior [ˈdʒuː.njə]

① *adj.* （父子同名的年幼者）小；年輕的

② *n.* 較年少者

搭 **junior college** 二專

同 **minor / inferior**

▶ William Ford Jr. will take over the company after his father retires.
小威廉福特在他父親退休之後，將會接管這家公司。

▶ My brother is two years my junior, but he is taller than me.
我的弟弟小我兩歲，但是他比我身高高很多。

---

keen [kiːn] *adj.* 銳利的；熱心的；敏銳的

同 **eager / earnest**

實用片語
keen on doing something 熱切地想…

▶ Eagles are known for their keen vision.
老鷹以他們銳利的眼光而出名。

▶ I am not very keen on going shopping; I prefer to rest at home.
我不愛購物，我比較喜歡在家休息。

---

kindly [ˈkaɪnd.li] *adj.* 親切的；和藹的

搭 **kindly face** 和善的面容

同 **gentle / good-hearted**

▶ The kindly neighbor offered us a watermelon.
這位親切的鄰居給我們西瓜吃。

99

kindness [ˈkaɪnd.nəs] *n.* 友善；仁慈；和藹

同 **hospitality / humanity**

▶ I was happy with the kindness being shown here.
我對這裡人們展現的友善感到開心。

knuckle [ˈnʌk.əl]

① *n.* 關節
② *v.* 用指關節敲打

▶ I can't take my ring off because my knuckles are swollen.
我無法把我的戒指拿下來，因為我的手指關節腫起來了。

▶ The butcher knuckled the piece of beef until it became tender.
那位肉販不斷用指關節敲打著那塊牛肉，一直到它變得軟嫩為止。

---

labor [ˈleɪ.bɚ]

① *n.* 勞動
搭 **labor intensive** 勞力密集
同 **activity / employment**
② *v.* 努力；艱苦地幹活
同 **work / effort**

實用片語
labor at 埋頭工作，苦幹

▶ I wasn't paid enough for my labor because the job took longer than I expected.
我的工資不及於我所付出的勞力，因為這份工作所花的時間比我預期的還要久。

▶ Gillian labored for weeks on her research paper.
紀琳恩為她的研究報告努力了三個星期。

▶ He is laboring at fixing the house.
他正埋頭維修房子。

---

laboratory / lab [ˈlæb.rə.tɔːr.i] *n.* 實驗室

▶ Stan works in a lab all day, testing blood.
史丹整天在實驗室裡做著檢測血液的工作。

---

lag [ˈlæg]

① *v.* 落後；延遲
同 **delay / idle**
實用片語
lag behind 落後，延遲
② *n.* 延遲；落後；衰退

▶ The horse lagged behind all of the others in the race.
那匹馬在競賽中，遠遠落後其他所有的馬匹。

▶ Rick is lagging behind in her project.
瑞克的專案延遲了。

▶ During the TV broadcast, there was a lag between the audio and the singer's words.
在電視的轉播當中，歌手的聲音和嘴形之間有點延遲。

Exercise 46

I. Derivatives

1. Kate bought the new house purely as an _____ (invest).
2. During World War II, France suffered severely due to the German _____ (invade) of Europe.
3. Susie experienced an increasing sense of _____ (isolate) after all the other family members had gone.
4. There is no evidence of her direct _____ (involve) in this murder case.
5. I will never forget the _____ (kind) my friends showed me in my time of financial difficulty.

II. Vocabulary Choice

(A) kind   (B) investigation   (C) leg   (D) jealous   (E) keen

(F) jealousy   (G) lag   (H) investment   (I) irregular   (J) labor

1. Although Grandma Ruth is already 80 years old, her eyes are still _____ .

2. The buses from this neighborhood are _____ and it angers the residents because they sometimes have to a long time.
3. There is always a _____ between thinking and reality.
4. _____ has ruined many friendships.
5. There will be a full _____ to find out what caused the plane crash.

landmark [ˈlænd.mɑːrk] *n.* 地標

搭 **historical landmark** 古蹟型地標
同 **monuments / milestone**

▶ This website has pictures of the world's most famous landmarks.
這個網站有所有世界聞名的地標的照片。

---

landscape [ˈlænd.skeɪp]

① *n.* 風景
同 **mural / photograph**
② *v.* 從事景觀美化或園藝工作

▶ Many artists travel to Arizona to paint the state's unusual landscape.
很多藝術家旅行到亞利桑拿州去畫這州獨特的風景。

▶ Margie hired a professional to help landscape her yard.
瑪姬雇用了一位專家來幫她的庭院做園藝設計。

---

landslide [ˈlænd.slaɪd] *n.* 坍方；山崩

搭 **landslide victory** 大獲全勝
同 **avalanche / mudslide**

▶ Following the heavy rains, the mountain villages are now at risk for landslides.
在下過一場大雨之後，山上的小村落面臨著土石流坍方的危險。

---

largely [ˈlɑːrdʒ.li] *adv.* 大部分地；主要地

同 **mostly / broadly**

▶ The painter's early pieces were largely ignored. His later works, however, made him famous.
這位畫家早期的作品大部分都被忽略掉了。然而他的近作卻使他聲名大噪。

---

lately [ˈleɪt.li] *adv.* 最近

同 **newly / recently**

▶ Lately, I've been getting up earlier than usual.
我最近比以往還要早起。

---

launch [lɑːntʃ] *v.* 推出；發射；積極投入

搭 **launch new products** 新產品上市
同 **commence / propel**

launch into 投入

▶ The company launched their new website three months ago.
那家公司在三個月前推出了他們的新網站。

▶ The professor launched into the topic after a short introduction.
簡短介紹後，教授便投入主題中。

lavatory [ˈlæv.ə.tɔːr.i] *n.* 盥洗室；廁所

▶ Wash your hands after you go to the lavatory.
在你去過廁所後，請洗手。

---

lawful [ˈlɑː.fəl] *adj.* 合法的
圁 **authorized / legal**

▶ It was decided that the search of Thad's car was not lawful.
上面已經決定，搜尋賽德的汽車是不合法的。

97
lead [liːd] *n.* 領導；領先地位
圁 **advantage / point**

▶ Carrie took the lead for our team's presentation and did a good job.
凱蕊主導我們小組的簡報而且表現得很優秀。

---

leading [ˈliː.dɪŋ] *adj.* 主要的；帶領的；先進的
搭 **a leading company** 首屈一指的公司
圁 **dominant / principal**

▶ Alan works for the leading law firm in the city.
亞倫在本市裡最主要的法律事務所上班。

L

---

leaflet [ˈliː.flət] *n.* 小葉；傳單
圁 **flyer / pamphlet**

▶ The leaflet advertised a new kind of skin product.
這傳單廣告著新的護膚產品。

---

lean [liːn]
① *v.* 靠；傾斜
圁 **bow / incline**

實用片語
lean back 後躺，後仰

② *adj.* 精瘦的；無脂肪的
圁 **skinny / thin**

▶ Don't lean on the door. Someone might open it.
請不要靠在門上。可能會有人要開門進來。

▶ Lean back and make yourself comfortable.
往後躺並讓您自己感到舒服。

▶ My mom eats mostly lean meat and vegetables.
我媽媽吃的大部分是瘦肉和蔬菜。

---

learned [ˈlɜː.nɪd] *adj.* 博學的；有學問的
搭 **learned profession** 需高深學問之職業
圁 **accomplished / well-educated**

▶ The learned scholar has written a very interesting book.
那位博學的學者寫了一本很有趣的書。

---

learner [ˈlɜː.nɚ] *n.* 學習者

▶ We are all learners everyday of our lives.
我們大家在生活中天天都是學習者。

learning [ˈlɜː.nɪŋ] *n.* 學習；學問

搭 **learning process** 學習進度

同 **education / training**

▶ Ms. Tsai's teaching methods make learning enjoyable.
蔡小姐的教學方式使得學習變得很有樂趣。

---

lecture [ˈlek.tʃɚ]

① *n.* 授課

搭 **formal lecture** 正式講課

同 **lesson / speech**

② *v.* 給…講課

同 **teach / address**

實用片語
lecture at 對…說教

▶ Each week, I have a two-hour lecture in psychology.
每個星期我要教授一堂兩個小時的心理學。

▶ The doctor lectured us on the importance of keeping our hands clean.
醫生為我們上了一課「保持雙手乾淨的重要性」。

▶ Don't lecture at me all the time.
不要一直向我說教。

---

lecturer [ˈlek.tʃɚ.ɚ] *n.* 講師；演講者

同 **instructor / professor**

▶ The guest lecturer gave an interesting speech on musical changes through the years.
客座講師發表了一篇歷年來音樂風格改變的有趣演講。

101
legend [ˈledʒ.ənd]

n. 傳說；傳奇故事；傳奇人物

搭 **ancient legend** 古老傳說

同 **folklore / mythology**

▶ Each country has their own popular legends.
每個國家都有大家耳熟能詳的傳奇故事。

---

leisurely [ˈleʒ.ɚ.li]

① *adj.* 悠閒的

同 **languid / lazy**

② *adv.* 悠閒地；從容不迫地

同 **casually / lazily**

▶ We took a leisurely stroll around the lake.
我們繞著湖邊，享受悠閒的漫步。

▶ We talked and walked leisurely around the park.
我們繞著公園，悠閒地談天及散步。

---

98 95
license [ˈlaɪ.səns]

① *n.* 執照

搭 **marriage license** 結婚證書

同 **certificate / privilege**

② *v.* 領有執照；許可；發執照給…

▶ You'll have to take a driving test in order to get a driver's license.
你必須先通過路考，才能拿到駕駛執照。

▶ John is licensed to marry people.
約翰有執照可以為人證婚。

lighten [ˈlaɪ.tən] *v.* 變亮;發亮

同 **brighten / light up**

實用片語
lighten someone's wallet 花大筆錢

▶ After the storm, the sun came out and lightened the sky.
暴風雨過後,太陽出現了並且照亮了整片天空。

▶ That hotel is going to lighten your wallet.
那間旅館會讓你花大錢(很貴)。

---

limitation [ˌlɪm.əˈteɪ.ʃən] *n.* 限制

搭 **overcome limitation** 克服限制

同 **circumspection / inhibition**

▶ Even though Linda's arm was broken, she worked around the limitations.
雖然琳達的手斷了,但是她仍在受限的情況下工作。

---

liquor [ˈlɪk.ɚ] *n.* 酒;含酒精飲料

▶ This store doesn't sell liquor, but you can buy other drinks here.
這家店不賣酒,但是你可以在這裡買到其他的飲料。

---

literary [ˈlɪt.ə.rer.i] *adj.* 文學界的;文學的

同 **classical / scholarly**

▶ A literary agent can help get your book published.
文學代理人可以幫你出書。

---

literature [ˈlɪt.ə.ə.tʃɚ] *n.* 文學;文學作品

▶ In college, Joan studied Chinese literature.
在大學裡,瓊安主修中國文學。

L

Exercise 47

I. 中英對應

_____ 1. 酒（含酒精飲料） (A) liquid   (B) light
                                          (C) liquor   (D) liqueur

_____ 2. 傳說 (A) legacy   (B) legend
                          (C) legal   (D) legendary

_____ 3. 廁所 (A) laboratory   (B) labyrinth
                          (C) lavender   (D) lavatory

_____ 4. 傾斜 (A) lean   (B) lead
                          (C) leaf   (D) leaflet

_____ 5. 推出 (A) lunch   (B) laugh
                          (C) launch   (D) laundry

II. Derivatives

1. After the typhoon, _____ (land) buried several houses and cause a lot of damage.

2. Jennifer Lawrence has been nominated for an Oscar as Best Actress in a _____ (lead) role four times already.

3. My sister is studying English _____ (literary) at a university in the United States.

4. Danna and her husband enjoyed a _____ (leisure) picnic lunch in New York's Central Park.

5. Many women in Africa and Asia use skin products to _____ (light) their skin because they believe that light skin is more beautiful.

Unit 48

loan [loʊn]

① *n.* 貸款

[搭] **loan shark** 放高利貸者

[同] **mortgage / credit**

② *v.* 借出

▶ Bradley took out a loan to buy a new car.
布萊德利貸了一筆款去買部新車。

▶ I can't loan you the money until I get paid.
我在領薪水之前無法借你錢。

97

location [loʊˈkeɪ.ʃən] *n.* 位置

▶ The restaurant is now in a new location.
這家餐廳已經搬到新的地方了。

---

locker [ˈlɑː.kɚ] *n.* 置物櫃

▶ You can leave your belongings in the locker while you exercise.
你運動的時候，可以將你的個人用品留在置物櫃裡。

---

logic [ˈlɑː.dʒɪk] *n.* 邏輯

[同] **philosophy / rationale**

▶ I don't understand the logic behind the mayor's decision to close more schools.
市長決定要關閉更多的學校，而我完全不了解這個決定背後的邏輯。

98

logical [ˈlɑː.dʒ.ɪ.kəl] *adj.* 合理的；邏輯上的

[搭] **logical reasoning** 邏輯關係

[同] **compelling / rational**

▶ Grady didn't offer any logical reasons for why he wanted us to change our plans.
葛拉帝並沒有提供他為何要我們改變計畫的合理原因。

99

loneliness [ˈloʊn.li.nəs] *n.* 孤獨；寂寞

[同] **alienation / emptiness**

▶ He started to feel the loneliness after being left alone.
他被單獨留下之後開始感到孤單。

---

loop [luːp]

n. （線、繩等繞成的）圈，環；環狀物

▶ She pulled the sewing needle through many loops.
她把縫衣針穿過許多的圓圈。

---

lorry [ˈlɔːr.i] *n.* （英國）卡車；貨車

▶ The men packed our belongings onto their lorry.
這些人把我們所有的物品都裝運上他們的卡車。

L

lotion [ˈloʊ.ʃən] *n.* 乳液;較稀的乳液

▶ Hand lotion will help you with your dry skin.
護手霜會改善你的乾性肌膚。

---

lousy [ˈlaʊ.zi] *adj.* 很糟糕的;差勁的

同 **miserable / awful**

實用片語
lousy with 擁有大量的

▶ The plumber did a lousy repair job. Now I'll have to hire someone else.
那個水電工的修理得很差勁。現在我必須再去請別人來修。

▶ Mr. Chen is lousy with money.
陳先生有大筆金錢。

---

loyal [ˈlɔɪ.əl] *adj.* 忠誠的

搭 **loyal customers** 忠誠客戶
同 **devoted / trustworthy**

▶ Tom has been a loyal customer of ours for more than 20 years.
湯姆是來我們超過二十年以上的忠實顧客。

---

loyalty [ˈlɔɪ.əl.tj] *n.* 忠誠;忠心

同 **faith / obedience**

▶ My loyalty to the airline was rewarded with bonus miles to use toward a free trip.
我對那家航空公司的忠誠度讓我得到紅利里程數,可以換一趟免費旅程。

---

luckily [ˈlʌkɪli] *adv.* 幸運地

同 **by chance / happily**

▶ The event planners luckily had a backup plan.
這位活動策劃者幸虧有備份計畫。

---

lunar [ˈluː.nɚ] *adj.* 農曆的;陰曆的

▶ All of my family will come over tonight to celebrate Lunar New Year.
我所有的家人今晚都會過來慶祝農曆新年。

---

(103)
luxurious [lʌgˈʒʊr.i.əs] *adj.* 奢華的;奢侈的

搭 **luxurious hotel** 高檔飯店
同 **extravagant / lavish**

▶ The hotel is filled with luxurious decorations.
這家飯店到處充滿奢華的裝飾。

---

(95)
luxury [ˈlʌk.ʃɚ.i] *n.* 奢華;奢侈

同 **affluence / extravagance**

實用片語
in the lap of luxury 生活闊綽,奢侈

▶ Living a life of luxury is not the most important goal in life.
過著奢華的生活並不是人生最重要的目標。

▶ Linda lives in the lap of luxury.
琳達生活闊綽。

lychee [ˈliːˌtʃiː] *n.* 荔枝

▶ Lychees are a juicy and delicious fruit.
荔枝是多汁又美味的水果。

---

(101)

machinery [məˈʃiːˌnə.i] *n.* 機器；機械

▶ It's time to replace the older machinery with some newer equipment.
該是把老舊的機器汰換為一些新的設備的時候了。

---

madam / ma'am [ˈmæd.əm / mɑːm]
n. 女士；小姐

▶ Your car is waiting, Madam Secretary.
國務卿女士，你的車已經在外面等候了。

---

(101)

magnetic [mægˈnetˌɪk] *adj.* 磁性的
搭 **magnetic material** 有吸力的材質
同 **irresistible / seductive**

▶ The charming girl has a magnetic personality.
那迷人的女孩具有很吸引人的特質。

---

(96)

magnificent [mægˈnɪf.ə.sənt]
adj. 壯觀的；極好的
搭 **absolutely magnificent** 相當壯觀
同 **excellent / gorgeous**

▶ The festival offers a magnificent selection of international foods.
這個慶典提供了相當壯觀的國際美食選擇。

M

---

(98) (96)

mainly [ˈmeɪn.li] *adv.* 通常；主要地；大部分地
同 **primarily / essentially**

▶ Kevin mainly enjoys spending his summers in Spain.
凱文通常在西班牙度過夏天。

---

makeup [ˈmeɪk ʌp] *n.* 化妝品

▶ I think Allie wears too much makeup.
我覺得愛麗上妝上得太濃了。

---

(100)

manual [ˈmæn.ju.əl]
① *adj.* 手動的
同 **human / hand-operated**
② *n.* 手冊；簡介
搭 **instruction manual** 教學手冊
同 **guidebook / reference book**

▶ I learned how to type on a manual typewriter.
我學會了如何使用手動打字機打字。

▶ The manual will explain how to use your new phone.
這本手冊會解釋如何操作你的新手機。

manufacture [ˌmæn.jəˈfæk.tʃɚ]

① *v.* 製造;加工

搭 **manufacture products** 製造產品

同 **make / produce**

② *n.* 製造

▶ The company manufactures tires.
這家公司生產製造輪胎。

▶ The manufacture of cloth has changed over the years.
布料的製造方式在過去幾年內已經有所改變。

Exercise 48

I. 中英對應

_____ 1. 磁性的 (A) magnet   (B) magnetic   (C) marathon   (D) margin

_____ 2. 差勁的 (A) lazy   (B) lorry   (C) lucky   (D) lousy

_____ 3. 壯觀的 (A) magnet   (B) magazine   (C) magnify   (D) magnificent

_____ 4. 手動的 (A) manufacture (B) material   (C) manual   (D) manage

_____ 5. 置物櫃 (A) locker   (B) looker   (C) lock   (D) luck

II. Derivatives

1. It is _____ (logic) to assume that shareholders will attend the annual meeting because they have always done so in past.

2. The couple spent a fortune on their honeymoon because they stayed in a _____ (luxury) 5-star hotel in Dubai.

3. Richard didn't come to the party last night _____ (main) because he had to work overtime.

4. It is dangerous to drive or operate _____ (machine) after drinking alcohol.

5. I was impressed by the _____ (loyal) of the staff to their company when they offered to work overtime without pay.

Unit 49

manufacturer [ˌmæn.jəˈfæk.tʃɚ.ɚ]

n. 製造廠;製造者

同 **vendor / producer**

▶ The manufacturers are required to meet all safety guidelines.
所有的製造廠都被要求要達到安全的規定。

---

marathon [ˈmer.ə.θɑːn] *n.* 馬拉松賽跑

▶ My brothers will run in next month's marathon.
我的兄弟們會參加下個月的馬拉松賽跑。

100

margin [ˈmɑːr.dʒɪn] *n.* 頁邊空白處;邊緣

搭 **increase margin** 增加獲利

同 **edge / limit**

實用片語
by a wide margin 差距拉大

▶ The teacher wrote some helpful comments in the margin.
老師在頁邊空白處寫了一些很有用的評語。

▶ We won the contest by a wide margin.
我們以大幅差距贏得競賽。

---

married [ˈmer.id] *adj.* 已婚的;婚姻的

搭 **married couple** 已婚伴侶

同 **marital / mated**

實用片語
married above someone's station
高攀某人

▶ My grandparents have been married for fifty years.
我的祖父母結婚至今已經五十年了。

▶ Joan is marrying above her station.
瓊高攀了人家了。

---

104 103

maturity [məˈtʊr.ə.tʃ] *n.* 成熟

搭 **level of maturity** 成熟度

同 **wisdom / full bloom**

▶ Some researchers believe that girls' brains reach maturity earlier than boys' brains.
有些研究人員認為女孩的頭腦比男孩的頭腦更早達到成熟度。

104

maximum [ˈmæk.sə.məm]

① *n.* 最大限度;最大值

同 **ceiling / peak**

② *adj.* 最大(多、高、量)的

同 **maximal / superlative**

▶ Tony's credit card has a $6,000 limit, and he has already reached the maximum.
東尼的信用卡最高的刷卡額度是六千元,而他已經達到最高的額度了。

▶ According to my diet plan, I ate my maximum number of calories today.
根據我的節食計畫,我今天吃的已經達到我的卡洛里極限。

measure [ˈmeʒ.ə] *n.* 措施；手段；策略

搭 **reliable measure** 可靠的方式

同 **strategy / means**

實用片語
in a measure 某些程度

▶ The measures were designed to keep everyone safe.
這些措施是設計維護大家的安全。

▶ I sometimes think that success depends in a measure on good luck.
我有時認為成功也要靠一定程度的好運。

---

mechanic [məˈkæn.ɪk]
n. 技師；機械工；修理工

同 **machinist / repairman**

▶ My auto mechanic works on European cars.
我的汽車技師專門修理歐洲車。

---

mechanical [məˈkæn.ɪ.kəl] *adj.* 機械的

同 **automated / automatic**

▶ Our plane was delayed because of mechanical problems.
我們的飛機因為機械問題的緣故而延誤了。

---

memorable [ˈmem.ər.ə.bəl]
adj. 難忘的；值得紀念的

搭 **memorable experience** 難忘的經驗

同 **impressive / momentous**

▶ Our trip to Australia was filled with many memorable moments.
我們的澳洲之旅充滿了許多難忘的時光。

---

memorandum [ˌmem.əˈræn.dəm]
n. （正式）公務便條；備忘錄

同 **announcement / message**

▶ A memorandum was sent out introducing the new boss.
公司發出公告來介紹新的老闆。

---

memorial [məˈmɔːr.i.əl]

① *adj.* 追悼的；紀念的

搭 **memorial hospital** 紀念醫院

同 **remembering / celebrative**

② *n.* 紀念碑；紀念物

▶ Eddie's family had a memorial service for his father.
艾迪的家人為他的父親舉行了一個追思儀式。

▶ The town built a memorial to honor those who died in the war.
這個小鎮蓋了一座紀念碑來紀念那些死於戰爭的人。

---

mercy [ˈmɝː.si] *n.* 慈悲

搭 **mercy killing** 安樂死

同 **blessing / goodwill**

▶ The prisoners begged those who had captured them for mercy.
囚犯央求那些逮捕他們的人手下留情。

M

mere [ˈmɪr] *adj.* 僅僅的

同 **sheer / minor**

實用片語
mere trifle 小意思，小錢

▶ Skipper saves a mere five percent each month.
史奇博每個月只能存到百分之五。

▶ The snacks cost a mere trifle.
這點心只是小意思（這很便宜）。

---

merit [ˈmer.ɪt] *n.* 價值

搭 **artistic merit** 藝術特質

同 **talent / value**

實用片語
judge something on its own merits
按事實本身判斷

▶ Nick's ideas had some merit, but we'll need to consider them carefully.
尼克的點子有些參考價值，但我們仍然要仔細地考慮一下。

▶ We have judge this plan on its own merits.
我們讓評審按事實本身判斷這個計劃。

97

messenger [ˈmes.ɪn.dʒɚ] *n.* 送信人；使者

同 **courier / mediator**

▶ A messenger arrived with a telegram for Cindy.
一位信差送來一封電報給欣蒂。

---

messy [ˈmes.i] *adj.* 凌亂的；髒亂的

同 **untidy / sloppy**

▶ I don't know how you can find anything on your messy desk.
我不知道你怎麼能在凌亂的書桌上找到任何東西。

---

microscope [ˈmaɪ.krə.skoʊp] *n.* 顯微鏡

▶ You can see tiny germs by using a microscope.
使用顯微鏡，你就可以看到微小的微生物。

---

midday [ˌmɪdˈdeɪ] *n.* 正午；中午

▶ Why don't we go grab lunch during midday?
我們中午很快地吃個午餐吧？

---

mild [maɪld] *adj.* 溫和的

搭 **mild symptom** 輕微的症狀

同 **soft / temperate**

▶ Kevin has many friends because he has a mild temper.
凱文有很多朋友因為他個性溫和。

---

milkshake [ˈmɪlk.ʃeɪk] *n.* 奶昔

▶ Chris ordered a chocolate milkshake for dessert.
克力斯點了一杯巧克力奶昔當甜點。

---

mineral [ˈmɪn.ər.əl] *n.* 礦物；礦物質

▶ Mountain spring water often contains a variety of minerals.
山泉水通常含有各式各樣的礦物質。

minimum [ˈmɪn.ə.məm]

① *n.* 最低限度；最小值

同 **margin / merest**

實用片語

keep something to a minimum

壓至最低，最小化

② *adj.* 最小（少、低）的

搭 **minimum payment** 最低薪資

同 **minimal / least possible**

---

minister [ˈmɪn.ə.stɚ] *n.* 牧師；部長

---

ministry [ˈmɪn.ə.stri] *n.* 服事

▶ We'll keep the store's prices to a minimum because the students don't have much money.

我們會盡量把店裡的價錢壓到最低，因為學生們不太有錢。

▶ The budget should be kept to a minimum.

預算應壓到最低。

▶ In some places, the minimum age for a driver's license is 16.

在某些地方，取得駕照的最低年齡是十六歲。

▶ The minister from our church performed our wedding ceremony.

我們教會的牧師為我們主持結婚典禮。

M

▶ Our church has ministry for the homeless every weekend.

我們的教會每個週末都有針對遊民的服事。

Exercise 49

I. Vocabulary Choice

(A) mechanic   (B) maximum   (C) mature   (D) minimum   (E) maturity

(F) merit   (G) memorial   (H) mercy   (I) memorandum   (J) mechanical

1. The criminal appealed to the judge for _____ , but he refused because the crime had been so horrific.

2. NT$15 is the _____ adult fare on buses.

3. Several flights were cancelled because of _____ problems with one of the airplanes.

4. Ellen's plan has gradually come to _____ and she was finally able to fulfil her dream of traveling abroad for a year.

5. Our supervisor has prepared a _____ outlining our need for a new royalty system and everyone must read it.

II. 中英對應

_____ 1. 最大值 (A) maximum   (B) minimum   (C) median   (D) maximal

_____ 2. 礦物質 (A) miner   (B) mineral   (C) mirror   (D) minor

_____ 3. 牧師   (A) ministry   (B) miniskirt   (C) minister   (D) miniseries

_____ 4. 手段   (A) meaning   (B) mention   (C) measure   (D) messenger

_____ 5. 顯微鏡 (A) microwave   (B) microphone (C) Microsoft   (D) microscope

Unit 50

(97)

mischief [ˈmɪs.tʃɪf] *n.* 搗蛋；頑皮；惡作劇

同 **misconduct / playfulness**

實用片語
make mischief 惡作劇

▶ Every time I turn my back, the twins get into mischief.
每次我一轉身，那對雙胞胎就開始搗蛋。

▶ Don't listen to his gossip; he's trying to make mischief.
不要聽他八卦；他試圖惡作劇。

---

(98)

miserable [ˈmɪz.ɚ.ə.bəl] *adj.* 痛苦的；不幸的

搭 **miserable life** 悲慘的生活

同 **gloomy / pathetic**

實用片語
make someone miserable 讓人苦不堪言

▶ This cold has made me feel miserable all week.
這次感冒讓我整個星期都很痛苦。

▶ My boss is making me miserable.
我的老闆讓我苦不堪言。

---

misfortune [ˌmɪsˈfɔːr.tʃən] *n.* 不幸

同 **disadvantage / discomfort**

實用片語
misfortunes never come singly 禍不單行

▶ With the loss of their business, the family has suffered a great deal of misfortune.
由於事業經營失敗，他們一家遭遇到極大的不幸。

▶ I lost my job. Well, misfortunes never come singly; my wife lost hers too.
我工作丟了。好吧，禍不單行；我太太也丟了她的工作。

---

mislead [ˌmɪsˈliːd] *v.* 誤導；把…帶錯方向；誤導

同 **misguide / misinform**

實用片語
mislead about 誤導

▶ The witness mislead the police officer by giving him false information.
那位目擊者把錯誤的資料給了警察，誤導他辦案的方向。

▶ I think you've misled me about the price.
我認為你是跟我亂報價吧。

---

misleading [mɪsˈliː.dɪŋ] *adj.* 使人誤解的；誤導的

搭 **misleading statement** 誤導的說詞

同 **ambiguous / puzzling**

▶ The story was misleading, and it confused the readers.
這篇故事會誤導人，它把讀者搞混了。

M

misunderstand [ˌmɪs.ʌn.dəˈstænd] *v.* 誤解

搭 **completely misunderstand** 完全會錯意

同 **confuse / misconstrue**

► I misunderstood the instructions and completed the wrong exercise.
我誤解了指示而做完錯誤的練習。

99

moderate [ˈmɑd·ər·ɪt] *adj.* 中等的;適度的

搭 **moderate competition** 適度的競爭

同 **conservative / modest**

► You'll find some items with moderate prices, but most are very expensive.
你可以找到一些中等價位的品項,但是大部分的東西都很昂貴。

---

103 102 100

modest [ˈmɑː.dɪst] *adj.* 謙虛的

同 **humble / moderate**

► Lucy is an excellent violinist, but she is very modest about her abilities.
露西是個非常優秀的小提琴家,但是她對她的才能卻表示的很謙虛。

---

modesty [ˈmɑː.dɪ.sti] *n.* 謙虛

同 **decency / reticence**

► Peter's modesty prevented him from telling everyone about his perfect test score.
彼得的謙虛讓他沒有對大家宣布他考滿分的消息。

99

monitor [ˈmɑː.nə.tɚ]

① *n.* (學校的)班長;監督員

同 **supervisor / overseer**

② *v.* 監控;監聽;監視

搭 **monitor effectiveness** 監督成效

同 **supervise / manage**

► The class monitor wrote down the names of everyone who cheated.
班長把那些作弊的人名一一記下來。

► The board will monitor the situation to see if changes should be made.
董事會將會監控所有的狀況,然後再決定是否需要做些改變。

---

monthly [ˈmʌn.θli]

① *adj.* 每月一次的

② *adv.* 每月一次地

③ *n.* 月刊

► Our English class has weekly quizzes and a monthly test.
我們的英文課每週有小測驗,每月有個大考。

► Until Angie feels better, she will need to go to the doctor monthly.
在安姬覺得比較舒服以前,她必須每個月去看一次醫生。

► You can find news and information about our town in the local monthly.
你可以在本地的月刊裡讀到有關我們鎮上的新聞和資訊。

103

monument [ˈmɑːn.jə.mənt] *n.* 紀念碑;紀念館

搭 **national monument** 國家紀念館

▶ Washington, D.C. is famous for its many monuments.
華盛頓首府以它的幾個紀念碑／館而聞名。

---

moreover [ˌmɔːrˈoʊ.vɚ] *adv.* 此外;並且

同 **likewise / furthermore**

▶ Derek is a good actor. Moreover, he's a good musician.
德瑞克是個好演員,此外他還是個好的音樂家。

---

mostly [ˈmoʊst.li] *adv.* 大多數地

同 **largely / chiefly**

▶ The restaurant serves mostly Asian food, but they have some Western food too.
這家餐廳賣的大多數是亞洲菜色,但他們也有賣一些西餐。

---

103 **101** **98**

motivate [ˈmoʊ.t̬ə.veɪt] *v.* 給⋯動機;激勵

搭 **motivate employees** 激勵員工

同 **incline / persuade**

▶ What motivated you to move to London?
什麼事情鼓動你搬到倫敦?

---

motivation [ˌmoʊ.t̬əˈveɪ.ʃən] *n.* 動機;刺激

搭 **generate motivation** 產生動機

同 **encouragement / inclination**

▶ My main motivation for going back to school was to find a better job.
我打算回到學校再進修的動機是想找一份更好的工作。

---

mountainous [ˈmaʊn.tən.əs] *adj.* 多山的

搭 **mountainous region** 多山地區

同 **highland / alpine**

▶ Switzerland's mountainous region is beautiful!
瑞士的山區非常漂亮。

---

moustache [ˈmʌs.tæʃ] *n.* 八字鬍

▶ The man grew a moustache and beard.
那位男士留了八字鬍及絡腮鬍。

---

mow [moʊ] *v.* 割草;收割

同 **trim / cut**

實用片語
mow someone down 壓過,輾過

▶ This week, it's Bob's turn to mow the lawn.
這星期輪到鮑伯割草了。

▶ That speeding car almost mowed the kid down.
那輛超速行駛的車差點輾過這小孩。

M

MTV / music television

[ˈmjuː.zɪk / ˈtel.ə.vɪʒ.ən] *n.* 音樂電視

▶ The singer's newest video is on MTV.
那位歌手的最新影片正在音樂電視台上演。

---

muddy [ˈmʌd.i] *adj.* 泥濘的

同 grubby / mucky

實用片語
muddy the waters 攪亂局面，增加混亂

▶ Please don't walk across the floor with your muddy shoes.
請你不要穿著那雙沾滿泥巴的鞋子走過地板。

▶ These figures are confusing; they simply muddy the waters.
這些數字令人混淆；它們只是增加混亂而已。

---

multiple [ˈmʌl.tə.pəl] *adj.* 多的；複合的

搭 multiple choice 選擇題

同 different / numerous

▶ Kara drives too fast and has received multiple speeding tickets over the past month.
卡拉愛開快車，她已經在過去的一個月內收到了許多的超速罰單。

---

murderer [ˈmɝː.dɚ.ɚ] *n.* 兇手

實用片語
murmur against 埋怨，對⋯有微詞

▶ The police caught and arrested the murderer.
警察抓到並逮捕了兇手。

▶ The whole team is murmuring against the manager.
所有團隊成員都對經理有所微詞。

---

(101)

murmur [ˈmɝː.mɚ]

① *v.* 低聲說話

搭 murmur softly 輕聲談話

同 mumble / grumble

② *n.* 低沈持續的聲音；細語

同 buzz / muttering

▶ I could hear the student murmur something, but I couldn't understand what he said.
我可以聽到那位學生在低聲說話，但卻聽不清楚他到底說了什麼。

▶ Penny could hear a murmur of voices outside her hospital door.
潘妮可以聽到她的病房外有著輕輕的說話聲。

---

mustache [ˈmʌs.tæʃ] *n.* 小鬍子

▶ Sean looks completely different without his mustache.
西恩剃掉鬍子後，完全像另外一個人。

Exercise 50

I. 中英對應

_____ 1. 謙虛　　(A) moderate　　　　(B) modify

　　　　　　　　(C) modern　　　　　(D) modesty

_____ 2. 痛苦的　(A) misery　　　　　(B) misfortune

　　　　　　　　(C) miserable　　　　(D) misleading

_____ 3. 泥濘的　(A) murmur　　　　　(B) murder

　　　　　　　　(C) mud　　　　　　(D) muddy

_____ 4. 誤導　　(A) misleading　　　(B) mislead

　　　　　　　　(C) misunderstand　(D) misunderstood

_____ 5. 激勵　　(A) motivate　　　　(B) monitor

　　　　　　　　(C) motivation　　　(D) mostly

II. Vocabulary Choice

(A) moderate　(B) modest　(C) mature　(D) murmuring　(E) maturity

(F) monument　(G) monitor　(H) murderer　(I) multiple　(J) misfortune

1. There are a lot of people _____ over the new government's policy on gay marriage.

2. The restaurant is _____ in its charges and most of the dishes are affordable.

3. "The Teardrop" _____ was donated by Russia as a memorial for the victims of 9/11.

4. The _____ in the parking lot showed a man trying to break into a car, so the security called the police.

5. The young man suffered _____ injuries in the car accident.

㉑ **eminent** [ˈɛmənənt] *adj.* 出眾的、著名的

例 She has eventually become an eminent lawyer.
她最終變成一個出眾的律師。

imminent [ˈɪmənənt] *adj.* 逼近的、即將發生的

例 A super typhoon is imminent.
一個超級颱風即將逼近。

㉒ **emission** [iˈmɪʃən] *n.* 排出物質、放射

例 The factory is trying to reduce its emission of smoke.
那工廠試著要減少煙塵的排放。

omission [oˈmɪʃən] *n.* 遺漏、疏忽、失職

例 There is one noticeable omission in your business report.
你商務報告內有一個明顯的疏失。

㉓ **envelop** [ɪnˈvɛləp] *v.* 包住、裹住、蓋住、圍繞

例 The queen enveloped herself in a dark long cloak.
女王用深色的長斗篷將自己裹住。

envelope [ˈɛnvəˌlop] *n.* 信封、封皮、封套

例 She opened the envelope and withdrew a check.
她將信封打開並取出支票。

㉔ **equable** [ˈɛkwəbəl] *adj.* 穩定的、平和的

例 In Taiwan the climate is pretty equable.
在台灣氣候算滿穩定的。

equitable [ˈɛkwətəbəl] *adj.* 公平的、公正的

例 The two parties finally reached an equitable settlement.
兩方總算達成一個公正的結果了。

㉕ **fatal** [ˈfetl] *adj.* 致命的、極嚴重的

例 He suffered a fatal disease, after returning from the jungle.
他自叢林回來後，就得了致命的疾病。

fateful [ˈfetfəl] *adj.* 重大的、決定命運的

例 Something happened to him in that fateful year.
在那個重要的一年他發生了些事。

Unit 51

(102) (99)

mutual [ˈmjuː.tʃu.əl] *adj.* 共同的；互相的

搭 **mutual benefit** 雙方互利

同 **bilateral / reciprocal**

▶ Their mutual interest in music drew them together and helped them become good friends.
他們對音樂的共同興趣拉近了他們的距離，並且幫助他們成為好朋友。

mysterious [mɪˈstɪr.i.əs] *adj.* 神秘的

同 **secret / weird**

▶ Doctors still haven't identified the source of the mysterious illness.
醫生仍然無法找出那個神秘怪病的來源。

namely [ˈneɪm.li] *adv.* 也就是；意即

同 **that is / for example**

▶ The hotel provided breakfast, namely pastries and juice.
飯店提供早餐，也就是麵包以及果汁。

(104)

nationality [ˌnæʃ.ənˈæl.ə.ţi / ˌnæʃ.nælˈæl.ə.ţi]
n. 國籍

▶ Be sure to list your nationality on the application.
請務必在申請表格上列出你的國籍。

(103) (97)

naturally [ˈnætʃ.ɚ.ə.li] *adv.* 自然地；天生地

搭 **behave naturally** 表現自然（行動）

同 **generally / typically**

實用片語
come naturally to 與生俱來

▶ Children naturally learn how to walk when they grow older.
小孩子開始長大時自然會學會走路。

▶ The ability to solve problems comes naturally to her.
她處理問題的能力是與生俱來的。

nearsighted [ˌnɪrˈsaɪ.ţɪd] *adj.* 近視的

同 **purblind / shortsighted**

▶ Amber is nearsighted and can't see things clearly that are far away.
安柏近視，所以看不清楚遠方的事物。

(103) (98)

necessarily [ˈnes.ə.ser.ɪl.i]
adv. 必然地；必需地

同 **positively / actually**

▶ One bad grade doesn't necessarily mean you will fail the class.
一次的壞成績並不一定表示你會被當掉。

needy [ˈniː.di] *adj.* 貧窮的

搭 **poor and needy** 弱勢需幫助

同 **down-and-out / indigent**

▶ Donald is known for helping needy families.
唐納以樂於幫助貧窮的家庭而出名。

---

(104) (102) (99) (98) (96) (95)

neglect [nɪˈglekt]

① *v.* 忽視

同 **bypass / overlook**

實用片語
neglect to do 疏於…

② *n.* 忽略

同 **oversight / disrespect**

▶ I know you are busy, but you shouldn't neglect your health.
我知道你很忙碌，但是你不應該忽視你的健康。

▶ I neglected to water the flowers.
我疏於幫花澆水。

▶ Your neglect to study for the exam will probably result in a failing grade.
由於你忽略考前的準備，你很可能會考不及格。

---

(104) (96)

negotiate [nəˈgoʊ.ʃi.eɪt] *v.* （就…）磋商；談判

搭 **negotiate a settlement** 談判協議

同 **haggle / settle**

實用片語
negotiate with 與…協商，談判

▶ The two sides are trying to negotiate a fair price for the house.
雙方正在為這個房子議論出一個公平的價格。

▶ We need to negotiate with them further.
我們需要與他們進一步協商。

---

nevertheless/nonetheless
[ˌnev.ɚ.ðəˈles / ˌnʌn.ðəˈles] *adv.* 儘管如此；仍然

同 **regardless / after all**

▶ You are healthy. Nonetheless, you still need to exercise.
你很健康。儘管如此，你仍然需要運動。

---

newcomer [ˈnuːˌkʌm.ɚ] *n.* 新來的人；新手

同 **novice / outsider**

▶ Let's all give the newcomer a warm welcome!
讓我們熱烈歡迎新人！

---

nightmare [ˈnaɪt.mer] *n.* 噩夢

▶ Joan's 5-year-old son has nightmares every night.
瓊安五歲大的兒子每晚都會做噩夢。

---

nonsense [ˈnɑːn.sens] *n.* 胡說

▶ Larry told me some nonsense about his dog eating his homework.
賴瑞就愛胡說八道，他告訴我他的狗把他的作業給吃掉了。

normally [ˈnɔːr.mə.li] *adv.* 通常；正常地

搭 **behave normally** 正常表現

同 **as a rule / generally**

▶ I would normally eat a big breakfast in the morning.
我通常在早上會吃一頓豐富的早餐。

---

noun [ˈnaʊn] *n.* 名詞

▶ Today, I want you to make sentences with this new list of nouns.
今天，我要你使用這些新的名詞來造些句子。

---

nowadays [ˈnaʊ.ə.deɪz] *adv.* 當今

▶ Nowadays, it seems like everyone is on their cellphone all the time.
現今，似乎每個人隨時都在使用手機。

---

nuclear [ˈnuː.kliː.ə] *adj.* 核子的；核心的

▶ Many leaders fear that the country is developing a nuclear bomb.
很多領袖都害怕那個國家正在發展核子彈。

---

(103)

numerous [ˈnuː.mə.rəs] *adj.* 為數眾多的

搭 **numerous species** 多數物種

同 **vast / ample**

▶ We've had numerous issues with the new software.
那套新的軟體帶給我們好多的問題。

---

nursery [ˈnɜː.sə.i] *n.* 育兒室；幼兒園

▶ Kaitlyn painted the nursery in pretty shades of blue.
凱特琳將育兒室粉刷上一層漂亮的水藍色。

---

nursing [ˈnɜː.sɪŋ] *n.* 護理；看護；養育

▶ Stephanie loves helping people and is studying nursing.
史緹芬妮熱衷助人而且正在唸護理科。

---

nylon [ˈnaɪ.lɑːn] *n.* 尼龍

▶ Our mountain climbing ropes are very strong but light. They're made of nylon.
我們的登山繩索很堅固但是很輕。它是用尼龍做成的。

---

obedience [oʊˈbiː.di.əns] *n.* 服從

搭 **blind obedience** 盲從

同 **conformity / meekness**

▶ We took our dog to school for him to learn obedience.
我們把狗帶去訓練學校學習服從。

obedient [oʊˈbiː.di.ənt] *adj.* 聽話的；服從的

同 **loyal / attentive**

---

(102) (99)

objection [əbˈdʒek.ʃən] *n.* 反對

搭 **strong objection** 極力反對

同 **rejection / doubt**

▶ Phil's 7-year-old son is not very obedient.
菲爾的七歲兒子不太聽話。

- -

▶ The proposal was discussed and voted on. There were no objections.
這個提案已經被討論過而且也完成投票。完全沒有反對的意見。

Exercise 51

I. 中英對應

_____ 1. 惡夢　　(A) nightclub　　　　(B) nightgown
　　　　　　　　 (C) nightfall　　　　　(D) nightmare

_____ 2. 近視的　(A) neglect　　　　　(B) nearsighted
　　　　　　　　 (C) nevertheless　　　(D) necessarily

_____ 3. 幼兒園　(A) nurse　　　　　　(B) nursing
　　　　　　　　 (C) nursery　　　　　 (D) nuclear

_____ 4. 談判　　(A) negotiator　　　 (B) negotiate
　　　　　　　　 (C) neglect　　　　　 (D) negative

_____ 5. 核心的　(A) unclear　　　　　(B) numerous
　　　　　　　　 (C) newcomer　　　　 (D) nurture

II. Vocabulary Choice

(A) mystery　(B) obedient　(C) neglect　(D) namely　(E) naturally

(F) mysterious　(G) needy　(H) obedience　(I) objection　(J) negotiate

1. Many celebrities and famous individuals such as politicians, movie stars and rockers, have died in _____ circumstances.

2. The emperor demands unquestioning _____ from his people. Those who do not listen are severely punished.

3. This building has fallen into a state of _____ because no-one has lived there for many years.

4. The organization collected money to help _____ families in the poorest parts of the country.

5. I learned an important lesson from the Bible today, _____ that people look at the outward appearance, but God looks at the heart.

objective [əbˈdʒek.tɪv]

① *adj.* 客觀的

同 **open-minded / impartial**

② *n.* 目標；任務

搭 **objective analysis** 客觀的分析

同 **target / goal**

▶ Researchers hope the tests will provide accurate and objective information.
研究員們希望這個測試能夠提供精準及客觀的數據。

▶ Frank's objective is to finish school in three years.
法蘭克的目標就是在三年內完成學業。

---

 observation [ˌɑːb.zɚˈveɪ.ʃən] *n.* 觀察

同 **inspection / review**

▶ The man has been under the observation of doctors for days.
那個男人已經入院接受醫生的觀察好幾天了。

---

 obstacle [ˈɑːb.stə.kəl] *n.* 障礙物

搭 **come across obstacle** 超越障礙

同 **hitch / bump**

▶ My biggest obstacle to going back to school is the tuition.
我重回學校唸書的最大障礙就是學費。

---

 obtain [əbˈteɪn] *v.* 獲得

搭 **obtain knowledge** 獲得知識

同 **gain / acquire**

實用片語
obtain for 幫…取得，拿取

▶ I have finally been able to obtain the resources needed to finish my paper.
我最後終於能夠取得所需的資源來完成我的報告。

▶ I promised I would obtain a kitten for you.
我保證會幫你得到一隻小貓。

---

 obviously [ˈɑːb.vi.əs.li] *adv.* 明顯地；顯然地

同 **certainly / visibly**

▶ From the look on his face, Mark obviously enjoys the cake.
從馬克臉上的表情看來，他顯然很喜歡這個蛋糕。

---

occasional [əˈkeɪ.ʒən.əl / əˈkeɪʒ.nəl]
adj. 偶爾的

搭 **occasional visitor** 偶爾拜訪者

同 **random / casual**

▶ During Mark's occasional visits, he always insists on preparing dinner.
馬克偶然來拜訪時，都會堅持他做晚餐。

occupation [ˌɑː.kjəˈpeɪ.ʃən] *n.* 職業；佔據

搭 **well-paid occupation** 高收入工作

同 **job / career**

▶ Many occupations require a college degree.
很多的職業都會要求你具備大學文憑。

---

occupy [ˈɑkjəˌpaɪ] *v.* 佔據

搭 **occupy attention** 攫住注意力

同 **take up / engage**

實用片語
occupy by 佔用

▶ Drake's car used to occupy that space, until he sold it.
德拉克賣掉車子以前，都是停在那個位子。

▶ While waiting, I occupied myself by reading.
等候的時候，我把時間用在閱讀。

---

offend [əˈfend] *v.* 激怒；冒犯

同 **disturb / irritate**

實用片語
offend against 觸犯

▶ Emily was offended by Stan's comments about "dumb blondes".
艾蜜莉因著史丹對「金髮笨娃」的評論而被激怒了。

▶ We don't want to offend against anyone.
我們不想觸犯任何人。

---

offense [əˈfens] *n.* 罪過；犯法；得罪

搭 **criminal offense** 犯罪行為

同 **misdeed / wrongdoing**

▶ The ruler had his opponents arrested for no particular offense.
那位統治者逮捕了反對他的人，即使他們沒有觸犯任何法律。

---

offensive [əˈfen.sɪv] *adj.* 令人反感的；冒犯的

同 **shocking / abusive**

▶ Jacob's behavior was very offensive.
雅各的行為真是令人反感。

---

oneself [ˌwʌnˈself] *pron.* 自己；本身

▶ One can admire oneself in front of a mirror.
人可以在鏡子面前欣賞自己。

---

opener [ˈoʊ.pən.ɚ] *n.* 開罐器

實用片語
eye opener 開眼界

▶ It'll be easier to open up that bottle with an opener.
用開罐器打開那個瓶子會比較容易。

▶ His presentation was a real eye opener for me.
他的簡報真的讓我開眼界。

O

104

opening [ˈoʊp.nɪŋ] *n.* 開啟；職缺

搭 **grand opening** 盛大開幕

同 **vacancy / opportunity**

▶ The opening of the door made a loud noise.
開門的聲音很大聲。

---

opera [ˈɑː.pɚ.ə] *n.* 歌劇

實用片語
soap opera 肥皂劇

▶ Opera tells a story through music.
歌劇就是透過音樂說故事。

▶ My mother watches soap operas all day long.
我媽媽一整天只是看肥皂劇。

---

104 100 98 96

operation [ˌɑː.pɚˈreɪ.ʃən] *n.* 手術；操作

搭 **perform operation** 動手術

同 **surgery / enterprise**

▶ After my father broke his shoulder, he needed an operation.
爸爸在摔斷了肩膀之後，必須動一個手術。

---

103 102

oppose [əˈpoʊz] *v.* 對抗；反對

同 **argue / defend**

實用片語
oppose to 反對…

▶ Our team will oppose the district's top team.
我們的團隊將會對抗本區的冠軍隊。

▶ They are strongly opposed to my suggestions.
他們嚴正反對我的建議。

---

oral [ˈɔːr.əl]

① *adj.* 口述的

搭 **oral exam** 口試

同 **vocal / spoken**

② *n.* 口試

▶ The final test will include an oral exam.
期末考將會包括一項口試。

▶ We will have our English orals at the end of the semester.
我們在學期結束前會舉行英文口試。

100

orbit [ˈɔːr.bɪt]

① *n.* 運行軌道

② *v.* 繞軌道運行

▶ The rocket is now entering the Earth's orbit.
火箭現在已經進入地球的運行軌道。

▶ The satellite will orbit the Earth for the next ten years.
人造衛星會在未來的十年內繞著地球的軌道運行。

---

orchestra [ˈɔːr.kə.strə] *n.* 管弦樂隊

▶ Deana plays violin in the community orchestra.
迪娜在社區的管弦樂隊裡拉小提琴。

99

organic [ɔːˈgæn.ɪk] *adj.* 有機體的；器官的

同 **living / essential**

---

103 **102**

otherwise [ˈʌð.ə.waɪz]
adv. 不同地；以另外的方式

同 **differently / or else**

---

ought [ˈɑːt] *aux v.* 應該

---

ourselves [ˌaʊ.əˈselvz / ˌaʊrˈselvz]
pron. 我們自己

---

outcome [ˈaʊtˌkʌm] *n.* 結果

搭 **eventual outcome** 最終結果

同 **conclusion / reaction**

▶ Samples containing organic matter are being tested in the lab.
含著有機成分的樣本正在實驗室裡接受化驗。

- -

▶ Lizzie thought the movie was great. Josh thought otherwise.
莉絲覺得那部電影很棒。賈許卻不以為然。

- -

▶ I ought to wait until my laundry is finished.
我應該等到衣服洗好。

- -

▶ We couldn't blame ourselves for what happened.
我們不該為已經發生的事來責怪自己。

- -

▶ The family was anxious to hear the outcome of the court decision.
那家人急著聽到法院定案的結果。

O

Exercise 52

I. 中英對應

_____ 1. 明顯地   (A) obviously   (B) obstacle   (C) obtain   (D) observe

_____ 2. 器官的   (A) organize   (B) organic   (C) organization   (D) organizer

_____ 3. 手術   (A) operator   (B) operate   (C) opera   (D) operation

_____ 4. 職業   (A) occupy   (B) occupied   (C) occupation   (D) occasional

_____ 5. 職缺   (A) opening   (B) opener   (C) open   (D) openly

II. Vocabulary Choice

(A) observe   (B) observations   (C) occasional   (D) oval   (E) obtain

(F) oral   (G) offensive   (H) obedience   (I) obstacle   (J) occupation

1. There is no _____ too big to overcome.

2. The company received complaints because their advertisement was _____ to women.

3. Isaac Newton made great _____ about gravity and he became a great scientist.

4. In the world of business today, unlike in the past, an _____ agreement is not enough to secure a deal.

5. Tina likes an _____ glass of wine before she goes to bed.

outstanding [ˌaʊtˈstæn.dɪŋ] *adj.* 傑出的

搭 **outstanding achievement** 傑出的成就

同 **superior / magnificent**

▶ Susan gave an outstanding performance in the concert.
她在音樂會上的表現是非常傑出。

---

oval [ˈoʊ.vəl]

① *adj.* 橢圓形的；蛋形的

② *n.* 橢圓形；卵形物

▶ The diamond in Laura's beautiful ring is oval-shaped.
鑲在琳達漂亮戒指上的鑽石是橢圓形的。

▶ The children are learning to recognize circles, squares and ovals.
小朋友開始學習認識圓形，正方形以及橢圓形。

101

overcome [ˌoʊ.vɚˈkʌm] *v.* 戰勝；克服

搭 **overcome barrier** 克服障礙

同 **overwhelm / survive**

▶ Our team has had several losses, but we can overcome next week's team.
我們的球隊輸掉了幾場，但是我們會戰勝下星期的球隊。

96

overlook [ˌoʊ.vɚˈlʊk] *v.* 眺望；俯瞰

搭 **overlook the river** 往下鳥瞰河面

同 **look out on / look over**

▶ We stopped the car and overlooked the small village below.
我們停下車來，眺望下面的小村落。

---

overnight [ˌoʊ.vɚˈnaɪt]

① *adv.* 整夜地；通宵地

② *adj.* 一整夜的

搭 **overnight train** 過夜火車

▶ Make your spaghetti sauce now, and keep it in the refrigerator overnight.
你可以現在做義大利麵醬，然後將它放在冰箱一整晚。

▶ The Chens took an overnight trip to Kaohsiung.
陳家人去高雄旅遊兩天一夜。

---

overtake [ˌoʊ.vɚˈteɪk] *v.* 超越；趕上

同 **catch up with / outdistance**

▶ The horse came from the rear, overtook all the others and won the race.
那匹馬從後面追趕上來，超越了其他所有的賽馬而贏得冠軍。

O

overthrow [ˌoʊ.vəˈθroʊ] *v.* 推翻

同 **conquer / overturn**

▶ The rebels overthrew the corrupt government.
那些反抗者推翻了腐敗的政府。

---

oxygen [ˈɑːk.sɪ.dʒən] *n.* 氧氣

▶ The patient isn't getting enough oxygen to her brain.
那位病人的頭腦缺乏氧氣。

---

p.m. / pm / P.M. / PM [ˌpiːˈem] *adv.* 下午

▶ The meeting will begin at 7:00 p.m. and finish at 9:00 p.m.
那個會議會從午後七點開始，直到九點才結束。

---

pace [peɪs]

① *n.* 一步

搭 **walking pace** 行走速度

同 **clip / measure**

② *v.* 踱步；慢慢地走

同 **trot / gallop**

實用片語
at a snail's pace 緩慢，龜速

▶ Walk 30 paces to the north, and you'll find buried treasure under the tree.
往北方走三十步，你將會發現埋在樹下的寶物。

▶ My dad has been pacing the floor, waiting for my sister to return home.
我爸爸一直來回地踱步，等著妹妹回家。

▶ Jenny works at a snail's pace.
珍妮工作龜速，動作很慢。

---

pail [peɪl] *n.* 桶

▶ Go to the river and fill this pail with water.
去河邊，把桶子裝滿水。

---

panel [ˈpæn.əl] *n.* 門板；儀錶盤

▶ The doors are a natural color, but the panels are painted white.
這些門都是天然的顏色，但是門板都被漆成白色。

---

parachute [ˈper.ə.ʃuːt]

① *n.* 降落傘

② *v.* 跳傘

同 **bounce / dive**

▶ Do you ever worry that your parachute won't open?
你曾經擔心過你的降落傘會打不開嗎？

▶ The soldiers parachuted into the war-torn area.
那些士兵們跳傘進入遭受戰爭破壞的地區。

---

paragraph [ˈper.ə.græf] *n.* 段落

▶ Your article should be six paragraphs long.
你的文章必須要有六個段落長。

parking ['pɑːr.kɪŋ] *n.* 停車；停車處

實用片語
valet parking 代客停車

▶ Parking is very difficult during the morning hours.
上午時間非常難停車。

---

partial ['pɑːr.ʃəl] *adj.* 部分的

同 **limited / imperfect**

實用片語
partial to 偏心

▶ Lannie has only a partial understanding of today's math assignment.
今天的數學作業，蘭尼只了解一部分。

▶ The teacher is partial to female students.
老師對女學生偏心。

103
participation [pɑːrˌtɪs.əˈpeɪ.ʃən] *n.* 參加

搭 **encourage participation** 鼓勵參與

同 **attendance / cooperation**

▶ Our teacher strongly believes in class participation.
我們的老師深信課堂參與的重要性。

---

participle ['pɑːr.tɪ.sɪ.pəl] *n.* 分詞

▶ A participle can function as an adjective.
分詞也可以當成形容詞來使用。

---

104 95
particularly [pɚˈtɪk.jə.lɚ.li] *adv.* 特別；尤其

同 **especially / chiefly**

▶ I like all candy, but I particularly love chocolate.
我喜歡所有的糖果，但是偏愛巧克力。

102
partnership ['pɑːrt.nɚ.ʃɪp] *n.* 合夥（合作）關係

同 **relationship / alliance**

▶ The partnership between our two companies has been mutually beneficial.
我們兩家公司的合夥關係讓我們彼此互惠。

---

passive ['pæs.ɪv] *adj.* 消極的；被動的

搭 **passive smoking** 吸二手煙

同 **static / inactive**

▶ Winston's passive behavior causes people to think he is a weak person.
溫斯頓的被動行為使別人認為他是個軟弱的人。

---

pasta ['pɑː.stə] *n.* 義大利麵；通心麵

▶ Let's have pasta tonight. We can have fish tomorrow.
我們今晚吃義大利麵。明天再吃魚。

---

pebble ['peb.əl] *n.* 小卵石

▶ The beach is covered in tiny white pebbles.
海灘上鋪滿了許多小小的白石頭。

P

peculiar [pɪˈkjuːl.jə]

adj. 奇怪的;罕見的;獨特的

同 distinct / strange

---

pedal [ˈped.əl]

① *n.* 踏板
② *v.* 踩踏板,常指騎腳踏車

▶ My car is making a peculiar noise. I hope it's not a serious problem.
我的汽車發出奇怪的聲音。希望不是個大問題。

▶ The piano pedals no longer work.
鋼琴的踏板已經無法使用了。

▶ Pedaling up the hill was hard work and very tiresome.
騎自行車上山是很辛苦的,也很累人。

Exercise 53

I. 中英對應

_____ 1. 降落傘　(A) paragraph　(B) parade　(C) parachute　(D) paradise

_____ 2. 罕見的　(A) peculiar　(B) pebble　(C) perspective　(D) personal

_____ 3. 被動的　(A) passion　(B) passage　(C) passionate　(D) passive

_____ 4. 儀表盤　(A) panel　(B) panic　(C) pail　(D) penal

_____ 5. 推翻　(A) overtake　(B) overthrow　(C) overtime　(D) overheat

II. Derivatives

1. Mark eventually decided to go into _____ (partner) with his younger brother last year so that they could expand his company overseas.

2. The Paris hotel we stayed in _____ (over) the Musée d'Orsay and the Seine river.

3. Our team won because of her _____ (participate) in this competition.

4. I hope we can find a _____ (park) space close to the movie theatre because I do not want to walk so far .

5. I like all her movies, but her latest film is _____ (particular) good.

Unit 54

peer [ˈpɪr]

① *n.* 同儕；同輩；（地位、能力等）同等的人

搭 **peer pressure** 同儕壓力

同 **associate / companion**

② *v.* 凝視；端詳

同 **peep / stare**

實用片語
peer about 四處張望

▶ Jon's peers aren't always very good examples.
瓊恩的同儕並不都是好榜樣。

▶ The cat peered at the mouse from behind the sofa.
那隻貓從沙發後面凝視著小老鼠。

▶ Jack peered about, looking for a place to sit.
傑克四處張望，尋找坐下的地方。

---

penalty [ˈpen.əl.ti] *n.* 刑罰；懲罰

搭 **impose penalty** 開罰單

同 **fine / amends**

▶ His penalty for drinking and driving was one week in jail.
他酒駕所得到的刑罰就是在牢裡度過一星期。

---

percent / per cent [pɚˈsent] *n.* 百分之⋯

▶ Thirty percent of our students come from other countries.
我們學生當中，有百分之三十是來自其他國家。

---

percentage [pɚˈsen.tɪdʒ] *n.* 百分率

同 **portion / ratio**

▶ A small percentage of adults are unable to read.
有小部分的成年人是不識字的。

---

perfection [pɚˈfek.ʃən] *n.* 完美

同 **ideal / precision**

實用片語
cook to perfection 將⋯煮到完美

▶ My mother spent hours preparing the food, and everything was cooked to perfection.
我媽媽花了數小時準備食物，她煮的每一道菜都是完美的。

▶ The dinner was cooked to perfection.
晚餐被烹調至完美。

---

perfectly [ˈpɝ.fekt.li] *adv.* 完美地；十足地

搭 **perfectly accurate** 完全正確

同 **entirely / fully**

▶ She sang the song perfectly.
她那首歌唱地太完美了！

perfume [pɚˈfjuːm]

① *n.* 香水

② *v.* 灑香水於；使充滿香氣

搭 **costly French perfume** 昂貴的法國香水

同 **bouquet / incense**

▶ Dolores' perfume is too strong. I can smell it outside her office.
陶樂瑞的香水太濃了。我在她辦公室外面就聞到了。

▶ Joanie perfumed the thank you cards to give them a nice fragrance.
瓊妮把香水灑在感謝卡上，讓卡片發出輕柔的香味。

---

permanent [ˈpɚːmə.nənt] *adj.* 永久的

同 **durable / perpetual**

▶ Please put this in your files as my permanent address.
請把我的永久地址放進你的檔案裡。

---

persuasion [pɚˈsweɪ.ʒən] *n.* 說服力；說服

同 **seduction / prejudice**

▶ It took a lot of persuasion to convince Abby to sing a solo.
我們花了好大的說服力才說服艾比表演獨唱。

---

persuasive [pɚˈsweɪ.sɪv]

adj. 有說服力的；勸說的

搭 **persuasive argument** 具說服力的

同 **convincing / inspiring**

▶ You will have to be more persuasive if you hope to sell anything.
你如果想要把產品推銷出去，就必須要更具有說服力。

P

---

pessimistic [ˌpes.əˈmɪs.tɪk] *adj.* 悲觀的

搭 **pessimistic view** 悲觀的看法

同 **depressed / discouraged**

▶ Glenn is so pessimistic; he finds something negative to say about everything.
格蘭是個很悲觀的人；他對每件事都有負面的說法。

---

petal [ˈpet̬.əl] *n.* 花瓣

▶ The little girl sprinkled flower petals down the center of the aisle.
小女孩把花瓣灑在走道的中間。

---

petrol [ˈpet.rəl] *n.* （英國）汽油

同 **diesel fuel / oil**

▶ We made sure the car had enough petrol before we set out.
我們出發前已經確定汽車有足夠的汽油。

phenomenon [fə'nɑː.mə.nɑːn] *n.* 現象

搭 **observe phenomenon** 觀察現象

同 **circumstance / anomaly**

▶ The phenomenon of black holes in space is not completely understood.
外太空的黑洞現象仍然無法讓人完全理解。

---

philosopher [fɪ'lɑː.sə.fɚ] *n.* 哲學家

▶ Socrates was a famous Greek philosopher.
蘇格拉底是位有名的希臘哲學家。

---

philosophical [ˌfɪl.ə'sɑː.fɪ.kəl] *adj.* 哲學的

▶ These philosophical discussions aren't very worthwhile. We need some practical solutions.
這些哲學的討論不太值得花費時間，我們需要一些實際的解決方案。

---

philosophy [fɪ'lɑː.sə.fi] *n.* 哲學

▶ Meghan is majoring in philosophy in school.
梅格翰在學校主修哲學。

---

photography [fə'tɑː.grə.fi] *n.* 攝影術

同 **beaux arts / graphic arts**

▶ Grant likes taking photos, so he hopes to study photography in the future.
葛蘭特很喜歡拍照，所以他希望將來能夠學習攝影。

---

physical ['fɪz.ɪ.kəl] *adj.* 身體的

同 **bodily / personal**

▶ In addition to your fatigue, are you experiencing any other physical problems?
你除了疲憊之外，是否還有什麼其他身體上的問題？

---

physician / doctor [fə'zɪʃ·ən / 'dɑːk.tɚ] *n.* 醫生；內科醫生

同 **specialist / surgeon**

▶ An experienced physician will perform Kate's surgery.
一位資深的醫師將會為凱蒂動手術。

---

physicist ['fɪz·ə·sɪst] *n.* 物理學家

▶ The German physicist left the country before the war.
那位德國的物理學家在戰爭之前就離開了國家。

---

physics ['fɪz.ɪks] *n.* 物理學

▶ His uncle is a professor of physics at Harvard University.
他的叔叔是哈佛大學的物理學教授。

pianist [ˈpɪːənˌɪst] *n.* 鋼琴家；鋼琴演奏者

▶ A famous pianist gave a concert at our school.
一位著名的鋼琴家在我們學校開了一場音樂會。

---

pickpocket [ˈpɪkˌpɑːkɪt] *n.* 扒手

▶ When you go through the market at night, you have to watch for pickpockets stealing your purse.
當你在夜間走過市場時，千萬要小心扒手偷走你的錢包。

---

pioneer [ˌpaɪəˈnɪr]

① *n.* 拓荒者；先鋒
搭 **pioneer technique** 先驅技術
同 **guide / innovator**
② *v.* 作先鋒；倡導；成為開拓者
同 **develop / explore**

▶ Long before this area was settled, my ancestors were some of the early pioneers.
遠在人們到這裡定居之前，我的祖先們就是早期的拓荒者。

▶ Wernher von Braun pioneered the development of rockets that took people into space.
華納・馮布朗是設計火箭的先驅，並且將人類送上外太空。

Exercise 54

I. 中英對應

_____ 1. 永久的　　(A) permanent　　(B) permission
　　　　　　　　　(C) performance　　(D) persuasion

_____ 2. 現象　　　(A) phantom　　　(B) pharmacy
　　　　　　　　　(C) phenomenon　　(D) penalty

_____ 3. 先鋒　　　(A) pilot　　　　(B) pianist
　　　　　　　　　(C) pickpocket　　(D) pioneer

_____ 4. 悲觀的　　(A) pessimist　　(B) pessimistic
　　　　　　　　　(C) pessimism　　(D) passageway

_____ 5. 內科醫生　(A) philosopher　(B) physicist
　　　　　　　　　(C) physician　　(D) pickpocket

II. Derivatives

1. Many people believe the presidential candidate because of her _____ (persuade) arguments.

2. According to recent research by the National Taiwan University, the _____ (percent) of babies born in Taiwan has been rising since 2011.

3. Isaac Newton, Albert Einstein and Niels Bohr were the greatest _____ (physic) of their time.

4. World famous author Leo Tolstoy wrote in his work, Anna Karenina that "If you look for _____ (perfect), you'll never be content."

5. Sarah used Jewish _____ (philosophe) views to guide her life.

Unit 55

pirate [ˈpaɪr.ət]

① *n.* 海盜

② *v.* 從事劫掠

▶ Pirates are always looking for the next ship to attack.
海盜們總是在尋找下一艘船來攻擊。

▶ The movie is about a ship that was pirated in the Indian Ocean.
這部電影是有關一艘在印度洋遭海盜劫掠的船。

 95

plentiful [ˈplen.tʃ.fəl] *adj.* 豐盛的；豐富的

[搭] **plentiful resources** 大量資源
[同] **bountiful / generous**

▶ Our hosts were nice, and the food was plentiful.
接待我們的主人非常親切，而且食物也很豐盛。

---

plot [plɑːt]

① *n.* 陰謀

[搭] **murder plot** 謀殺陰謀
[同] **conspiracy / design**

② *v.* 策劃；密謀
[同] **conspire / operate**

[實用片語]
plot out 描繪出

▶ Their plot to kill the president was discovered in time to prevent it.
他們打算刺殺總統的陰謀被即時發現，而得以被制止。

▶ A small group is plotting to overthrow the government.
有一小群人正在策劃要推翻政府。

▶ We need to plot out a new strategy.
我們需要描繪出新的策略。

---

plural [ˈplʊr.əl]

① *adj.* 多種的；複數的
[同] **multiple / dual**

② *n.* 複數

▶ In our country, we are allowed to have plural citizenship.
在我們國家裡，我們可以擁有多重國籍。

▶ "Children" is the plural of "child."
「Children」是「child」的複數形。

---

pocket money [ˈpɑː.kɪt ˌmʌn.i] *n.* 零用錢

▶ I have a little pocket money that you can use.
我有一點零用錢可以給你用。

100

poisonous [ˈpɔɪ.zən.əs] *adj.* 有毒的

[同] **deadly / noxious**

▶ I'm afraid to swim in the lake because of the poisonous snakes.
我很害怕在湖裡游泳，因為裡面有毒蛇。

polish [ˈpɑːlɪʃ]

① v. 擦亮；變光滑

搭 **polish shoe** 擦亮皮鞋

同 **brighten / burnish**

實用片語
polish up 磨光，磨亮

② n. 亮光劑；磨光

▶ Don't forget to polish your shoes for tomorrow's interview.
你明天有個面談，不要忘了把皮鞋擦亮喔。

▶ We polished up the silver before using it for the dinner party.
在晚宴前，我們把要使用的銀器磨亮了。

▶ The polish makes the table look clean and shiny.
這個亮光劑使得這張桌子又乾淨又光亮。

---

pollution [pəˈluːʃən] n. 污染

同 **deterioration / impurity**

▶ The pollution in the air made it difficult to breathe.
污染的空氣使人呼吸困難。

---

popularity [ˌpɑːpjəˈlerətɪ] n. 知名度；流行

同 **fame / reputation**

▶ The music group's popularity makes it hard for them to travel.
這個音樂團隊的知名度使他們難以旅行。

---

portable [ˈpɔːrtəbəl] adj. 可攜帶的

搭 **portable computers** 攜帶型電腦

同 **compact / lightweight**

▶ His portable speakers were easy to bring to the party.
他的可攜帶式喇叭很方便帶到派對。

---

porter [ˈpɔːrtə]

n. 行李員；（車站、機場等的）搬運工

▶ The porter helped me with my luggage.
行李員幫我提行李。

---

portray [pɔːrˈtreɪ] v. 描繪（人物）；扮演

同 **characterize / interpretstar**

實用片語
portray as 塑造成

▶ The painting portrayed life in ancient Rome.
這幅畫描繪了古羅馬人的生活。

▶ Ben hopes to portray himself as a gentleman.
班想把自己塑造成一位紳士。

---

possess [pəˈzes] v. 擁有

搭 **possess properties** 擁有財產

同 **occupy / own**

▶ Bill Gates possesses great wealth.
比爾蓋茲擁有雄厚的財力。

possession [pəˈzeʃ.ən] *n.* 私人所有物；擁有

同 **assets / belongings**

▶ The stolen ring was found in his possession.
被竊的戒指在他的私人所有物中被發現了。

---

⁹⁷ **possibly** [ˈpɑː.sə.bli] *adv.* 也許；可能

搭 **possibly dangerous** 潛在危險
同 **perhaps / maybe**

▶ We will possibly visit France if there's enough time.
如果時間充裕，我們有可能去法國。

---

postal [ˈpoʊ.stəl] *adj.* 郵政的

▶ The postal worker delivered the package.
郵局人員送來了包裹。

---

powerless [ˈpaʊ.ɚ.ləs]
adj. 無力量的；無權力的

同 **incapable / passive**

▶ The secretary was powerless to change the company rules.
這位秘書無權更改公司的政策。

---

¹⁰¹ **precise** [prɪˈsaɪs] *adj.* 精確的

搭 **precise answer** 精準的答案
同 **actual / proper**

▶ The witness gave a precise description of the thief.
目擊證人對小偷給了精確的描素。

---

¹⁰⁴ ¹⁰³ ⁹⁸ **predict** [prɪˈdɪkt] *v.* 預測

搭 **predict accurately** 準確地預測
同 **foresee / forecast**

▶ Mark predicts that a storm will hit tomorrow.
馬克預測明天將有暴風雨襲擊。

---

preferable [ˈpref.ɚ.ə.bəl]
adj. 更合意的；更好的

同 **desirable / preferred**

▶ Susie feels a window seat is preferable to a middle seat.
蘇西覺得靠窗位子比中間的位子更合她意。

---

pregnancy [ˈpreg.nən.si] *n.* 懷孕

▶ Women should avoid smoking during pregnancy.
女人在懷孕期間應該避免抽煙。

---

⁹⁵ **pregnant** [ˈpreg.nənt] *adj.* 懷孕的

同 **abundant / anticipating**

▶ Sally is pregnant and will have her baby in April.
莎莉懷孕了而且她的寶寶四月會出生。

P

prepared [prɪˈperd] *adj.* 有準備的

搭 **carefully prepared** 仔細地準備

同 **arranged / planned**

▶ Sara left the prepared food on the table for her husband.
莎拉為先生準備好食物，放在桌上。

---

preposition [ˌprep.əˈzɪʃ.ən] *n.* 介系詞

▶ Common prepositions include at, from and with.
常見的介系詞包括「at」、「from」以及「with」。

---

presentation [ˌprez.ənˈteɪ.ʃən] *n.* 簡報；授予

搭 **presentation skills** 簡報技巧

同 **demonstration / proposal**

▶ His presentation to the new employees lasted thirty minutes.
他對新進員工所做的簡報持續三十分鐘。

Exercise 55

I. Derivatives

1. The factory claims it is not responsible for the air _____ (pollute) that has made people in the town sick.

2. The _____ (possess) of a degree does not mean you will be success in life.

3. Mr. Lee gave an interesting _____ (present) on modern art and Christianity.

4. According to the weather forecast, there will be showers and _____ (possible) a thunderstorm this afternoon.

5. Kevin is considering buying a new _____ (port) power bank because his cell phone's battery runs out very quickly.

II. 中英對應

_____ 1. 有毒的　(A) poisonous　(B) polish　(C) poison　(D) possession

_____ 2. 精確的　(A) precise　(B) precious　(C) previous　(D) presence

_____ 3. 描繪　(A) porter　(B) portray　(C) postal　(D) portable

_____ 4. 懷孕　(A) presentation (B) pregnancy　(C) privacy　(D) pressure

_____ 5. 更好的　(A) preferable　(B) preference (C) prefer　(D) preface

presently [ˈprez.ənt.li] *adv.* 目前；不久；此刻

同 **immediately / currently**

▶ Presently, the room is being used.
這個房間目前有人正在使用。

---

preservation [ˌprez.ɚˈveɪ.ʃən] *n.* 保存；維護

同 **conservation / protection**

▶ The preservation of the ancient city is important to the country.
對國家而言，保存古蹟是非常重要的。

---

99 98

preserve [prɪˈzɝːv] *v.* 維護；保存

搭 **preserve heritage** 保存遺產

同 **safeguard / conserve**

實用片語
preserve against 保護…使免受（危害）

▶ The government is trying to preserve the environment.
政府正在努力維護環境。

▶ I use sun block to preserve my skin against the harmful effects of the sun.
我用防曬乳保護皮膚免受太陽的有害效應危害。

96

prevention [prɪˈven.ʃən] *n.* 防範；預防

同 **avoidance / determent**

▶ Washing one's hands is important in the prevention of spreading germs.
洗手對於防範細菌擴散而言非常重要。

---

prime [ˈpraɪm]

① *adj.* 最主要的；最初的

搭 **prime responsibility** 主要任務

② *n.* 黃金時期；初期

同 **opening / greenness**

實用片語
in someone's prime 極盛時期

▶ The prime goal of our company is to make money.
公司最主要的目標就是賺錢。

▶ Michael Jordan won five NBA titles during the prime of his career.
麥可・喬丹在他職業生涯的黃金時期榮獲五次 NBA 最有價值球員獎。

▶ Ms. Jones retired in her prime.
瓊斯太太在她的極盛時期退休。

---

104 103

primitive [ˈprɪm.ə.t̬ɪv] *adj.* 原始的；簡陋的

搭 **primitive condition** 原始狀態

同 **primeval / undeveloped**

▶ With no power or water, the conditions of the campground were primitive.
沒電又沒水，露營區的狀況非常簡陋。

---

100 96

privacy [ˈpraɪ.və.si] *n.* 隱私

同 **concealment / retreat**

▶ We respected the family's privacy after their father died.
在他們的父親過世後，我們決定尊重他們的隱私。

privilege [ˈprɪv.əl.ɪdʒ]

① *n.* 殊榮；特權

搭 **special privilege** 特殊待遇

同 **allowance / authorization**

② *v.* 給予…特權

▶ It was a privilege to be invited to meet the president.
能被邀請面會總統真是一項殊榮。

▶ The tax laws privilege the wealthy.
稅法總是給予有錢人特權。

97

procedure [prəˈsiː.dʒɚ] *n.* 程序

同 **conduct / scheme**

▶ Tom followed the company's procedure for requesting time off.
湯姆按照公司的程序申請休假。

proceed [proʊˈsiːd] *v.* 前進；繼續進行

搭 **proceed directly** 直接進行

同 **go ahead / advance**

▶ The police didn't allow us to proceed past the accident.
警察不允許我們通過意外現場。

99

production [prəˈdʌk.ʃən] *n.* 產量；生產

同 **construction / manufacture**

▶ The drought impacted the production of wheat.
旱災影響了小麥的產量。

101 99 95

productive [prəˈdʌk.tɪv]

adj. 有效率的；多產的

搭 **productive discussion** 有效的討論

同 **constructive / energetic**

▶ The office was quiet, so I had a very productive day.
辦公室裡很安靜，所以我這一天非常有效率。

profession [prəˈfeʃ.ən]

n. （指受過專業訓練的）職業；工作

同 **situation / career**

▶ Popular professions in this area include doctor, teacher and nurse.
在這個地區受歡迎的專業抱括醫生，教師以及護士。

96

professional [prəˈfeʃ.ən.əl]

① *adj.* 職業的；專業的

搭 **professional engineer** 專業的工程師

同 **competent / experienced**

② *n.* 專業人士；專家

▶ Jean is a professional singer and performs often.
琴恩是位職業歌手而且經常表演。

▶ I can't fix the sink, so I called a professional.
我無法修好水槽，只好找專家來。

P

professor [prəˈfes.ə-] *n.* 教授

搭 **chemistry professor** 化學教授

同 **instructor / advisor**

▶ Alex will meet with his professor after class.
艾力士下課後會和教授碰面。

---

96 95

profitable [ˈprɑː.fɪ.t̬ə.bəl] *adj.* 有利潤的

同 **beneficial / rewarding**

▶ Our business wasn't profitable, so we closed the store.
我們的生意不賺錢，所以我們結束營業。

---

prominent [ˈprɑː.mə.nənt] *adj.* 突出的；顯著的

同 **outstanding / arresting**

▶ It's easy to recognize Bill from his prominent eyebrows.
從比爾突出的眉型來看，一眼就能讓人認出他來。

100

promising [ˈprɑː.mɪ.sɪŋ]
adj. 有前途的；大有可為的

搭 **promising future** 前景看好

同 **encouraging / up-and-coming**

▶ After graduating with honors, she has a promising career ahead of her.
她以優等成績畢業，未來的職業生涯是非常看好的。

---

promotion [prəˈmoʊ.ʃən] *n.* 升遷；晉級

同 **advancement / jump**

▶ After working hard for years, Steve received a promotion to vice president.
史提夫在辛苦工作多年之後，終於被升遷為副總裁。

---

103 102

prompt [prɑːmpt]

① *adj.* 立即的：（付款）即時的

搭 **prompt reply** 立即回應

同 **immediate / punctual**

② *v.* 鼓動；促使

搭 **prompt change** 促進改變

同 **encourage / trigger**

③ *n.* 提詞；提醒

同 **help / reminder**

▶ The invitation asked for a prompt reply.
這分邀請函要求立即的回應。

▶ I had to prompt Susan to share her story with the class.
我必須要鼓動蘇珊跟同學們分享她的故事。

▶ The actor forgot his line and needed a prompt.
這位演員忘了他的台詞，因此需要別人提詞。

---

pronoun [ˈproʊ.naʊn] *n.* 代名詞

▶ Common pronouns include his, her, he and she.
常見的代名詞包括 his、her、he 以及 she。

pronunciation [prəˌnʌn.siˈeɪ.ʃən] *n.* 發音

▶ John's poor pronunciation made it difficult for the other students to understand him.
約翰糟糕的發音使得班上其他同學很難聽懂他。

---

[100] [99]

properly [ˈprɑː.pɚ.li] *adv.* 適當地；恰當地

搭 **prepare properly** 適當的準備
同 **rightly / suitably**

▶ If you don't properly clean the desk, it won't be clean!
如果你不確實地擦桌子，桌子就不會乾淨！

---

[99]

prosper [ˈprɑː.spɚ] *v.* 成功；繁榮

同 **catch on / flourish**

實用片語
prosper from 繁榮

▶ I hope your son will prosper in his new job.
我希望你的兒子在新的工作有所成就。

▶ I hope you prosper from your new business.
我希望你的新事業會蓬勃發展。

---

prosperity [prɑːˈsper.ə.tj]
n. 生意興隆；繁榮；興盛

搭 **create prosperity** 創造繁榮
同 **accomplishment / success**

▶ After years of prosperity, the company wasn't used to falling sales.
這家公司在多年的榮景之後，很難接受下滑的業績。

P

Exercise 56

I. Derivatives

1. This year has been the author's most _____ (produce) year so far in her career with three novels waiting to be published.

2. My friend is a _____ (profession) singer and he makes a lot of money by performing at weddings.

3. Most people hope to have a life of happiness and _____ (prosper).

4. The convenient store is planning a big _____ (promote) for its seasonal products.

5. Over the years, her small restaurant has developed into a highly _____ (profit).

II. 中英對應

_____ 1. 有前途的　　(A) prominent　　　　(B) promise
　　　　　　　　　　　(C) prompting　　　　(D) promising

_____ 2. 防範　　　　(A) prevention　　　 (B) preposition
　　　　　　　　　　　(C) previous　　　　 (D) preservation

_____ 3. 發音　　　　(A) pronoun　　　　 (B) pronounce
　　　　　　　　　　　(C) pronouncement　 (D) pronunciation

_____ 4. 特權　　　　(A) primitive　　　 (B) privacy
　　　　　　　　　　　(C) principle　　　　(D) privilege

_____ 5. 即時的　　　(A) promote　　　　 (B) promptly
　　　　　　　　　　　(C) prompt　　　　　(D) prominent

prosperous [ˈprɑː.spɚ.əs]

adj. 成功的；富裕的；繁榮的

搭 **prosperous economy** 繁榮的經濟

同 **flourishing / wealthy**

▶ Sam is a prosperous businessman.
山姆是位成功的生意人。

---

protein [ˈproʊ.tiːn] *n.* 蛋白質

▶ The doctor said to add more eggs to your diet for protein.
醫生說要飲食中要多加一些雞蛋以攝取蛋白質。

---

104 97

protest [proʊˈtest]

① *n.* 抗議

搭 **street protest** 街頭抗議

同 **objection / question**

② *v.* 抗議；對…提出異言

同 **declare / object**

▶ The citizens filed a protest against the government's decision.
市民們對於政府的決策提出抗議。

▶ The workers protested the boss's decision to cut their pay.
員工們紛紛抗議老闆減薪的決策。

P

---

proverb [ˈprɑː.vɝːb] *n.* 諺語

搭 **old proverb** 古老諺語

同 **motto / saying**

▶ Ancient proverbs offer timeless wisdom.
古老的諺語提供不朽的智慧。

---

psychological [ˌsaɪ.kəˈlɑː.dʒɪ.kəl]

adj. 心理學的

▶ She picked a psychological topic for her research paper.
她挑了一個心理學的主題作為她的研究報告。

---

psychologist [saɪˈkɑː.lə.dʒɪst] *n.* 心理學家

▶ Talking to a psychologist might help you with your problems.
找個心理學家談談，或許會幫助你解決困難。

---

psychology [saɪˈkɑː.lə.dʒi] *n.* 心理學

▶ Psychology involves the study of behavior.
心理學涉及行為科學。

publication [ˌpʌb.ləˈkeɪ.ʃən] *n.* 出版

同 **broadcasting / publishing**

not for publication 勿公開

▶ The publication of his first book was cause for celebration.
為他處女作出版而慶祝一番。

▶ This report is not for publication.
請勿公開此報告。

---

publicity [pʌbˈlɪs.ə.tj] *n.* 宣傳；關注

同 **distribution / attention**

▶ His award received widespread publicity in his hometown.
他得獎的消息在他的家鄉得到大肆的宣傳。

---

publish [ˈpʌb.lɪʃ] *v.* 出版

搭 **publish a survey** 做調查

同 **broadcast / distribute**

▶ The editor made several changes to the book before he published it.
編輯在出版這本書之前，做了多次的更改。

---

publisher [ˈpʌb.lɪ.ʃə] *n.* 出版商；出版者

搭 **magazine publisher** 雜誌出版商

同 **compositor / typographer**

▶ The publisher told Sam that his book needed to be rewritten.
出版商告訴山姆，他的書必須重新寫過。

---

pursuit [pəˈsuːt] *n.* 追蹤；追求

同 **inquiry / quest**

in pursuit 追求

▶ The pursuit of the suspect took the police all over town.
為了追蹤嫌犯，警察滿城地跑。

▶ Frank spends most of his energy in pursuit of wealth.
法蘭克花了他大多數的精力在追求財富。

---

quake [kweɪk]

① *v.* 顫抖；哆嗦

同 **pulsate / shrink**

② *n.* 震動；搖晃

同 **quaker / temblor**

▶ Fear from the shocking news caused her to quake.
受到這個駭人新聞的驚嚇，她全身顫抖。

▶ The large truck passing our building caused a brief quake.
這輛大卡車經過我們的大樓前面造成短暫的震動。

---

qualified [ˈkwɑː.lə.faɪd]

adj. 合格的；有資格的；有限制的

搭 **qualified candidate** 合格的候選人

同 **eligible / suitable**

qualified for 符合資格

▶ She wasn't qualified, so she wasn't offered the job.
由於她資歷不合格，所以沒有拿到那份工作。

▶ Sorry, but you are not qualified for this job.
抱歉，但你不符此份工作的要求。

queue [kjuː] *n.* 行列；長隊

同 **chain / line**

實用片語
queue up 排隊等候

▶ The queue to buy movie tickets was very long.
排隊買電影票的隊伍非常的長。

▶ We have to queue up to buy tickets for the play.
我們必須排隊等候這場表演的票。

---

quilt [ˈkwɪlt]

① *n.* 被子

② *v.* 作拼布被

▶ The thick quilt kept the children warm.
這條厚厚的被子讓小朋友們保暖。

▶ Dee's grandma quilted her a blanket.
娣的祖母幫她縫製了一條拼布被。

---

quotation [kwoʊˈteɪ.ʃən] *n.* 語錄；引文；引用

同 **excerpt / reference**

▶ He kept an inspiring quotation on his desk.
他在桌上放了一句激勵人心的語錄。

---

rage [reɪdʒ]

① *n.* 狂怒

同 **exasperation / madness**

② *v.* （暴風雨）肆虐；發怒

同 **boil over / rampage**

▶ His fit of rage scared the child.
他的狂怒驚嚇了小孩。

▶ The storm raged through the countryside.
暴風雨肆虐了整個鄉村。

---

raincoat [ˈreɪn.koʊt] *n.* 雨衣

▶ The raincoat kept him dry in the storm.
雨衣讓他在暴風雨中不被淋濕。

95
rainfall [ˈreɪn.fɑːl] *n.* 降雨

▶ The heavy rainfall resulted in many closed roads.
傾盆大雨造成許多道路的封閉。

---

100 97
rarely [ˈrer.li] *adv.* 很少地；難得地

搭 **rarely happen** 鮮少發生

同 **seldom / not often**

▶ My parents rarely eat at expensive restaurants.
我的父母很少在昂貴的餐廳吃飯。

99
readily [ˈred.əl.i]

adv. 迅速地；心甘情願地；輕而易舉地

同 **freely / at once**

▶ The new employee readily accepted his new jobs.
這位新員工很快接受了他的新任務。

Q
R

realistic [ˌriːəˈlɪs.tɪk] *adj.* 實際的；現實的

搭 **realistic assessment** 現實的評估

同 **practical / real**

▶ Her dream of becoming a movie star wasn't realistic.
她想要成為電影明星的夢想並不實際。

---

104 103 102 97

rebel [ˈreb.əl] *n.* 叛逆的人；造反者

同 **opponent / secessionist**

▶ Billy is a rebel and refuses to listen to the teacher.
比利是個叛逆的人，他拒絕聽從他的老師。

rebel [rɪˈbel] *v.* 反抗；反叛

同 **overthrow / resist**

實用片語
rebel against 叛逆，反叛

▶ No one dared to rebel against the teacher's strict rules.
沒有人敢反抗老師嚴格的規定。

▶ Jones rebelled against his parents.
她瓊斯反抗他的父母。

101

rebuild [ˌriːˈbɪld] *v.* 重振經濟

搭 **rebuild economy** 現實的評估

同 **fix / reconstruct**

▶ Construction workers had to rebuild the broken bridge.
建築工人必須重建毀壞的橋樑。

Exercise 57

I. Derivatives

1. Abraham Maslow was a famous American _____ (psychology) who was best known for creating Maslow's Hierarchy of Needs.

2. "It is more blessed to give than to receive," is a famous _____ (quote) from the Bible.

3. Amanda's job is creating _____ (public) for the new movies released by her company.

4. Smartphones are _____ (ready) available nowadays and you can buy them almost anywhere.

5. That the boss expects to hire people to work for him for so little money, isn't _____ (realist).

II. Multiple Choice

(   ) 1. The flight attendants of China Airlines __ against unreasonable work contracts.
   (A) protected   (B) protein   (C) protested   (D) proceeded

(   ) 2. Jean passed her exam recently, so she is a __ accountant now.
   (A) Qualify   (B) qualified   (C) qualities   (D) quality

(   ) 3. The heavy __ ruined our camping plan this weekend.
   (A) rainbow   (B) rainforest   (C) raincoat   (D) rainfall

(   ) 4. The businessman told the reporter it was the scariest __ he had ever experienced. Everything shook for two minutes.
   (A) quick   (B) quake   (C) quarrels   (D) quilts

(   ) 5. The aim of this donation is to help the families to __ their houses which were destroyed in the typhoon.
   (A) rebuild   (B) realistic   (C) rebel   (D) readily

Unit 58

recall [ˈriːˌkɑːl]

① v. 召回；回憶

同 **reminisce / evoke**

實用片語
recall something to 提醒了…；想起某事…

② n. 回收；回想

▶ The factory recalled all the workers back to the shop.
工廠召回所有的工人回到廠裡工作。

▶ What you just mentioned recalled an old song to me.
你剛提到的讓我想起一首老歌。

▶ The company announced a recall of its faulty product.
這家公司發佈瑕疵品回收的公告。

---

reception [rɪˈsepˌʃən] n. 招待會

搭 **business reception** 商業招待會

同 **buffet / gathering**

▶ After the wedding ceremony, we attended the reception.
結婚典禮結束後，我們去參加喜宴。

---

recipe [ˈresˌəpi] n. 做法；食譜；處方

搭 **mouth-watering recipe** 美味的料理

同 **method / program**

實用片語
a recipe for 產生…之原因

▶ My mother's recipe for chocolate cake is a family secret.
我媽媽的巧克力蛋糕食譜是家裡的祖傳秘方。

▶ Living with my husband's family was a recipe for disaster.
與先生的家人同住是產生災難的原因。

---

recite [rɪˈsaɪt] v. 朗讀；背誦

同 **declaim / perform**

▶ The children recited a poem during the performance.
小朋友在表演當中，朗讀了一首詩。

---

 103 102 96

recognition [ˌrekˌəgˈnɪʃən] n. 肯定；認出

同 **acceptance / concession**

▶ In recognition of your efforts, we are giving you this award.
我們為了肯定你的努力，在此頒給你這個獎項。

102

recovery [rɪˈkʌvˌəˌri] n. 康復；恢復

搭 **complete recovery** 完全康復

同 **improvement / recuperation**

實用片語
on the road to recovery 恢復

▶ Luke's recovery from his broken leg will take a long time.
路加的斷腿要完全康復，要花很久的時間。

▶ Don't worry. I am on the road to recovery.
別擔心，我正恢復良好。

recreation [ˌrek.riˈeɪ.ʃən] *n.* 休閒活動；娛樂

同 **amusement / relaxation**

▶ The elderly couple went to the park for some recreation.
這對老夫妻到公園裡做休閒活動。

101

recycle [ˌriːˈsaɪ.kəl] *v.* 回收再利用

搭 **recycle waste** 回收廢棄物
同 **convert / reclaim**

▶ The liquid recycles after it passes through the system.
這些液體在經過這套設備後可以回收再利用。

---

reduction [rɪˈdʌk.ʃən] *n.* 減少

同 **contraction / devaluation**

▶ The company announced a reduction in everyone's salary.
公司宣佈所有的員工都將面對減薪。

---

refer [rɪˈfɜ] *v.* （醫院裡的）轉診

▶ Her general doctor referred her to a bone doctor.
她的家醫科醫師把她轉診給一位骨科醫師。

---

reference [ˈref·ər·əns] *n.* 參考

搭 **reference letter** 推薦信
同 **endorsement / recommendation**

▶ Bob didn't get the job, but they kept his information for future reference.
鮑伯沒有得到工作；但公司保留他的申請資料以便將來作為參考。

---

reflect [rɪˈflekt] *v.* 反射

同 **echo / reverse**

實用片語
reflect on 反映於…

▶ The light reflects off the mirror and makes it hard to see.
從鏡中反射出來的亮光讓人看不清楚。

▶ Paula reflected on the events of the past few days.
寶拉回想這些天發生的事件。

99

reflection [rɪˈflek.ʃən] *n.* 映射；反射

搭 **accurate reflection** 確實反映
同 **image / impression**

▶ The baby was surprised to see his own reflection in the window.
小嬰兒看見自己在玻璃窗上的反射的模樣；感到驚訝。

98

reform [rɪˈfɔːrm]

① *v.* 改革；改正
同 **rehabilitate / renovate**
② *n.* 革新方案；改良
搭 **practical reform** 實際改造

▶ The government hopes to reform the complicated tax system.
政府希望能夠改革這套複雜的稅收制度。

▶ The new president promised to fight for health-care reform.
新任總統承諾將致力於醫療體系的革新。

R

refresh [rɪˈfreʃ] *v.* 重新溫習；使清新；恢復精神

搭 **refresh my memory** 提醒／提示記憶

同 **exhilarate / rejuvenate**

實用片語
refresh with 提神，恢復精力

▶ Tina needs to refresh her memory of French before her trip to France.
緹娜必須在她前往法國旅遊之前，重新溫習她的法文。

▶ After a long run, I like to refresh myself with a bottle of iced tea.
長跑後，我想要來一罐冰茶提神。

---

refreshment [rɪˈfreʃ.mənt] *n.* 提神物；飲食

同 **snack / pick-me-up**

實用片語
liquid refreshment 提神飲料（酒水）

▶ Apples make for great refreshment on a hot day.
在炎熱的天氣中，蘋果有很好的提神效果。

▶ After a busy day, he needs some liquid refreshment.
忙碌的一天後，他需要一些提神飲料。

---

refugee [ˌref.jəˈdʒiː] *n.* 難民

▶ After leaving their home country, the refugees were welcomed by their neighbor.
這些難民在離鄉背井之後，得到他們鄰國的歡迎。

---

refusal [rɪˈfjuː.zəl] *n.* 拒絕；否決

搭 **outright refusal** 全然否決

同 **defiance / rejection**

▶ The boss's refusal to give Tim a raise only made him work harder.
老闆拒絕為提姆加薪，反而讓提姆更加努力工作。

---

regarding [rɪˈɡɑːr.dɪŋ] *prep.* 有關於

同 **respecting / as regards**

▶ The principal asked to speak with me regarding my son's behavior.
校長要求和我談論有關於我兒子在校行為的事。

---

register [ˈredʒ.ə.stɚ]

① *v.* 登記註冊

同 **enroll / record**

實用片語
register for 註冊，登記

② *n.* 登記簿；名冊

▶ On her birthday, Amy will register to vote for the first time.
艾咪會在她生日當天為首次的投票去登記註冊。

▶ I need to register for five courses next term.
我下學期要修五門課。

▶ When we arrived at the wedding, we wrote our names in the register.
當我們抵達婚禮會場時，我們在客人登記簿裡簽名。

registration [ˌredʒ.əˈstreɪ.ʃən] *n.* 登記；註冊

[搭] **meeting registration** 會議登記

[同] **booking / enrollment**

▶ Registration for college courses takes place online.
大學選課的註冊登記可以透過網路進行。

---

regulate [ˈreg.jə.leɪt] *v.* 調整；管理；控制

[同] **conduct / govern**

▶ Regulating working conditions for factory workers is a difficult job.
為廠房的工作人員調整工作環境是一項困難的工作。

---

regulation [ˌreg.jəˈleɪ.ʃən] *n.* 規定；規章

[搭] **traffic regulation** 交通法規

[同] **law / principle**

▶ Joe didn't realize that using his own computer was against company regulations.
喬伊不知道，使用他自己的電腦違反了公司的規定。

---

rejection [rɪˈdʒek.ʃən] *n.* 拒絕；退回

[同] **elimination / repudiation**

▶ After his rejection from the football team, Tony joined the orchestra.
東尼遭足球隊拒絕之後，轉而加入管弦樂團。

---

related [rɪˈleɪ.tɪd]
adj. 相關的；有關的；有親戚關係的

[搭] **loosely related** 不直接相關

[同] **complementary / pertinent**

實用片語
related to 與…有關係

▶ The meeting was about sales and other related issues.
這個會議是有關業務及其他一些相關的主題。

▶ I wonder if John is related to you?
我在想約翰是否與你有關係？

R

Exercise 58

I. 中英對應

_____ 1. 難民　(A) refuse　　(B) refugee　　(C) refuge　　(D) refund

_____ 2. 朗讀　(A) recipe　　(B) reflect　　(C) recycle　　(D) recite

_____ 3. 減少　(A) redemption　(B) redirection　(C) reduction　(D) redial

_____ 4. 拒絕　(A) rejection　(B) rejoicing　(C) rejoin　　(D) rejoice

_____ 5. 參考　(A) reflection　(B) reform　　(C) refusal　　(D) reference

II. Derivatives

1. The driver sped through the red light and was fined for breaking traffic _____ (regulate).

2. Women are employed in _____ (relative) less dangerous jobs, hence they experience fewer job-related injuries and death than men.

3. Hayao Miyazaki was presented with Academy Honorary Award in _____ (recognize) his years of contributions to the motion picture industry.

4. The doctor said that Sarah will make a quick and full _____ (recover) from the operation.

5. According to the pastor, the Biblical word "witness" has the meaning of "Christians' life being a _____ (reflect) of God's glory to the world around us."

relative [ˈrel.ə.t̬ɪv]

① *adj.* 相對的;相較之下的

同 **corresponding / proportionate**

② *n.* 親戚

▶ He enjoyed the relative quiet of his uncle's farm.
他非常享受在叔叔農場裡那樣相對寧靜的日子。

▶ We visited our relatives during Chinese New Year.
我們在農曆過年時去拜訪我們的親戚。

 relatively [ˈrel.ə.t̬ɪv.li] *adv.* 相對地

搭 **relatively inexpensive** 相對便宜

同 **somewhat / quite**

▶ It was a relatively small problem, but it still made Jan angry.
相較之下這只是個小問題,但它還是讓珍相當生氣。

relaxation [ˌriː.lækˈseɪ.ʃən] *n.* 放鬆

同 **loosening / mitigation**

▶ Do you think vacations are for adventure or relaxation?
你認為休假的目的是為了冒險還是為了放鬆?

  relieve [rɪˈliːv] *v.* 減輕;緩和;解除

搭 **relieve ache** 消除疼痛

同 **comfort / diminish**

實用片語
relieve someone of 減輕,緩和

▶ Take this medicine to relieve the pain.
服用這個藥來減輕疼痛。

▶ The maid relieved me of my household chores.
女傭幫我減少了不少家務。

R

reluctant [rɪˈlʌk.tənt] *adj.* 不情願的;勉強的

同 **circumspect / hesitant**

實用片語
reluctant to 不情願,不甘願

▶ He was reluctant to help the stranger.
他很不情願去幫助陌生人。

▶ Carol is reluctant to take on more responsibilities.
卡蘿不想承擔更多責任。

 remark [rɪˈmɑːrk]

① *v.* 談到;談論;評論

同 **declare / mention**

實用片語
address remarks 發表意見,演說

▶ She remarked that she liked the man's hat.
她談到她很喜歡那位男士的帽子。

▶ The CEO addressed his remarks to everyone.
這位執行長向所有人發表意見。

② n. 注目;注意;察覺

搭 **encouraging remark** 鼓勵的話語

同 **commentary / opinion**

▶ The museum is worthy of remark.
那家博物館真是值得注目。

remarkable [rɪˈmɑːr.kə.bəl]

adj. 引人注目的;值得注意的

同 **marvelous / striking**

▶ His performance in the play was remarkable.
他在劇中的表現真是引人注目。

97

remedy [ˈrem.ə.di]

① n. 療法;治療

搭 **effective remedy** 有效的療法

同 **medicine / countermeasure**

② v. 治癒;醫治

同 **assuage / relieve**

▶ Her mother's remedy for a cold is chicken soup.
她媽媽對於感冒的療法就是喝雞湯。

▶ The doctors were able to remedy his disease after he received months of treatment.
在經過數月的治療之後,醫生終於能夠治癒他的疾病。

repeatedly [rɪˈpiː.t̬ɪd.li] 一再重複地;多次

同 **regularly / often**

▶ I repeatedly called until you answered the phone.
我一再重複地打電話給你直到你接電話。

repetition [ˌrep.əˈtɪʃ.ən] n. 背誦;重複

搭 **constant repetition** 持續重覆

同 **recurrence / reiteration**

▶ He memorized his lines after weeks of repetition.
經過幾個星期的背誦之後,他終於記得他的台詞了。

reporting [rɪˈpɔː(r)tɪŋ] n. 報導

同 **broadcasting / coverage**

▶ The politician criticized the reporting about nuclear power.
那位政界人士批評有關核能的報導。

representation [ˌrep.rɪ.zenˈteɪ.ʃən]

n. 代理;代表

同 **image / portrayal**

▶ The lawyer decided to provide representation to the man.
這位律師決定代表這位男士。

102 **101**

reputation [ˌrep.jəˈteɪ.ʃən] n. 名譽;好名聲

搭 **build up reputation** 建立起名聲

同 **fame / prestige**

實用片語

reputation for 有…名聲

▶ The restaurant had a reputation for delicious food.
這家餐廳以它的美食而出名。

▶ Mary has a reputation for being kind.
瑪莉因為仁慈而出名。

rescue [ˈres.kjuː]

① v. 營救；援救

同 **preserve / recover**

實用片語
come to one's rescue 拯救某人

② n. 營救

同 **recovery / salvage**

▶ The firemen rescued the kitten stuck in the tree.
消防人員救出困在樹上的小貓咪。

▶ While I was drowning, the lifeguard came to my rescue.
救生員在我掉進水裡的時候過來救了我。

▶ The rescue of the hikers who got lost during the storm was celebrated by everyone.
在暴風雨中失蹤的登山客得到營救後，大家都歡欣鼓舞。

research [ˈriː.sɝːtʃ]

① n. 研究

搭 **market research** 市場調查

同 **analysis / inquiry**

② v. 作學術研究；調查

搭 **research extensively** 大規模地研究

同 **consult / investigate**

實用片語
research into 對某事研究

▶ The scientist's research uncovered some unexpected facts.
科學家的研究揭發了一些令人出乎意料的事實。

▶ Carol went to the library to research the history of trains.
凱蘿到圖書館去做有關火車歷史的學術研究。

▶ Our team has decided to research into the 2nd World War.
我們團隊決定研究「第二次世界大戰」主題。

researcher [riː.sɝː.tʃər] n. 研究員

▶ The researchers sent surveys to all the students.
研究員將問卷寄給所有的學生。

resemble [rɪˈzem.bəl] v. 長的像；類似

同 **feature / parallel**

實用片語
resemble someone in 跟某人很像

▶ My family often tells me that I resemble my grandfather when he was young.
我的家人經常告訴我，我長的很像我祖父年輕的時候。

▶ You resemble my sister in the way you walk.
你走路的方法跟我姊的很像。

reservation [ˌrez.ɚˈveɪ.ʃən]

n. 未給予；保留（意見）；預訂（房間或席座）

搭 **hotel reservation** 飯店預定

同 **booking / restriction**

實用片語
make a reservation 預定，預約

▶ His mother's reservation of praise made Henry think she didn't like his performance.
亨利的媽媽沒有給他讚美，讓亨利以為媽媽不喜歡他的表演。

▶ I've made a reservation for a table for two.
我已經預約了兩人的桌子。

R

resign [rɪˈzaɪn]

v. 聽任；順從；不得不接受

同 **relinquish / surrender**

實用片語
resign from 離職，辭職

▶ I resigned myself to a long wait in the doctor's office.
我只好在醫生診療室外慢慢地等候。

▶ Andy has resigned from his job.
安迪已經辭掉他的工作了。

---

resignation [ˌrez.ɪgˈneɪ.ʃən]

n. 辭職；放棄（工作）

同 **departure / termination**

▶ Jim's resignation took the office by surprise.
吉姆的辭職讓公司的人大吃一驚。

---

resistance [rɪˈzɪs.təns] *n.* 排斥；抵抗

搭 **drug resistance** 抗藥性

同 **defiance / protection**

實用片語
path of least resistance 阻力最小的道路

▶ Her suggested changes were met with strong resistance.
她所建議的改變遭到強烈的排斥。

▶ I like challenges and won't take the path of least resistance.
我喜歡挑戰而且不會選阻力最小的道路。

---

resolution [ˌrez.əˈluː.ʃən] *n.* 堅定；決心

同 **decision / settlement**

▶ My mom faced her disease with resolution and optimism.
我媽媽用堅定以及樂觀的態度來面對疾病。

103

resolve [rɪˈzɑːlv]

① *v.* 下定決心；決定

搭 **resolve conflict** 排解衝突

同 **conclude / propose**

② *n.* 決心；堅定的信念

同 **courage / firmness**

▶ After his heart attack, Bob resolved to lose weight.
鮑伯在心臟病發作之後，下定決心要減肥。

▶ His tireless resolve ensured he would one day be a great pianist.
他孜孜不倦的信念確保他將來會成為一位偉大的鋼琴家。

---

respectable [rɪˈspek.tə.bəl]

adj. 體面的；值得尊敬的

搭 **eminently respectable** 非常值得尊崇

同 **honorable / modest**

▶ Mark was given a respectable position in the company.
馬克在公司裡得到一個很體面的職位。

---

respectful [rɪˈspekt.fəl]

adj. 有禮貌的；恭敬的；尊重人的

同 **admiring / obedient**

▶ Removing your hat is a respectful way of greeting a lady.
和女士打招呼時脫下帽子是很有禮貌的。

Exercise 59

I. Derivatives

1. Gary handed in his _____ (resign) to his boss and he will be leaving the company at the end of the month.

2. Ben's New Year's _____ (resolute) this year are giving up smoking and exercising at least three times a week.

3. Jackie tries to avoid unnecessary _____ (repeat) in her writing because it could bore the readers.

4. Mother Teresa was truly a _____ (remark) woman and great servant of humanity.

5. Littering in the street is not a _____ (respect) thing to do.

II. 中英對應

_____ 1. 不情願的   (A) relevant   (B) reluctant
                            (C) relocate   (D) relative

_____ 2. 抵抗   (A) resident   (B) residence
                            (C) resign   (D) resistance

_____ 3. 代理   (A) representation   (B) representative
                            (C) representable   (D) representational

_____ 4. 保留（意見）   (A) resemble   (B) rescue
                            (C) reservation   (D) remedy

_____ 5. 緩和   (A) reliable   (B) relieve
                            (C) related   (D) relax

restless [ˈrest.ləs] *adj.* 焦躁不安的;求變的

同 **edgy / uneasy**

▶ The restless children just could not sit still!
那些孩子就是坐不住,根本沒辦法安靜坐好!

---

restore [rɪˈstɔːr] *v.* 恢復

搭 **restore morale** 重振士氣

同 **rebuild / reestablish**

實用片語
restore to 回復,恢復原狀

▶ The police finally restored peace to the city.
警察終於讓整個市區恢復到平靜。

▶ Please restore this room to its original state.
請將此房間恢復原狀。

99
restriction [rɪˈstrɪk.ʃən] *n.* 限制;約束

同 **constraint / regulation**

▶ The store put a restriction on how many items could be purchased per person.
這家商店限制每個人可購買的總件數。

97
retain [rɪˈteɪn] *v.* 保持;保留

搭 **retain influence** 維持影響力

同 **contain / maintain**

實用片語
retain over 保有…對

▶ The man retained possession of his dog after his divorce.
這位男士在離婚後保有小狗的所有權。

▶ Mr. Chen tried to retain control over Jack.
陳先生試圖保有對傑克的控制。

---

retire [rɪˈtaɪr] *v.* 退休;退職

搭 **retire early** 提早退休

同 **relinquish / separate**

實用片語
retire from 自…退休,退下

▶ William retired on his 70th birthday and went traveling.
威廉在他七十大壽時退休並且啟程去旅行。

▶ When do you plan to retire from your job, dad?
爸爸,你計劃何時退休?

103
retirement [rɪˈtaɪr.mənt] *n.* 退休;隱居

搭 **retirement pension** 退休年金

同 **evacuation / withdrawal**

▶ After retirement, the couple spent more time with their grandchildren.
這對夫婦在退休之後,花更多時間與孫子女們相處。

96

retreat [rɪˈtriːt]

① *v.* 躲避；隱退

同 **backtrack / hide**

② *n.* 隱退；隱避處

搭 **holiday retreat** 假期休憩

同 **haven / resort**

▶ Leann was tired and decided to retreat to her room early.
黎安非常的累，她決定提早躲回房間。

▶ We hope to make a retreat to the country after life in the big city.
在大城市生活一段時間後，我們希望能隱退到鄉下去。

---

reunion [ˌriːˈjuːnjən] *n.* 重聚；團聚；再聯合

搭 **university reunion** 大學同學會

同 **homecoming / reconciliation**

▶ After their reunion, the classmates promised to stay in touch.
在重聚之後，同學們彼此承諾要保持聯繫。

---

reunite [ˌriːjuːˈnaɪt] *v.* 使再聯合；使重聚

同 **reconvene / rejoin**

▶ Matt reunited with his family after living abroad.
麥特結束旅居國外，終於和家人團聚了。

---

revenge [rɪˈvendʒ]

① *n.* 報復；報仇

搭 **revenge attack** 反擊

同 **reprisal / retribution**

② *v.* 報復；替…報仇

同 **avenge / get back at**

take revenge 反抗，報仇

▶ Tina's mother told her not to take revenge on her brother after he hit her.
緹娜的媽媽告訴她，不可以因為弟弟打她而對他報復。

▶ He sought to revenge the unjust action against him.
他為他所受的不公平待遇尋求報復的機會。

▶ Linda plans to take revenge on her cheating boyfriend.
琳達計畫要報復她不忠的男友。

---

104 **101** **98**

revise [rɪˈvaɪz] *v.* 修改；修正

搭 **revise policy** 修改政策

同 **modify / change**

▶ Tom spent several weeks revising his essay.
湯姆花了好幾個星期去修改他的文章。

---

revision [rɪˈvɪʒən] *n.* 校訂；修正

同 **improvement / modification**

▶ After many revisions, Mia's novel is ready to be published.
米雅的小說在經過多次的校訂之後，終於要出版了。

R

95

revolution [ˌrev.əˈluː.ʃən] *n.* 繞轉；旋轉

搭 **political revolution** 政治改革
同 **cycle / circumvolution**

▶ The roller coaster made several revolutions before coming to a stop.
雲霄飛車在旋轉數圈之後，終於停下來了。

---

revolutionary [ˌrev.əˈluː.ʃən.er.i]

① *adj.* 革命的
同 **radical / subversive**

② *n.* 革命者

▶ Jim enjoyed studying revolutionary figures in American history.
吉姆非常喜歡閱讀美國歷史上的革命人物。

▶ The revolutionaries worked together to overthrow the government.
這群革命人士合力把政府給推翻了。

104

reward [rɪˈwɔːrd]

① *n.* 獎勵；報償；獎賞
搭 **reap reward** 收穫成果
同 **award / dividend**

② *v.* 報答；獎勵
同 **compensate / take care of**

實用片語
reward for 頒獎

▶ One reward of exercise is increased energy.
運動的獎勵就是有更多的精力。

▶ Larry rewarded his dog after it learned a new trick.
賴利在愛犬學會一項新把戲後就獎勵牠。

▶ I'd like to reward you for your excellent performance.
因為你卓越的表現，我想要頒獎給你。

---

rewrite [ˌriːˈraɪt] *v.* 重寫；改寫

搭 **rewrite substantially** 大量改寫
同 **revise / modify**

▶ I had to rewrite this sentence over and over.
我需要一再改寫這個句子。

---

rhyme [raɪm]

① *n.* 同韻語；押韻
② *v.* 作押韻詩

▶ He couldn't think of a rhyme for piano.
他想不出和鋼琴押同韻的字。

▶ Her poem rhymed "sweet" with "neat."
她的詩裡面「sweet」和「neat」同韻。

---

rhythm [ˈrɪð.əm] *n.* 節奏；韻律

搭 **steady rhythm** 平穩的韻律
同 **movement / pattern**

▶ The rhythm of the waves put him to sleep.
海浪的節奏使他入睡。

roast [roʊst]

① *v.* 烘烤

同 **broil / swelter**

② *adj.* 烘烤的

③ *n.* 烘烤

- ▶ Tammy roasted the chicken in the oven.
  譚咪把雞放在烤箱裡烤。
- ▶ Tammy served roasted duck on Christmas.
  譚咪在聖誕節招待烤鴨。
- ▶ Samuel served roast for Easter.
  撒母耳在復活節招待烤肉。

---

rob [rɑːb] *v.* 搶劫

搭 **rob a bank** 搶銀行

同 **mug / hijack**

實用片語
rob someone blind 洗劫一空

- ▶ Ken robbed the bank.
  肯恩搶劫銀行。
- ▶ The clerk was robbing the old man blind.
  店員把這老人洗劫一空。

---

robber [ˈrɑːbɚ] *n.* 強盜

- ▶ The robber sneaked into the hotel and stole a glass vase.
  強盜潛入旅館，偷了一只玻璃花瓶。

---

robbery [ˈrɑːbɚ.i] *n.* 搶案

- ▶ There was a robbery in our neighborhood last night.
  昨晚我們住家附近發生搶案。

---

robe [roʊb]

① *n.* 長袍

② *v.* 穿著

- ▶ Every graduate must wear a robe on the day of graduation.
  每位畢業生在畢業當天必須穿長袍。
- ▶ Leslie was robed in a blanket.
  萊絲莉披著一條毯子。

---

rocket [ˈrɑːkɪt]

① *n.* 火箭

② *v.* 飛快行進；向前急衝

同 **escalate / take off**

實用片語
rocket into 飛速進入…

- ▶ Not many people have the opportunity to watch a rocket take off.
  只有少數人有機會看見火箭起飛升空。
- ▶ Cindy just rocketed through all of her homework.
  珊蒂剛剛飛快寫完了她的家庭作業。
- ▶ The train rocketed into the darkness.
  火車飛速進入黑暗之中。

---

romance [ˈroʊ.mæns] *n.* 羅曼史；戀愛關係

- ▶ Abby and Al's romance started in college.
  艾碧和艾爾的羅曼史從大學時期開始。

R

Exercise 60

I. Derivatives

1. Leah's colleagues held a party to celebrate her _____ (retire).

2. Radio, the internet, television, the airplane and the personal computer are considered the most _____ (revolution) inventions of the 20th century.

3. There are speed _____ (restrict) on the highways and freeways in Taiwan.

4. Their pastor is making several _____ (revise) to his sermon.

5. This man was arrested and charged with armed _____ (rob).

II. Multiple Choice

(   ) 1. Tom served ___ for Easter. Everyone loves it.
  (A) roar (B) route (C) roast (D) root

(   ) 2. The church went on a ___ at a bed and breakfast resort in the mountains.
  (A) restore (B) retain (C) retire (D) retreat

(   ) 3. A lot of modern poetry is not written in ___ .
  (A) rhythm (B) rhyme (C) rewrite (D) reunite

(   ) 4. Jesus taught us to love people as we love ourselves, even our enemies; and not take ___ , if others mistreat or offend us.
  (A) revenge (B) reverse (C) revenue (D) revelation

(   ) 5. Linda deserves a day off as a ___ for working so hard.
  (A) rewind (B) rewrite (C) reward (D) remedy

㉖ **fictional** [ˈfɪk.ʃən.əl] *adj.* 小說的、虛構的

例 I love the story even though it's a fictional one.
我喜歡那個故事,即便那是虛構的。

fictitious [fɪkˈtɪʃ.əs] *adj.* 虛構的、假的

例 All the characters in the novel are fictitious.
此小說內的所有角色都是虛構的。

㉗ **final** [ˈfaɪ.nəl] *adj.* 最後的、最終的

例 I'd like to make one final point please.
我還要提最後一個要點。

finale [fɪˈnɑː.li] *n.* 終曲、末章

例 She sung a rather touching song for the finale.
她在終曲時獻唱了一首動人的歌。

㉘ **historic** [hɪˈstɔːr.ɪk] *adj.* 歷史上著名的、有重大歷史意義的

例 That historic building was damaged by fire last year.
那棟古蹟在去年一場火災中受損了。

historical [hɪˈstɔːr.ɪk] *adj.* 歷史(學)的

例 She is interested in reading historical novels.
她對讀歷史故事有興趣。

㉙ **impractical** [ɪmˈpræk.tɪ.kəl] *adj.* 不切實際的、不現實的

例 My brother is full of weird and impractical ideas.
我弟弟總是有很多奇怪又天馬行空的點子。

impracticable [ɪmˈpræk.tɪ.kə.bəl] *adj.* 不能實行的

例 Such ambitious goals would be highly impracticable.
如此龐大的目標真的很難被實現。

㉚ **inhuman** [ɪnˈhjuː.mən] *adj.* 無人性的、非人類的

例 His treatment of his workers was totally inhuman.
他對員工的待遇真的很沒人性。

inhumane [ˌɪn.hjuːˈmeɪn] *adj.* 無人情味的、不人道的

例 The dog was kept in inhumane conditions.
那隻狗受到不人道的對待。

Unit 61

romantic [roʊˈmæn.tɪk]

① *adj.* 浪漫的

搭 **a romantic story** 羅曼蒂克的故事

同 **dreamy / exotic**

② *n.* 浪漫的人

▶ Let's go to a restaurant that has a romantic atmosphere.
我們去一間有浪漫氣氛的餐廳吧。

▶ Kendra is so romantic.
肯卓是個非常浪漫的人。

---

rot [rɑːt]

① *v.* 腐敗

同 **corrode / decay**

② *n.* 腐朽；腐敗

▶ Sandy couldn't use the apples in her fruit salad because they had started to rot.
珊蒂不能在水果沙拉裡放入蘋果，因為蘋果已經開始腐爛了。

▶ The rot spread all over the bathroom.
整個廁所都朽壞了。

---

rotten [ˈrɑː.tən] *adj.* 腐爛的

搭 **rotten apple** 壞傢伙

同 **sour / moldy**

▶ As Daniel was looking in his refrigerator, he found some rotten cherries.
丹尼爾在檢查冰箱時，發現一些腐爛的櫻桃。

99

rough [rʌf]

① *adj.* 粗糙的

同 **harsh / bumpy**

② *adv.* 粗糙地；粗暴地

搭 **rough surface** 粗糙的表面

同 **uncertain / inexact**

③ *n.* 粗糙

④ *v.* 毆打；使變粗糙

▶ My father sanded the table so that it was no longer rough.
我爸爸用砂紙把桌子磨光，這樣桌子就不粗糙了。

▶ The engine on the scooter runs rough.
這台機車的引擎發動得不順。

▶ Sally wiped her hand across the rough of the table.
莎麗用手擦過桌子粗糙的表面。

▶ Martin roughed up his brother.
馬丁毆打他的兄弟。

---

104 **102** **96**

roughly [ˈrʌf.li] *adv.* 粗暴地；大體上地

同 **approximately / around**

▶ The boy roughly tackled his friend during the game.
那位男孩在比賽的時候粗暴地擒抱摔倒他的朋友。

route [ru:t]

① *n.* 路線

搭 **indirect route** 迂迴路線

同 **direction / road**

② *v.* 按規定路線發送

同 **transmit / send**

實用片語
route to 照路線發送

▶ We took another route home during the storm.
暴風雨來時，我們繞道回家。

▶ His mail was routed to the wrong house.
他的信件被送錯到別人家。

▶ I will route a copy of the agenda to you.
我會將議程副本發送給你。

---

routine [ru:'ti:n]

① *n.* 例行公事

搭 **establish routine** 建立起常規

同 **task / duty**

② *adj.* 例行的

同 **habitual / ordinary**

▶ It's important to get into a routine of cleaning your bathroom everyday.
每天固定清潔浴室是很重要的。

▶ It's time for me to go for my routine visit to the dentist.
我固定去看牙醫的時間到了。

---

rug [rʌg] *n.* 小地毯

▶ Sandy bought a new rug for her living room last week.
珊蒂上週為她的客廳添置一條小地毯。

---

ruin ['ru:.ɪn]

① *v.* 毀滅；使毀壞

搭 **ruin her career** 毀了職涯

同 **damage / destroy**

實用片語
ruin of 毀滅

② *n.* 毀滅；崩潰

搭 **financial ruin** 金融崩盤

同 **collapse / downfall**

▶ The fire ruined all our photos.
一場大火燒毀我們所有的照片。

▶ Your bad decision will be the ruin of this team.
你的錯誤決定將會毀了這個團隊。

▶ The abandoned home fell into ruin.
那棟廢棄的屋子倒榻全毀。

R

rumor [ˈruː.mə]

① *n.* 謠言
同 **gossip / lie**
② *v.* 謠傳

▶ I heard a rumor that Jack and Candy are getting married.
我聽到一個謠言說傑克和荻蒂要結婚了。

▶ It was rumored that Zack was quitting.
據說柴克要辭職了。

---

rural [ˈrʊr.əl] *adj.* 農村的；田園的

搭 **rural village** 鄉下農村
同 **country / natural**

▶ He preferred a rural lifestyle over living in a city.
他喜歡鄉村的生活步調勝於都市的生活。

---

rust [rʌst]

① *n.* 鏽
② *v.* 生鏽
同 **corrode / stale**

實用片語
rust up 生鏽

▶ Be careful! There's a lot of rust on the nail.
小心！釘子上有很多鏽。

▶ Remember, when left in the rain, bikes will rust.
記住，腳踏車若放在外面淋雨，就會生鏽。

▶ The walls had rusted up.
牆壁已經生鏽了。

---

rusty [ˈrʌs.ti] *adj.* 生鏽的

搭 **rusty iron** 鐵生鏽
同 **decayed / corroded**

▶ Samuel was walking along the beach when he found a rusty, old coin.
撒母耳沿著海邊走時，發現一只生鏽的古老硬幣。

---

sack [sæk] *n.* 袋

▶ There's a big sack of rice sitting in the barn.
穀倉裡面放了一大袋米。

---

sacrifice [ˈsæk.rə.faɪs]

① *n.* 祭品；獻祭
② *v.* 獻祭；犧牲；獻出
同 **suffer / offer**

實用片語
sacrifice to 為…犧牲

▶ Jewish priests offered animals as a sacrifice.
猶太的祭司將動物獻上成為祭品。

▶ The animal was sacrificed to God.
那隻動物被獻祭給上帝。

▶ Many parents sacrifice their own ambitions to put their children's education first.
多數父母犧牲自己的野心，而以顧全小孩教育為優先。

sadden [ˈsæd.ən] *v.* 使悲傷；使難過

搭 **sadden greatly** 非常傷心

同 **distress / dishearten**

▶ The news of Abe's death saddened his co-workers.
亞伯死亡的消息讓他的同事感到十分悲傷。

---

safely [ˈseɪf.li] *adv.* 安全地

同 **harmlessly / securely**

▶ We hoped that everyone on the trip would arrive safely.
我們希望參加旅行的每個人都能平安抵達。

---

sailing [ˈseɪ.lɪŋ] *n.* 航海；航行

搭 **sailing boat** 帆船

▶ Bob studied sailing last summer.
鮑柏去年夏季學習航海。

---

sake [seɪk] *n.* 緣故；目的

同 **reason / objective**

▶ For the sake of the children, please stop yelling.
為了小孩子的緣故，請停止叫喊。

---

salary [ˈsæl.ə.i] *n.* 薪水

搭 **starting salary** 起薪

同 **wage / income**

▶ Mabel's salary is low, but she loves her job.
梅波的薪水雖然低，但是她熱愛她的工作。

---

salesperson /salesman / saleswoman

[ˈseɪlz.pɝː.sən / ˈseɪlz.mən /ˈseɪlz.wʊm.ən]

n. （男／女）售貨員、推銷員

同 **representative / sales specialist**

▶ The salesperson helped us find the right vacuum cleaner.
那位售貨員幫我們找到最合適的吸塵器。

---

satellite [ˈsæt̬.əl.aɪt] *n.* 人造衛星；衛星

▶ The satellite orbited earth.
人造衛星繞著地球運轉。

96

satisfaction [ˌsæt̬.ɪsˈfæk.ʃən] *n.* 滿足；滿意

▶ Anna found satisfaction in her new job.
安娜對她的新工作感到十分滿足。

---

satisfactory [ˌsæt̬.ɪsˈfæk.tə.i] *adj.* 令人滿意的

搭 **satisfactory conclusion** 滿意的結論

同 **adequate / suitable**

▶ Joe found the fish and chips to be quite satisfactory.
裘對英式炸魚和薯條的滋味很滿意。

---

saucer [ˈsɑː.sɚ] *n.* 淺碟

▶ Steve placed the teacup on the saucer before he poured the tea.
史蒂夫把茶倒入杯中前，先把茶杯放在淺碟上。

S

Exercise 61

I. Derivatives

1. Exercise has become part of Lily's daily _____ (route).
2. We had to smash the door open because the lock was _____ (rust) and the key did not fit anymore.
3. Sherry and Gloria are _____ (rough) the same age.
4. The team is trying hard to find a _____ (satisfy) solution to the problem that would make everyone happy.
5. The boys' dormitory smelled of _____ (rot) eggs.

II. 中英對應

_____ 1. 緣故　(A) sack　　(B) sake　　(C) suck　　(D) sock

_____ 2. 崩潰　(A) rude　　(B) ruin　　(C) rule　　(D) rush

_____ 3. 謠言　(A) rumor　　(B) rural　　(C) rubber　　(D) rubbish

_____ 4. 犧牲　(A) satisfy　　(B) scarce　　(C) sacrifice　　(D) sacrificial

_____ 5. 衛星　(A) satellite　　(B) settlement　　(C) settle　　(D) sailing

sausage [ˈsɑː.sɪdʒ] *n.* 香腸

▶ The cook added some sausage to the potato soup.
廚師在馬鈴薯湯裡加了些香腸。

---

savings [ˈseɪ.vɪŋ] *n.* 存款
搭 **savings account** 存款帳戶
同 **hoard / funds**

▶ You should open up a savings account at the bank.
你應該在銀行裡開個戶頭。

---

saying [ˈseɪ.ɪŋ] *n.* 格言；言論；諺語
同 **byword / proverb**
實用片語
go without saying 不用多說…

▶ Many old sayings are still true today.
許多古老的格言到現在都還是很有道理。

▶ It goes without saying that there's no shortcut to success.
不用多說，成功沒有捷徑。

103
scale [skeɪl] *n.* 魚鱗；刻度；規模
搭 **international scale** 國際規模
同 **ratio / range**

▶ Please remove the scales of the fish before you cook it.
請你在煮魚之前，先去除魚鱗。

97
scarce [skers] *adj.* 缺乏的
搭 **remain scarce** 持續不足
同 **rare / limited**

▶ Fresh water is scarce in some African countries.
在非洲一些國家中，淡水相當缺乏。

S

---

102 101 99 96 95
scarcely [ˈskers.li] *adv.* 幾乎不
同 **slightly / hardly**

scarcely ever 鮮少，極少

▶ We scarcely had enough money to pay for the meal.
我們差一點沒有足夠的錢付那頓飯。

▶ Since having kids, I scarcely ever get the chance to watch movies.
有小孩後，我鮮少有機會看電影。

---

scarecrow [ˈsker.kroʊ] *n.* 稻草人

▶ Some farmers like to place a scarecrow in their yards to keep the birds away.
有些農夫喜歡在園圃裡放一個稻草人，來防止鳥類靠近。

scarf [skɑːrf] *n.* 圍巾

實用片語
scarf out 狼吞虎嚥

▶ In the winter, Sandy never leaves the house without wearing a scarf.
珊蒂在冬天出門一定會戴圍巾。

▶ I scarf out whenever we have Chinese food.
吃中餐時我總是狼吞虎嚥。

---

scary [ˈsker.i] *adj.* 恐怖的；嚇人的
同 **creepy / shocking**

▶ Children should never watch scary movies.
小孩絕對不可以看恐怖電影。

---

104 98

scatter [ˈskæt̬.ɚ]

① *v.* 散佈
同 **spread / distribute**

② *n.* 散佈

▶ The flock of pigeons scattered as the dog ran toward them.
這隻狗跑向那群鴿子時，鴿子就散開了。

▶ The scatter of papers made a big mess on my desk.
我桌上四散的文件看起來很亂。

---

scenery [ˈsiː.nɚ.i] *n.* 風景
同 **landscape / setting**

▶ The mountain scenery was breathtaking.
山上的風景真是令人驚嘆。

---

schedule [ˈskedʒ.uːl]

① *n.* 日程表
搭 **ambitious schedule** 排滿行程
同 **timetable / agenda**

② *v.* 排定
搭 **schedule an appointment** 約個會議
同 **arrange / plan**

▶ Katrina found the movie schedule online.
卡崔娜在網路上找到電影時刻表。

▶ Kendra scheduled her car payment for the first day of every month.
肯卓把每月第一天定為汽車貸款還款日。

---

scholar [ˈskɑː.lɚ] *n.* 學者
同 **expert / academic**

▶ Only the best scholars apply to Harvard University.
只有最優異的學者會申請哈佛大學。

---

scholarship [ˈskɑː.lɚ.ʃɪp] *n.* 獎學金
搭 **apply for scholarship** 申請獎學金
同 **grant / award**

▶ Sandy was awarded a full scholarship to Stanford University.
珊蒂獲頒全額獎學金進入史丹佛大學就讀。

schoolboy [ˈskuːlˌbɔɪ] *n.* 男學生

實用片語
schoolboy error 明顯基本的錯誤

▶ All the schoolboys had to wear the same uniform.
所有學童必須穿相同的制服。

▶ Several schoolboy errors were discovered in this textbook.
這本教科書中找出了好幾個明顯基本的錯誤。

---

schoolmate [ˈskuːlˌmeɪt] *n.* 同校同學

▶ My schoolmate and I help each other with our classwork.
我和我的同校同學互相幫忙彼此的作業。

---

scientific [ˌsaɪənˈtɪf.ɪk] *adj.* 科學的

搭 **scientific evidence** 科學證據

同 **logical / systematic**

▶ There is scientific proof that the world is round.
有科學證據證明地球是圓的。

---

scold [skoʊld]

① *v.* 叱責；責罵

同 **admonish / blame**

實用片語
scold for 責罵

② *n.* 愛埋怨指責的女人；好罵人的女人

▶ She scolded the young boy when he hit his sister.
當小男孩動手打她妹妹時，她大聲叱責他。

▶ The mother scolded her child for misbehaving at school.
這位媽媽責罵他的小孩在校行為不檢。

▶ I asked my mom to stop being such a scold.
我請媽媽不要再當個愛埋怨指責的女人。

---

scoop [skuːp]

① *n.* 勺子

② *v.* 用勺舀

▶ Jamie couldn't find the scoop for the flour.
傑米找不到舀麵粉的勺子。

▶ Martin scooped some chocolate ice cream into a bowl for his sister.
馬丁幫他的姊妹舀了些巧克力冰淇淋到她碗裡。

---

scout [skaʊt]

① *n.* 偵查者；童子軍

② *v.* 偵查

搭 **scout talent** 星探

同 **explore / inspect**

實用片語
scout around 偵查，四處看看

▶ The scout made it back to camp right before the sun set.
這位偵察員剛好在日落前趕回營地。

▶ Tommy scouted out the area looking for a good place to hide the flag.
湯米偵查這個地區，想要找尋一個理想地點來藏旗子。

▶ You stay here and I will scout around.
你待在這，而我將四處看看。

S

scratch [skrætʃ]

① v. 刮出（痕跡）；抓；搔

同 claw / scrawl

② n. 抓痕；擦傷

▶ The end of the table scratched the wall.
桌子的尾端刮到了牆壁。

▶ The cat left a long scratch on the boy's face.
那隻貓在小男孩的臉上留下一道很長的抓痕。

scream [skriːm]

① v. 尖叫

搭 scream loudly 大聲尖叫

同 screech / shout

② n. 尖叫

搭 high-pitched scream 高音頻的尖叫

▶ Sally screamed at the sight of the bear.
莎莉一看見熊就尖叫。

▶ Jesse immediately called the police when she heard the scream.
潔西聽見尖叫聲時，立刻就報警。

screw [skruː]

① n. 螺絲

② v. 旋；轉動

同 crumple / pucker

實用片語
screw something up 將某事搞砸

▶ I need to buy some screws at the store.
我需要在這間店裡買些螺絲。

▶ The repairman screwed the desk together.
修理工人把桌子旋緊。

▶ Don't screw it up this time, okay?
這次別搞砸了，好嗎？

screwdriver [ˈskruːˌdraɪ.və-] n. 螺絲起子

▶ The man used a screwdriver to replace the light bulb.
那位男士使用螺絲起子來更換電燈泡。

scrub [skrʌb]

① v. 刷洗；擦洗

搭 scrub thoroughly 徹底刷洗

同 brush / mop

② n. 刷洗；擦洗

▶ Stacy scrubbed the floor for an hour before the dirt finally came off.
史黛西刷洗地板一個小時之後，才把汙垢刷掉。

▶ Give the bathtub a good scrub.
把浴缸好好刷洗一下。

Exercise 62

I. 中英對應

_____ 1. 恐怖的　(A) scale　　(B) scare　　(C) scary　　(D) scarf

_____ 2. 尖叫　　(A) scream　(B) screen　(C) screw　　(D) scatter

_____ 3. 排定　　(A) scholar　(B) schedule　(C) scheme　(D) schoolboy

_____ 4. 偵查　　(A) scold　　(B) scope　　(C) score　　(D) scout

_____ 5. 抓痕　　(A) scratch　(B) scrape　(C) scratchy　(D) scratchback

II. Derivatives

1. Danna could _____ (scarce) believe it when Denny said he wanted to marry her.

2. Daniel won a _____ (scholar) to Oxford University, so his parents would not suffer financially.

3. Iris ran into a famous _____ (school) at the supermarket who she has not seen for many years.

4. Italy has truly amazing _____ (scene) that is a must-see when visiting the country.

5. Scientists have tried many different ways of predicting earthquakes, including using _____ (science) instruments and fish, but so far it is still impossible.

sculpture [ˈskʌlp.tʃɚ]

① *n.* 雕塑品

② *v.* 雕刻

搭 **modern sculpture** 現代雕刻

同 **sculpt / carve**

▶ Sculpture was a popular form of art in ancient Rome.
在古羅馬時代，雕塑品是一項很受歡迎的藝術。

▶ She sculptured a lion in her art class.
她在藝術課堂上雕刻出一隻獅子。

---

seafood [ˈsiː.fuːd] *n.* 海鮮

▶ I like to eat seafood at a particular Japanese restaurant.
我喜歡在特定的日式餐廳吃海鮮。

---

seagull/gull [ˈsiː.gʌl / gʌl] *n.* 海鷗

▶ The seagulls flew over the beach looking for food.
海鷗飛在海灘上尋找食物。

---

seal [siːl]

① *v.* 捕海豹；密封

② *n.* 封印；圖章

搭 **seal of approval** 批准印章

實用片語
seal the deal 結案

③ *n.* 海豹；封

④ *v.* 確認；正式核准

同 **confirm / establish**

▶ Make sure you seal the envelope before putting it in the mailbox.
在把信件投入信箱之前，要確定它已密封。

▶ The king put his seal on the peace agreement.
國王在和平協議書上蓋上他的印璽。

▶ Let's seal the deal now.
我們現在結案吧。

▶ Since the windows don't have a good seal, cool air usually leaks in.
因為這個窗戶的密封度不好，所以冷空氣往往會滲進來。

▶ The leaders of the two countries sealed the agreement in their meeting.
兩國領袖用握手來確認達成協議。

---

seaside [ˈsiː.saɪd] *n.* 海邊

搭 **seaside resort** 海邊渡假村

同 **shore / beach**

▶ My family would often visit the seaside to have fun.
我的家人經常去海邊玩。

secondary [ˈsek.ən.der.i] *adj.* 第二的

同 **insignificant / unimportant**

▶ This broken toilet is definitely more of a secondary concern.
這個故障的廁絕對是次要的事。

---

security [səˈkjʊr.ə.tj] *n.* 安全（感）

同 **guarantee / insurance**

▶ Please don't go out at night because this area has poor security.
請不要在晚上出門，因為這個地區治安很差。

---

seek [siːk] *v.* 尋找；追求

搭 **seek employment** 找尋工作機會

同 **explore / investigate**

實用片語
seek someone out 尋找

▶ Kelly went to the library seeking for a book about whales.
凱莉到圖書館找一本關於鯨魚的書籍。

▶ We need to seek someone out to do the work for us.
我需要找人替我們做這件工作。

---

seize [siːz] *v.* 抓

搭 **seize opportunity** 抓住機會

同 **catch / snatch**

實用片語
seize the moment 抓住當下

▶ The brave knight quickly seized the sword.
這位勇敢的騎士立刻抓起寶劍。

▶ Jim is a good businessman because he always seizes the moment.
吉姆是一個善於抓住時機的優秀商人。

---

seldom [ˈsel.dəm] *adv.* 很少

同 **rarely / hardly**

▶ Although Zack enjoys playing the piano, he seldom practices.
雖然柴克喜歡彈鋼琴，但卻很少練習。

---

senior [ˈsiː.njɚ]

① *adj.* 老的；年長的

搭 **senior citizen** 老年人

同 **elder / leading**

② *n.* 年長者

同 **elder / pensioner**

實用片語
senior moment 老人忘事，暫時失憶

▶ People often confuse Jay with his father, Jay senior.
人們常常誤把小傑當成是他的爸爸老傑。

▶ She is ten years my senior.
她比我年長十歲。

▶ I had a senior moment and forgot his name.
我暫時失憶，忘了他的名字。

S

98

sensible [ˈsen.sə.bəl] *adj.* 明智的；合情理的

搭 **strategically sensible** 合理策略

同 **intelligent / rational**

▶ Going to the beach right now sounds like a sensible idea.
現在去海灘聽起來是個明智的主意。

---

103 **102** **100** **98**

sensitive [ˈsen.sə.tʃɪv] *adj.* 敏感的

搭 **sensitive information** 敏感資料

同 **nervous / susceptible**

▶ Kathy seems to be very sensitive to her surroundings.
凱蒂似乎對周遭的事物很敏感。

---

separation [ˌsep.əˈreɪ.ʃən] *n.* 分離

同 **disengagement / partition**

▶ What do you think caused the separation between her parents?
你認為造成她父母離異的原因是什麼？

---

settler [ˈset.lə] *n.* 移居者；殖民者

同 **colonist / immigrant**

▶ The early American settlers dealt with harsh conditions.
早期到美洲的移民者面對艱難的生存條件。

---

104 **99**

severe [səˈvɪr] *adj.* 嚴重的

搭 **especially severe** 尤其嚴重

同 **serious / far-reaching**

▶ She gave the boy a severe punishment.
她很嚴重地處罰那位小男孩。

---

sew [soʊ] *v.* 縫合

同 **stitch / bind**

實用片語
sew up 解決，決定

▶ Samuel sewed his button onto his jacket without any help.
撒母耳不靠別人的幫忙，自己就把鈕扣縫在夾克上。

▶ Let's sew up this contract today.
我們今天敲定這個合約吧。

---

sex [seks] *n.* 性別

▶ We should teach children to be respectful of the opposite sex.
我們應該教導孩童尊重不同性別的人。

---

sexual [ˈsek.sjʊəl] *adj.* 性的

▶ Sexual harassment can be avoided.
性騷擾是可以避免的。

---

sexy [ˈsek.si] *adj.* 性感的

▶ Cathy looked really sexy in her blue, strapless dress.
凱蒂穿這件藍色無肩帶洋裝看起來真性感。

shade [ʃeɪd]

① n. 陰涼處；陰影
② v. 蔽蔭；遮蔽
同 conceal / darken

實用片語
put in the shade 相形失色，相形見絀

▶ Park the car in the shade.
把汽車停在陰涼處。

▶ That line of trees shades the sidewalk.
那排樹木替人行道蔽蔭。

▶ Jack's good performance put mine in the shade.
傑克的優秀表現讓我相形失色。

---

shadow [ˈʃæd.oʊ]

① n. 影子
搭 giant shadow 大面積陰影
同 dark / gloom
② v. 遮蔽；產生陰影
同 dim / overshadow

▶ As a kid, Sandy used to run after her shadow.
珊蒂小時候經常追著自己的影子跑。

▶ The trees shadowed the rocks.
這些樹遮蔽了岩石。

---

shady [ˈʃeɪ.di] adj. 陰涼的；多蔭的

搭 shady corner 陰涼的角落
同 leafy / shadowy

實用片語
shady past 不光彩的過去

▶ Let's find a shady area to sit and eat our lunch.
我們來找個陰涼的地方坐下來吃午餐吧。

▶ Don't go out with someone with a shady past.
不要跟有不光彩過去的人來往。

---

shallow [ˈʃæl.oʊ] adj. 淺的

同 hollow / flat

▶ The water in the lake is way too shallow.
這湖中的水實在太淺了。

---

shame [ʃeɪm]

① n. 可惜；羞恥
搭 feel shame 感到丟臉
同 contempt / humiliation
② v. 使感到羞恥
同 discredit / humiliate

實用片語
put to shame 使蒙羞

▶ It's such a shame that Brandon decided not to come on the trip.
布蘭登決定不參加旅行，真的好可惜。

▶ Benny shamed his mother.
班尼使他的母親蒙羞。

▶ Your kindness has put us to shame.
你的仁慈讓我們蒙羞。

S

Exercise 63

I. Derivatives

1. Jonathan Livingston Seagull is a story about a _____ (sea) learning about life and flight, and a homily about self-perfection.

2. The man walked along in the _____ (shade) hoping no one would notice him.

3. Kylie takes her work performance seriously and is very _____ (sense) to criticism from her boss.

4. Taipei bus companies have security equipment specially designed to stop _____ (sex) harassment such as whistles and special bells.

5. Love and marriage give children a sense of _____ (secure) and belonging.

II. Vocabulary Choice

(A) shame   (B) sealed   (C) shame   (D) separation   (E) senior

(F) secondary   (G) seize   (H) seldom   (I) severe   (J) seek

1. Many families in Taiwan nowadays have to endure long periods of _____ due to the husband/father working in China to earn a living.

2. It is such a _____ that my brother wouldn't join my birthday party because he has to work overtime tonight.

3. The post office clerk _____ the box with tape.

4. "Ask and it will be given to you; _____ and you will find;" is one of the great scripture quotes in the Bible.

5. Good pet owners think that a pet's health is what matters, the cost of the treatment is of _____ importance.

96

shameful [ˈʃeɪm.fəl] *adj.* 可恥的

搭 **shameful secret** 不可告人之秘密

同 **embarrassing / immoral**

▶ The man's shameful behavior embarrassed his family.
那位男人可恥的行為讓家人感到非常丟臉。

---

shampoo [ʃæmˈpuː]

① *n.* 洗髮精

② *v.* 洗頭髮

▶ I need to go to the store to buy some special shampoo for my hair.
我要到店裡為我的頭髮買特殊的洗髮精。

▶ Before cutting my hair, the stylist first shampooed my hair.
在剪頭髮之前，美髮師先幫我洗頭。

---

shave [ʃeɪv]

① *v.* 剃毛髮

② *n.* 剃刀

▶ Joey shaves his face every morning before work.
裘伊每天早晨上班前都會先刮鬍子。

▶ That shave felt so good.
修面感覺好舒服。

---

shaver [ˈʃeɪ.vɚ] *n.* 電動剃刀；理髮師

▶ I'm going to buy my dad a new shaver for his birthday.
我要幫爸爸買一支新的電動刮鬍刀作他的生日禮物。

102

shelter [ˈʃel.tɚ]

① *n.* 遮蔽處；避難所

搭 **temporary shelter** 臨時避難處

同 **safety / sanctuary**

② *v.* 遮擋；使掩蔽；躲避

同 **harbor / protect**

▶ We ran under the shelter during the rainstorm.
暴風雨時，我們跑到可遮蔽的地方躲雨。

▶ The tree sheltered the children from the hot sun.
大樹幫小朋友們遮擋酷熱的太陽。

---

shepherd [ˈʃep.ɚd] *n.* 牧羊人

▶ The shepherd stayed out all night watching his sheep.
牧羊人整夜在外看守他的羊群。

S

shift [ʃɪft]

① *v.* 轉移

同 **transfer / move**

實用片語
shift over 移過去

② *n.* 變動；轉換

搭 **profound shift** 大量轉變

同 **switch / deviation**

實用片語
shift for 照顧，保護自己

▶ We shifted the work to Sam because Judy was too busy.
我們把工作移轉給山姆，因為裘蒂實在是太忙了。

▶ Can you shift over a bit please?
你可以移過去一點嗎？

▶ The coach made a shift and replaced his best player.
教練做了一個調動，把最佳的球員換掉了。

▶ You are 18 years old, and need to shift for yourself.
你 18 歲了，需要保護自己了。

---

shiny [ˈʃaɪni] *adj.* 閃耀的；發光的

同 **sparkling / polished**

▶ Timothy found a shiny coin on the side of the road.
提摩太在路邊找到一只閃亮的硬幣。

---

shopkeeper [ˈʃɑːpˌkiːpɚ] *n.* （小商店）店主

同 **owner / vendor**

▶ The shopkeeper closed his store at 6 p.m.
商店老闆在晚上六點打烊。

---

shopping [ˈʃɑːpɪŋ] *n.* 購物

▶ Shopping can either be fun or boring.
購物可以很好玩，也可能很無聊。

---

shortcut [ˈʃɔːrtkʌt] *n.* 捷徑

搭 **no shortcut to success** 成功無捷徑

同 **alternative / bypass**

▶ We took a shortcut home to save time.
我們走捷徑回家以便節省時間。

---

shorten [ˈʃɔːr.tən] *v.* 縮短

同 **lessen / trim**

▶ Because of the weather conditions, we decided to shorten our trip.
因為氣候的因素，我們決定縮短旅程。

103
shortly [ˈʃɔːrt.li] *adv.* 不久

搭 **reply shortly** 稍後回應

同 **quickly / before long**

▶ Shortly after we arrived, we sat down and ate dinner.
我們抵達後不久，就坐下來吃晚餐。

shortsighted [ʃɔːrtˈsaɪ.tɪd] *adj.* 近視的
同 **nearsighted / myopic**

▶ She is shortsighted and needs to wear glasses.
她有近視，必須要戴眼鏡。

shovel [ˈʃʌv.əl]
① *n.* 鏟子
② *v.* 用鏟子鏟

▶ The gardener used a shovel to dig a hole in the front yard.
這位園丁用鏟子在前院挖了一個洞。

▶ My dad shoveled all the dirt into the truck.
我爸爸把所有泥土鏟進卡車中。

shrink [ʃrɪŋk] *v.* 收縮
搭 **shrink dramatically** 大幅縮水
同 **diminish / narrow**
實用片語
shrink back 退縮

▶ Unfortunately, my shirt shrunk after I washed it.
很不幸地，我洗完襯衫洗後，它縮水了。

▶ The dog shrank back in fear.
這隻狗因恐懼而退縮。

shrug [ʃrʌg]
① *v.* 聳肩（表疑惑、無奈等）
同 **lug / snatch**
實用片語
shrug off 蔑視，不屑
② *n.* 聳肩

▶ I asked him a difficult question, and he just shrugged his shoulders.
我問他一個困難的問題，而他只是聳聳肩。

▶ Linda shrugged off Mr. Lin's advice.
琳達蔑視林先生的建議。

▶ Jack was embarrased by the question and responded with a shrug.
傑克對於提出的問題感到很尷尬，只好以聳聳肩來回應。

shuttle [ˈʃʌt.əl]
① *n.* 短程接駁車
搭 **shuttle train** 接駁車 / 區間車
同 **shuttle bus / spacecraft**
② *v.* 短程穿梭往返

▶ The shuttle to the airport will take twenty minutes.
到機場的接駁車一趟要花二十分鐘。

▶ The hotel shuttled us to the airport.
飯店的接駁車載送我們到機場。

sickness [ˈsɪk.nəs] *n.* 生病；疾病
搭 **sickness absence** 病假
同 **illness / disease**

▶ Be careful, his sickness can be very contagious.
小心，他的病傳染性相當高。

S

sigh [saɪ]

① v. 嘆氣
② n. 嘆息

▶ Sandy sighed and then shared the news about her wedding with her mom.
珊蒂嘆了一下氣，然後就向媽媽透露她要結婚了。

▶ After a long sigh, Sandy finally had the courage to speak.
珊蒂長嘆一口氣之後，終於有勇氣開口說話了。

sightseeing [ˈsaɪtˌsiː.ɪŋ] n. 觀光

同 trek / tour

▶ We will be sightseeing in Paris for two weeks.
我們會花兩星期在巴黎觀光。

signal [ˈsɪg.nəl]

① n. 示意；信號
搭 warning signal 警告訊號
同 sign / indication
② v. 發信號

實用片語
signal for 發出訊號，示意

▶ My scuba diving instructor uses several signals to communicate.
我的水肺潛水教練用幾種手勢來溝通。

▶ When I signal, start walking towards me.
當我比手勢時，你就開始朝著我走過來。

▶ Please signal for the waiter and get the check.
請示意服務生拿帳單來。

signature [ˈsɪg.nə.tʃɚ] n. 簽名

搭 signature movement 招牌舞步

▶ Put your signature at the bottom of the form.
請在這張表格底下簽名。

significance [sɪgˈnɪf.ə.kəns] n. 重要性

同 importance / gravity

▶ The picture of his father held great significance to him.
他爸爸的照片對他而言是非常重要。

significant [sɪgˈnɪf.ə.kənt]

adj. 重要的；顯著的
搭 significant feature 重點特性
同 essential / vital

▶ There has been some significant changes that have been made to the company.
公司做出一些重大的改變。

Exercise 64

I. 中英對應

_____ 1. 牧羊人   (A) shell   (B) shelter   (C) shepherd   (D) sheep

_____ 2. 嘆氣   (A) sign   (B) sight   (C) signal   (D) sigh

_____ 3. 轉換   (A) shirt   (B) shift   (C) ship   (D) shine

_____ 4. 短程接駁車   (A) shutdown   (B) shuffle   (C) shuttle   (D) shrug

_____ 5. 避難所   (A) shelter   (B) shield   (C) shelf   (D) shellfish

II. Derivatives

1. Tina is _____ (short) and she has to wear contact lenses to see far.

2. The discovery of the new cancer-fighting drug is of great _____ (signify) for millions of suffering patients.

3. I plan to go _____ (sight) in Italy for two weeks.

4. I gave an electric _____ (shave) to my dad as a Father's Day gift.

5. The clerk asked me to make my _____ (sign) on the credit card slip.

96

similarity [ˌsɪm.əˈler.ə.tj] *n.* 類似；相似

同 **closeness / connection**

▶ What are some of the similarities between Thailand and Korea?
泰國與韓國之間有哪些相似之處？

---

sin [sɪn]

① *n.* 罪

搭 **confess sin** 認罪

同 **evil / wrongdoing**

② *v.* 犯罪

▶ It is a sin to steal.
偷竊是一種罪。

▶ Sally sinned when she stole the microwave.
當莎莉偷竊了微波爐時，就犯罪了。

---

101 99

sincere [sɪnˈsɪr] *adj.* 真誠的

同 **heartfelt / forthright**

▶ Susan is always available to help. She is a sincere friend.
蘇珊隨時願意幫助別人，她是一位真誠的朋友。

---

96 95

sincerely [sɪnˈsɪrlɪ] *adv.* 誠心地；真誠地

搭 **apologize sincerely** 誠心地道歉

同 **truly / deeply**

▶ She sincerely apologized for hurting my feelings.
她因為傷害了我的感受而真誠心地向我道歉。

---

sincerity [sɪnˈser.ə.tj] *n.* 真誠；誠心誠意

同 **frankness / impartiality**

▶ The boy's sincerity convinced his mother that he really wanted a pet.
這位小男孩的真誠讓他的媽媽確定，他真的想要一隻寵物。

---

103 102

singular [ˈsɪŋ.gjə.lə-]

① *adj.* 單一的；單數的

同 **extraordinary / uncommon**

② *n.* 單數

▶ The singular tree stood out among the small bushes.
那唯一的一棵樹在小草叢中非常突出。

▶ She used the plural form of the word instead of the singular.
她使用這個字的複數型態而不是單數型態。

sip [sɪp]

① *v.* 啜飲

搭 **sip gratefully**　優雅地飲用

同 **imbibe / quaff**

實用片語
sip on　小口喝，酌飲

② *n.* 單數

▶ Deborah sipped on her coffee all afternoon.
戴博拉整個下午都在啜飲咖啡。

▶ She was sipping on a cocktail at the bar.
她正在吧檯小口啜飲雞尾酒。

▶ After only one sip, Katherine decided that she didn't like the drink.
凱瑟琳才喝一小口，就確定她不喜歡那杯飲料。

site [saɪt]

① *n.* 地點

② *v.* 設置；為⋯選址

同 **location / spot**

▶ This is a perfect site for the new building.
這裏是蓋那座新大樓的最佳地點。

▶ The company sited their new factory next to the river.
公司把新廠的地點設置在河邊。

103
situation [ˌsɪtʃ.uˈeɪ.ʃən] *n.* 情況；處境

搭 **involve in situation**　參與其中

同 **condition / position**

實用片語
chicken and egg situation　雞生蛋，蛋生雞

▶ Since she wasn't honest, Sally found herself in a very difficult situation.
莎莉因為不誠實，而發現自己陷入困境了。

▶ It's a chicken and egg situation.
這是雞生蛋，蛋生雞的問題。

skate [skeɪt]

① *n.* 溜冰鞋

② *v.* 溜冰

實用片語
sketch out　概述，草擬

▶ Jenny went to the store to buy some skates for her friend's birthday party.
珍妮去商店為朋友的生日派對購買溜冰鞋。

▶ Since it is so beautiful outside, Maria decided to go skating in the park.
因為戶外實在好美，瑪利亞決定去公園溜冰。

▶ Please sketch out your ideas.
請概述你的想法。

skating [ˈskeɪ.tɪŋ] *n.* 溜冰

▶ Who would like to go skating this Saturday?
這星期六誰要去溜冰？

101
sketch [sketʃ]

① *n.* 草圖；素描

▶ They drew a quick sketch of what the kitchen could look like.
他們很快地畫了一張廚房可能樣式的草圖。

② v. 草擬；概略地敘述

搭 **sketch roughly** 隨意擬出

同 **delineate / lay out**

▶ Court sketched out his idea for the party.

寇特草擬出他對派對的點子。

---

ski [ski:]

① n. 滑雪板

② v. 滑雪

▶ Katie gave her granddaughter some new skis.

凱蒂送給她孫女新的滑雪板。

▶ Over the holiday, Marvin went to the mountains to go skiing.

馬文在假期時去山上滑雪。

---

skip [skɪp]

① v. 跳；略過

同 **bounce / hop**

② n. 跳；省略

▶ Susan skipped all the way to school.

蘇珊一路蹦蹦跳跳到學校。

▶ The child gave a skip of happiness when he saw his mother coming.

小孩看到媽媽來了之後，就開心得跳了起來。

---

skyscraper [ˈskaɪˌskreɪ.pɚ] n. 摩天大樓

▶ If you visit New York, you should definitely check out some of the skyscrapers.

如果你造訪紐約，一定要去一些摩天大樓。

---

slave [sleɪv]

① n. 奴隸

實用片語
be a slave to 受控於，奴役於

② v. 拼命工作；苦幹

同 **toil / labor**

實用片語
slave away 做牛做馬

▶ Many of the early American Founding Fathers had slaves.

許多早期美國開國元勳都有奴隸。

▶ I don't want to be a slave to any devices.

我不想受控於任何裝置。

▶ Beatrice slaved over the cookies all day long.

畢翠絲整天都在辛苦地做餅乾。

▶ Construction workers slave away under the intense sun.

建築工人在烈日下做牛做馬。

---

sled [sled] v. 划雪橇

▶ The kids enjoyed sledding in the snow.

小孩子們很喜歡在下雪時划雪撬。

---

sledge [sledʒ] n. 雪橇

▶ The dogs pulled the sledge through the snow.

狗在雪中拉著雪橇。

sleeve [sliːv] *n.* 袖子

▶ Make sure to roll up your sleeves before you start rolling out the pizza dough.
在開始？披薩餅皮之前，務必把袖子捲起來。

---

sleigh [sleɪ]

① *n.* 雪橇

② *v.* 駕雪橇；乘坐雪橇

▶ The horse pulled our sleigh through the heavy snow.
那匹馬在大雪之中拉著我們的雪橇。

▶ People enjoy sleighing around the park.
大家都喜歡乘雪橇繞公園。

---

slice [slaɪs]

① *n.* 薄片

② *v.* 切成薄片

▶ At the birthday party, Sarah cut the cake into 15 slices.
莎拉在生日派對上把蛋糕切成 15 片。

▶ At the birthday party, Sarah sliced the cake right down the middle.
在生日派對上，莎拉從蛋糕中間切下去。

---

slight [slaɪt]

① *adj.* 輕微的

搭 **slight difference** 些許的不同

同 **minor / slim**

② *v.* 藐視；冷落

同 **disparage / scorn**

③ *n.* 怠慢；輕蔑

同 **affront / rejection**

▶ The slight wind wasn't enough to power our kite.
這陣微風不足以讓我們的風箏往上飛。

▶ He felt slighted when he wasn't invited to the party.
當他沒被邀請去參加派對時，他感到被藐視了。

▶ We apologized for the slight against Joe and invited him to join the team.
我們為怠慢喬伊這事道歉，並且邀請他參加團隊。

---

slightly [ˈslaɪt.li] *adv.* 輕微地

搭 **slightly different** 些許不同

同 **kind of / lightly**

▶ I slightly scratched the side of your car.
我輕微地刮傷了你的汽車的側邊。

---

(103)

slippery [ˈslɪp.ɚ.i] *adj.* 滑的

同 **greasy / sleek**

實用片語
slippery as an eel 滑如泥鰍

▶ Be careful! The rocks in the water are very slippery.
小心！水中的石頭非常滑。

▶ I think John is as slippery as an eel.
我認為約翰油滑如泥鰍（個性矯情）。

S

slogan [ˈsloʊ.gən] *n.* 標語；口號

搭 **advertising slogan** 廣告詞

同 **saying / motto**

▶ The company's slogan is written on the building.
公司的口號就標記在大樓的外面。

Exercise 65

I. 中英對應

_____ 1. 啜飲　(A) sit　　　(B) side　　(C) sip　　(D) sin

_____ 2. 滑的　(A) smoky　　(B) slippery　(C) slope　(D) smooth

_____ 3. 單數　(A) singular　(B) signal　(C) single　(D) singer

_____ 4. 薄片　(A) slight　　(B) slide　(C) slice　(D) slipper

_____ 5. 滑雪　(A) skip　　　(B) sketch　(C) skate　(D) ski

II. Derivatives

1. It is very true what the proverb says:, "Misfortunes test the
_____ (sincere) of friends."

2. Janelle is pretty good at ice _____ (skate).

3. I Anna is thinking of going on a husky _____ (sled) adventure
to see the Northern Lights of the Arctic.

4. Fanny was _____ (slight) upset because Phoebe forgot their
appointment and stood her up yesterday.

5. New York City is famous for its _____ (sky); and One World
Trade Center is the tallest building in New York and the United States.

slope [sloʊp] *n.* 斜坡；傾斜

同 **ramp / incline**

▶ Let's climb up the slope near the building.
我們去爬靠近大樓的那個斜坡吧。

---

smog [smɑ:g] *n.* 煙霧

同 **smoke / fog**

▶ The heavy smog made it difficult to breathe.
煙霧實在太濃了，令人難以呼吸。

---

smoky [ˈsmoʊ.ki]
adj. 冒煙的；煙霧彌漫的；煙灰色的

▶ Our entire family gathered around the smoky fireplace.
我們全家聚在煙霧瀰漫的壁爐四周。

---

smooth [smu:ð]

① *adj.* 平滑的

② *adj.* 平靜的；平滑的

搭 **smooth transition**　順暢的轉移

同 **even / slippery**

實用片語
smooth away　撫平

▶ As she was walking through the water, Cynthia found several smooth rocks.
當辛西亞走過水中時，她發現幾顆平滑的石頭。

▶ The ocean looks very smooth today.
今天海洋看起來很平靜。

▶ Please smooth away the wrinkles.
請撫平皺褶。

---

snap [snæp]

① *v.* 折斷；猛咬

同 **crack / fracture**

② *n.* 折斷；猛咬

▶ I snapped the twig into two pieces.
我把樹枝折斷成兩節。

▶ Did you hear that snap?
你聽到那個斷裂聲嗎？

---

sneeze [sni:z]

① *v.* 打噴嚏

實用片語
sneeze into　對…打噴嚏

② *n.* 噴嚏（聲）

▶ The cat hair made Julie sneeze.
貓毛使得茱莉打噴嚏。

▶ Please sneeze into a tissue.
打噴嚏時請用面紙。

▶ The man's loud sneeze could be heard in the entire office.
整個辦公室都可以聽到那位先生響亮的打噴嚏聲。

---

snowman [ˈsnoʊ.mæn] *n.* 雪人

▶ Do you want to build a snowman?
你想做一個雪人嗎？

sob [sɑːb]

① *v.* 啜泣；哭訴

搭 **sob silently** 暗自飲泣

同 **cry / wail**

實用片語
sob something out 哽咽地說出

② *n.* 啜泣聲

▶ The man's wife sobbed loudly at the news of his death.
那位先生的妻子一聽到丈夫過世的消息，馬上嚎啕大哭。

▶ He sobbed out his sad story.
他哽咽地說出他的故事。

▶ After a long sob, the woman dried her eyes.
整在一陣長長的啜泣聲後，那位女士擦乾了眼淚。

---

socket [ˈsɑːkɪt] *n.* 插槽；插座

▶ I screwed the light bulb into the socket.
我把燈泡轉進插槽裡。

---

softball [ˈsɑːftbɑːl] *n.* 壘球

▶ She loves to play softball on Saturdays.
她非常喜歡在星期六時打壘球。

100
software [ˈsɑːftwer] *n.* （電腦）軟體

▶ The new computer comes equipped with free software.
這台新的電腦已經附有免費的軟體。

---

solar [ˈsoʊlɚ] *adj.* 太陽的

同 **cosmic / stellar**

▶ We heat our home with solar energy.
我們利用太陽能使屋子暖起來。

---

solid [ˈsɑːlɪd] *adj.* 固體的

搭 **solid idea** 確切意見

同 **compact / firm**

▶ Most 2-year-old kids eat solid food.
大多數兩歲的孩子都吃固體食物。

S

---

someday [ˈsʌmdeɪ] *adv.* 有朝一日

▶ Someday, I am going to have my own airplane.
有朝一日我會擁有自己的飛機。

---

somehow [ˈsʌmhaʊ] *adv.* 不知怎地

▶ Even though she woke up late, somehow, Samantha managed to make it to work on time.
雖然珊曼莎睡過頭，但不知怎地，她順利地準時上班。

---

sometime [ˈsʌmtaɪm] *adv.* 在某個時候；日後

▶ I really think that we should take a trip to Jiufen sometime.
我真的覺得我們應該找時間去九份。

somewhat [ˈsʌm.wɑːt] *adv.* 有點；稍微

▶ After the 20 KM hike, Peter was somewhat tired.
彼得在健行 20 公里之後，有點累了。

---

sophomore [ˈsɑː.fə.mɔːr] *n.* 二年級學生

▶ After a tough first year, he looked forward to being a sophomore.
經過難熬的第一年，他很期待成為二年級的學生。

---

sore [sɔːr]

① *adj.* 疼痛的

搭 **sore throat** 喉嚨痛

同 **aching / painful**

② *n.* 痛處

同 **pain / ache**

實用片語
a sore loser 輸不起的人

▶ It isn't unusual to have sore legs after running 21 KM.
跑完 21 公里之後，雙腿出現酸痛是正常的。

▶ Sandy has 15 sores on her legs.
珊蒂的腿上有 15 處痛處。

▶ Don't be such a sore loser, Tom.
湯姆，不要這麼輸不起。

---

sorrow [ˈsɔːr.oʊ]

① *n.* 悲傷

搭 **express sorrow** 表達遺憾

同 **misery / remorse**

② *v.* 悲傷

▶ The pastor constantly prayed for Eddy during his time of sorrow.
艾迪在傷痛期間，這位牧者不斷地為他禱告。

▶ Kevin sorrowed over the loss of his mother.
凱文為失去母親而感到悲傷。

---

sorrowful [ˈsɔːr.ə.fəl] *adj.* 悲傷的

同 **distressing / lugubrious**

▶ The boy's face looked sorrowful after his goldfish died.
小男孩的金魚死了之後，他的表情看起來很悲傷。

---

souvenir [ˌsuː.vəˈnɪr] *n.* 紀念品

▶ We brought back souvenirs from our trip to Italy.
我們到義大利旅遊，帶回了紀念品。

---

spade [speɪd] *n.* 鏟子

▶ The farmer used a spade to weed his garden.
農夫用鏟子除去園中的雜草。

---

spaghetti [spəˈget.i] *n.* 義大利麵條

▶ We are eating spaghetti for dinner tonight.
我們今晚晚餐會吃義大利麵。

spare [sper]

① *adj.* 備用的;多餘的

搭 **spare moment** 閒暇時間

同 **unoccupied / unused**

② *n.* 備用品(輪胎)

③ *v.* 使免於受傷;使不受破壞

▶ The spare tire is in the trunk of the car.
汽車的備用輪胎在車子的行李箱裡面。

▶ Jill has a flat tire, but thankfully she has a spare.
吉兒有個輪胎沒氣了,不過幸好她有一個備胎。

▶ The tornado spared our house during the storm.
在暴風中,龍捲風沒有吹倒我們的房子。

S

Exercise 66

I. 中英對應

_____ 1. 疼痛的   (A) sore   (B) sort   (C) sour   (D) sort

_____ 2. 折斷   (A) snail   (B) snack   (C) snake   (D) snap

_____ 3. 壘球   (A) software   (B) softball   (C) softback   (D) softcover

_____ 4. 打噴嚏   (A) sneeze   (B) snap   (C) snowman   (D) sneak

_____ 5. 太陽的   (A) solo   (B) solid   (C) solar   (D) solely

II. Vocabulary Choice

(A) souvenir   (B) sorrow   (C) spaghetti   (D) spade   (E) software

(F) spare   (G) sobbing   (H) sophomore   (I) sometime   (J) someday

1. Jason hides his _____ house key under the mat.

2. I ordered a _____ dish and a vegetable salad with Thousand Island dressing for dinner.

3. Vivian is a junior and her younger brother, Isaac is a _____ in the same high school.

4. Cindy found her sister _____ in the bathroom because she broke their mother's favorite antique vase.

5. The boys dreamed of _____ respectively becoming a famous actor, singer and president.

Unit 67

spark [spɑːrk]

① *n.* 火花

[搭] **produce spark** 產生火花

[同] **flicker / glitter**

② *v.* 發出火花；發動

[同] **precipitate / set off**

[實用片語]
bright spark 出類拔萃者，精明的人

▶ When I plugged in the lamp, it caused a spark.
當我把燈插上插座，瞬間冒出火花。

▶ The toaster overheated and sparked.
小烤箱因為過熱而冒出火花。

▶ Jim is the bright spark of the family.
吉姆是家中出類拔萃者。

---

sparkle [ˈspɑːr.kəl]

① *v.* 發火花；閃耀

[同] **twinkle / glow**

② *n.* 閃耀；閃爍

[搭] **a sparkle in your eyes** 眼內的光芒

[同] **glimmer / glitz**

▶ The car scraped against the pavement and sparkled.
汽車刮擦路面而發出火花。

▶ The bright light created a sparkle in my mirror.
明亮的光線在我的鏡子產生一道亮光。

---

sparrow [ˈsper.oʊ] *n.* 麻雀

▶ The sparrow sang loudly from the treetops.
麻雀在樹上大聲歌唱。

---

spear [spɪr]

① *n.* 矛；魚叉

② *v.* 用尖物刺；用矛刺

▶ The warrior carried a spear into battle.
戰士帶著長矛上戰場。

▶ I speared the meat to see if it was cooked enough.
我去刺一下肉，看看它到底煮熟了沒。

---

specialized [ˈspeʃ.ə.laɪz] *adj.* 專門的；專業的

[搭] **specialized technique** 專業技術

[同] **functional / particular**

▶ May is studying a specialized area of medicine.
梅正在專攻醫學界的一項專門領域。

---

species [ˈspiː.ʃiːz] *n.* 種類

[同] **breed / division**

▶ Endangered species are protected from hunters.
瀕臨絕種動物受到保護，不讓獵人獵殺。

S

specific [spəˈsɪf.ɪk] *adj.* 特定的

搭 **specific details** 明確的細節

同 **distinct / special**

▶ Is there anything specific I should bring tonight?
我今晚需要帶什麼特定的東西來嗎？

---

spice [spaɪs]

① *n.* 香料

同 **salt / seasoning**

② *v.* 增添風味；加香料

實用片語
spice up 增加風味，增添情趣

▶ The baker uses some special spices during the Christmas holiday.
聖誕節期間，這位糕點師傅會用一些特別的香料。

▶ Amanda added some ginger to spice up the apple cider.
阿曼達加了些薑，來提升蘋果汁的味道。

▶ That necklace really spices up your dress.
那條項鍊為你的洋裝更添風情。

---

spicy [ˈspaɪ.si] *adj.* 辛辣的；加香料的

搭 **mildly spicy soup** 微辣的湯

同 **hot / seasoned**

▶ His soup was so spicy that it made his eyes water.
他的湯太辣了，讓他不住流眼淚。

---

spill [spɪl] `

① *v.* 使濺出；使溢出

同 **scatter / dribble**

② *n.* 溢出

搭 **oil spill** 漏油

▶ As Katherine reached for the potato chips, she accidentally spilled her milk.
凱瑟琳伸手去拿洋芋片時，不小心把牛奶撒出來了。

▶ Make sure you clean up your spill right away.
務必要立刻清除灑出來的東西。

---

spin [spɪn]

① *v.* 旋轉

搭 **spin freely** 自由地旋轉

同 **twist / roll**

實用片語
take a spin 兜風

② *n.* 旋轉

▶ If I spin too fast, I will get dizzy.
我如果轉得太快，就會頭暈目眩。

▶ I just got a new car. Do you want to take it for a spin after work?
我剛買新車，所以你想兜個風嗎？

▶ The dancer added a complicated spin to her dance.
這位舞者在她的舞碼中增加了一個複雜的旋轉舞姿。

---

spiritual [ˈspɪr.ə.tʃu.əl] *adj.* 精神的；心靈的

搭 **spiritual strength** 心靈力量

同 **divine / metaphysical**

▶ John felt a spiritual power guide him during his difficult time.
約翰在他困難的時候，感受到一股屬靈的力量在引領他。

spit [spɪt]

① *v.* 吐（口水等）

② *n.* 口水

▶ Peter spit out the food because it tasted bad.

彼得把食物吐出來，因為實在太難吃了。

▶ Why is there so much spit in the sink?

為什麼水槽中有這麼多口水？

---

spite [spaɪt] *n.* 惡意

同 contempt / gall

▶ Jessie definitely stole the chicken from her neighbor in spite.

潔西一定是出於惡意而偷走鄰居的雞。

---

splash [splæʃ]

① *v.* 濺；潑

搭 splash water 噴灑水

同 drench / spray

② *n.* 濺；潑

同 burst / dash

▶ As soon as they jumped into the pool, the boys started splashing the girls.

男孩們一跳入泳池中，就開始向女孩們潑水。

▶ As soon as he jumped into the pool, there was a big splash.

他一跳進游泳池中，就濺起很大的水花。

103

splendid [ˈsplen.dɪd] *adj.* 絢麗多彩的；燦爛的

搭 splendid opportunity 絕佳的機會

同 dazzling / grand

▶ Bryan bought his mother a splendid bunch of flowers.

布萊恩買給他媽媽一束絢麗多彩的鮮花。

---

split [splɪt]

① *v.* 切開；剝開

同 break / isolate

實用片語
split in 分裂，拆分

② *n.* （分出的）一份；裂縫

同 crack / chasm

▶ The boys split the cake in half.

男孩子們將蛋糕切成兩半。

▶ The vase dropped and split in quarters.

這花瓶掉落且裂成好幾片。

▶ Jonathan felt his split of the money was less than his brother's.

強納森覺得他那份錢比弟弟的來得少。

---

spoil [spɔɪl] *v.* 損壞

搭 utterly spoil 徹底破壞

同 wreck / rot

▶ Don't leave the meat out for too long, or else, it will spoil.

不要把肉放在外面太久，不然會腐壞。

---

sportsman / sportswoman

[ˈspɔːrts.mən / ˈspɔːrts.wʊm.ən] *n.*

（男）運動員 / 女運動員

▶ I was an active sportsman in college, playing golf and tennis regularly.

我在大學時是個非常活躍的運動員，經常地打高爾夫球以及網球。

S

sportsmanship ['spɔ:rts.mən.ʃɪp]

n. 運動家精神

同 **fairness / honesty**

> ▶ Mike showed good sportsmanship by helping the injured player off the field.
> 邁克幫助受傷的球員離場，充分展現出良好的運動家精神。

sprain [spreɪn]

① *v.* 扭傷

實用片語
sprain one's ankle 扭傷腳踝

② *n.* 扭傷

> ▶ Zack sprained his ankle while playing football last Saturday.
> 柴克上星期六踢足球時扭傷腳踝。

> ▶ Grace sprained her ankle while playing basketball.
> 葛瑞絲在打籃球時扭傷腳踝。

> ▶ It is important that you put some ice on that sprain.
> 要放些冰塊在扭傷處，這很重要。

spray [spreɪ]

① *n.* 噴霧

同 **sprayer / sprinkler**

② *v.* 噴灑（霧或水珠等）

同 **dust / smear**

實用片語
spray with 在⋯灑水

> ▶ Kelly uses a special spray in her bathroom.
> 凱莉在她的浴室裡噴上一種特別的噴霧。

> ▶ Shaun sprayed the kitty with water to keep her from scratching the couch.
> 肖恩用水噴小貓，防止牠抓沙發。

> ▶ Linda sprayed the flowers with water.
> 琳達在花上灑水。

sprinkle ['sprɪŋ.kəl]

① *v.* 灑（水等）

同 **smear / strew**

② *n.* 稀疏的小雨；灑

> ▶ Melody sprinkled some salt and pepper onto her chicken and rice.
> 美樂蒂在她的雞肉飯上撒上鹽和胡椒。

> ▶ The nice sprinkle cooled us off.
> 這場稀稀疏疏的小雨真的很不錯，因為它讓我們涼快下來。

spy [spaɪ]

① *n.* 間諜

同 **detective / agent**

② *v.* 刺探

同 **snoop / observe**

實用片語
spy on 暗中監視

> ▶ The spy's positive report gave the soldiers hope that they could win this battle.
> 間諜的正向報告帶給士兵們希望，讓他們相信能夠贏得這場戰役。

> ▶ Jeremy set out to spy on his brother and sister in the other room.
> 傑爾米起身到另一個房間窺探他的哥哥和妹妹。

> ▶ Do we need to send someone to spy on the competitor's sales force?
> 我們需要派人暗中監視競爭者的銷售人員嗎？

squeeze [skwi:z]

① *v.* 擠；榨；壓

搭 **squeeze tightly** 緊捏

同 **cram / grip**

實用片語
squeeze by 擠過去

② *n.* 捏；榨；壓

▶ Although it was difficult, Vicky squeezed every last bit of toothpaste out of the tube.
儘管很困難，但維琪還是把牙膏擠地一點不剩。

▶ I squeezed by the crowd in the train station.
我在車站中從人群中擠過去。

▶ Mr. Smith gave his wife a gentle hand squeeze and then left for work.
史密斯先生輕輕地捏了一下他太太的手，然後就離開去工作了。

S

Exercise 67

I. 中英對應

_____ 1. 運動家精神   (A) sportsman   (B) sportswoman

                               (C) sportswear   (D) sportsmanship

_____ 2. 切開   (A) spit   (B) split

                               (C) spoil   (D) spite

_____ 3. 灑（水等）   (A) sprain   (B) spray

                               (C) sprinkle   (D) spread

_____ 4. 口水   (A) spin   (B) spit

                               (C) spite   (D) split

_____ 5. 濺；潑   (A) splash   (B) splendid

                               (C) split   (D) spice

II. Vocabulary Choice

(A) spite   (B) spiritual   (C) splash   (D) split   (E) spy

(F) squeeze   (G) sprain   (H) spoils   (I) spin   (J) splendid

1. After praying, Daniel felt a _____ renewal in his life.

2. Esther can _____ on her toes like a ballet dancer.

3. We had a _____ holiday in the Rocky Mountain National Park this summer.

4. The James Bond movies, about a British Secret Service agent codenamed '007', have been named the best _____ films of all time in a poll of film fans.

5. We'd better eat the fruit before it _____ .

stab [stæb]

① v. 刺；戳

同 **prick / stick**

實用片語
stab someone in the back 暗中中傷

② n. 刺；戳

同 **jab / twinge**

▶ The soldier stabbed the lion.
這士兵刺殺獅子。

▶ Don't stab me in the back.
不要暗中中傷我。

▶ Paul bled a lot from a stab he got in a fight last night.
保羅昨夜打架時被刺了一刀，流了很多血。

---

stable [ˈsteɪ.bəl] adj. 穩定的

搭 **stable structure** 穩定的架構

同 **steady / solid**

▶ Since the platform isn't stable, you should not climb on it.
因為這舞台不穩，你不應該爬上去。

---

stadium [ˈsteɪ.di.əm] n. 體育場；競技場

同 **field / gymnasium**

▶ Over 15,000 people piled into the stadium to watch the softball game.
超過 15,000 人湧入體育場觀看這場壘球賽。

104
staff [stæf]

① n. 員工；工作人員

② v. 配備職員

▶ There are about 25 people on staff at that church.
那間教會有大約 25 位員工。

▶ The summer camp was staffed with 15 people.
這個夏令營有十五位工作人員。

---

staircase [ˈster.keɪs]

n. （有扶手欄杆的）樓梯；樓梯間

▶ Noah ran up the staircase to his bedroom.
諾亞跑上樓回到他的臥房。

---

stale [steɪl] adj. 不新鮮的；腐壞的

同 **hackneyed / threadbare**

▶ Rick threw out the stale bread.
里克丟掉不新鮮的麵包。

---

stare [ster]

① v. 注視；瞪

搭 **stare wordlessly** 無言凝視

同 **glare / gawk**

▶ It is very rude to stare at people.
盯著人看是很不禮貌的。

S

實用片語

stare at 凝視著

② *n.* 凝視

▶ Everyone in the conference room turned to stare at Jack.
會議室中的所有人都轉過去凝視傑克。

▶ The teacher gave an intent stare when the students started talking during the test.
當學生在考試時一開始說話，老師就目不轉睛地凝視著他們。

---

starve [stɑːrv] *v.* 挨餓

搭 **starve to death** 餓得半死

同 **fast / reduce**

實用片語
starve for 渴望，急需

▶ Can we eat now? I am starving.
我們現在可以吃了嗎？我很餓。

▶ The young child is starved for attention.
年輕的孩子渴望被關注。

---

statue [ˈstætʃ.uː] *n.* 雕像

搭 **Statue of Liberty** 自由女神像

同 **figure / sculpture**

▶ Let's pose like a statue for the picture.
我們來擺個像雕像的姿勢來拍照。

100

status [ˈsteɪ.təs] *n.* 地位；身分

搭 **social status** 社經地位

同 **standing / position**

▶ His status in the company changed after his promotion.
他升遷之後，在公司的身份地位也改變了。

---

steady [ˈsted.i]

① *adj.* 穩固的

同 **solid / reliable**

② *v.* 使穩固

實用片語
go steady with someone 與某人穩定發展

③ *adv.* 穩固地

▶ The ladder isn't very steady.
這個梯子不太穩。

▶ Gabe steadied the boat as Winston climbed in.
凱柏穩住船身，讓溫斯頓爬進船內。

▶ Mary has been going steady with Jack for a month now.
瑪莉現在已經跟傑克穩定發展一個月了。

▶ Grace and Frank have been going steady for six months.
葛雷絲和法蘭克已經穩定交往六個月了。

steady [ˈstɛdi] *n.* 情侶；穩固

▶ Grace is Marlin's steady.
葛瑞絲是馬林的情人。

steep [sti:p] *adj.* 陡峭的

搭 **relatively steep** 相當陡峭

同 **sharp / lifted**

▶ Ryan ended up walking his bike up the hill since it was so steep.
萊恩最後只好扛著他的腳踏車爬坡，因為太陡了。

---

stem [stem]

① *n.* 莖；柄

② *v.* 源自；抽去…的莖

▶ Mom cut the stem off the rose and pinned it to my chest.
媽媽把玫瑰花的莖剪掉，然後把花別在我的胸前。

▶ His promotion stems from hard work.
他的升遷來自於她的賣力工作。

---

stepchild [ˈstep.tʃaɪld] *n.* 繼子；繼女

▶ Fanny needed to leave the party early to pick her stepchild up from school.
凡尼需要早點離開派對去學校接她的繼子。

---

stepfather [ˈstep.fɑː.ðɚ] *n.* 繼父

▶ Sandy has started to see her stepfather like her real father.
珊蒂已經開始視她的繼父為自己的親生父親。

---

stepmother [ˈstep.mʌð.ɚ] *n.* 繼母

▶ Many people these days have stepmothers.
現今許多人都有繼母。

---

stereo [ˈster.i.oʊ] *n.* 立體音響

▶ The officer bought a new stereo for his car.
這位官員為自己的汽車買了一台新音響。

---

sticky [ˈstɪk.i] *adj.* 黏的

同 **tacky / ropy**

實用片語
in a sticky situation 棘手狀況

▶ The candy was really sticky.
這個糖果很黏。

▶ I found myself in a sticky situation when I caught my colleague stealing money.
當我發現同事偷錢時，我讓自己陷入窘境。

---

103 102

stiff [tɪf] *adj.* （僵）硬的

搭 **stiff shoulders** 僵硬的肩頸

同 **hard / rigid**

實用片語
bore someone stiff 令人厭煩

▶ The collar was so stiff Amanda couldn't bend it.
這衣領很僵硬，阿曼達無法把它折起來。

▶ This movie bored me stiff.
這部電影令我厭煩。

S

sting [stɪŋ]

① *n.* 刺痛；螫針

② *v.* 螫；叮

實用片語
sting for 敲詐

▶ If you put some ice on your arm, it will take away the sting.
如果你放些冰在手臂上，就不會刺痛了。

▶ I was stung by a bee last summer.
去年夏天我被蜜蜂螫了。

▶ That guy stung me for 100 dollars.
那傢伙敲詐我 100 元。

---

stingy [ˈstɪn.dʒi] *adj.* 吝嗇的

同 **greedy / selfish**

▶ The stingy woman refused to share her wealth with others.
那位吝嗇的女人拒絕跟別人分享她的財富。

---

stir [stɝː]

① *v.* 攪拌；攪動

同 **blend / disturb**

實用片語
stir someone up 撥弄，挑起

② *n.* 攪拌；騷動

搭 **considerable stir** 大幅騷動

同 **furor / fuss**

▶ Stir the sugar and butter together until it is smooth.
把糖和奶油攪拌在一起，直到調勻為止。

▶ The speech stirred the crowd up.
這場演講挑動了群眾的情緒。

▶ The cook gave one last stir and then poured the batter into the baking pan.
廚師攪拌最後一次後，就把麵糊倒入烤盤中。

---

stitch [stɪtʃ]

① *n.* 縫線；一針

② *v.* 縫；繡

同 **fasten / sew**

實用片語
stitch up 縫合

▶ Katrina is having a difficult time keeping her stitches in a line.
卡翠娜不會縫一直線。

▶ My mom stitched my name on my backpack.
我媽媽在我的背包上繡上我的名字。

▶ I'll ask my mom to stitch up my shirt.
我會叫媽媽縫好我的襯衫。

---

stocking [ˈstɑː.kɪŋ] *n.* 長襪

▶ Make sure that you wear stockings tomorrow morning.
你明天早上務必穿長襪。

---

stomach [ˈstʌm.ək] *n.* 胃；腹部

▶ Adam left work early because he was having pain in his stomach.
亞當提前下班，因為他胃痛。

Exercise 68

I. 中英對應

_____ 1. 樓梯間　(A) stare　　　　(B) staircase　(C) star　　　(D) start

_____ 2. 腹部　　(A) stomachache　(B) storm　　(C) stomach　(D) stormy

_____ 3. 吝嗇的　(A) stingy　　　　(B) sting　　　(C) sticky　　(D) stinky

_____ 4. 縫線　　(A) stir　　　　　(B) stiff　　　(C) strip　　　(D) stitch

_____ 5. 雕像　　(A) status　　　　(B) statue　　(C) state　　　(D) station

II. Vocabulary Choice

(A) staff　　(B) stale　　(C) starving　　(D) stare　　(E) steep

(F) stem　　(G) sting　　(H) stiff　　(I) steady　　(J) stereo

1. Good _____ communication is essential to business success.

2. Scorpions use their _____ to capture prey and to defend themselves.

3. We should stop wasting food; over millions of people on this planet are

　_____ .

4. You have to have a _____ hand and good eyes to be a surgeon.

5. The boy's sadness _____ from losing his new toy.

stool [stu:l] *n.* 凳子

▶ Uncle Joe bought a new stool for the dining room table.
裘叔叔為餐桌買了一張新凳子。

---

storey [ˈstɔːr.i] *n.* （英國）樓層
[同] **floor / level**

▶ His room is on the second storey of the house.
他的房間位於這棟房子的二樓。

---

stormy [ˈstɔːr.mi] *adj.* 暴風雨的；暴風的
[搭] **stormy weather** 暴風雨天氣
[同] **murky / rainy**

▶ Because it is really stormy today, we are going to have to cancel the picnic.
因為今天的暴風雨天候，我們得取消野餐才行。

---

storyteller [ˈstɔːr.iˌtel.ɚ]
n. 講故事的人；故事作者

▶ Bill is a fascinating storyteller.
比爾是個很會吸引人的說故事專家。

---

strategy [ˈstræt̬.ə.dʒi] *n.* 策略
[搭] **develop strategy** 發展策略
[同] **approach / project**

▶ What is your strategy for making more money this year?
今年你賺更多錢的策略是什麼？

---

(95)

strength [streŋθ] *n.* 力氣；力量
[搭] **gather strength** 凝聚力量
[同] **power / stability**
實用片語
on the strength of 以…某實力，強項

▶ Joey didn't have the strength to carry the heavy box up the stairs.
裘伊沒有力氣扛沉重的箱子到樓上。

▶ Linda was hired on the strength of her excellent English ability.
琳達因為卓越的英文實力而獲雇用。

---

strengthen [ˈstreŋ.θən] *v.* 加強；變強大
[同] **enlarge / reinforce**

▶ Drinking milk strengthens your bones.
多喝牛奶能夠強化骨頭。

---

strip [strɪp]
① *n.* 長條
實用片語
strive for 爭取

▶ Cut the chicken into strips.
請把雞肉切成條狀。

▶ Companies strive for higher profits.
所有公司都在爭取更高的利潤。

② v. 脫去
搭 **completely strip away** 完全脫去
同 **peel / tear away**

▶ Felix stripped off his shirt as he ran past his house.
菲力克斯跑過他的房子時脫下自己的襯衫。

---

strive [straɪv] v. 努力；奮鬥
同 **endeavor / go all out**

▶ She is striving to be a better student.
她非常努力的要成為一位更優秀的學生。

---

(97)

stroke [stroʊk]

① n. 打擊
同 **blow / hit**
② v. （用手）撫摸
同 **brush / caress**

▶ He knocked the boy over with one stroke.
他出手一擊就把男孩給打倒了。

▶ The mother stroked her little boy's hair.
那位媽媽輕輕撫摸她的小兒子的頭髮。

---

(97)

structure [ˈstrʌk.tʃɚ]

① n. 構造；組織
搭 **reorganize structure** 重新規劃架構
同 **complex / formation**
② v. 安排；組織

▶ It is very difficult to get anything done because of the company's structure.
因為公司這樣的組織結構，我們很難完成任何事情。

▶ How do you like to structure your day?
你希望怎麼安排自己的一天？

---

stubborn [ˈstʌb.ɚn] adj. 頑固的
同 **determined / unshakable**

▶ Keith is so stubborn; he refuses to take his medication.
凱斯非常固執；他拒絕吃藥。

---

studio [ˈstuː.di.oʊ] n. 工作室；錄音室

▶ Amanda teaches piano in her studio.
阿曼達在自己的工作室教授鋼琴。

---

stuff [stʌf]

① n. 材料；東西
② v. 填塞
同 **fill / shove**

▶ Sandy has so much stuff she can't fit it all into five boxes.
珊蒂有好多東西，她無法把所有東西都塞進五個箱子裡。

▶ My mom stuffed our Christmas stockings with lots of goodies.
我媽媽在我們聖誕節的長筒襪裡塞滿好東西。

S

style [staɪl]

① *n.* 風格;流行式樣

搭 **dress in style** 打扮有型

同 **mode / sophistication**

② *v.* 設計;給…造型

實用片語
in style 流行,別具風格

> Sally looked through the magazine to find some of the latest clothing styles.
> 莎莉翻閱雜誌,找尋一些最近流行的服飾樣式。

> The princess has her hair styled differently everyday.
> 公主每天都有不同的髮型。

> This dress isn't in style any more.
> 這件洋裝不再流行了。

---

submarine [ˌsʌb.məˈriːn]

① *n.* 潛水艇

同 **submersible / U-boat**

② *adj.* 海底的

> The sailors used a submarine to reach the sunken ship.
> 水手們利用潛水艇到達沈船的地方。

> The submarine vessel carried many sailors.
> 這艘潛水艇載了大批的水手們。

---

substance [ˈsʌb.stəns] *n.* 物質

搭 **chemical substance** 化學物質

同 **material / object**

> There isn't a lot of substance in this container.
> 這個容器裡的物質不多。

---

suburb [ˈsʌb.ɝːb] *n.* 市郊;近郊

搭 **affluent suburb** 富裕的地區

同 **environs / hinterland**

> The journalist lives in the suburb of Philadelphia.
> 這位新聞記者住在費城的郊區。

---

suck [sʌk]

① *v.* 吸

② *n.* 吸

> It was difficult to suck the ice-cream through the straw.
> 用吸管吸冰淇淋是很難的。

> Take one last suck of the drink.
> 吸完最後一口飲料。

---

suffer [ˈsʌf.ɚ] *v.* 受苦

同 **grieve / endure**

實用片語
suffer from 遭受,患有…

> Sally suffered from a minor heart attack.
> 莎莉受輕微心臟病之苦。

> Lisa suffers from insomnia and takes sleeping pills at night.
> 麗莎受失眠之苦,睡前都要吃安眠藥。

suffering [ˈsʌf.ɚ.ɪŋ]

n. （身體、精神上的）痛苦；折磨；苦難

同 **difficulty / discomfort**

▶ The medicine should reduce his suffering.
這個藥應該可以減輕他的痛苦。

102

sufficient [səˈfɪʃ.ənt] *adj.* 足夠的

搭 **sufficient understanding**
　　足夠的認知 / 瞭解

同 **enough / ample**

▶ We have a sufficient amount of help for the party next weekend.
下週末的派對我們有足夠的幫手。

103　97

suggest [səˈdʒest] *v.* 建議

同 **mishap / hazard**

實用片語
suggest something to someone
推薦某物給某人

▶ I suggest that you drink at least 8 glasses of water before the race.
我建議你賽跑前先喝至少八杯水。

▶ Jack suggested the ERP software to all his clients.
傑克向他所有的客戶推薦 ERP 軟體。

---

suggestion [səˈdʒes.tʃən] *n.* 建議

搭 **reject suggestion** 拒絕提議

同 **invitation / advice**

▶ She took my suggestion and cut her hair.
她接受了我的建議，把頭髮剪短。

---

suicide [ˈsuː.ə.saɪd] *n.* 自殺

▶ The police officer stopped the student from committing suicide.
警察阻止了這位學生自殺。

S

Exercise 69

I. Derivatives

1. A good _____ (story) can keep the attention of small children as well as antsy, busy businessmen.

2. Susan's battle against cancer has _____ (strength) her faith in God.

3. Candy bears her pain bravely even though she is _____ (suffer) severely from cancer.

4. Nancy has some good _____ (suggest) for bridal shower presents.

5. Sailing can be very dangerous on _____ (storm) seas and many ships have been destroyed.

II. 中英對應

_____ 1. 頑固的   (A) studio   (B) stubborn   (C) stunning   (D) stumble

_____ 2. 足夠的   (A) suffering   (B) substance   (C) sufficient   (D) suggest

_____ 3. 填塞   (A) staff   (B) stuff   (C) staffing   (D) stuck

_____ 4. 海底的   (A) submarine   (B) substance   (C) suburb   (D) substitute

_____ 5. 打擊   (A) strive   (B) strike   (C) strong   (D) stroke

97

suitable [ˈsuː.ṭə.bəl] *adj.* 適合的

同 **convenient / qualified**

▶ Unfortunately, I don't think that Jeremy is suitable for this particular teaching position.
不巧的是，我不認為傑爾米適合這個教職。

---

sum [sʌm]

① *n.* 總數；總和

同 **total / amount**

② *v.* 總計

▶ The sum of 2 plus 2 is 4.
二加二的總和是四。

▶ After summing up the points, it was determined that Rebecca was the winner.
在總計分數之後，利百加成了冠軍。

---

summarize [ˈsʌm.ə.raɪz] *v.* 作總結

搭 **summarize the results** 歸納結果

同 **encapsulate / epitomize**

▶ Please summarize the story for me because I don't have time to read it.
請為我把故事做個總結，因為我實在沒有時間去讀它。

---

summary [ˈsʌm.ɚ.i] *n.* 摘要；總結

同 **prospectus / rehash**

▶ As soon as you finish the book, I need you to write a short summary.
你寫完這本書之後，我需要你寫一篇簡短的摘要。

---

summit [ˈsʌm.ɪt] *n.* 山頂；峰頂

同 **peak / crest**

實用片語
at the summit of success
事業頂峰，如日中天

▶ Four hours later, the boy scouts made it to the summit.
四小時之後，男童子軍抵達山頂。

▶ The company is presently at the summit of success.
這間公司正如日中天。

---

sunbathe [ˈsʌn.beɪð] *v.* 作日光浴

▶ We sunbathed at the beach.
我們在海灘上作日光浴。

---

sunlight [ˈsʌn.laɪt] *n.* 陽光；日光

搭 **strong sunlight** 光線強烈

同 **sunshine / dawn**

▶ The sunlight was shining brightly today.
今天的陽光很強。

S

superior [sə`pɪr.i.ɚ]

① *adj.* 優秀的；上級的

同 **exceptional / significant**

② *n.* 上司

同 **manager / supervisor**

▶ Felix sees himself as a superior teacher.
菲力克斯視自己為一位優秀的老師。

▶ My dad is definitely the superior of the two officers.
我爸爸當然是兩位軍官的上司。

---

supporter [sə`pɔːr.tɚ]

n. 支撐物；支持者；援助者

搭 **loyal support** 忠誠支持

同 **follower / proponent**

▶ The supporters help keep the building in place.
這些支撐物有助於固定住這棟建築。

---

suppose [sə`poʊz] *v.* 假定；以為

同 **expect / presume**

▶ I suppose that she is not at home. Nobody answered the phone.
我認為她不在家。沒人接電話。

---

supposed [sə`poʊzd]

adj. 被信以為真的；假定的

同 **assumed / putative**

▶ The supposed food shortage had us all worried.
原本誤以為食物短缺，害我們大家都很擔心。

---

surely [`ʃʊr.li] *adv.* 確實地；無疑地

搭 **surely right** 確定正確

同 **certainly / definitely**

實用片語
slowly but surely 緩慢穩定地

▶ People will surely miss you while you are away.
你不在時大家一定會想念你的。

▶ I've been working on my project slowly and surely.
一直緩慢穩定地進行我的專案。

---

surf [sɝːf]

① *n.* 碎浪

搭 **ride surf** 衝浪

同 **swell / wave**

② *v.* 作衝浪運動；在網路上搜尋資料

同 **search / seek**

實用片語
surf the Net 上網

▶ The swimmer almost drowned in the violent surf.
游泳的人差點被巨浪給滅頂。

▶ Dan surfed the big waves of Hawaii.
丹恩在夏威夷衝浪。

▶ He spends two hours a day surfing the Net.
他每天花兩小時上網。

surfing [ˈsɝː.fɪŋ] *n.* 衝浪

▶ This beach is perfect for surfing.
這個沙灘非常適合衝浪！

surgeon [ˈsɝː.dʒən] *n.* 外科醫生

▶ The surgeon operated on the man's damaged heart.
外科醫生為那位男士的受損心臟開刀。

95
surgery [ˈsɝː.dʒɚ.i] *n.* 外科手術

▶ Cameron had surgery to fix his shoulder.
卡麥榮接受外科手術來修復他的肩膀。

103 102
surrender [səˈren.dɚ]

① *n.* 投降
同 **give in / renounce**

實用片語
surrender to 投降

② *n.* 投降；屈服
搭 **unconditional surrender** 無條件投降
同 **abandonment / renunciation**

▶ The soldiers surrendered the city to their enemies.
這些士兵投降，把城市拱手讓給敵人。

▶ The thief surrendered to the police.
這小偷跟警察投降。

▶ The general demanded the enemy's surrender.
將軍命令敵方投降。

98
surround [səˈraʊnd] *v.* 圍繞
同 **circle / inundate**

▶ The pack of dogs surrounded the little girl.
一群狗圍著這個小女孩。

surroundings [səˈraʊn.dɪŋz] *n.* 環境
搭 **peaceful surroundings** 安寧的氛圍
同 **atmosphere / environs**

▶ After ten years, Mark needed a change in surroundings.
已經過了十年了，馬克需要換個新環境。

survey [ˈsɝː.veɪ]

① *v.* 勘測；調查
同 **poll / sampling**

② *n.* 調查；勘測
搭 **extensive survey** 大規模調查
同 **analysis / inspection**

▶ Before buying the property, Jamie surveyed the land.
傑米在購買這塊地之前先做了勘測。

▶ It took Ken 5 minutes to fill out the survey at the restaurant.
肯恩花了五分鐘的時間在餐廳填寫問卷調查。

S

survival [sə·ˈvaɪ.vəl] *n.* 存活；倖存

同 **continuity / endurance**

▶ Jamie thought that his survival was more important than his dog's.
傑米認為，自己的存活比寵物狗的存活更重要。

---

survivor [sə·ˈvaɪ.vɚ] *n.* 生還者；存活者

同 **endurer / outlaster**

▶ There was only one survivor from the shipwreck.
只有一個人從船難中生還。

---

suspect [səs·ˈpekt]

① *v.* 懷疑

搭 **strongly suspect** 強烈懷疑

同 **consider / speculate**

實用片語
suspect of 懷疑某事

② *n.* 嫌疑犯

③ *adj.* 可疑的

▶ Who do you suspect ate the cookies?
你懷疑誰吃了餅乾？

▶ They suspect the clerk of stealing.
他們懷疑這店員偷竊。

▶ There are three suspects in the courtroom.
法庭中有三位嫌疑犯。

▶ A suspect bag was found at the airport.
只在機場找到一個可疑的袋子。

---

suspicion [sə·ˈspɪʃ.ən] *n.* 懷疑

同 **conjecture / mistrust**

▶ Sally's quiet nature aroused my suspicion.
莎莉安靜的性格引起我的懷疑。

---

suspicious [sə·ˈspɪʃ.əs] *adj.* 可疑的

同 **incredulous / mistrustful**

實用片語
suspicious character 可疑人物

▶ Lynn was suspicious that her neighbor's dog tore up her yard.
琳恩懷疑是鄰居的狗把她的院子給破壞了。

▶ There is a suspicious character standing in the hallway.
有個可疑人物站在走廊上。

Exercise 70

I. Derivatives

1. Lisa likes to _____ (sun) and relax on the beach over the weekend.
2. The meeting was _____ (suppose) to start at 3:00 p.m. but it was postponed.
3. Luke averages an hour a day or more _____ (surf) on the net.
4. The deaths of the old couple, found on the Tamsui River bank this afternoon, is being treated as _____ (suspicion).
5. The _____ (surgery) performed an operation to remove the woman's breast tumor.

II. Multiple Choice

(   ) 1. A recent ___ found that 60% of people are not satisfied with the performance of our new government.
(A) surf (B) survey (C) surface (D) survive

(   ) 2. Thousands of ___ went to the Taichung Intercontinental Baseball Stadium for the 2015 WBSC Premier12.
(A) supports (B) suppliers (C) supporters (D) staff

(   ) 3. The bank robbers finally ___ to the police.
(A) suspected (B) surprised (C) surrounded (D) surrendered

(   ) 4. My brother was fined a ___ of NT$12000 due to over speeding last year.
(A) sum (B) summarize (C) summary (D) summit

(   ) 5. The police ___ the singer has some connection with a drug dealer.
(A) suspicion (B) suspects (C) suspicious (D) surrounds

㉛ **loose** ['lus] *adj.* 鬆的、寬的、鬆散的

例 Young people like to wear loose jeans as they are more comfortable.
年輕人喜歡穿寬鬆的牛仔褲,因為那比較舒適。

lose ['luz] *v.* 丟失、喪失

例 If you lose your credit card, inform the bank immediately.
若你遺失信用卡,馬上告知銀行。

㉜ **luxurious** [lʌɡˈʒʊr.i.əs] *adj.* 奢侈的、豪華的

例 Ian is a gentleman with luxurious tastes.
宜安是有奢華品位的紳士。

luxuriant [lʌɡˈʒʊr.i.ənt] *adj.* 繁茂的、濃密的

例 Tall and luxuriant plants grew along the street.
高又濃密的植物種在道路兩旁。

㉝ **momentary** [ˈmoʊ.mən.tər.i] *adj.* 短暫的、瞬間的

例 Larry experienced a momentary loss of consciousness.
賴瑞經歷了短暫的失去意識。

momentous [məˈmen.ṭəs] *adj.* 重大的、重要的

例 That's one of the most momentous decisions I've ever made.
那是我做過最重大的決定之一。

㉞ **moral** [ˈmɔːr.əl] *n.* 道德、品行

例 Nowadays people have noticed a decline in moral standards.
現今人們已意識到道德水準的下降。

morale [məˈrɑːl] *n.* 士氣、鬥志

例 Can you share with me how to boost staff's morale?
你可以跟我方享提高員工士氣的方法嗎?

㉟ **motive** [ˈmoʊ.ṭɪv] *n.* 動機、主旨、目的

例 We need to find out his motive for killing the old man.
我們要找出他殺死那老人的動機。

motif [moʊˈtiːf] *n.* (藝術、文學作品等之)主題

例 We chose a rug with a flower motif.
我們選了一組有花色的地墊。

sway [sweɪ]

① *v.* 搖擺；搖動

搭 **sway slightly** 輕微地搖晃

同 **swing / move**

實用片語
sway someone to 影響，動搖

② *n.* 晃動；搖擺

同 **clout / amplitude**

▶ We swayed to the beat of the music.
我們跟著音樂的拍子搖擺起來。

▶ I can't sway Mary to my position.
我無法動搖瑪莉，說服她同意我的立場。

▶ The sway of the boat made the boy feel sick.
船身的晃動使得小男孩暈船。

---

swear [swer] *v.* 發誓

搭 **swear solemnly** 鄭重地發誓

同 **affirm / depose**

▶ I swear to tell the truth.
我發誓只說事實。

---

sweat [swet]

① *n.* 汗水

② *v.* 出汗

搭 **sweat profusely** 大量出汗

同 **glow / swelter**

實用片語
no sweat 不費力

▶ Steve was dripping with sweat after his run.
史提夫跑完步後在流汗。

▶ Kelly really seems to sweat a lot.
凱莉似乎流很多的汗。

▶ You'd like a red shirt? No sweat.
你想要一件紅上衣？沒問題。

---

swell [swel]

① *v.* 腫脹

同 **balloon / expand**

② *n.* 腫脹

同 **crescendo / boost**

▶ Katherine's finger swelled after she was bitten by a spider.
凱瑟琳的手指被蜘蛛咬後腫起來。

▶ Because of the swelling on her leg, Anna wasn't able to go running.
安娜因為腳腫脹而不能去跑步。

---

swift [swɪft] *adj.* 快速的

搭 **swift movement** 輕巧的行動

同 **rapid / speedy**

實用片語
swift as the wind 敏捷，快速

▶ Cheetahs are very swift animals.
獵豹是非常敏捷的動物。

▶ The new train will be swift as the wind.
新的列車將會相當快速。

S

swimsuit [ˈswɪm.suːt] *n.* 泳衣

> ► Don't forget to bring your swimsuit to the beach!
> 別忘了帶你的游泳衣去海邊！

---

switch [swɪtʃ]

① *n.* 開關

同 **about-face / alteration**

② *v.* 打開（或關掉）開關

搭 **switch emphasis** 轉移重點

同 **convert / replace**

實用片語
switch out 關掉

> ► I can't seem to find the switch for the light.
> 我找不到燈的開關。
>
> ► Joey and James switched seats on the airplane.
> 裘伊和詹姆士在飛機上互換座位。
>
> ► Please switch the light out when you leave.
> 離開時請關燈。

---

sword [sɔːrd] *n.* 劍

> ► At one time, people used swords as a weapon to defend themselves.
> 人們曾經用劍來當作防衛的武器。

---

syllable [ˈsɪl.ə.bl̩] *n.* 音節

> ► The word telephone has three syllables.
> 「telephone」這個字有三個音節。

---

sympathetic [ˌsɪm.pəˈθet̬.ɪk]
adj. 同情的；有同情心的

搭 **sympathetic understanding** 同情瞭解

同 **affectionate / interested**

> ► She gave the man a sympathetic hug after his wife's death.
> 在這位男士的妻子過世之後，她給了他一個同情的擁抱。

---

sympathy [ˈsɪm.pə.θi] *n.* 同情；同情心

同 **compassion / kindness**

> ► We sent Bill a card to show our sympathy.
> 我們寄給比爾一張卡片傳達我們的慰問。

---

symphony [ˈsɪm.fə.ni] *n.* 交響樂

> ► The musician wrote a beautiful symphony.
> 這位音樂家譜了一首美妙的交響曲。

---

syrup [ˈsɪr.əp] *n.* 糖漿

> ► The kids poured thick syrup on their pancakes.
> 小朋友們把濃稠的糖漿淋在煎餅上。

system [ˈsɪs.təm] *n.* 系統

搭 **workable system** 可行的系統

同 **arrangement / scheme**

實用片語
beat the system 挑戰現有制度

▶ Jamie updated the system on his computer.
傑米更新自己的電腦系統。

▶ Nancy often gets in trouble when she tries to find ways to beat the system.
南西常常為了鑽漏洞而惹禍上身。

---

systematic [ˌsɪs.təˈmæt̪ˌɪk] *adj.* 有系統的

同 **precise / methodical**

▶ He came up with a systematic plan for improving the business.
他想出一個有系統的計畫以帶動他的生意。

---

tablecloth [ˈteɪ.bəl.klɑːθ] *n.* 桌布

▶ She spilled her grape juice and ruined the tablecloth.
她打翻了她的葡萄汁而且把桌布給弄髒了。

---

tablet [ˈtæb.lət] *n.* 藥片；平板電腦

▶ Seth went looking for grandfather's tablet.
賽斯去找爺爺的平板電腦。

---

tack [tæk]

① *n.* 大頭釘

② *v.* 用大頭釘釘

▶ Sam used a tack to hang his picture on the wall.
山姆用大頭釘把照片掛在牆上。

▶ I helped my dad tack the carpet in place.
我幫助爸爸把地毯釘好。

---

tag [tæg]

① *n.* 標籤

② *v.* 加標籤

同 **identify / adjoin**

▶ According to the tag, this shirt is on sale.
標籤上說這件襯衫是減價出售。

▶ My friend's dog has been tagged as dangerous.
我朋友的狗的標籤上寫牠是危險的。

---

tailor [ˈteɪ.lɚ]

① *n.* 裁縫師

② *v.* 縫製

同 **accommodate / adapt**

▶ Stephanie brought her coat to a tailor to be fixed.
史蒂芬妮拿大衣去給裁縫師修改。

▶ My aunt tailored the dress just for me.
我阿姨特別為我縫製這件洋裝。

T

talented [ˈtæl.ən.tɪd] *adj.* 有天份的

搭 **talented musician** 有才能的音樂家

同 **skilled / brilliant**

▶ Gabe is very talented in music.
蓋伯在音樂方面非常有天份。

---

tame [teɪm]

① *adj.* 溫順的；馴服的

同 **harmless / manageable**

② *v.* 馴養

同 **restrain / suppress**

▶ My cat doesn't always seem very tame.
我的貓不是一直都很溫順。

▶ Teddy spent several months trying to tame the wild horse.
泰迪花了幾個月的時間試圖馴服這匹野馬。

---

tap [tæp]

① *v.* 輕拍；輕敲

搭 **tap lightly** 清拍

同 **knock / pat**

實用片語
What's on tap for today. 今天有何新鮮事。

② *n.* 輕敲；輕拍

同 **spigot / valve**

③ *n.* 水龍頭

④ *n.* 輕拍

同 **spigot / valve**

⑤ *v.* 輕拍

搭 **tap gently** 輕輕拍打

同 **knock / pat**

▶ He tapped me on the shoulder and asked me for the time.
他輕拍我的肩膀，問我當時的時間。

▶ Let's check my schedule and see what's on tap for today.
我確認一下我的行程表，看今天有何新鮮事。

▶ The cat's tap on the window lets us know she wants to come in.
貓咪在窗戶上輕敲讓我們知道牠想要進來。

▶ Turn off the tap. Don't let the water run.
把水龍頭關掉，不要讓水一直流個不停。

▶ Do you like the sound of tap?
你喜歡輕輕拍打的聲音嗎？

▶ The teacher gently tapped the student on the shoulder.
老師輕拍學生的肩膀。

---

tax [tæks]

① *n.* 稅

搭 **tax collector** 收稅人員

同 **tariff / duty**

② *v.* 課稅

同 **burden / charge**

▶ Taxes seem to be so high in the States.
美國的稅金似乎很高。

▶ In America, the government taxes the people on their property.
在美國，政府徵收人民房地產稅。

tease [ti:z]

① *v.* 戲弄；取笑

同 **harass / nudge**

實用片語
tease someone about 戲弄某人

② *n.* 戲弄；取笑

▶ Boys always seem to like to tease girls.
男生似乎總是喜歡戲弄女生。

▶ Stop teasing him about his clothes.
停止取笑他的衣服了。

▶ That was such a good tease.
那個玩笑很好笑。

Exercise 71

I. 中英對應

_____ 1. 藥片　　(A) table　　　　(B) tablecloth　　(C) tabletop　　(D) tablet

_____ 2. 溫順的　(A) time　　　　(B) tame　　　　(C) temper　　　(D) tack

_____ 3. 加標籤　(A) take　　　　(B) tape　　　　(C) tag　　　　(D) tap

_____ 4. 開關　　(A) switch　　　(B) swift　　　　(C) sword　　　(D) swim

_____ 5. 糖漿　　(A) symphony　(B) syrup　　　　(C) system　　　(D) symbol

II. Derivatives

1. Both Scarlett Johansson and Natalie Portman are beautiful and
   _____ (talent) actresses in Hollywood.

2. You have to change into your _____ (swim) and put on your
   swim cap before getting into the swimming pool.

3. Daniel is very _____ (system) in his approach to work and he
   cannot stand chaos.

4. My mother covered the table with a plastic _____ (table)
   before she put our dinner on it.

5. Because Teresa also suffers from gum disease, she is very
   _____ (sympathy) about my problem.

97
technical [ˈtek.nɪ.kəl] *adj.* 技術的

搭 **technical know-how** 技術專業

同 **professional / specialized**

▶ Once again, we seem to be having technical problems.
我們好像又再次出現技術上的問題了。

---

technician [tekˈnɪʃ.ən] *n.* 技術人員；技師

同 **consultant / professional**

▶ We called a technician to fix the computer.
我們請技術人員來修理電腦。

---

101 99
technique [tekˈniːk] *n.* 技巧；技術

同 **procedure / method**

▶ Charlotte uses a very special teaching technique in her classroom.
夏綠蒂在課堂上用一種很特殊的教學技巧。

---

technological [ˌtek.nəˈlɑː.dʒɪ.kəl]
adj. 科技的；技術的

同 **mechanical / scientific**

▶ Technological advances in 3D printing have helped doctors save people's lives.
3D列印的科技突破幫助醫生們拯救更多的生命。

---

technology [tekˈnɑː.lə.dʒi] *n.* 科技

搭 **implement technology** 運用科技

同 **automation / machinery**

▶ It seems like technology is always being updated.
科技似乎一直在更新。

T

---

telegram [ˈtel.ə.græm] *n.* 電報

▶ A telegram arrived with bad news from overseas.
收到來自海外一封壞消息的電報。

95
telegraph [ˈtel.ə.græf]

① *n.* 電報
② *v.* 打電報給⋯

▶ Telegraphs were popular in the 19th century.
電報在十九世紀時是很受歡迎的。

▶ People telegraphed messages before they had telephones.
在他們有電話以前，人們都是透過電報傳遞消息。

---

telescope [ˈtel.ə.skoʊp] *n.* 望遠鏡

▶ She used a telescope to view the planets.
她用望遠鏡來觀察行星。

televise [ˈtel.ə.vaɪz] *v.* 用電視播送

> That accident will be televised on the news channel.
> 那個意外將會在電視新聞頻道上播出。

---

temper [ˈtem.pɚ] *n.* 脾氣

同 **mood / temperament**

> Freddie has a very bad temper today.
> 佛萊帝今天脾氣很壞。

---

(95)
temperature [ˈtem.pɚ.ə.tʃɚ] *n.* 溫度

同 **condition / climate**

> Kelly has a very high temperature this evening.
> 凱莉今晚的體溫很高。

---

(99)(97)
temporary [ˈtem.pə.rer.i] *adj.* 暫時的

搭 **temporary employment** 臨時雇用
同 **limited / momentary**

> Jim's time in Korea is only temporary.
> 吉姆只是暫時留在韓國。

---

(103)
tend [tend] *v.* 傾向於⋯

同 **incline / favor**

實用片語
tend to 意圖

> Everyone tends to get a little tired after several hours of hard work.
> 大家在努力工作數小時之後都變得有點疲累。

> We tend to believe whatever we are told.
> 我們試圖相信別人告訴我們的任何事。

---

(104)(100)(98)
tendency [ˈten.dən.si] *n.* 傾向；趨勢

搭 **growing tendency** 日益增加之趨勢
同 **movement / trend**

> I have a tendency to laugh when I am nervous.
> 我有一緊張就會笑的傾向。

---

tender [ˈten.dɚ] *adj.* 溫柔的；柔軟的

同 **delicate / supple**

實用片語
tender age 年紀輕

> My mom has a very tender heart.
> 我媽媽有溫柔的心腸。

> It's a great advantage to learn languages at a tender age.
> 年紀輕的時候是學習語言的好機會。

---

tense [tens]

① *adj.* 緊繃的；緊張的

搭 **tense atmosphere** 緊張的氣氛
同 **rigid / stiff**

> My shoulder muscles are very tense.
> 我的肩膀肌肉十分緊繃。

② *v.* 繃緊；覺得緊張；使拉緊

實用片語
tense up 緊張

▶ Tia tenses up when she is frightened.
提雅一害怕就全身繃緊。

▶ When the police stopped his car, Simon tensed up.
當警察攔下他的車，西門緊張了起來。

---

tension [ˈtɛn.ʃən] *n.* 緊張；拉緊

同 **pressure / strain**

▶ Massage can reduce tension in your muscles.
按摩能夠幫助紓解你肌肉的緊張。

---

terrify [ˈtɛr.ə.faɪ] *v.* 使恐懼

搭 **absolutely terrify** 極度害怕
同 **dismay / horrify**

▶ The loud noise terrified the child.
巨大的聲響嚇壞了那個小孩。

---

territory [ˈtɛr.ə.tɔːr.i] *n.* 領土；地區

同 **district / area**

▶ When you paintball, you need to stay in your territory.
你玩漆彈遊戲時，要留在你的領土範圍。

---

terror [ˈtɛr.ə] *n.* 恐怖

搭 **spread terror** 散佈恐懼
同 **horror / intimidation**

▶ She screamed in terror.
她感到恐怖而尖叫。

---

text [tɛkst] *n.* 正文

▶ Please copy the text of the book into your notebook.
請將書本的內容抄寫在你的筆記本上。

T

---

thankful [ˈθæŋk.fəl] *adj.* 感謝的

同 **grateful / contented**

實用片語
be thankful for 對⋯感恩

▶ I am very thankful for my mom and dad.
我很感謝我的父母。

▶ We are not rich, but we have enough. We should be thankful for small blessings.
我們並不富有，但至少我們有足夠的食物。我們要因為小確幸而感恩。

---

theme [θiːm] *n.* 主題；話題

搭 **principal theme** 主要議題
同 **matter / thought**

▶ The theme of the conference was innovation.
這次大會的主題是創新。

theory [ˈθɪr.i] *n.* 理論

同 **ideology / understanding**

實用片語
in theory 理論上

---

thirst [θɝ:st] *n.* 渴望

▶ Based upon the scientist's theory, rats can't swim.
根據科學理論，老鼠不會游泳。

▶ Home schooling, in theory, is good for children.
理論上，在家自學對小孩是好的。

- -

▶ Kevin has a great thirst for knowledge.
凱文有很強的求知慾。

Exercise 72

I. Derivatives

1. _____ (techno) advancements in filmmaking expand the creative potential of the filmmaker.

2. Both male and female cats can spray and mark their _____ (terrain) with their urine.

3. There are three lighting _____ (technic) in this movie crew.

4. She has a _____ (tend) to avoid conflict by just keeping quiet.

5. The _____ (temper) in Taipei rose to 38.7 degrees Celsius on June 1st, 2016, the city's highest record in June for the past 120 years.

II. 中英對應

_____ 1. 溫柔的　(A) tend　　　(B) tension　　(C) tense　　(D) tender

_____ 2. 電報　　(A) telephone　(B) telegraph　(C) televise　(D) telescope

_____ 3. 主題　　(A) theory　　(B) text　　　(C) theme　　(D) therapy

_____ 4. 使恐懼　(A) terrible　(B) terrify　　(C) terrific　(D) territory

_____ 5. 暫時的　(A) temporary　(B) temperature　(C) temper　(D) temptation

thorough [ˈθɝː.oʊ] *adj.* 徹底的

搭 **thorough preparation** 妥善準備

同 **complete / intensive**

▶ Despite a thorough search, the ring was lost.

儘管經過徹底的搜索，戒指還是遺失了。

---

thoughtful [ˈθɑːt.fəl]

adj. 思慮周全的；周到的

同 **careful / considerate**

▶ She gave a thoughtful response to his question.

對於他的問題，她提供了一個非常周全的回答。

---

thread [θred]

① *n.* 線

同 **filament / string**

② *v.* 穿（針、線）

搭 **silk thread** 絲線

實用片語
lose the thread 抓不到要點，亂了頭緒

▶ I need four different colors of thread for my sewing project.

我的縫紉作業需要四種不同顏色的線。

▶ Some people have a difficult time threading a needle.

有些人很難把線穿到針裡。

▶ The movie was so long that I soon lost the thread.

那電影太長我一下就亂了頭緒。

---

threat [θret] *n.* 威脅；恐嚇

同 **hazard / menace**

實用片語
be threatened with 受到威脅

▶ Those dogs are really not a threat.

這些狗真的沒有危險性。

▶ Many animals are now threatened with extinction.

許多動物現在都面臨絕種的威脅。

---

102 99

threaten [ˈθret.ən] *v.* 威脅；恐嚇

搭 **threaten safety** 威脅到安全

同 **imperil / warn**

▶ Frank threatened his neighbor with a knife.

法蘭克用刀威脅他的鄰居。

---

thunderstorm [ˈθʌn.dɚ.stɔːrm] *v.* 大雷雨

▶ The violent thunderstorm scared the children.

這個猛烈的大雷雨把小孩子們給嚇壞了。

tickle [ˈtɪk.əl]

① v. 搔癢
同 enchant / gratify

② n. 癢

tide [taɪd] n. 潮水;潮汐

同 stream / torrent

實用片語
go with the tide 順勢而行

tidy [ˈtaɪ.di]

① adj. 整潔的
同 orderly / neat

② v. 整理
搭 tidy the room 清理房間
同 groom / frame

實用片語
tidy up 清理

99 tight [taɪt]

① adj. 緊的
同 sturdy / compact

② adv. 緊地

實用片語
tighten the purse strings
拉緊錢包帶,花錢謹慎

tighten [ˈtaɪ.tən] v. 使變緊

搭 tighten muscle 拉緊肌肉
同 narrow / stiffen

timber [ˈtɪm.bɚ] n. 木材

▶ My dad loves to tickle my mom.
我爸爸喜歡搔我媽媽癢。

▶ I am going to give you a good tickle.
我會幫你好好的搔癢。

▶ Since the tide is high, we should be very careful when climbing over the rocks.
因為潮水很高,我們應該小心爬過這些石頭。

▶ Don't fight fate. Just go with the tide.
不要與命運對抗。就順勢而為。

▶ It is important to keep your room tidy.
保持你的房間整潔是很重要的。

▶ Since we have guests coming tonight, make sure you tidy up your room.
因為我們今晚有客人要來,你務必要整理你的房間。

▶ I will tidy up the conference room later.
我稍後將會清理會議室。

▶ The lid was so tight, I couldn't get it off.
蓋子蓋得很緊,我打不開。

▶ Hold my hand tight.
抓緊我的手。

▶ After losing his job, he had to tighten the purse strings.
丟掉工作後,他必須謹慎花錢。

▶ Jim tightened the peanut butter jar before putting it back in the fridge.
吉姆把花生醬放回冰箱之前先把罐子扭緊。

▶ Uncle Harry went out to buy some more timber.
哈利叔叔出去買更多木材。

T

timetable [ˈtaɪmˌteɪ.bəl]

n. （公車、火車等的）時刻表；時間表

▶ Jon checked the timetable to see when the train arrives.
裘恩查了一下時刻表，看看火車幾點進站。

---

timid [ˈtɪm.ɪd] 膽小的；羞怯的

同 shy / fearful

▶ The kitten was timid around the large dog.
那隻小貓咪在大狗的旁邊，就變得很膽小。

---

tiresome [ˈtaɪr.səm] *adj.* 使人疲勞的

同 boring / exhausting

▶ Bob's long meetings were tiresome.
鮑伯的冗長會議總是讓人感到疲倦。

---

tissue [ˈtɪʃ.uː] *n.* 面紙；組織

▶ Can you pass me a tissue for my nose?
你可以遞一張面紙讓我擦鼻子嗎？

---

tobacco [təˈbæk.oʊ] *n.* 菸草

▶ It is not a good idea to chew tobacco.
嚼菸草不是好主意。

---

103 102

tolerable [ˈtɑː.lə.ə.bəl] *adj.* 可容忍的

同 allowable / bearable

▶ The pain was tolerable, so she was able to go to work.
她還可以忍受那個痛，所以她才能夠去上班。

104

tolerance [ˈtɑː.lə.əns] *n.* 容忍；寬容

搭 degree of tolerance 忍受度

同 patience / resilience

▶ It is difficult for some people to show tolerance towards others.
對某些人而言，要容忍他人是很困難的。

---

tolerant [ˈtɑː.lə.ənt] *adj.* 寬容的；忍受的

同 forbearing / permissive

▶ Her tolerant attitude made it easy for her to work with others.
她寬容的態度使她跟別人非常容易共事。

97

tolerate [ˈtɑː.lə.reɪt] *v.* 寬容；忍受

同 accept / condone

▶ The teacher will not tolerate misbehavior in class.
那位老師絕對不會寬容在教室裡的不當行為。

---

tomb [tuːm] *n.* 墳墓

▶ The dead body was placed in a tomb.
這具屍體被放進墳墓裡。

ton [tʌn] *n.* 公噸

▶ A killer whale weighs 2 tons.
一隻殺人鯨重兩公噸。

---

tortoise [ˈtɔːr.təs] *n.* 龜

▶ If you go to the desert, you might see a big tortoise.
如果你去那處沙漠，也許會看見一隻大烏龜。

₉₈

toss [tɑːs]

① *v.* 拋；擲

[搭] **toss a coin** 擲硬幣

[同] **cast / throw**

[實用片語]
toss up 丟擲

② *n.* 拋；擲

[同] **cast / heave**

▶ Katrina came home from school and tossed her shirt on the floor.
卡翠娜從學校回家，她把襯衫扔到地板上。

▶ The referee tossed up a coin to see which team would go first.
裁判丟擲錢幣決定哪一隊先攻。

▶ Although it was a good toss, Susie still didn't catch the ball.
雖然那一球投得很好，蘇茜還是沒接到。

T

Exercise 73

I. 中英對應

_____ 1. 整潔的 (A) tide   (B) tight   (C) tickle   (D) tidy

_____ 2. 面紙 (A) threat   (B) timetable (C) tissue   (D) timber

_____ 3. 拋；擲 (A) ton   (B) toss   (C) tortoise   (D) tolerate

_____ 4. 墳墓 (A) tomb   (B) tobacco   (C) ton   (D) thunderstorm

_____ 5. 膽小的 (A) timid   (B) timber   (C) tiresome   (D) tight

II. Derivatives

1. Government agencies in Europe need to _____ (tight) the screws on illegal immigrants.

2. It is dangerous to stand under a tree during a _____ (thunder) as you could be struck by lightning.

3. Preparing for administrative work can be _____ (tire).

4. The terrorists _____ (threat) to kill the hostages unless the police did as they asked.

5. When she lost her job, it was her friends who made her life _____ (tolerate).

103

tough [tʌf] *adj.* 堅固的；牢固的

搭 **tough challenge** 困難的挑戰

同 **solid / vigorous**

▶ The tough fabric was not damaged in the heavy rain.
這塊堅固的布料沒有被大雨給毀損。

tourism [ˈtʊr.ɪ.zəm] *n.* 旅遊；觀光

同 **journey / travel**

▶ Megan wrote a book on tourism in France.
梅根寫了一本關於法國旅遊的書。

tourist [ˈtʊr.ɪst] *n.* 觀光客

搭 **tourist attractions** 旅遊景點

同 **visitor / sightseer**

實用片語
tourist trap 敲竹槓商店

▶ Have you noticed that tourists usually take lots of pictures?
你注意到觀光客通常都拍許多的照片嗎？

▶ That shop looked like a tourist trap.
那間店看來像是敲竹槓的商店。

102

tow [toʊ]

① *v.* 拖；拉

同 **haul / draw**

實用片語
in tow 隨後拉著…

② *n.* 拖；拉

▶ Frank towed his sailboat across America.
法蘭克拖著他的帆船橫越美國。

▶ The mother walked with two children in tow.
這位母親走著，身後還拉著兩個小孩。

▶ Sally asked her friend for a tow.
莎莉請她的朋友幫她拖車。

trace [treɪs]

① *v.* 追查；追蹤

同 **seek / follow**

實用片語
sink without trace 消聲匿跡

② *n.* 痕跡

搭 **detect trace** 偵查到痕跡

同 **footprint / relic**

▶ The rescue crew traced the trail up the mountain looking for the missing boy.
救援隊追查林間小道一直到山上，為要尋找失蹤的男孩。

▶ They enjoyed brief success and sank without trace a few months later.
他們享受短暫的成功，然後在幾個月後便銷聲匿跡了。

▶ There is no trace that anyone has ever been to this part of the beach.
沒有跡象顯示有任何人曾經來過海灘的這處地區。

T

trader [ˈtreɪ.də] *n.* 商人

同 **businessman / dealer**

▶ When traveling to California, I met a gold trader.
我到加州旅行時，遇見了一個黃金交易商。

101

tragedy [ˈtrædʒ.ə.di] *n.* 悲劇

同 **mishap / failure**

▶ Shakespeare wrote many famous tragedies.
莎士比亞寫了許多有名的悲劇。

---

tragic [ˈtrædʒ.ɪk] *adj.* 悲劇的

搭 **tragic consequence** 悲慘的後果

同 **disastrous / terrible**

▶ Hamlet is a famous tragic hero.
哈姆雷特是位出名的悲劇英雄。

---

trail [treɪl]

① *n.* 蹤跡；路徑

同 **path / track**

② *v.* 拖曳；跟蹤

同 **follow / chase**

實用片語
hit the trail 上路，出發

▶ Unfortunately, this mountain range doesn't have any trails.
遺憾地是，這個山脈沒有任何的小徑。

▶ The dog's leash trailed behind him.
狗兒的皮鏈拖在牠的後面。

▶ It's getting late. Let's hit the trail.
快遲到了。我們出發吧。

---

training [ˈtreɪ.nɪŋ] *n.* 訓練

搭 **participate in training** 參與訓練

同 **drill / guidance**

實用片語
keep in training 保持身體健康狀態

▶ His training was a long and tough process.
他的訓練是漫長且艱辛的過程。

▶ You should keep in training, so you will look good in your wedding dress.
你應該要持續健身，這樣穿婚紗才會好看。

---

101 96

transfer [ˈtræns.fɚ]

① *v.* 轉讓；轉移；調動

同 **change / convert**

實用片語
transfer from 調職到⋯

② *n.* 調動；遷移

搭 **technology transfer** 技術轉移

同 **removal / relocation**

▶ She transferred ownership of the car to her son.
她把她的汽車所有權轉讓給她的兒子。

▶ The company transferred Jenny from Tokyo to Taipei.
公司把珍妮從東京調職到台北。

▶ His job transfer means he has to move out of the country.
他的工作調動表示他必須搬到國外。

100 **96**

transform [trænsˈfɔːrm] *v.* 改變；將…改成…

搭 **transform the world** 顛覆世界

同 **revamp / remodel**

實用片語
transform someone to 某人轉變成…

▶ We transformed the garage into a gym.
我們將車庫改成健身房。

▶ Time had transformed Linda from a child to a young lady.
時間讓琳達從一個孩子轉變成一個年輕小姐。

---

translate [trænsˈleɪt] *v.* 翻譯

同 **decipher / reword**

實用片語
translate into 自…翻譯成…

▶ Doris translated the book into English.
桃樂絲把那本書翻譯成英文。

▶ Please translate this from English into Chinese.
請把這個從英文翻成中文。

103

translation [trænzˈleɪ.ʃən] *n.* 翻譯；譯文

▶ The translation of the Bible into the African language took many years.
把聖經翻譯成非洲語言的工作花了好多年的時間。

---

translator [trænzˈleɪ.tə] *n.* 翻譯者

▶ Jim worked as a translator at the museum.
吉姆在博物館裡當翻譯人員。

96

transport [ˈtræn.spɔːrt]

① *v.* 運輸

搭 **transport goods** 運送貨物

同 **deliver / ship**

實用片語
transport from 自…載到…

② *n.* 運輸

▶ Since I have a car, it will be very easy to transport all the groceries from the store.
因為我有車，所以很容易從商店運送所有的食品雜貨。

▶ He transported us from the office to the airport.
他從辦公室載我們到機場。

▶ The transport of goods was a very difficult task.
運送貨物是一件非常艱難的任務。

95

transportation [ˌtræn.spəˈteɪ.ʃən]
n. （交通工具的）接送；運輸；輸送

搭 **public transportation system**
大眾交通系統

同 **portage / shipment**

▶ We arranged transportation from the airport to the hotel.
我們會安排機場到飯店的接送。

T

trash [træʃ]

① *n.* 垃圾

② *v.* 丟掉

▶ Once again, Sally forgot to throw away her trash.
莎莉又忘了倒垃圾。

▶ Aunt Betty trashed the broken glass.
貝蒂姑姑把碎玻璃丟掉。

---

traveler [ˈtræv.əl.ɚ] *n.* 旅客

同 **sightseer / passenger**

▶ There aren't many travelers who come through Wilmington, NC.
從北卡威明頓過來的遊客不多。

---

traveling [ˈtræv.əl.ɪŋ] *n.* 旅行

搭 **traveling cost** 旅遊花費

同 **trip / journey**

▶ Traveling is fun if you like to experience different cultures.
旅行很好玩，如果你喜歡體驗不同文化的話。

---

tray [treɪ] *n.* 托盤

▶ Melody served breakfast on a tray.
美樂蒂把早餐放在一個托盤上。

97

tremble [ˈtrem.bəl]

① *v.* 顫抖

同 **shake / vibrate**

實用片語
tremble with 發抖

② *n.* 顫抖

▶ Ken trembled at the sight of his father.
肯恩一看見他爸爸就發抖。

▶ During the earthquake, the dog trembled with fear.
地震時，這隻狗因恐懼而發抖。

▶ There was a slight tremble in his voice when he started speaking.
當他開始說話時，聲音有點顫抖。

---

tremendous [trɪˈmen.dəs] *adj.* 巨大的

同 **huge / gigantic**

▶ She had a tremendous amount of work to finish.
她手上有大量的工作要完成。

98

trend [trend] *n.* 趨勢

搭 **analyze trend** 分析情勢

同 **direction / tendency**

▶ Over the years, there has been an upward trend in clothing sales.
這些年來，服飾的銷售量一直呈現往上增加的趨勢。

---

tribal [ˈtraɪ.bəl] *adj.* 部落的；種族的

同 **national / inborn**

▶ Nancy wore tribal clothing to her son's wedding ceremony.
南希穿著她部落的服裝去參加兒子的婚禮。

Exercise 74

I. 中英對應

_____ 1. 托盤　(A) trap　　(B) trade　　(C) tray　　(D) trail

_____ 2. 蹤跡　(A) trail　　(B) trial　　(C) track　　(D) trade

_____ 3. 垃圾　(A) trash　　(B) track　　(C) train　　(D) trace

_____ 4. 趨勢　(A) tremble　(B) trend　　(C) tread　　(D) treat

_____ 5. 追查　(A) trade　　(B) track　　(C) trap　　(D) trace

II. Derivatives

1. This hospital provides on-the-job _____ (train) for nurses.

2. The September 11, 2001, terror attacks was a terrible _____ (tragic) and one of the worst in American history.

3. The Rukai people appeared in full _____ (tribe) dress to welcome us when we arrived in their village.

4. The audience got a _____ (tremble) surprise when the movie star arrived at the theater to greet them.

5. A translator's duty is to keep his or her _____ (translate) as faithful as possible to the original book.

tribe [traɪb] *n.* 部落

同 **clan / group**

▶ If you go to Hualien, you will meet people from various tribes.
如果你去花蓮，就會遇見不同族群的人。

---

tricky [ˈtrɪk.i] *adj.* 難處理的；狡猾的

搭 **tricky questions** 預防意外發生
同 **risky / thorny**

▶ These math problems can be a little tricky.
這些算術問題可能會有點難。

---

(101)

triumph [ˈtraɪ.əmf]

① *n.* 勝利

搭 **personal triumph** 個人成功
同 **victory / achievement**

② *v.* 戰勝；獲得勝利

同 **conquer / overcome**

實用片語
triumph over 贏過，勝過

▶ The president celebrated his triumph in the election.
總統慶祝他在選舉中獲得勝利。

▶ The team triumphed over its rival.
這一隊戰勝了他們的對手。

▶ Our team triumphed over all the other competitors.
我們的團隊勝過所有其他競爭者。

---

troop [truːp]

① *n.* 部隊

同 **army / crew**

② *v.* 成群結隊地走；聚集

實用片語
troop in 一齊湧入

▶ By 8 in the morning, the troop had already left for Iraq.
到早上八點時，部隊已經離開往伊拉克去了。

▶ The students all trooped into the classroom.
所有學生都成群結隊走進教室。

▶ Many students trooped in and sat down.
許多學生一起湧入並坐下。

---

tropical [ˈtrɑː.pɪ.kəl] *adj.* 熱帶的

搭 **tropical fruit** 熱帶水果
同 **hot / lush**

▶ Since Hawaii is a tropical island, you might find lots of palm trees.
夏威夷因為是熱帶島嶼，所以你可以在那裡看見許多的棕櫚樹。

---

troublesome [ˈtrʌb.əl.səm] *adj.* 令人煩惱的

同 **alarming / irritating**

▶ The pain in Grandpa's heart was troublesome to the family.
爺爺的胸痛讓家人感到十分煩惱。

trunk [trʌŋk] *n.* 樹幹

▶ A redwood tree has a very thick trunk.
紅杉有非常粗壯的樹幹。

---

truthful [ˈtruːθ.fəl] *adj.* 誠實的；真實的
搭 **truthful answer** 誠心的回應
同 **straightforward / realistic**

▶ My sister is always very truthful about how she feels.
我的姊妹總是說出自己真實的感受。

---

tub [tʌb] *n.* 桶；盆

▶ You can use this tub to wash your dog.
你可以用這個桶子來沖洗你的狗兒。

---

tug [tʌg]
① *v.* 用力拉
同 **drag / draw**
實用片語
tug at 拉，扯
② *n.* 拉

▶ Fanny tugged on the rope so hard that it broke.
凡尼用力拉繩子，繩子就斷了。

▶ The child tugged at his mother to go home.
孩子拉著他媽媽回家。

▶ After a good tug, Sally broke the rope.
經過用力一拉，莎莉把繩子拉斷了。

---

tug of war [ˌtʌg əv ˈwɔːr] *n.* 拔河

▶ The children used a long rope to play tug-of-war.
小朋友們拿了一條長長的繩索來玩拔河。

---

tulip [ˈtuː.lɪp] *n.* 鬱金香

▶ Katie went to the flower market to buy some red tulips.
凱蒂去花市買一些紅色鬱金香。

---

tumble [ˈtʌm.bəl]
① *v.* 跌倒
搭 **price tumble** 價格崩盤
同 **slump / descend**
② *n.* 翻滾；翻觔斗；跌倒

▶ The gymnast tumbled over the carpet.
體操運動員跌落在地毯上。

▶ The gymnast performed a scary tumble.
體操運動員表演了一個危險的翻滾動作。

---

tummy [ˈtʌm.i] *n.* 腹部；胃

▶ If you want a flat tummy, do sit ups everyday.
如果你想有個平坦的腹部，就每天做仰臥起坐。

T

tune [tuːn]

① *n.* 曲調

同 **theme / piece**

② *v.* 調音

▶ The boys sang the same tune all the way home.

男孩們在回家的路上一直唱著同一支曲子。

▶ Ellen must tune her violin before she plays it.

愛倫在拉小提琴前必須先調音。

---

tutor [ˈtuː.tə]

① *n.* 家庭教師

搭 **private tutor** 私人家教

同 **lecturer / mentor**

② *v.* 當⋯的教師；指導

▶ The English tutor will arrive in 20 minutes.

英文家庭教師將會在二十分鐘內抵達。

▶ Fanny tutors 25 children every week.

凡尼每週指導 25 位孩童。

---

twig [twɪg] *n.* 細樹枝

▶ We found a twig that fell off of a tree.

我們找到一根從樹上掉下的細樹枝。

---

twin [twɪn] *n.* 雙胞胎之一

▶ One twin had a different personality than the other.

雙胞胎其中一位的個性與另外一位不同。

---

twinkle [ˈtwɪŋ.kəl]

① *v.* 使閃耀

實用片語

twinkle with 閃爍著

② *n.* 光芒；閃爍

搭 **eye twinkle** 眼中閃光芒

同 **blink / light up**

▶ The stars twinkled at night.

星星在夜晚閃閃發亮。

▶ Her eyes twinkled with laughter.

她眼中閃爍著笑意。

▶ The stars caused a twinkle in the sky.

星星在天空裡放光芒。

---

104 100

twist [twɪst]

① *v.* 扭轉

同 **screw / swivel**

② *n.* 扭轉

搭 **twist face** 扭曲的臉

同 **curve / bend**

▶ She had to twist the towel to get the water out.

她必須擰乾毛巾，把水擠出。

▶ Jennifer gave the lid of the jar a twist to tighten it.

珍妮佛把罐子的蓋子扭緊。

typewriter [ˈtaɪpˌraɪ.tɚ] *n.* 打字機

▶ My dad still writes with his typewriter.
我爸爸仍然使用打字機來寫東西。

---

⑨⑦

typical [ˈtɪp.ɪ.kəl] *adj.* 典型的

同 **classic / ordinary**

▶ Tom's nickname is Mr. Yes because his typical response to every question is "yes."
湯姆的綽號是「好先生」，因為他對每個問題的回應都是「好」。

---

typist [ˈtaɪ.pɪst] *n.* 打字員

▶ Terry worked as a typist in a legal office.
泰瑞在法律事務所當打字員。

---

unable [ʌnˈeɪ.bəl] *adj.* 不能的；無法的

搭 **totally unable** 完全沒辦法

同 **incapable / weak**

▶ The man with a broken leg was unable to walk.
那男子一隻腿斷了，無法走路。

---

unaware [ˌʌn.əˈwer] *adj.* 不知道的；未察覺的

同 **unconcerned / careless**

▶ I was unaware that the restaurant had closed.
我不知道那家餐廳已經結束營業了。

T

Exercise 75

I. Derivatives

1. Christians should be _____ (truth) in words and deeds.

2. This hot and spicy cuisine is very _____ (type) of the food in Sichuan province of China.

3. The naughty boy in my class is a really _____ (trouble) child.

4. Most bestselling authors write their books on computer, but some like Danielle Steel and George R. R. Martin still use a _____ (type) to type their stories.

5. Bananas, lemons and papayas are _____ (tropic) fruits.

II. Multiple Choice

(   ) 1. My father likes to sink into a hot ___ after dinner.
      (A) tug (B) tub (C) tube (D) tune

(   ) 2. Julie has ___ her ankle so she won't be able to run in the race.
      (A) twinkled (B) twig (C) twisted (D) twittered

(   ) 3. The man lost his balance and ___ over the edge of the cliff.
      (A) tumor (B) tummy (C) trembled (D) tumbled

(   ) 4. Jimmy's parents employed a ___ to teach him English.
      (A) tutor (B) traveler (C) technician (D) trader

(   ) 5. The lights of the town ___ in the distance.
      (A) twin (B) twig (C) twinkled (D) twilight

unbelievable [ˌʌn.bɪˈliː.və.bəl]

adj. 令人難以置信的

搭 **almost unbelievable** 幾乎買不到

同 **impossible / unthinkable**

▶ Seeing Bryan on the plane was an unbelievable coincidence.
在飛機上見到布萊恩真是件令人難以置信的事。

---

unconscious [ʌnˈkɑːn.ʃəs]

adj. 失去知覺的

同 **senseless / insensible**

▶ The accident knocked her unconscious.
這件意外讓她完全失去知覺。

---

underpass [ˈʌn.dɚ.pæs] *n.* 地下道

▶ The van was abandoned in the underpass.
那部廂型車被遺棄在地下道裡。

102
understanding [ˌʌn.dɚˈstæn.dɪŋ]

n. 瞭解;諒解

搭 **thorough understanding** 徹底瞭解

同 **insight / realization**

實用片語
reach an understanding with
與…達成共識

▶ Your understanding of the situation is greater than mine.
你對整個事件的瞭解比我還清楚。

▶ We were able to reach an understanding with our customer.
我們可以跟客戶達成共識。

---

underwater [ˌʌn.dɚˈwɑː.tɚ] *adv.* 在水面下

▶ Scuba diving takes place underwater.
深海潛水必須在水面下進行。

---

underweight [ˌʌn.dɚˈweɪt] *adj.* 重量不足的

同 **starved / bony**

▶ The baby was underweight at birth.
這位嬰兒出生時體重過輕。

---

unexpected [ˌʌn.ɪkˈspek.tɪd]

adj. 意想不到的;突如其來的

同 **unforeseen / sudden**

實用片語
expect the unexpected 防範於未然

▶ The storm was unexpected and took the town by surprise.
暴風雨突如其來,讓全鎮的人大吃一驚。

▶ I know you are well-prepared, but be sure to expect the unexpected.
我知道你準備妥當,但仍要確定以防範於未然。

U

unfortunate [ʌnˈfɔːr.tʃən.ət]

adj. 不幸的;令人遺憾的

搭 **unfortunate incident** 不幸的事件

同 **sadly / unluckily**

▶ The unfortunate accident left Mary without a car.
這個不幸的意外使得瑪莉失去了她的車。

---

unfortunately [ʌnˈfɔːr.tʃən.ət.li]

adv. 遺憾地;不幸地

同 **sadly / regrettably**

▶ Unfortunately, I cannot find my house keys.
非常遺憾地,我就是找不到家裡的鑰匙。

---

unfriendly [ʌnˈfrend.li]

adj. 不友善的;有敵意的

搭 **environmentally unfriendly products**
對環境有害的商品

同 **hateful / against**

▶ The unfriendly customer talked in a rude manner.
這位不友善的顧客說話很不禮貌。

---

union [ˈjuː.nj.ən] *n.* 聯盟;結合

同 **concord / joint**

▶ The student union got together for a meeting.
學生會聚集在一起開會。

---

unique [juːˈniːk] *adj.* 獨特的;唯一的

搭 **unique selling point** 特殊賣點

同 **exclusive / different**

▶ The teacher praised Jack's unique style of dancing.
老師稱讚傑克獨特的舞風。

---

unite [juːˈnaɪt] *v.* 使團聚;使聯合

同 **merge / unity**

實用片語
unite for 合力,合作

▶ They tried to unite the puppy with his parents.
他們試圖讓小狗和牠的父母團聚。

▶ We will unite for a great gala party.
我們將合力舉辦盛大的晚宴派對。

---

united [juːˈnaɪ.tɪd]

adj. 聯合的;統一的;團結的

同 **linked / integrated**

▶ The united groups worked together to succeed.
這些聯合團體一起合作以獲取成功。

---

unity [ˈjuː.nə.tɪ] *n.* 團結;統一;一致

搭 **restore unity** 重新團結起來

同 **consensus / integrity**

▶ The unity of the group was hard to break.
那個團隊的團結很難加以瓦解。

universal [ˌjuː.nəˈvɝː.səl]
adj. 共同的;普遍的;世界性的
同 **worldwide / extensive**

▶ Christians hold a universal belief that God loves everyone.
所有的基督徒都有共同的信念,就是神愛世人。

---

universe [ˈjuː.nə.vɝːs] *n.* 宇宙

▶ There are many stars in the universe.
宇宙中有許多的恆星。

---

university [ˌjuː.nəˈvɝː.sə.tj] *n.* 大學
搭 **famous university** 有名的大學
同 **school / college**

實用片語
university of life 生命大學

▶ Tom went to university to study physics.
湯姆進大學念物理系。

▶ Jenny has learned more from the university of life than from any schools she attended.
比起任何她上過的學校,珍妮從生命大學中學到的更多。

---

unknown [ʌnˈnoʊn] *adj.* 未知的
同 **foreign / unexplored**

實用片語
unknown quantity 未知數,不確定熟識之人

▶ I tried to figure out what the unknown problem was.
我試著想找出那個未知的問題究竟是什麼。

▶ Joe is an unknown quantity.
喬伊是個未知數。

---

unless [ənˈles] *conj.* 除非

▶ You cannot succeed unless you work hard.
除非你努力去作,否則就無法成功。

---

unlike [ʌnˈlaɪk] *prep.* 和…不同;不像

▶ My cat is unlike the other cats in the neighborhood.
我的貓跟鄰近地區的貓不同。

---

unlikely [ʌnˈlaɪ.kli] *adj.* 不太可能的
同 **unbelievable / rare**

▶ It's unlikely that he will get to the party on time.
我覺得他不可能會準時抵達派對。

---

untouched [ʌnˈtʌtʃt]
adj. 未受影響的;未觸動過的;保持原樣的
搭 **virtually untouched** 幾乎無污染
同 **unharmed / undamaged**

▶ The village in the mountains remained untouched by the storm.
山上的小村莊沒有受到暴風雨的影響。

U

unusual [ʌnˈjuː.ʒu.əl]

adj. 不尋常的；稀有的；獨特的

同 **noteworthy / special**

 96

upload [ʌpˈloʊd] *v.* 上傳（檔案）

搭 **upload file** 上傳檔案
同 **transfer / transmit**

▶ Can you hear that unusual sound coming from outside?
你可以聽見外面傳來的不尋常聲音嗎？

- -

▶ Adam uploaded his file to the server.
亞當將他的檔案上傳到伺服器。

Exercise 76

I. Derivatives

1. It is late and it's pretty _____ (unlike) that she'll show up.

2. _____ (unfortunate), I didn't bring any cash, or else I would have bought the books for your birthday gift.

3. That the Earth moves around the Sun is a _____ (universe) truth that no one disputes.

4. Brothers and sisters should live together in _____ (unite) and not fight all the time.

5. The English Bible study group is aimed at helping people to develop a deeper _____ (understand) of the Bible through learning English.

II. 中英對應

_____ 1. 獨特的   (A) uniform   (B) unit

                          (C) unique   (D) unite

_____ 2. 稀有的   (A) untouched   (B) unusual

                          (C) unlikely   (D) unusable

_____ 3. 失去知覺的   (A) unaware   (B) unconscious

                          (C) unconditional   (D) unclear

_____ 4. 意想不到的   (A) unexplored   (B) uneven

                          (C) unemployed   (D) unexpected

_____ 5. 有敵意的   (A) unfriendly   (B) unfriended

                          (C) unfruitful   (D) unframed

upset [ʌpˈsɛt]

① *v.* 使難過；使生氣；使心煩意亂

同 **distrub / unsettle**

實用片語
upset someone's plans 打亂某人計劃

② *n.* 難過；生氣；心煩意亂

同 **bother / disorder**

③ *adj.* 心煩意亂的

搭 **deeply upset** 極度沮喪

同 **distressed / confused**

▶ Kyle's decision to drop out of college upset his mom.
凱爾從大學休學的決定，讓他媽媽很難過。

▶ I don't want to upset your plans, but I need you to change the meeting date.
雖然不想打亂你的計劃，但我需要你改變會議日期。

▶ Ellen went through an upset when she lost her job.
艾倫丟掉工作之後，心情相當難過。

▶ Carl got upset when he lost his new phone.
卡爾遺失了新手機後，覺得很心煩。

---

urban [ˈɝ.bən] *adj.* 都市的

搭 **urban community** 都市社會

同 **downtown / city**

▶ Urban life is very convenient.
都市的生活真的是非常便利。

---

urge [ɝːdʒ]

① *v.* 力勸；催促；極力主張

同 **encourage / suggest**

實用片語
urge someone to do 鼓勵某人做某事

② *n.* 強烈的慾望

同 **craving / drive**

▶ We urged him to see a doctor.
我們催促他去看醫生。

▶ I urge you to give diving a try.
我鼓勵你試著潛水看看。

▶ He resisted the urge to eat a second piece of cake.
他按捺住自己想要吃第二塊蛋糕的強烈慾望。

---

104 97 96 95

urgent [ˈɝdʒənt] *adj.* 緊急的

搭 **increasingly urgent** 越發緊急

同 **pressing / compelling**

▶ She gave him an urgent message.
她給他一個緊急的訊息。

---

usage [ˈjuː.sɪdʒ] *n.* 用量；用法

同 **method / operation**

▶ Water usage increases in the summer.
夏天裡水的用量會增加。

useless [ˈjuːsləs] *adj.* 無用的；無價值的

搭 **completely useless** 完全無用處

同 **worthless / futile**

▶ My watch is useless because it doesn't work anymore.
我的手錶沒用了，因為它壞了。

---

vacant [ˈveɪkənt] *adj.* 空的

同 **bare / empty**

▶ She parked her car in the vacant parking space.
她把車子開到有空位的停車格裡。

---

vain [veɪn] *adj.* 徒勞的；無益的

同 **useless / fruitless**

實用片語
take someone's name in vain 以某人名義

▶ Peter made a vain attempt to win Emily's heart.
彼得想贏得艾蜜莉的芳心，結果徒勞無功。

▶ I heard someone taking my name in vain.
我聽到有人濫用我的名義。

---

valuable [ˈvæljəbəl] *adj.* 貴重的；值錢的

搭 **valuable experience** 有價值的經驗

同 **worthwhile / beneficial**

▶ He could not let go of his valuable things.
他無法捨棄自己的貴重物品。

---

van [væn] *n.* 廂型車

▶ Everyone took the van to go on a road trip.
大家都搭上廂型車準備來一趟公路旅行。

---

vanish [ˈvænɪʃ] *v.* 消失

搭 **suddenly vanish** 突然消失

同 **melt / dissolve**

實用片語
vanish away 消失（被搶光）

▶ The cards will vanish in front of your eyes!
卡片將會在你眼前消失！

▶ The cookies vanished away when the hungry kids walked in the kitchen.
當這飢腸轆轆的孩子走進廚房時，餅乾馬上就消失了。

---

variety [vəˈraɪəti] *n.* 多樣化；變化

同 **mixture / variation**

▶ He likes to listen to a variety of music.
他喜歡聽各種不同的音樂。

U

various [ˈver.i.əs] *adj.* 各種各樣的

搭 **various aspects** 各式角度

同 **enlist / assorted**

► My aunt has various kinds of perfume.
我阿姨有各種不同的香水。

---

vary [ˈver.i] *v.* 使不同

同 **differ / alter**

實用片語
vary between 在…間顯得不同

► The types of songs will vary as you change radio stations.
轉到不同的廣播頻道，就會聽到不同類型的歌曲。

► The unemployment rate widely varies between different industries.
失業率在不同產業間差異頗大。

---

vase [veɪs] *n.* 花瓶

► Do not knock over the flower vase!
不要打翻花瓶！

---

vast [ˈvæst] *adj.* 廣大的

搭 **vast quantity** 數量龐大

同 **immense / infinite**

► Canada covers a vast area of North America.
加拿大佔地北美洲很廣大一塊面積。

---

vegetarian [ˌvedʒ.ɪˈter.i.ən] *n.* 素食主義者

► Carolyn is a vegetarian and avoids meat and fish.
凱若琳是個素食主義者，所以她不吃魚和肉。

---

vehicle [ˈviː.ə.kəl] *n.* 車輛；運載工具

同 **wagon / automobile**

► Please keep your arms and legs inside the vehicle at all times.
請勿把手腳伸出車外。

---

verb [vɝːb] *n.* 動詞

► Verbs are action words.
動詞是帶有行動的字彙。

---

verse [vɝːs] *n.* 詩句

► The verse from that poem was very beautiful.
那首詩有一句非常美。

---

very [ˈver.i] *adj.* （強調）就…；正好；確實的

► The hero defeats the dragon at the very end of the movie.
就在電影的尾聲，英雄打敗了那條龍。

vessel [ˈves.əl] *n.* 容器;船

同 **tanker / craft**

▶ He used the jar as a vessel for the wine.
他拿水瓶來當裝酒的容器。

---

vest [vest] *n.* 背心

▶ All the men must wear a vest with their tuxedos.
所有男士穿著禮服都必須搭配背心。

---

vice president [ˌvaɪs ˈprez.ɪ.dənt] *n.* 副總統

▶ The vice president had a big responsibility while the president was away.
總統不在時,副總統的責任重大。

---

victim [ˈvɪk.təm] *n.* 受害者;遇難者

搭 **innocent victim** 無辜的受害者

同 **sufferer / pushover**

實用片語
a fashion victim 時裝奴(穿名牌時裝但不合適)

▶ The poor woman was a victim of that car crash.
這個很可憐的婦人是那場車禍的受害者。

▶ Daniel is always broke because he is a fashion victim always buying new clothes.
丹尼爾是個流行受害者(時裝奴),因為他不停地買新衣服所以總是很窮。

V

Exercise 77

I. 中英對應

_____ 1. 詩句   (A) verse   (B) verb   (C) venue   (D) version

_____ 2. 徒勞的   (A) vanish   (B) vacant   (C) vain   (D) van

_____ 3. 車輛   (A) vertical   (B) vehicle   (C) verify   (D) vegetarian

_____ 4. 背心   (A) vase   (B) vast   (C) vest   (D) verse

_____ 5. 正好   (A) versus   (B) various   (C) vary   (D) very

II. Vocabulary Choice

(A) usage   (B) vegetarian   (C) variety   (D) vacant   (E) valuable

(F) various   (G) useless   (H) vast   (I) victims   (J) vase

1. Pokemon Go players flocked to Beitou Park in _____ numbers and left behind large amounts of trash.

2. Over 7,000 marine animals, including sea otters, dolphins and seabirds were among the _____ of the oil spill.

3. Cable TV offers a wide _____ of TV programs and channels.

4. There are some major distinctions between American and British English _____ such as punctuation and dates.

5. The work experience in the UK as an exchange student was very _____ to her career after graduation.

vinegar [ˈvɪn.ə.gɚ] *n.* 醋

實用片語
sour as vinegar 味酸如醋

▶ She used vinegar to make the sour soup.
她加了醋來做酸湯。

▶ This milk is as sour as vinegar. Throw it out !
這牛奶味道酸得跟醋一樣。丟了吧！

100 98

violate [ˈvaɪ.ə.leɪt] *v.* 違反

搭 **violate the law** 違反法律
同 **disrupt / defy**

實用片語
a shrinking violet 羞怯，畏首畏尾

▶ The man violated the law by driving too fast.
那位男士開車超速因此違法。

▶ I don't think Mary is a shrinking violet.
我不認為瑪莉很羞怯。

violation [ˌvaɪ.əˈleɪ.ʃən] *n.* 違法；違反
同 **offense / breaking**

▶ His traffic violation cost him a lot of money.
他因為交通違法被罰了不少錢。

violence [ˈvaɪə.ləns] *n.* 暴力

搭 **domestic violence** 家庭暴力
同 **intensity / assault**

▶ The violence in the area caused everybody to be uneasy.
這地區的暴力情況讓每個人感到不安。

violent [ˈvaɪə.lənt] *adj.* 暴力的；猛烈的
同 **vicious / brutal**

▶ All the authorities tried to calm the violent man.
所有專家都試圖安撫有暴力的男子。

violet [ˈvaɪə.lət]

① *n.* 紫蘿蘭
② *adj.* 紫蘿蘭色的

▶ My mother grows many violets in her garden.
我媽媽在她花園種了很多紫蘿蘭。

▶ He wore a violet jacket over his yellow shirt.
他在黃襯衫外面套上一件紫羅藍色的夾克。

virgin [ˈvɝː.dʒɪn]

① *n.* 處男；處女
② *adj.* 處女的；貞潔的

▶ Paul plans to remain a virgin until he gets married.
保羅打算結婚之前要維持處男的狀況。

▶ The Bible speaks of Jesus' virgin birth.
聖經上提到耶穌是處女所生的。

V

virtue [ˈvɝ:.tʃuː] *n.* 美德

搭 **inherit virtue** 遺傳到美德

同 **ethic / goodness**

實用片語
Virtue is its own reward. 善有善報。

▶ Patience is a virtue.
耐心是一項美德。

▶ Q: I help you and you'll pay me right?
A: Virtue is its own reward.
Q: 我幫助你，然後你會付我錢對嗎？
A: 善有善報。

---

103 102
virus [ˈvaɪ.rəs] *n.* 病毒

▶ He's taking medicine to fight a virus.
他正在服藥來對抗病毒。

---

visible [ˈvɪz.ə.bəl] *adj.* 可看見的

搭 **visible spectrum** 可見光譜

同 **obvious / noticeable**

▶ You cannot miss the visible designs on that wall.
你一定會看見那個牆上的顯眼圖案。

101
vision [ˈvɪʒ.ən] *n.* 視力

實用片語
tunnel vision 一孔之見，目光短淺

▶ Her poor vision did not allow her to see very far.
她糟糕的視力讓她無法看得很遠。

▶ The boss has tunnel vision about sales. He refuses to adopt new methods.
老闆對於業務開發的目光短淺。他不願意嘗試新的做法。

97
visual [ˈvɪʒ.u.əl] *adj.* 視覺的

搭 **visual effect** 視覺效果

同 **optical / imaged**

▶ He has visual problems and cannot see well.
他有視覺障礙，所以無法看很清楚。

---

vital [ˈvaɪ.t̬əl]
adj. 維持生命所必需的；重要的；生命的

同 **crucial / significant**

▶ Your heart is a vital organ.
你的心臟是個活命的重要器官。

---

vitamin [ˈvaɪ.t̬əmɪn] *n.* 維生素

▶ I take my vitamins everyday to stay healthy.
我每天吃維生素來保持健康。

98
vivid [ˈvɪv.ɪd] *adj.* 鮮明的

搭 **vivid imagination** 鮮明的圖像

同 **colorful / striking**

▶ The vivid lights can be seen by everybody here.
這裡每個人都能看見鮮明的燈光。

volcano [vɑːlˈkeɪnoʊ] *n.* 火山

▶ The volcano last erupted in 1980.
這座火山上次在 1980 年爆發。

 volume [ˈvɑːl.juːm] *n.* 冊；音量

▶ She found the first volume of her textbook in the library.
她在圖書館找到她的第一冊課本。

99 **voluntary** [ˈvɑː.lən.ter.i] *adj.* 自發的；自願的
同 **willing / intended**

▶ I made a voluntary decision to leave the company.
我離開公司的決定是我自己提出來的。

104 98 **volunteer** [ˌvɑː.lənˈtɪr]

① *n.* 志工；自願者
搭 **volunteer worker** 志工

② *v.* 自願（做）
同 **enlist / offer services**

▶ We need two volunteers to work in the booth.
我們需要兩位志工到攤位上服務。

▶ Tony volunteered to donate blood.
東尼自願去捐血。

vowel [vaʊəl] *n.* 母音

▶ Common vowels include a, e, and o.
普通的母音包括 a、e 以及 o。

98 **voyage** [ˈvɔɪ.ɪdʒ]

① *n.* 航行
同 **excursion / travel**

② *v.* 旅行

實用片語
maiden voyage 首航

▶ Her voyage across the sea lasted two weeks.
她的跨海之旅花了兩個星期完成。

▶ The family voyaged across the Pacific Ocean.
他們一家人旅行跨越太平洋。

▶ The Titanic sank on its maiden voyage.
鐵達尼號在首航中沉沒。

wag [wæg]

① *v.* 搖擺
搭 **wag the dog** 搖尾乞憐
同 **shake / vibrate**

② *n.* 搖擺

▶ A dog will wag its tail if it is happy!
狗狗如果快樂就會搖尾巴。

▶ He did a finger wag after scoring a basket for his team.
他為球隊上籃得分後，就搖動一下手指。

wage(s) [weɪdʒ(s)] *n.* 薪水

搭 **maximum wage** 最高薪資

同 **income / salary**

實用片語
freeze someone's wages 工資凍結

▶ The new worker was happy with his wage.
她新職員對他的薪水很滿意。

▶ The company froze everybody's wages.
公司凍結所有人的薪資。

---

wagon [ˈwæg.ən] *n.* 四輪馬車

實用片語
on the wagon 戒酒

▶ That wagon on the road is being pulled by a horse.
路上的那輛馬車是由馬來拉動的。

▶ No, I don't drink beer. I am on the wagon.
不了，我不喝啤酒。我在戒酒。

---

waken [ˈweɪ.kən] *v.* 叫醒

同 **arise / arouse**

▶ It was nearly impossible to waken the bear from his sleep.
要叫醒沉睡中的熊幾乎是不可能的。

Exercise 78

I. 中英對應

_____ 1. 紫羅蘭　(A) violate　(B) violent　(C) violin　(D) violet

_____ 2. 火山　(A) volume　(B) volcano　(C) volunteer　(D) vocabulary

_____ 3. 貞潔的　(A) virgin　(B) virtue　(C) virus　(D) vital

_____ 4. 搖擺　(A) wage　(B) wagon　(C) wag　(D) wagon

_____ 5. 叫醒　(A) wagon　(B) waken　(C) waffle　(D) wages

II. Derivatives

1. Some teachers and helpers at the English Bible Study class are
   helping out on a _____ (volunteer) basis.

2. Many fruits, such as apples, bananas, mangos, oranges and
   watermelons, contain several essential _____ (vital).

3. Amanda appreciates the _____ (vision) arts and she has taken
   courses in ceramics and photography and painting.

4. The shooting stars tonight should be _____ (vision) to the
   naked eye.

5. Verbal abuse, or verbal _____ (violent) may not cause
   physical damage, but it can cause severe emotional pain and scarring.

Unit 79

walnut [ˈwɑːl.nʌt] *n.* 胡桃

▶ The cookie contains chopped walnuts.
這個餅乾裡面加了碎胡桃。

---

waltz [wɑːls] *n.* 華爾滋（舞）

實用片語
waltz into 輕快地走近

▶ They danced the waltz at their wedding.
他們在婚禮上跳華爾滋。

▶ Ariel waltzed into the room and said hello.
艾瑞爾輕快地走進房間並說哈囉。

103
wander [ˈwɑːn.dɚ]

① *v.* 閒逛；漫遊；徘徊

搭 **wander aimlessly** 無目標地漫遊

同 **amble / stray**

實用片語
wander around 閒逛

② *n.* 閒逛；漫遊；徘徊

▶ We had a short wander through the museum.
我們在博物館裡閒逛了一下。

▶ It's fun to wander around in a strange city.
在陌生的城市中閒逛很有趣。

▶ The wander around the park gave me time to think.
繞著公園漫步讓我有時間思考。

---

warmth [wɔːmθ] *n.* 溫暖；暖和

同 **passion / kindness**

▶ Come and feel the warmth around the campfire.
來感受一下營火四周的溫暖。

104
warn [wɔːrn] *v.* 警告

搭 **warn the public** 警告大眾

同 **remind / signal**

實用片語
warn about 警告，警示

▶ I have to warn you, those animals are dangerous!
我必須警告你，那些動物很危險！

▶ I need to warn you about John.
我要警告你小心約翰這人。

---

warning [ˈwɔːr.nɪŋ] *n.* 警報；警告

同 **caution / indication**

▶ The government issued a warning about the typhoon.
政府發布了颱風警報。

---

warship [ˈwɔːr.ʃɪp] *n.* 軍艦；艦艇

▶ The sailors honored the retired warship.
這些水手們向這艘退役的軍艦致敬。

washing ['wɑː.ʃɪŋ] *n.* 洗；洗滌

搭 **washing machine** 洗衣機
同 **cleaning / laundry**

▶ The dishes in the sink needed some washing.
水槽中的盤子需要洗一洗。

---

watchman ['wɑːtʃ.mən] *n.* 看守人；巡夜者

同 **guard / patrolman**

▶ A watchman was placed on each side of the tower.
這座塔的每一側都安置了一位看守人。

---

wax [wæks]

① *n.* 蠟
② *v.* 上蠟

▶ The wax from the candle started to slowly melt away.
蠟燭上的蠟開始慢慢地融化。

▶ He would often wax his car to keep it polished.
他常常把車子打蠟，保持光亮。

---

weaken ['wiː.kən] *v.* 變弱

同 **dilute / lessen**

▶ The boxer patiently waited to weaken her opponent.
拳擊手耐心等待讓對手體力變差。

---

wealth [welθ] *n.* 財富

搭 **wealth gap** 貧富差異
同 **property / treasure**

實用片語
roll in wealth 極為富裕

▶ The millionaire offered his wealth to a good cause.
百萬富翁把他的財富捐給一個很有意義的志業。

▶ Leo's family has been rolling in wealth for years.
里歐的家族多年來一直極為富裕。

---

wealthy ['wel.θi] *adj.* 富裕的

搭 **wealthy family** 富裕的家庭
同 **rich / affluent**

▶ That wealthy man bought himself a new car.
那個富人替自己買了一輛新車。

---

weave [wiːv]

① *v.* 編織
同 **unite / knit**

實用片語
weave in and out 穿梭其間

② *n.* 織物

▶ I like to weave all kinds of fabric.
我喜歡編織各式各樣的織物。

▶ The bike is weaving in and out of traffic.
腳踏車在車流中穿梭其間。

▶ The pattern of the weave complimented his outfit well.
編織品的圖案跟他的衣服很搭配。

W

web [web]

① *n.* 織物；網狀物

搭 **complex web** 複雜的網絡

同 **netting / lacework**

② *v.* 結網

▶ The web of her scarf was well-designed.
她的圍巾的織物圖案設計很棒。

▶ The bed was webbed by a mosquito net.
這張床被蚊帳罩著。

---

website [ˈweb.saɪt] *n.* 網站

搭 **educational website** 教育網站

同 **network / internet**

▶ She found the company's address on their website.
她在這家公司的網站上找到公司的地址。

---

weed [wiːd]

① *n.* 野草

② *v.* 除草

實用片語
weed out 淘汰，清除

▶ We saw some weeds growing near the flowers in our yard.
我們在院子中看到花朵附近有些雜草。

▶ The gardener tried to weed the lawn.
園丁嘗試除掉草坪上的雜草。

▶ I need to weed out the unqualified applicants.
我需要淘汰不合格的申請者。

---

weekly [ˈwiː.kli]

① *adj.* 每週的

② *adv.* 每週一次

③ *n.* 週刊

搭 **weekly meeting** 週會

同 **journal / magazine**

▶ Mary has weekly staff meetings.
瑪麗有固定的員工週會。

▶ Mary meets weekly with her staff.
瑪麗每個星期和他的員工開一次會。

▶ The magazine used to be a daily but now it's a weekly.
這本雜誌原本是日刊，但現在改成為週刊。

---

weep [wiːp] *v.* 哭泣

同 **sob / grieve**

實用片語
weep for joy 喜極而泣

▶ Many people will weep at the funeral.
許多人會在喪禮上哭泣。

▶ I was so happy; I wept for joy.
我太高興了；我喜極而泣。

---

welfare [ˈwel.fer] *n.* 福利

搭 **social welfare** 社會福利

同 **well-being / benefit**

▶ The boss is concerned about the welfare of her employees.
老闆很關心她員工的福利。

---

westerner [ˈwes.tɚ.nɚ]
n. 西方人；美國西部人

▶ The westerner had a strong accent when he spoke.
這位西方人說話時有很濃厚的口音。

wheat [wiːt] *n.* 小麥

▶ I like to buy foods made of whole grains and wheat.
我喜歡買全麥穀物做成的食物。

---

whichever [wɪˈtʃɛv.ɚ]
pron. 無論哪個;無論哪些

▶ Please choose whichever you would like to take!
請隨意挑選你要的!

---

whip [wɪp]

① *n.* 鞭子
② *v.* 鞭打
同 **bash / beat**

▶ They used a whip to discipline the animals.
他們用鞭子來管教動物。

▶ The teacher would whip the students if they didn't behave.
學生如果不守規矩,老師就會鞭打他們。

101

whistle [ˈwɪs.əl]

① *n.* 口哨
② *v.* 吹口哨

實用片語
whistle-stop 小城鎮

▶ All the instructors used a whistle to keep everyone together.
所有教練都使用口哨集合大家。

▶ It took me a long time to learn how to whistle that song!
我花了很長的時間學會用口哨來吹那首歌曲!

▶ This town is just a whistle-stop.
這個鎮只是個小城鎮。

W

Exercise 79

I. Derivatives

1. Although Superman has many superpowers, kryptonite can _____ (weak) and even kill him.

2. Health _____ (warn) should not only appear on alcohol labels, but it should also appear in all alcohol advertisements.

3. This TV drama is about a beautiful and _____ (wealth) woman who seeks revenge for her framed father.

4. Daniel loves the _____ (warm) of his mother's embrace.

5. She writes a _____ (week) entertainment column for a popular movie website.

II. 中英對應

_____ 1. 福利　(A) wardrobe　(B) wellness　(C) warfare　(D) welfare

_____ 2. 哭泣　(A) weep　(B) weed　(C) whip　(D) wheat

_____ 3. 除草　(A) wheat　(B) weave　(C) weed　(D) week

_____ 4. 胡桃　(A) waltz　(B) walnut　(C) shock　(D) shrink

_____ 5. 口哨　(A) whisper　(B) whistle　(C) whiten　(D) whistler

Unit 80

wicked [ˈwɪk.ɪd] *adj.* 邪惡的
同 **evil / nasty**

▶ Everybody knew that the wicked witch was up to no good.
每個人都知道邪惡的巫婆只會做壞事。

---

wildly [ˈwaɪld.li] *adv.* 野生地;失控地;狂暴地
搭 **fluctuate wildly** 大幅波動
同 **fiercely / recklessly**

▶ The grass was growing wildly on the other side.
另一邊長了野生的草。

---

willow [ˈwɪl.oʊ] *n.* 柳樹

▶ We all met under the willow for shade after lunchtime.
午餐後我們都集合在柳樹下遮陽。

---

wink [ˈwɪŋk]
① *v.* 眨眼
實用片語
twenty winks 小睡,打個盹
② *n.* 眨眼
同 **twinkle / bat**

▶ The boy tried to wink at the girl sitting across from him.
男孩試圖向坐在對面的女孩眨眼。

▶ I'm going to go grab a quick twenty winks before everyone arrives.
在所有人抵達前,我要很快的打個盹。

▶ He gave them a wink to tell them to start.
他向他們眨個眼,示意要他們開始。

---

wipe [waɪp]
① *v.* 擦拭
搭 **wipe the floor** 擦地板
同 **brush / clean**
實用片語
wipe off 擦拭
② *n.* 擦拭

▶ They wiped the sweat off their faces after running.
他們跑步完之後,把臉上的汗水擦掉。

▶ Don't wipe your feet off on the carpet.
不要在地毯上擦腳。

▶ That old television screen needs a good wipe.
那台老電視機的螢幕需要好好擦拭一下了。

---

wisdom [ˈwɪzdəm] *n.* 智慧
搭 **pearl of wisdom** 名言金句
同 **knowledge / acumen**
實用片語
a pearl of wisdom 至理名言

▶ She gained her wisdom from all of her past experiences.
她從過往所有的經驗中獲得智慧。

▶ Thank you for that pearl of wisdom, Doris.
桃樂絲,感謝您的至理名言。

W

wit [ˈwɪt] *n.* 機智；風趣

同 **humor / fun**

實用片語
collect one's wits 鎮定下來

▶ He used his wits to figure out the puzzle.
他運用機智來破解謎題。

▶ Take a moment to collect your wits and tell us what happened.
花點時間鎮定下來，然後告訴我們發生什麼事。

---

witch / wizard [wɪtʃ / ˈwɪz.ə-d]

n. 女巫師 / 男巫師

▶ The little girl dressed up as a witch on Halloween.
小女孩在萬聖節當天打扮成女巫。

---

withdraw [wɪðˈdrɔ]

v. 抽回；提取（金錢）；撤退

搭 **withdraw cash** 提領現金
同 **detach / remove**

實用片語
withdraw from 自…提取

▶ She withdrew her hand when she found out I had a cold.
當她發現我感冒了，就把手給抽回去。

▶ Jack withdrew three thousand dollars from the ATM.
傑克從 ATM 提款機中提了三千元。

---

witness [ˈwɪt.nəs]

① *n.* 目擊者
同 **observer / spectator**
② *v.* 目睹；作證；目擊
搭 **witness the argument** 目睹了爭執經過
同 **observe / perceive**

▶ The police asked the witness about the accident.
警察詢問目擊者有關意外事件的情況。

▶ I witnessed a car accident and called the police.
我目睹了一場車禍，並且打電話報警。

---

workbook [ˈwɝ:k.bʊk] *n.* 習題簿；練習簿

▶ You must write your answers in your own workbook.
你一定要把答案寫在你自己的習題簿上面。

---

working [ˈwɝ:.kɪŋ]

adj. 正常運作的；操作的；工作的

搭 **working population** 勞動人口
同 **running / alive**

▶ I hope that his phone is a working device.
我希望他的電話是好的。

worldwide [ˈwɝːld.waɪd]

adj. 全世界的；遍及全球的

搭 **worldwide operation** 全球營運

同 **global / international**

▶ There was a worldwide celebration when the cure was found.
找到治癒的方法時，全世界都在歡慶。

---

(102)

worn [wɔ:rn]

adj. 用舊的；磨壞的；精疲力盡的

同 **shabby / tattered**

▶ The sweater looked old and worn.
那件毛衣看起來又舊又破。

---

worried [ˈwɝː.id] *adj.* 擔心的；憂慮的

同 **concerned / tense**

▶ My worried mother asked if I was doing fine.
擔心的母親問我是否一切都好。

---

worthless [ˈwɝː.θ.ləs]

adj. 一文不值的；無價值的；無用的

搭 **worthless opinion** 無價值的意見

同 **warren / pointless**

▶ My old computer is nearly worthless.
我的舊電腦幾乎是一文不值了。

---

wow [waʊ] *interj.* 哇！（讚嘆詞）

▶ Wow! Those fireworks are so amazing!
哇！那些煙火好棒！

---

(95)

wrap [ræp]

① *v.* 包；裹

實用片語

it's a wrap 結束，尾聲

② *n.* 圍巾；披肩；包裹物

同 **coat / blanket**

▶ He walked over to wrap a blanket around the baby.
他走過去用毯子把嬰孩包裹起來。

▶ After three years, it's a wrap for the mission.
經過三年，這是任務的尾聲了。

▶ My friend covered his bare head with a wrap.
我的朋友用圍巾把頭包起來。

---

wrapping [ˈræp.ɪŋ] *n.* 包裝紙；包裝材料

▶ She carefully tore the beautiful wrapping off the gift.
她將禮物外面那漂亮的包裝紙小心翼翼地撕開。

---

wreck [rek]

① *n.* 殘骸；失事

同 **destroy / ruin**

▶ After the storm, our yard was a wreck.
暴風雨過後，我們家的院子真是滿目瘡痍。

W

train wreck 一團亂，一團糟

② *v.* 毀壞；完全破壞

同 **crash / collapse**

---

wrinkle [ˈrɪŋ.kəl]

① *n.* 皺紋

同 **crinkle / fold**

② *v.* 皺起（鼻子）；起皺紋

搭 **wrinkle his nose** 皺了皺鼻子

iron out the wrinkles 撫平皺紋

---

wrist [rɪst] *n.* 手腕

---

writing [ˈraɪ.tɪŋ] *n.* 寫作；筆跡；作品；書寫

搭 **creative writing** 創意寫作

同 **article / document**

in writing 寫下

X-ray / x-ray [ˈeks.reɪ]

① *n.* X 光

② *v.* 照 X 光

---

yawn [jɑːn]

① *v.* 打呵欠

同 **doze / nap**

② *n.* 呵欠

▶ The project has become a complete train wreck.
專案已經完全變成一團亂。

▶ I wrecked the car when I hit the tree.
我撞上樹的時候，也把車給撞毀了！

▶ There is a wrinkle in my shirt, please iron it.
我的襯衫有一道折紋，請幫我燙一下。

▶ Tim wrinkled his nose after smelling my soup.
提姆聞了我的湯後，馬上皺起鼻子。

▶ I have to iron out the wrinkles in this shirt.
我必須燙平這件上衣的皺褶。

▶ It is important to have flexible wrists when playing drums.
打鼓時有靈活的手腕是很重要的。

▶ I'm not good at writing, but I practice to get better!
我不擅於寫作，但是我藉著練習來進步！

▶ Be sure to get the agreement in writing.
務必取得書面協議。

▶ Peter needs to go to the hospital and get an x-ray.
彼得需要去醫院照 X 光。

▶ After my accident, I went to x-ray my foot at the hospital.
發生意外之後，我去醫院照腳部 X 光。

▶ You will yawn if you become tired or bored.
如果你變得疲累或無聊時，就會打哈欠。

▶ The contagious yawn started a chain around the room.
這個有傳染性的哈欠開始讓所有室內的人都開始打呵欠。

yearly [ˈjɪr.li]

① *adj.* 每年的

搭 **yearly basis** 每年基準

同 **annual / yearlong**

② *adv.* 一年一度

同 **annually / once a year**

▶ We take a yearly vacation to Japan.
我們每年都到日本度假。

▶ He goes to the doctor yearly for a checkup.
他一年一次到醫生那裡做健康檢查。

---

yell [jel]

① *v.* 喊叫

實用片語
yell one's head off 喊破喉嚨

② *n.* 喊叫

搭 **yell hysterically** 歇斯底里地大叫

同 **screech / yelp**

▶ Everyone watching the movie yelled during the scary scene.
每個看到這部電影的人在出現恐怖場景時都會尖叫。

▶ Sandra was yelling her head off at the basketball game.
珊卓在籃球賽中喊破了喉嚨。

▶ The man let out a loud yell after hurting his finger.
那個人傷到自己的手指後放聲大叫。

---

yogurt [ˈjoʊ.gɚt] *n.* 優格；酸奶

▶ Yogurt is a healthy breakfast.
優格是健康的早餐食品。

---

yolk [joʊk] *n.* 蛋黃

▶ They prefer the moon cakes that have egg yolk inside.
他們比較喜歡裡面包蛋黃的月餅。

---

youngster [ˈjʌŋ.stɚ] *n.* 小孩

同 **teenager / youth**

▶ All the youngsters have so much energy!
所有青少年都充滿許多活力！

---

youthful [ˈjuː.θ.fəl] *adj.* 年輕的

同 **immature / underage**

▶ The youthful teacher is often mistaken for a student.
那位年輕的老師常常被誤以為是個學生。

---

zipper [ˈzɪp.ɚ]

① *n.* 拉鍊

同 **link / hookup**

② *v.* 拉上拉鍊

實用片語
zipper head 中分頭

▶ Every jacket that you see here have zippers on them.
這裡所有你看見的夾克都有拉鍊。

▶ He carefully zippered his bag along with his luggage.
他小心地拉上袋子與行李上的拉鍊。

▶ Some zipper head told me I couldn't come in without a suit.
某個中分頭男子跟我說沒穿西裝不能進來。

Y
Z

zone [zoʊn]

① *n.* 地區

搭 **free-trade zone** 自由貿易地區

同 **region / territory**

② *v.* 使分成區

實用片語
comfort zone 舒適圈

▶ That zone has a lot of tall houses and large yards.
那個地區有許多很高的房子和大院子。

▶ The players were zoned into a specific area.
隊員們被分到一個特定的區域。

▶ This job is a bit out of my comfort zone.
這個工作有點超出我的舒適圈（具有挑戰性）。

426

Exercise 80

I. 中英對應

_____ 1. 呵欠　(A) yell　　　(B) yard　　　(C) yacht　　　(D) yawn

_____ 2. 撤退　(A) withdraw　(B) withstand　(C) withhold　(D) withdrawn

_____ 3. 小孩　(A) younger　(B) youngster　(C) youthful　(D) yogurt

_____ 4. 皺紋　(A) wink　　　(B) wrist　　　(C) wrinkle　　(D) wrestle

_____ 5. 無用的　(A) worldwide　(B) worthless　(C) worthwhile　(D) worthiness

II. Derivatives

1. Jack can't take off his jacket because the _____ (zip) is stuck.

2. A guard at the museum noticed that some of the mummy's _____ (wrap) had been removed.

3. The Bible says, "The fear of the Lord is the beginning of _____ (wise), but fools despise _____ (wise) and teaching.

4. It is hard to read our boss's _____ (write).

5. Police asked the two _____ (wit) to the accident to come forward.

III. Vocabulary Choice

(A) worldwide　　(B) worn　　(C) worried　　(D) zoned　　(E) youthful

(G) yell　　(G) yearly　　(H) wrecked　　(I) wrist　　(J) wrap

1. The book royalties of this publisher are paid _____ based on the first publication date of the work.

2. The former tobacco factory has been _____ as a cultural park.

3. Our town has been _____ by the typhoon.

4. Everyone was really _____ when my sister didn't come home last night.

5. My father was _____ out after a day's work.

㊱ **official** [əˈfɪʃ.əl] *adj.* 官方的、正式的

例 An official announcement will be released tomorrow.
官方正式的公告明天會宣佈。

officious [əˈfɪʃ.əs] *adj.* 官腔的、多管閒事的

例 Jack is so officious that all other members try to avoid him.
傑克太愛管閒事導致其他同仁都離他遠遠的。

㊲ **partly** [ˈpɑːrt.li] *adv.* 部分地、不完全地

例 Mary is partly responsible for this mistake.
瑪莉要為此錯誤負一部份責任。

partial [ˈpɑːr.ʃəl] *adj.* 偏袒的、偏愛的

例 Jones is partial to a cup of coffee after dinner.
瓊斯偏好飯後喝杯咖啡。

㊳ **personnel** [ˌpɝː.sənˈel] *n.* 人員、員工

例 The company plans to hire extra security personnel.
公司規劃要聘請更多安全人員。

personal [ˈpɝː.sən.əl] *adj.* 個人的、私人的

例 Is it okay if I ask you a personal question?
我可以問你個私人問題嗎？

㊴ **precede** [priˈsiːd] *v.* 在⋯之前、優於

例 Mary preceded Mr. Smith into the conference room.
瑪莉在史密斯先生之前進入會議室。

proceed [proʊˈsiːd] *v.* 繼續進行、繼續做

例 Businesses are proceeding according to the original plan.
業務依照原有計劃進行。

㊵ **prescribe** [prɪˈskraɪb] *v.* 規定、開藥方

例 The doctor prescribed some medicine for her headache.
醫生為了她的頭痛症狀開了些藥。

proscribe [proˈskraɪb] *v.* 禁止、排斥

例 Torture of political prisoners are proscribed by international law.
凌虐政治犯是被國際法律所不容的。

④ **proof** [pruːf] *n.* 證據、物證

例 All applicants should provide proof of employment.
所有申請者都應該要提供工作證明。

prove [pruːv] *v.* 證明、證實

例 This piece of evidence could prove his innocence.
這個證據證明他是無辜的。

---

④ **purposefully** [ˈpɜː.pəs.fəl.i] *adv.* 有目的地、有決心地

例 Jack strode purposefully towards the battle ground.
傑克充滿決心地向戰場走去。

purposely [ˈpɜː.pəs.li] *adv.* 故意地

例 The boy did it purposely to attract his mother's attention.
男孩故意那麼做以吸引他媽媽的注意。

---

④ **raise** [reɪz] *v.* 舉起、抬起

例 He raised his voice in order to be heard.
為了讓別人聽見他，他刻意地提高音量。

rise [raɪz] *v.* 起床、上升、升起

例 Interest rates are expected to rise next month.
下個月利息就要上升了。

---

④ **refuse** [rɪˈfjuːz] *v.* 拒絕、謝絕

例 Mr. Goods refused to accept that unfair proposal.
古德先生拒絕接受那個不公平的提議。

refute [rɪˈfjuːt] *v.* 駁斥、反駁、駁倒

例 You can easily refute his weak argument.
你可以輕意地駁斥他那薄弱的論點。

---

④ **regretful** [rɪˈgret.fəl] *adj.* 懊悔的、遺憾的

例 I was not regretful about leaving the previous company.
我對離開前一間公司不會感到遺憾。

regrettable [rɪˈgreˌ.ə.bəl] *adj.* 使人悔恨的、令人遺憾的

例 That's a regrettable mistake you've made.
你犯了個令人惋惜的錯誤。

46 **rout** [raʊt] *v.* 潰敗、潰退

例 Our enemy was eventually routed.
我們的敵人被擊潰了。

route [ruːt / raʊt] *n.* 路、路線、路程

例 The route to success requires hard work.
通往成功的道路要由努力堆砌。

---

47 **sensible** [ˈsen.sə.bəl] *adj.* 通情達理的、明智的

例 Jack is a sensible manager and doesn't panic at all.
傑克是個很明智的經理，都不會手足無措。

sensitive [ˈsen.sə.ţɪv] *adj.* 敏感的、易受傷害的

例 Mary is pretty sensitive about her appearance and weight.
瑪莉對她的外形和體重很敏感。

---

48 **suit** [suːt] *n.* （一套）衣服

例 A special diving suit is required for this activity.
做此活動要穿特製的潛水裝。

suite [swiːt] *n.* 套房

例 We are planning to stay in a suite at the Ritz.
我們打算要住麗緻酒店的套房。

---

49 **uninterested** [ʌnˈɪn.tɚ.es.tɪd] *adj.* 不感興趣的

例 I told her my plans but she seemed uninterested.
我把計劃告訴她，但她似乎不感興趣。

disinterested [dɪˈsɪn.trə.stɪd] *adj.* 無私心的、公平的

例 Professors are expected to be impartial and disinterested.
教授應該不偏心且要做到公平。

---

50 **urban** [ˈɝː.bən] *adj.* 都市的

例 Most urban areas are busy and crowded.
多數的都市地區都很繁忙又擁擠。

urbane [ɝːˈbeɪn] *adj.* 文雅的

例 Mr. Jones maintained an urbane tone in his emails.
瓊斯先生在電郵內還是保有文雅的語氣。

附 錄
Appendix

►易混淆單字

你曾注意過某些單字明明長得不一樣,發音卻一模一樣嗎?
附錄特別整理出 50 組發音相同,意思與詞性卻不同,常被
搞混的單字,若能記下來,就不怕再誤用囉。

① **aid** [eɪd] *n.* 幫助
aide [eɪd] *n.* 助手

② **born** [bɔːrn] *v.* 出生〔過去分詞〕
borne [bɔːrn] *v.* 承擔〔過去分詞〕

③ **air** [er] *n.* 空氣、氣氛
heir [er] *n.* 繼承人

④ **brake** [breɪk] *v.* 煞車
break [breɪk] *v.* 違反

⑤ **aloud** [əˈlaʊd] *adv.* 出聲地
allowed [əˈlaʊd] *v.* 允許〔被動〕

⑥ **cash** [kæʃ] *n.* 現金
cache [kæʃ] *n.* 隱藏處

⑦ **ascent** [əˈsent] *n.* 上升、提高
assent [əˈsent] *v.* 同意

⑧ **cast** [kæst] *v.* 投（票）
caste [kæst] *n.* 階級制度

⑨ **ate** [eɪt] *v.* 吃〔過去式〕
eight [eɪt] *n.* 八

⑩ **ceiling** [ˈsiːlɪŋ] *n.* 最大限額、最高限制
sealing [ˈsiːlɪŋ] *v.* 封閉〔進行式〕

⑪ **aural** [ˈɔːrəl] *adj.* 聽覺的
oral [ˈɔːrəl] *adj.* 口頭的

⑫ **cell** [sel] *n.* 細胞、小房室
sell [sel] *v.* 出售

⑬ **band** [bænd] *n.* 樂團
banned [bænd] *v.* 禁止〔被動〕

⑭ **complement** [ˈkɑːm.plə.ment] *v.* 補足
compliment [ˈkɑːm.plə.ment] *n.* 問候、恭維

⑮ **bare** [ber] *adj.* 僅有的、不加裝飾的
bear [ber] *v.* 忍受

⑯ **council** [ˈkaʊn.səl] *n.* 委員會、地方議會
counsel [ˈkaʊn.səl] *n.* 辯護律師、法律顧問

⑰ **base** [beɪs] *n.* 基地、總部
bass [beɪs] *adj.* 低音的

⑱ **desert** [ˈdez.ət] *v.* 拋棄、離棄
dessert [ˈdez.ət] *n.* 甜點

⑲ **beach** [biːtʃ] *n.* 海灘
beech [biːtʃ] *n.* 山毛櫸

⑳ **dual** [ˈduː.əl] *adj.* 雙重（倍）的
duel [ˈduː.əl] *n.* 決鬥

㉑ **berth** [bɝːθ] *n.* 座位
birth [bɝːθ] *n.* 出生

㉒ **fare** [fer] *n.* 票價、費用
fair [fer] *adj.* 公平的

㉓ **board** [bɔːrd] *n.* 理事會
bored [bɔːrd] *adj.* 覺得厭煩的

㉔ **feet** [fiːt] *n.* 英呎〔複數〕
feat [fiːt] *n.* 功績

㉕ **find** [faɪnd] *v.* 發現
fined [faɪnd] *v.* 處以罰金（被動）

㉖ **real** [ˈriː.əl] *adj.* 現實的、實在的
reel [rɪəl] *v.* 滔滔不絕地講

㉗ **flour** [ˈflaʊ.ɚ] *n.* 麵粉
flower [ˈflaʊ.ɚ] *n.* 花

㉘ **rest** [rest] *n.* 休息
wrest [rest] *v.* 奪取

㉙ **foul** [faʊl] *adj.* 骯髒的、腐敗的
fowl [faʊl] *n.* 家禽（肉）

㉚ **sail** [seɪl] *v.* 航行、順利進行
sale [seɪl] *n.* 銷售（額）

㉛ **hair** [her] *n.* 頭髮
hare [her] *n.* 野兔

㉜ **soar** [sɔːr] *v.* 驟升
sore [sɔːr] *adj.* 酸痛的

㉝ **hall** [hɑːl] *n.* 會堂、大廳
haul [hɑːl] *n.* 一次獲得的量

㉞ **sole** [soʊl] *adj.* 唯一的
soul [soʊl] *n.* 人、靈魂

㉟ **hangar** [ˈhæŋ.ɚ] *n.* 飛機棚
hanger [ˈhæŋ.ɚ] *n.* 掛勾、衣架

㊱ **stair** [ster] *n.* 樓梯
stare [ster] *v.* 凝視

㊲ **lessen** [ˈles.ən] *v.* 減少、減輕
lesson [ˈles.ən] *n.* 教訓

㊳ **stationary** [ˈsteɪ.ʃə.ner.i] *adj.* 不動的
stationery [ˈsteɪ.ʃə.ner.i] *n.* 書寫文具、信封信紙

㊴ **morning** [ˈmɔːr.nɪŋ] *n.* 上午、早晨
mourning [ˈmɔːr.nɪŋ] *n.* 悲傷、服喪

㊵ **steak** [steɪk] *n.* 牛排
stake [steɪk] *n.* 風險、賭注

㊶ **pail** [peɪl] *n.* 桶、一桶的量
pale [peɪl] *adj.* 蒼白的

㊷ **steal** [stiːl] *v.* 偷竊
steel [stiːl] *n.* 鋼鐵

㊸ **pedal** [ˈped.əl] *n.* 踏板
peddle [ˈpæd.əl] *v.* 叫賣

㊹ **waist** [weɪst] *n.* 腰（身）
waste [weɪst] *n.* 浪費

㊺ **plain** [pleɪn] *adj.* 簡單的、樸素的
plane [pleɪn] *n.* 飛機

㊻ **wait** [weɪt] *v.* 等待
weight [weɪt] *n.* 重量

㊼ **pole** [poʊl] *n.* 杆、柱
poll [poʊl] *n.* 意見調查

㊽ **wave** [weɪv] *v.* 揮手
waive [weɪv] *v.* 放棄、撤回

㊾ **principal** [ˈprɪn.sə.pəl] *adj.* 首要的
principle [ˈprɪn.sə.pəl] *n.* 原則

㊿ **weather** [ˈweð.ɚ] *n.* 天氣
whether [ˈweð.ɚ] *conj.* 是否、…抑或…

解答
Answer

Answer 解答

Exercise 1

Ⅰ. ① accidental ② absolutely
③ accomplishment ④ accountant
⑤ acceptance

Ⅱ. ① F ② C ③ A ④ J ⑤ E

Exercise 2

Ⅰ. ① admirable ② actually ③ acquaintance
④ achievement ⑤ adjustments

Ⅱ. ① G ② B ③ D ④ A ⑤ I

Exercise 3

Ⅰ. ① Agency ② advertisements ③ adviser
④ aged ⑤ agreeable

Ⅱ. ① J ② A ③ F ④ D ⑤ H

Exercise 4

Ⅰ. ① C ② B ③ D ④ A ⑤ C

Ⅱ. ① amazing ② analysis ③ amusement
④ ambitious ⑤ annoying

Exercise 5

Ⅰ. ① appreciation ② appointment
③ application ④ apologize ⑤ apparently

Ⅱ. ① J ② G ③ A ④ I ⑤ C

Exercise 6

Ⅰ. ① assembly ② assignments ③ arrival
④ Association ⑤ assurances

Ⅱ. ① F ② C ③ B ④ I ⑤ H

Exercise 7

Ⅰ. ① attachment ② attractive ③ authority
④ awakened ⑤ automobile

Ⅱ. ① E ② G ③ B ④ I ⑤ A

Exercise 8

Ⅰ. ① H ② J ③ E ④ B ⑤ C

Ⅱ. ① C ② B ③ D ④ B ⑤ A

Exercise 9

Ⅰ. ① D ② A ③ D ④ A ⑤ C

Ⅱ. ① I ② B ③ G ④ E ⑤ A

Exercise 10

Ⅰ. ① F ② C ③ A ④ D ⑤ G

Ⅱ. ① D ② C ③ B ④ A ⑤ B

Exercise 11

Ⅰ. ① B ② D ③ C ④ A ⑤ C

Ⅱ. ① G ② E ③ J ④ F ⑤ D

Exercise 12

Ⅰ. ① I ② A ③ J ④ G ⑤ E

Ⅱ. ① candidates ② capacity ③ campaign
④ cabinet ⑤ calculator

Exercise 13

Ⅰ. ① C ② B ③ D ④ A ⑤ C

Ⅱ. ① A ② H ③ D ④ F ⑤ J

Exercise 14

Ⅰ. ① I ② B ③ F ④ A ⑤ D

Ⅱ. ① C ② A ③ D ④ B ⑤ C

Exercise 15

Ⅰ. ① B ② D ③ D ④ C ⑤ A

Ⅱ. ① I ② A ③ D ④ F ⑤ H

Exercise 16

Ⅰ. ① A ② C ③ D ④ B ⑤ C

Ⅱ. ① B ② C ③ A ④ H ⑤ J

Exercise 17

Ⅰ. ① commercial ② communication
③ commander ④ competitive
⑤ complicated

Ⅱ. ① C ② A ③ J ④ D ⑤ H

Exercise 18

Ⅰ. ① compositions ② conclusion
③ concentration ④ connections
⑤ confidence

Ⅱ. ① E ② F ③ A ④ H ⑤ C

Exercise 19

Ⅰ. ① B ② D ③ A ④ C ⑤ C

Ⅱ. ① consequently ② consistent
③ considerable ④ constructive
⑤ consultant

Exercise 20

Ⅰ. ① B ② A ③ D ④ A ⑤ A

Ⅱ. ① correspond ② cooperation
③ contribution ④ conventional
⑤ continuous

Exercise 21

Ⅰ. ① A ② C ③ B ④ D ⑤ A

Ⅱ. ① B ② F ③ D ④ A ⑤ I

Exercise 22

Ⅰ. ① A ② B ③ C ④ D ⑤ B

Ⅱ. ① F ② C ③ G ④ J ⑤ E

Exercise 23

Ⅰ. ① B ② H ③ D ④ J ⑤ F

Ⅱ. ① B ② D ③ C ④ A ⑤ B

Exercise 24

Ⅰ. ① C ② B ③ D ④ A ⑤ D

Ⅱ. ① dependent ② democratic ③ depression
④ Definition ⑤ demanding

Exercise 25

Ⅰ. ① B ② B ③ C ④ A ⑤ D

Ⅱ. ① destruction ② digestion ③ determination
④ devoted ⑤ digital

Exercise 26

Ⅰ. ① I ② B ③ A ④ G ⑤ C

Ⅱ. ① B ② C ③ A ④ D ⑤ C

Exercise 27

Ⅰ. ① A ② D ③ B ④ D ⑤ A

Ⅱ. ① disorder ② distribution ③ discovery
④ distinguished ⑤ dissatisfaction

Exercise 28

Ⅰ. ① B ② A ③ C ④ D ⑤ B

Ⅱ. ① B ② E ③ C ④ F ⑤ J

Exercise 29

Ⅰ. ① editor ② earnings ③ economist
④ educational ⑤ efficiency

Ⅱ. ① H ② D ③ B ④ F ⑤ J

Exercise 30

Ⅰ. ① embarrassment ② electrician
③ emphasized ④ emergency ⑤
employment

Ⅱ. ① C ② D ③ A ④ D ⑤ B

Exercise 31

Ⅰ. ① C ② A ③ C ④ C ⑤ A

Ⅱ. ① enforcement ② enlargement
③ environmental ④ engineering
⑤ engagement

Exercise 32

Ⅰ. ① establishment ② equipment ③ evaluation
④ essential ⑤ examinees

II．① B ② C ③ D ④ A ⑤ B

Exercise 33

I ．① explosion ② exhibition ③ experimental

④ expansion ⑤ exposure

II．① B ② J ③ A ④ C ⑤ G

Exercise 34

I ．① expressive ② facilities ③ fantastic

④ faithful ⑤ extremely

II．① I ② A ③ D ④ F ⑤ G

Exercise 35

I ．① A ② C ③ B ④ A ⑤ D

II．① J ② F ③ C ④ B ⑤ G

Exercise 36

I ．① B ② B ③ A ④ C ⑤ B

II．① C ② G ③ B ④ I ⑤ F

Exercise 37

I ．① C ② B ③ A ④ B ⑤ D

II．① fragrance ② fortunately ③ frightening

④ foundation ⑤ frequency

Exercise 38

I ．① B ② C ③ A ④ D ⑤ C

II．① furniture ② frozen ③ fundamental

④ frustration ⑤ fulfillment

Exercise 39

I ．① genuine ② gangsters ③ generosity

④ glorious ⑤ generations

II．① A ② D ③ B ④ C ⑤ A

Exercise 40

I ．① grammatical ② graceful ③ graduation

④ guilty ⑤ gratitude

II．① D ② B ③ A ④ C ⑤ B

Exercise 41

I ．① healthful ② Halt ③ Handicapped

④ hatred ⑤ hesitation

II．① B ② B ③ C ④ A ⑤ D

Exercise 42

I ．① honorable ② humanity ③ Hijacker

④ horrify ⑤ household

II．① C ② B ③ A ④ D ⑤ C

Exercise 43

I ．① B ② D ③ A ④ C ⑤ D

II．① identification ② imitation ③ impression

④ Immigration ⑤ Imaginative

Exercise 44

I ．① A ② D ③ B ④ C ⑤ D

II．① informative ② inspection

③ Industrialized ④ influential ⑤ infections

Exercise 45

I ．① D ② I ③ F ④ C ⑤ G

II．① intellectual ② Interruption ③ Intention

④ interaction ⑤ Intensity

Exercise 46

I ．① investment ② invasion ③ isolation

④ involvement ⑤ kindness

II．① E ② I ③ G ④ F ⑤ B

Exercise 47

I ．① C ② B ③ D ④ A ⑤ C

II．① landslides ② leading ③ literature

④ leisurely ⑤ lighten

Exercise 48

I ．① B ② D ③ D ④ C ⑤ A

II．① logical ② luxurious ③ mainly

④ machinery ⑤ loyalty

Exercise 49

I . ① H ② D ③ J ④ E ⑤ I

II . ① A ② B ③ C ④ C ⑤ D

Exercise 50

I . ① D ② C ③ D ④ B ⑤ A

II . ① D ② A ③ F ④ G ⑤ I

Exercise 51

I . ① D ② B ③ C ④ B ⑤ A

II . ① F ② H ③ C ④ G ⑤ D

Exercise 52

I . ① A ② B ③ D ④ C ⑤ A

II . ① I ② G ③ B ④ F ⑤ C

Exercise 53

I. ① C ② A ③ D ④ A ⑤ B

II . ① partnership ② overlooked ③ participation ④ parking ⑤ particularly

Exercise 54

I . ① A ② C ③ D ④ B ⑤ C

II . ① persuasive ② percentage ③ physicists ④ perfection ⑤ philosophical

Exercise 55

I . ① pollution ② possession ③ presentation ④ possibly ⑤ portable

II . ① A ② A ③ B ④ B ⑤ A

Exercise 56

I . ① productive ② professional ③ prosperity ④ promotion ⑤ profitable

II . ① D ② A ③ D ④ D ⑤ C

Exercise 57

I . ① psychologist ② quotation ③ publicity ④ readily ⑤ realistic

II . ① C ② B ③ D ④ B ⑤ A

Exercise 58

I . ① B ② D ③ C ④ A ⑤ D

II . ① regulations ② relatively ③ recognition ④ recovery ⑤ reflection

Exercise 59

I . ① resignation ② resolutions ③ repetition ④ remarkable ⑤ respectable

II . ① B ② D ③ A ④ C ⑤ B

Exercise 60

I . ① retirement ② revolutionary ③ restrictions ④ revisions ⑤ robbery

II . ① C ② D ③ B ④ A ⑤ C

Exercise 61

I . ① routine ② rusty ③ roughly ④ satisfactory ⑤ rotten

II . ① B ② B ③ A ④ C ⑤ A

Exercise 62

I . ① C ② A ③ B ④ D ⑤ A

II . ① scarcely ② scholarship ③ schoolmate ④ scenery ⑤ scientific

Exercise 63

I . ① seagull ② shadows ③ sensitive ④ sexual ⑤ security

II . ① D ② A ③ B ④ J ⑤ F

Exercise 64

I . ① C ② D ③ B ④ C ⑤ A

II . ① shortsighted ② significance ③ sightseeing ④ shaver ⑤ signature

Exercise 65

I . ① C ② B ③ A ④ C ⑤ D

II . ① sincerity ② skating ③ sledge ④ slightly ⑤ skyscrapers

Exercise 66

I . ①A ②D ③B ④A ⑤C

II . ①F ②C ③H ④G ⑤J

Exercise 67

I . ①D ②B ③C ④B ⑤A

II . ①B ②I ③J ④E ⑤H

Exercise 68

I . ①B ②C ③A ④D ⑤B

II . ①A ②G ③C ④I ⑤F

Exercise 69

I . ① storyteller ② strengthened ③ suffering
④ suggestions ⑤ stormy

II . ①B ②C ③B ④A ⑤D

Exercise 70

I . ① sunbathe ② supposed ③ surfing
④ suspicious ⑤ surgeon

II . ①B ②C ③D ④A ⑤B

Exercise 71

I . ①D ②B ③C ④A ⑤B

II . ① talented ② swimsuit ③ systematic
④ tablecloth ⑤ sympathetic

Exercise 72

I . ① Technological ② territory ③ technicians
④ tendency ⑤ temperature

II . ①D ②B ③C ④B ⑤A

Exercise 73

I . ①D ②C ③B ④A ⑤A

II . ① tighten ② thunderstorm ③ tiresome
④ threatened ⑤ tolerable

Exercise 74

I . ①C ②A ③A ④B ⑤D

II . ① training ② tragedy ③ tribal
④ tremendous ⑤ translation

Exercise 75

I . ① truthful ② typical ③ troublesome
④ typewriter ⑤ tropical

II . ①B ②C ③D ④A ⑤C

Exercise 76

I . ① unlikely ② Unfortunately ③ universal
④ unity ⑤ understanding

II . ①C ②B ③B ④D ⑤A

Exercise 77

I . ①A ②C ③B ④C ⑤D

II . ①H ②I ③C ④A ⑤E

Exercise 78

I . ①D ②B ③A ④C ⑤B

II . ① voluntary ② vitamins ③ visual
④ visible ⑤ violence

Exercise 79

I . ① weaken ② warnings ③ wealthy
④ warmth ⑤ weekly

II . ① D ②A ③C ④B ⑤B

Exercise 80

I . ①D ②A ③B ④C ⑤B

II . ① zipper ② wrappings ③ wisdom
④ writing ⑤ witnesses

III . ①G ②D ③H ④C ⑤B

單字索引
Index

單字索引

C

國家圖書館出版品預行編目(CIP)資料

完勝大考英語7000單字. 中級篇2001~4500字 / 空中英語教室編輯
群著. -- 三版. -- 臺北市：笛藤出版圖書有限公司, 2024.02
　　面；　公分
ISBN 978-957-710-910-1(平裝)
1.CST: 英語教學 2.CST: 詞彙 3.CST: 中等教育
524.38　112021305

全新修訂版

完勝大考！
英語7000單字

中級篇 | **2001~4500字**

 7000單字雲端服務
永久序號

2024年7月27日　三版第2刷　定價330元

著　　　者	空中英語教室編輯群
封面設計	王舒玗
總 編 輯	洪季楨
編　　　輯	林子鈺、葉雯婷
編輯協力	陳佳文、關慧芯
編輯企畫	笛藤出版
發 行 人	林建仲
發 行 所	八方出版股份有限公司
地　　　址	台北市中山區長安東路二段171號3樓3室
電　　　話	(02) 2777-3682
傳　　　真	(02) 2777-3672
總 經 銷	聯合發行股份有限公司
電　　　話	(02) 2917-8022 · (02) 2917-8042
製 版 廠	造極彩色印刷製版股份有限公司
劃撥帳戶	八方出版股份有限公司
劃撥帳號	19809050